UNHOLY CATHOLIC IRELAND

SPIRITUAL PHENOMENA
TANYA LUHRMANN and ANN TAVES, Editors

Unholy Catholic Ireland

Religious Hypocrisy, Secular Morality, and Irish Irreligion

HUGH TURPIN

Stanford University Press • Stanford, California

STANFORD UNIVERSITY PRESS
Stanford, California

©2022 by the Board of Trustees of the Leland Stanford Junior University. All rights reserved.

No part of this book may be reproduced or transmitted in any form or by any means, electronic or mechanical, including photocopying and recording, or in any information storage or retrieval system without the prior written permission of Stanford University Press.

Printed in the United States of America on acid-free, archival-quality paper

Library of Congress Cataloging-in-Publication Data
Names: Turpin, Hugh, author.
Title: Unholy Catholic Ireland : religious hypocrisy, secular morality, and Irish irreligion / Hugh Turpin.
Other titles: Spiritual phenomena.
Description: Stanford, California : Stanford University Press, 2022. | Series: Spiritual phenomena | Includes bibliographical references and index.
Identifiers: LCCN 2021055930 (print) | LCCN 2021055931 (ebook) | ISBN 9781503613157 (cloth) | ISBN 9781503633131 (paperback) | ISBN 9781503633148 (ebook)
Subjects: LCSH: Catholic Church–Ireland–Influence. | Ex-church members–Ireland–Catholic Church. | Catholics–Ireland–Attitudes. | Secularism–Ireland. | Irreligion–Ireland.
Classification: LCC BX1503 .T87 2022 (print) | LCC BX1503 (ebook) | DDC 282/.415–dc23/eng/20220128
LC record available at https://lccn.loc.gov/2021055930
LC ebook record available at https://lccn.loc.gov/2021055931

Cover design: George Kirkpatrick
Cover photo: Headstone in Mount Jerome Cemetery, Dublin. Hugh Turpin
Typeset by Newgen North America in 10/15 ITC New Baskerville Std

For Donna Marie and Sylvan

CONTENTS

List of Figures and Tables ix

Acknowledgments xi

INTRODUCTION 1

1 Secularization, the Desacralization of the Church, and the Emergence of Ethno-Catholic "Nones" 18

2 "Hostages of Catholicism": Quantifying the Nature and Scale of the Rejection of the Church 56

3 "For Emergency Use Only": The Waning of Religious Socialization 95

4 "A Load of Shite": Hidden Cultures of Catholic Unbelief 131

5 "This Is Our Rising": Secularization as a Second Struggle for "Irish Freedom" 154

6 "Awakening from Conscription": Ex-Catholicism as Anti-Nostalgic Moralized Authenticity 189

7 "Blessed Are Those Who Are Persecuted Because of Righteousness": Coping with a Spoiled Religious Identity 222

EPILOGUE. "Anyone Else Not Bothered?" 253

Methodological Appendix 259

Notes 265

Bibliography 301

Index 315

LIST OF FIGURES AND TABLES

Figures

Figure 2.1. *Ex-Catholics show extreme distrust of clergy*   66

Figure 2.2. *Evaluations by group of the Catholic Church as a force in Irish society*   68

Figure 2.3. *Differences in Catholic belief and general theism between groups*   79

Figure 2.4. *Domestic CRED exposure predicts orthodox Catholic belief*   81

Figure 2.5. *Domestic CRED exposure decreases as age decreases*   82

Figure 2.6. *Protesting the papal visit*   91

Figure 3.1. *"Sex Education for Girls": Angela spills the beans*   122

Figure 3.2. *"Father Ted" merchandise*   125

Figure 5.1. *Tuam revelations as moral counter to pro-life stance*   166

Figure 5.2. *Propaganda for the "Time to Tick No" campaign*   179

Figure 5.3. *Aftermath of the Tuam affair*   180

Figure 5.4. *Secular sodality pins*   187

Figure 6.1. *The "Angry Atheist" trope as deployed in a school religion textbook*   212

Tables

Table 2.1. *Catholicism, liminal Catholicism, and ex-Catholicism by age*   61

Table 2.2. *Catholic, liminal Catholic, and ex-Catholic differences in trust rankings for atheists, priests, and bishops*   65

Table 2.3. *Free list associations with the term "Irish Catholic Church"* 71

Table 2.4. *Rejection factors, from most to least important* 76

Table 2.5. *Differing rejection emphases between liminal and ex-Catholics* 76

Table 2.6. *Impact of clerical abuse on willingness to perform various CREDs* 84

Table 2.7. *Variables that best predict the rejection of Catholic belief and social identity* 86

ACKNOWLEDGMENTS

This book would not have been possible without a great many others. I will start with the academics. When I was just beginning, Tom Inglis, John Weafer, Marie Keenan, and Kevin Egan were all kind enough to provide me with advice about how (and where) to get started on a very large topic. When I was doing my PhD at Aarhus University and Queen's University Belfast, Armin Geertz, Kristoffer Nielbo, Uffe Schjødt, Jesper Sørensen, Gladys Ganiel, Liam Kennedy, Paulo Sousa, Lauren Swiney, and especially Jonathan Lanman gave me invaluable advice, support, and constructive criticism. Jonathan in particular has been an academic mentor of the first order, and both the book and I bear his intellectual imprint. I also owe much to my doctoral examiners, Harvey Whitehouse, Jesper Sørensen, Stephen Bullivant, and Dominic Bryan. Their critiques and thoughts on my original research contributed greatly to the book that was (eventually) to follow. I would also like to further thank Harvey, as well as Aiyana Willard and Jonathan Jong, for their guidance in various postdoctoral roles and because writing this book has sometimes distracted me from devoting my full attention to the projects for which they hired me. I also owe thanks to the Understanding Unbelief program and the Templeton Foundation for financial support to conduct further research. Marc Andersen has my gratitude for his help with statistical analysis and programming; any statistical rawness in Chapter 2 is mine, not his. Ben Purzycki has my thanks for his advice on analyzing the free list data in Chapter 2, as do Nayanika Ghosh and Mary Nolan for their work blind-coding it.

I am thankful to Ann Taves and Tanya Luhrmann for including the book in their Spiritual Phenomena series and for their insightful comments on its content and structure. The book's peer reviewers also provided excellent advice, so I would like to thank them too, whoever they are. I also owe a deep debt of gratitude to all at Stanford University Press who worked in various ways to bring the book to completion: Erica Wetter, Sunna Juhn, Emily E. Smith, Dylan Kyung-lim White, and Mimi Braverman spring to mind.

My family endured the writing process alongside me, and I must sincerely thank them for their forbearance and commiserate with them for their vicarious suffering. I would like to thank my parents, Tom and Nuala, for their support and for the discussions we shared about a time when they were alive but I was not. Father Aidan Keenan, my first cousin once removed, has my sincere thanks for his invaluable help at a critical juncture. My wife, Donna Marie, deserves special mention for her endless patience and for all the stimulating and incisive thoughts she has shared with me about the contents of this book (and everything else in life besides). I would also like to thank my friends and colleagues Adam Baimel, Dave Daly, Eoin Gill, Rohan Kapitany, Danny Lambert, Ailbhe Large, Paul Mulcahy, Aoileann Ní Riain, Selin Nugent, Leopold O'Shea, Sara Rahmani, Filip Uzarevic, Valerie van Mulukom, Ingela Visuri, and Arty Ward for stimulating conversations that have in various subtle ways shaped the development of my thought and therefore this book.

Finally, my most enduring gratitude is reserved for all those whom I interviewed, surveyed, talked to, and (not to be too creepy about it) watched over the course of the past six years. I could never fully express the complexity, variety, and subtlety of all I saw and heard. To appropriate one famous scholar of religion, this book is a map, not the territory. However much it must by necessity simplify, my deepest wish is that my informants feel that it does not mislead.

UNHOLY CATHOLIC IRELAND

INTRODUCTION

YOU HAVE 100% FAILED HUMANITY
—Graffiti at the entrance to a Dublin church, 2011

I found the slogan "You have 100% failed humanity" spray-painted in bright yellow in the doorway of a Catholic church near the docklands in Dublin. It was 2011, two years after the release of the Murphy Report, the results of a government commission tasked with investigating the clerical sexual abuse of minors in the Archdiocese of Dublin between 1974 and 2005. The report concluded that "the Dublin Archdiocese's preoccupations in dealing with cases of child sexual abuse, at least until the mid-1990s, were the maintenance of secrecy, the avoidance of scandal, the protection of the reputation of the Church, and the preservation of its assets. All other considerations, including the welfare of children and justice for victims, were subordinated to these priorities. The Archdiocese did not implement its own canon law rules and did its best to avoid any application of the law of the State."[1] The Murphy Report also revealed that two-thirds of the 325 cases investigated by the commission took place as recently as the 1990s and 2000s.

Disclosures such as these have profoundly altered the image of the Irish Catholic Church. For many of the public, the figure of the priest—still thought by a dwindling few to be the *alter Christus* through whom Christ himself can act—has become psychically enmeshed with the pedophile, modern society's most diabolical pariah. Beyond the culpability of individuals, the institutional Church has widely come to be viewed in a dim light for its role in enabling and covering up such abuses. Further revelations concerning the Catholic past, such as those revolving around repressive institutions including mother and baby homes, Magdalene laundries, and industrial schools, have been added to the disclosures of clerical abuse and its concealment. Rightly or wrongly, the Church has absorbed most of the blame for the oppressive, puritanical culture and copious abuses of the post-independence period. Surveys suggest that many now feel compelled to distance themselves from the Church and from the legacy of the deferent Catholic past. Religious attendance has declined rapidly. Catholic morality has been publicly repudiated in referenda on marriage equality and abortion. At the same time, the Church remains widely embedded in social institutions (most notably the education system), and a large majority of the population continue to describe themselves on census forms as Catholic. How do people justify their stances toward Catholicism in a society where what was once the guardian of public morality has toppled so far from grace that it can be felt to have "100% failed humanity" while nevertheless remaining almost inextricably intertwined in everyday life? How do people cultivate—or indeed salvage—virtue under these circumstances?

Ireland is now almost three decades into what might be termed the age of scandal. This period, defined by the collapse of the Church's moral status, began most notably with the 1992 media revelations of the clandestine affair of a prominent bishop. Layer upon layer and year after year since then, the scandals have grown ever darker. Indeed "the scandals" can seem like a wan euphemism for what is a vast and complex tapestry of moral violations associated with Church policies, personnel, state influence, and institutions. Wider society is also deeply implicated. It is now quite commonplace to encounter the belief that, historically, Irish Catholic culture itself was pathological: in the grip of a morality so rigorous that it failed to be humane and yet tacitly permitted sin in its most extreme form among religious elites. The desacralization of the Church has had profound implications, not only for the institution itself but also for contesting Irish representations of what it means to be a "good" or "moral" person. Over the period that this new image of the past has been formed, the number of Irish people claiming to reject religion outright has increased rapidly. According to some measures, over a quarter of the Irish population now does not affiliate with any religious tradition, and a great many of these people were once at least nominally Catholic, or their parents were. But this is rarely nonreligion of the apathetic variety found in a range of other European societies. Declaring oneself an ex-Catholic or nonreligious in Ireland is often a moral gesture of defiance against a pitch-black vision of the post-independence past, although many Catholics abhor the dark legacies of that era.

The causal links between growing Irish nonreligion and the proliferation of religious scandal are not as direct and simple as is sometimes inferred. As in any secularizing society, a complex web of factors has caused many Irish people to drift away from religion. As Ireland grew more prosperous, it would have been a miracle indeed if the country had not followed the rest of Western Europe into secularization, whether the scandals had happened or not. And so, even though growing disaffiliation is not simply a result of disgust with Ireland's clericalist past and the abuses it enabled, this factor is nevertheless critical to how Irish ex-Catholics view themselves and their position in history and society, with scandal coloring how "not being a religious person" manifests in an Irish context. In this book I chart the relationships between widespread perceptions of religious hypocrisy and the emergence and character of religious rejection among a growing subsection of the Irish "ethno-Catholic" majority. Drawing on anthropological and psychological insights into the complex constructs that we call religion and morality, I examine how this nonreligious stance is locked in interaction with various other Irish orientations toward Catholicism, ranging from loose and fairly indifferent cultural affiliation to devout commitment. In the process I consider how and why people adopt the different stances they do toward a "contaminated" religious tradition and how these stances influence one another. This involves looking in detail at the rhetorical strategies, personal narratives, capitulation to institutional impediments, and everyday behavior that are deployed to support these stances in a country where, as one recent immigrant discerningly phrased it, "A lot of life is lived in the unsaid and the words held back can be more important than the ones actually spoken."[2]

I never discovered the author of that yellow graffiti: whether they had been one of the thousands who had suffered directly at the hands of abusive religious, whether they had been a relative of one who had been abused, or whether they were simply an outraged member of the public. But the slogan's message was clear: Considerable numbers see the Irish Catholic Church as a hotbed of self-interest and perversity. Although voices from the pulpit had determined what it meant to be a "good Irish person" for decades during the twentieth century, that damning Vatican-yellow graffiti captured the contrast between the image of the Irish Catholic Church at its zenith 60 years earlier and its sullied counterpart in 2011. Over the course of about three decades, Catholicism had not just become increasingly peripheral, though this also had happened. A completely different picture of its moral value had been adopted by a large segment of the population. For growing numbers the Cross had become inverted. Holy Catholic Ireland had been turned on its head.

• • •

Decades before, during the height of the Church's authoritarianism, submission to the Church was a source of pride in a small, humbled postcolonial country with little else to its name. Post-independence Ireland was an Atlantic rock of faith, an isolationist bastion of religious purity defended with fervent zeal against Western European secularism and permissiveness. Much like some governments in Eastern Europe today—namely, Poland and Hungary—Ireland's political and ecclesiastical rulers were preoccupied with defending tradition from the liberalizing cultural trends that were sweeping through other European societies. One thing preoccupied the Church more than any other: sex. Sexuality in Catholic Ireland was a minefield of baffling contradictions and hypocrisies, public pieties, semiprivate subversions, and willful, or fearful, blindness and doublethink.[3] It can be difficult today to fully comprehend just how much the obsession with the sins of the flesh exerted a hold on Irish society. Desire was coupled to damnation, and, paradoxically enough, sex was in one way or another ever on the mind. Today, the contradictions between the pulpit-stoked prudishness of the Catholic past and the clerical sexual transgressions of that time are jarring in the extreme. Dedicated specialists have done excellent work unpicking the dense network of institutional, social, theological, historical, and psychological factors that combined to produce a clerical culture that was at once outwardly unchallengeable but inwardly dysfunctional.[4] It is also hard not to speculate on whether the sex-maddened fulminations delivered from Holy

Catholic Ireland's more extreme pulpits simply terrified people or provided a sublimated version of erotic titillation. Most likely both are true, depending on how much the circumstances of one's life and birth put one at risk of ostracism for "giving scandal."[5]

What exactly was the relationship between this sexually repressive, sex-obsessed culture and the abuse and oppression that it produced? And who is to blame? These historical questions are beyond the scope of this book,[6] but they form an important part of its background and should be borne in mind going forward. They represent how a contemporary collective representation of the moral system of Holy Catholic Ireland at its 1950s zenith (and for some decades before and after) became widely entrenched as an anti-model of how people should relate to sex, religion, and one another. This anti-nostalgic shadow image, and the role it plays in the modern rejection of religious affiliation and institutional influence, is what will primarily concern us here.

But Holy Catholic Ireland did not wake up one day and find itself suddenly gone, with socially liberal orthodoxies sprouting like snowdrops in its place. A buffer zone of sorts filled the space between the Holy Catholic "then" and the zealously liberalizing "now." By the early 1990s Irish society had largely reoriented toward materialistic priorities that eclipsed Catholic nationalism and religiously inspired sexual purity. The Church still had great influence, but it had had to exist in the preceding few decades within a state no longer interested in economic and cultural isolationism. Beginning in the 1970s the Church toned down the fulmination and projected a more tolerant and loving image. My own interest in the subject stems from coming into adolescence as an ostensible Catholic in the 1990s at what felt like the liminal crux of this national transformation. It was a confusing time that seemed full of ambiguity and contradiction as I witnessed the attitudes and behavior of peers and strangers change around me with a peculiar kind of acceleration, a frantic mental costume change carried out behind the ever more translucent screen of increasingly nominal Catholicism.

Growing up in such a time, mine was an upbringing of mixed signals. In my immediate family it was tacitly understood that Mass was something we did to placate the aged. My father was a somewhat scornful "Catholic atheist" who nevertheless loved going on architectural pilgrimages to Rome (and who, like James Joyce's character Stephen Daedalus, considered Catholicism both suffocating and yet, in its continental manifestations at least, infinitely superior to what he believed was the aesthetic dourness of Protestantism). Once a year he went to Mass at Christmas in Dublin's Pro Cathedral "for the music," as he told us—to go for the sermon would have been embarrassing. Religion was not something my mother, probably best described as a wavering agnostic, felt comfortable talking about; her experience of it in the past had been repressive, and yet she could not let it go, much as she sometimes seemed to want to. Somehow, she was reluctantly fused to it. Her version of Catholicism was utterly different from my father's; it was regretful, even resentful, and yet it offered some conduit to an inalienable, if at times reluctant, sense of the supernatural. So, instead of facing these irreconcilable feelings, she stayed at home and basted the turkey.

By the time I was at university, fortress Catholicism had been thoroughly penetrated by globalization and it was crumbling, without having quite reached the levels of collapse witnessed from the late 2000s onward. I saw the last residues of Holy Catholic Ireland's former rigor preserved in my grandmother, a self-abnegating middle-class Irish Catholic to her very core. She went to Mass every day, and her austere religious outlook was tacitly treated as an anachronism by my family but also as something so brittle that we were obliged to tolerate it at all costs. I remember well, when we were children, her vicelike grip around our wrists as she dragged my brother and me onto a dual carriageway and into oncoming traffic so we could get across the road to Mass on time—and this was only on a Tuesday morning. Her faith was strong—strong enough to bring the cars screeching to a halt. Later, she succumbed to Alzheimer's just before the Church's scandals truly got underway.

In my lifetime, as Catholicism further softened, it also weakened. At home and at school, I saw religion atrophy in real time in a way that would have disturbed my grandmother, had she been privy to it. In the early 1990s, at secondary school—"a school for the sons of Catholic gentlemen" as it proudly billed itself, though rugby was its true creed—any efforts by our religion teacher to steer conversations toward matters of faith would be met with glazed eyes and demands to watch another episode of *The Simpsons*, something that we often got to do as a treat (at religious instruction's expense). The man, a child of the 1960s, was palpably uncomfortable carrying out the Church's work of "faith formation" and generally acquiesced. Yet any skeptical questions on religion were met with hostility, not from the teacher, who was always an understanding and benevolent man, but rather from the other students. In the attitude of those boys, the tacit makeshift social ethos of that time of transition was crystallized. It was OK to be inwardly bored by Catholicism because it had grown irrelevant (or "naff," as we put it), but it was still not really OK to question it out loud. If Holy Catholic Ireland had become a paper-thin charade, it was also a social faux pas to pick at the wallpaper.[7]

This has long since ceased to be the case. The apogee of the Church's loss of control came between 2015 and 2018, the period of my doctoral fieldwork in Dublin, where I was examining whether there was a relationship between religious scandals and declining Catholic affiliation and what that relationship might be. As Ireland's bond to Catholicism continued to weaken with the results of public referenda that incrementally excised Catholic morality from the Constitution[8] and just as some felt that "the scandals" were finally becoming an exhausted thing of the past, the Church's image faltered yet further in 2017. In March of that year, the Commission of Investigation into Mother and Baby Homes confirmed that a "significant amount" of infant remains had been discovered in the subsurface chambers of a disused sewage system at a former mother and baby home in Tuam, County Galway. This home had been one of a network of such institutions run by religious congregations where women who became pregnant outside of marriage were effectively imprisoned and hidden away in shame until their babies were delivered. Many children were then given up for adoption by the nuns, frequently to Catholic families in the United States, in return for substantial cash donations to the religious order, with the mother's consent often obtained through coercion, if at all.[9] The commission had been established following the pioneering efforts of local historian Catherine Corless, whose research was picked up by national and international media in 2014. Her investigations had uncovered that almost 800 babies and young children had died at the Tuam home run by the Bon Secours Sisters from 1925 to 1961, and she raised suspicions that many had been improperly buried in the defunct sewage system at the back of the home. Despite statements from the Gardaí in 2014 that "these are historical burials going back to famine times" with "no suggestion of any impropriety,"[10] the 2017 announcement confirmed that the remains indeed dated to the period of the Bon Secours home. Tests furthermore indicated that the children had ranged in age from 35 fetal weeks to 3 years—they had undeniably been the socially stigmatized "children of sin" consigned to the nuns' care.

For decades, the news had been so dominated by clerical child abuse, ecclesiastical cover-ups, the uncooperativeness of the Vatican, and the Church's evasion of compensation for victims, that Irish people had perhaps become somewhat detached from their own roles in the scandals, or the roles of their ancestors and the political parties they still voted for. But in the late 2010s, in the media and from the conversations that I heard around me, the re-examination of Holy Catholic Ireland's repressive institutional infrastructure was growing, along with interest in the twin thorny issues of culpability and widespread social complicity. After all, many had known that these institutions existed, and everyone involved had been Irish. Some unquestionably bore more responsibility than others, but these gradations threatened to be elided by the political construction of an ambiguous, vaporous receptacle into which all levels of culpability (including that of the state) could be decanted and combined: "past society." In 2021 these discussions were activated once again following the publication of the Mother and Baby Homes Report, which detailed an "appalling level of infant mortality" that was double the rate in the general population. The report also confirmed that children in the homes had been subjected to medical experiments, being used in vaccine trials without parental or guardian consent. Between 1922 and 1998, when the last home closed in Cork, 9,000 children had perished in the 18 institutions investigated by the commission. Taoiseach Micheál Martin's response to the report in the Dáil drew criticism for emphasizing that the commission's findings should be a generalized source of shame for all of Irish society rather than for the Catholic Church, the implicated religious orders and, perhaps more important in the context of Martin's speech, the state itself. Shortly after his address, Martin's apology was criticized in the Dáil on these and similar grounds by Catherine Connolly, independent Galway West TD (Teachta Dála, a member of the Dáil), whose own counterspeech on the subject was viewed more favorably in the media. Connolly criticized the report's conclusions that there was no compulsion for women and girls to enter the homes or to give up their babies for adoption, despite the fact that this "bears no connection to the testimony given," which makes clear "the role of the priest, the role of the Church, the role of the County Council."[11] This somber grappling with the past, however, is only one stream of discourse in a country with a tarnished religious past. The fact is that many people have found their own far more irreverent ways of coping with Catholicism and its legacies: mocking its pieties and profanities and further trampling its already long-sullied claims to authority while often still participating in a nostalgic, expedient, or instrumental manner when it suits them.

The flipside of the decades-long revision of the past, then, is that people have unconsciously adapted to the slow piecemeal pace of its terrible revelations. Consternation, for some, may have even been eclipsed by a habituation bordering on apathy. People grow inured to political performances of contrition offsetting the shame of the past. Since the late 1990s, Bertie Ahern, Brian Cowen, Enda Kenny, Leo Varadkar, and Micheál Martin—that is, all of Ireland's taoisigh—have waxed lyrical on the same repentant note, and it is regarded in some quarters as more than a little ritualistic (whereas many others simply do not listen to Dáil speeches or the 9 o'clock news).[12] Ireland today is in some ways reckoning with itself. But for all its secularizing referenda, it has also developed the jaundiced attitude of a post-religious abuse society, replete with post-traumatic black humor that would have given my grandmother a stroke. Many people have learned to live with a deeply contaminated religious institution, and some may even relish how statuses have been reversed. When I was writing this book, someone who had just come back from his lavish but largely socially placatory church wedding (which he justified as follows: "Look, she would've gone spare if it hadn't happened sooner or later, her aul one was down our necks, and I'm not one for passing up a hooley in Marbella!") told me the following joke:

> Why is a priest like a pint of Guinness?
> I don't know.
> Because he's in black up to the neck, has a white collar, and if you get a bad one he'll rip the hole off you.

When this informant returned intact from Marbella, he told me that the Spanish priest had in fact turned out to be quite pleasant.

• • •

In the field, I found that ex-Catholicism was often just as much a position taken against such complex positions of detached lingering affiliation as it was a stance of opposition to the Church itself. As the spotlight of abuse has intensified, the ostensible complacency of "cultural Catholicism" has been dragged into conscious scrutiny. In some circles the laissez-faire relationship of Ireland's post-1990s "à la carte" Catholicism to what is increasingly framed as a morally bankrupt religious institution has become an object of disdain, described by some as an immorally amnesiac tolerance for the crimes of a humbled Church—so long as it remains in its place as a convenient service provider of children's rites of passage, weddings, funerals, intergenerational harmony, and a source of inspiration for light television comedy.

Arguably, the driving animus of this stance is not only the Church's sins but also the fact that they have taken place amid a series of tensions relating to secularization. Once, Archbishop John Charles McQuaid could tacitly dictate state moral policy,[13] but today the Irish Church has declined in power, eclipsed by a quintessentially neoliberal political elite that is eager to look socially progressive, entrepreneurial, and global but that is also saddled with a clientelist political system and the duty of placating the piety of older and more conservative voters. By hook or by crook, the Church has clung onto what it has left, particularly through hegemonic control of the education system and, until recently, certain reproductive issues. But its institutional grip is slipping fast, though not as fast as some would like. Under these circumstances, the fact that a large swath of the population—whether or not they actually agree with the Church—continue to affiliate for purely cultural or ethnic reasons has become an object of increased secularist critique.

Although it would be a stretch to call the Republic of Ireland a divided society, the tensions implicit in the situation feel closer to the surface now. Some sectors of Irish society dream of it being a paragon of purity again, but this time a progressive secular one: Wholly Woke Ireland, a cosmopolitan and caring prefect of modernity. Others disagree, seeing in the construction of the "new morality" the atomizing, capitalistic destruction of a traditional way of life under an imported and imitative smokescreen. Still others are happy right where things are. And when it comes to religion, many are like the figures in Graham Knuttel paintings, which came to typify the interior décor of Dublin's Celtic Tiger–era restaurants: keeping poker faces but looking sidelong at one another, judging and fearing judgment, aware that social status is in play.[14]

The scandals enter this picture as an affordance in a struggle over moral and social reorientation. They have changed the moral status of "being religious" in Ireland but have not led to the growth of Irish nonreligion by directly causing disaffiliation among previously devout Catholics. The story is more complex than this. As I show in the following chapters, religious hypocrisy and its relationship to Irish ex-Catholicism must be understood in the context of a background of waning culturally Catholic socialization, entrenched religious influence on laws and institutions, openly habitual yet seemingly inescapable affiliation, increasing wealth and cultural globalization, and the kind of reorientation toward progressive social trends visible in many affluent Western capitalist societies. The emergence of Irish people who consider themselves not belonging to a religion is fueled not only by the tension between contrasting religious and secular aspirations for society but also by the tension between secular moralism and a condition of mass religious indifference that has grown quietly inside the outer shell of Catholic affiliation. In some ways, the explicit rejection of Catholicism is another manifestation of Ireland's preoccupation with Catholicism. Even if circumstances present no other option, to position oneself in opposition to something is also to focus on it and allow it be a deep part of one's life.

• • •

In this book I have sought to describe Irish ways of being nonreligious during a particular time period (2017–2021), focusing on their relationships to the peculiarities of Irish history, Irish society, Irish scandal, and Irish secularization. This has involved over four years of surveys, interviews, ethnographic fieldwork, and innumerable conversations with anyone who would talk to me. As is standard anthropological practice, I have used pseudonyms wherever possible to maintain informant privacy, with the exception of high-profile public organizations and individuals that are too distinctive to conceal in this manner.

Each chapter in this book contributes to a portrait of the everyday moral dispute around religion in Ireland that has given birth to what I call the ex-Catholic stance. In Chapter 1, I lay out the background and context of Irish nonreligion, situating it within a complex scene of secularization and fragmenting consensus about what being a Catholic involves and who gets to decide. I also describe the decades-long scandals that have undermined the moral credibility of the Church, greatly strengthening the hand of secularists and massively weakening the already waning social standing of religious conservatives.

It is one thing to claim that Irish ex-Catholicism bears some relationship to the desacralization of the Church and that the Irish baptized-but-now-unaffiliated have been numerically underestimated, but it is another to provide evidence for this. In Chapter 2, therefore, I present findings from a small but in-depth representative survey of 248 baptized Catholics. Among other findings, the data suggest that the number of ex-Catholics has been underestimated because of natalist responding and that the rejection of Catholicism is highly morally motivated. Associational data vividly demonstrate that the swiftest association with the Catholic Church for ex-Catholics (who make up one-third of the sample) is pedophilia, followed soon after by conservativism and corruption. Among other things, the data show, first, that ex-Catholics are exceptionally distrustful of the clergy, judging them as less trustworthy than bankers and politicians; second, that they tend to have been brought up in households with little parental religious socialization; and, finally, that they tend to be more morally progressive and younger. But this strong religious antipathy cannot be explained by clerical abuse scandals alone, as these are a global phenomenon. The taint of clerical abuse has interacted with a complex social setting, and the subsequent ethnographic chapters illuminate how responses to clerical abuse operate within this scene of moral conflict. Using the 2018 papal visit as an example, I set the ethnographic scene at the end of Chapter 2 by drawing the reader's attention to the growth of two prominent, quietly antagonistic social stances: religious antipathy and religious apathy.

From Chapter 3 onward, the book is purely ethnographic. One key element in the decline of Irish Catholicism is the degree to which participation had already become a matter of almost open social conformity rather than spirituality or religiosity for a growing number of the population. The scandals did not arrive in a Catholic society at the zenith of its piety. This, in part, explains their power in an Irish context: People were ready to spurn the Church; they were fed up with its demands. In Chapter 3 I examine qualitative data drawn from an intergenerational sample of informants from two Dublin parishes. The data depict how Catholic socialization has been transformed, particularly in the home. Catholic doctrine and practices, if encountered at all, are now generally quarantined to experiences in the school system and swiftly abandoned afterward. From this perspective, the cultural and liberalized forms of Catholicism described as emerging in the 1990s can be reconceptualized as a transient and increasingly inertial connection: the sacred canopy of Holy Catholic Ireland has become flimsy and peripheral. This dissolution of relevance foreshadowed the rejection that was to come by replacing an omnipresent, if frequently oppressive, experience of religiosity with one that was vague and disconnected from everyday routines and concerns. As one religious commentator phrased it, for the majority, Irish Catholicism had become something "for emergency use only" before the scandals even arrived on the scene. It is often also openly instrumental and sometimes nakedly tongue in cheek.

However, thin as religious Catholicism has become, the growth in Irish nonreligion is not without its impediments, even among those who actively deride the Church and scorn religious participation. Much of this links to all those aspects of Irish Catholicism that are decidedly *not* religious and therefore have relatively little to do with the Church and its moral collapse—that is, the deep importance of "Catholicism" as a symbol of local, familial, and national identity. Far from being sheeplike or unaware, cultural Catholic stances that absorb the perception of a morally tarnished Church have emerged. In Chapter 4 I focus in more detail on a case study that illustrates one particularly extreme form of cultural Catholicism encountered in the field: concealed cultural Catholic atheism among working-class self-identified Catholic men. These men primarily construct Catholic doctrine as "a load of shite," consider the Church a hypocritical and power-hungry business enterprise, and maintain that they participate in Catholic rituals and practices primarily out of a desire to ensure social harmony by preventing distress to weaker members of the community who need the crutch of religion to get by. In the context of what one informant described as "a tradition that is expected and has to be respected" and against which one "has no argument," atheism emerges as a private matter that should not be allowed to interfere with traditional social ties. This ethic of harmony, and the manner in which it has already successfully assimilated Church scandal, is likely a considerable impediment to the missionary objectives of purist ex-Catholicism.

The moral battlefield of Irish secularization, however, shows signs of generating new collective representations of what it means to be a "good Irish person." These secularization battles have become particularly heightened since 2014, leading almost to what might be described as an Irish culture war around the intertwinement of church and state. The Church holds on tenaciously to its influence at an institutional level, constituting a kind of progress-inhibiting structural force that exacerbates the antipathy of the nonreligious and other secularists. In the ensuing public battles to sway the more ambiguous middle, newspapers, broadcast TV and radio, social media, and the streets are filled with rhetoric around the turpitude of the Church. Therefore in Chapter 5 I draw on field data from various rallies and marches in Dublin and on interviews and secondary and online sources to describe the tense social dynamics of the lingering institutional influence of Catholicism, particularly in the educational realm and, until recently, in legal restrictions over abortion. The ideological field is dominated by secularist and traditionalist actors who vie for influence over a more blasé culturally Catholic middle in order to retain or eradicate Church influence on social institutions and laws. Religious conservatives describe a culture that is hostile to faith and make such statements as "Church-bashing is the new Brit-bashing." Secularist rejoinders focus on hypocrisy and admonish antagonists to "look up the dictionary definition of persecution . . . before passing judgment on people legitimately criticizing religion in the public sphere." Scandal has altered the moral stature of these two antagonists. The entrenched nature of Irish Catholic identity, perceived by some as another layer of Irish Catholic hypocrisy (given how little it relates to orthodoxy or moral commitment), continues to frustrate secular activists, particularly as baptism and census affiliation are used by religious conservatives to argue that Catholic institutional influence has numerical support. This conflict has led to a powerful secularist moral narrative that taps potent preexisting tropes around Ireland as a plucky underdog fighting its way toward a long-deferred but deeply romanticized dream of liberation. This allows the construction of public representations of secularization as a kind of new Irish freedom struggle.

Ex-Catholics are those who have most emphatically embraced this new normative vision of what it means to be a responsible Irish citizen in the 2020s. In Chapter 6 I describe ex-Catholicism in detail, drawing on key informant testimony and discourse in a number of real-world and online secularist communities to illustrate how it is primarily oriented around the moralized repudiation of both the Catholic Church and the cultural Catholic default presumed to keep it in power. Ex-Catholics often position themselves in opposition to cultural Catholics—whom they frequently construct as irresponsible, inauthentic, and complicit enablers of a corrupt and harm-causing institution—and describe themselves as a minority who bravely resist the easy comforts of low-cost social conformity. As one ex-Catholic informant said of her religiously apathetic sister after the baptism of her niece, "I am disgusted. . . . Surely baptizing your child is a vote to keep the reins in the hands of the Church?" Scandal powerfully amplifies this stance, and it becomes more pronounced and more socially active when there is a scandal outbreak. These dynamics are described through the example of the Tuam mother and baby home scandal of 2016–2017 and the reactions it generated. Overall, ex-Catholics are often best described as adhering to a normative stance that I describe as anti-nostalgic moralized authenticity: The past is a bleak hellscape of clericalist Catholic oppression; people have a moral obligation to rid the present of the Church's lingering influence; and one's religious status ought to be determined individualistically by one's beliefs rather than relationally by what one was born as.

In Chapter 7 I turn to an examination of how the moral taint has affected devout Catholics, beginning with priests and then moving on to members of the laity. Overall, although scandal draws secularists together and empowers cultural Catholics to seize a position of greater autonomy, it also exacerbates underlying tensions as the devout grapple with a new situation in which the moral rectitude of their close ties to the Church can be openly challenged by those who are "anti-Church, anti-God, anti-everything for the sake of being anti," as one informant put it. This has created an inward turn in devout Irish Catholicism: It has become withdrawn, self-conscious, broken up into increasingly idiosyncratic subcultures, and far less suitable for intergenerational transmission. The scandals have ushered in a fragmenting process as Catholics pursue a variety of idiosyncratic methods of salvaging moral status. Some cope with the taint by localizing it in a rival Catholic faction. Others quarantine it to direct perpetrators, and some counter-weaponize it by deflecting to experiences of personal victimhood and portraying secularists as opportunistic aggressors unmotivated by genuine moral concern. But in the face of a powerfully reinforced and coherent secularist moral narrative, it is unclear how much intergenerational traction these fragmented Catholic stances will have. On the other hand, the process of secularization has moved on from highly emotive issues such as abortion to the more complex and less powerfully affective issue of Church educational control. The intensity, success, and duration of Ireland's coming secularization battle around education remains impossible to predict. And at a larger level, fragmentary geopolitical forces at work in the British Isles may, in time, reopen old wounds and reactivate Catholicism not so much as a religion but as an ethnic designation. As a result, the future distribution of nonreligion and cultural Catholicism remains impossible to foresee. But for all this uncertainty or perhaps because of it, Ireland is one of the most complex and compelling places in the world today to study the moralized rejection of religion.

CHAPTER 1

SECULARIZATION, THE DESACRALIZATION OF THE CHURCH, AND THE EMERGENCE OF ETHNO-CATHOLIC "NONES"

Secularization did not arrive in Ireland simply because of the moral contamination of the Church. It developed piece by piece, a complex tapestry of disenchantment. Beneath a veneer of Catholic hegemony, Irish religion had been growing more brittle for decades. The scandals, then, acted as a kind of coup de grâce. They were unleashed by other prior secularizing processes, like methane deposits released by melting permafrost. But when they came, they fed back into, hastened, and colored Irish secularization. The scandals combined with existing tensions around residual Church influence in a semi-secularized society to powerfully alter the appeal of different social stances, and they undermined the previously unquestionable rectitude of maintaining some kind of connection to Catholicism, no matter how loose. Nor has their influence ended. Today, the tainted tide can seem to recede at intervals, revealing Irish Catholicism as merely comprising inoffensive rites of passage and a harmless source of comfort to a large but aging devout minority. Then, with a sudden swell, it can surge through the media and public consciousness in a septic wave of controversy, pitching all sorts of different stances against one another. Since the desacralization of the Church, no one has the social authority to define what "Catholic" means anymore, and it is not always clear whether it needs to mean anything definite at all. Although it may seem oxymoronic, most Irish Catholics are now Catholic in their own way, and ideological cohesiveness has apparently switched sides to a growing nonreligious minority that is acutely aware of itself as not-Catholic.

Once, Irish Catholicism was deeper in its levels of popular commitment, more static, more uniform, and much more constricting. This was not an immemorial condition. Irish Catholicism was heightened from the mid-nineteenth to the mid-twentieth century. In the decades after independence, Ireland became a fortress of deferent Catholic piety—"the most Catholic country in the world." In the opening decades of the twenty-first century, it is now a fairly typical socially liberal Western European state. But though the transformation may look complete, tensions exist just beneath the surface of this societal makeover, and the past has not simply vanished. In this chapter I establish this context by summarizing existing knowledge on the historic amplification of Irish religiosity, the factors that subsequently led to Irish secularization, the revelations and reappraisals collectively known as the scandals, and the growth in Irish nonreligion that coincided with them. At a theoretical level, I also discuss how and why phenomena such as the scandals may have contributed to this increase in Irish Catholic disaffiliation.

The Foundations of Holy Catholic Ireland

By the time Irish freedom was won in 1921, "Irishness" had become fused to a rigorous version of Catholicism. This ethnoreligious melding had deep foundations. The plantation of large numbers of Protestant settlers since the time of Elizabeth I and consequent experiences of religious persecution—in particular the Penal Laws[1]—set the groundwork for the amalgamation of national and religious identity that would later come to full fruition in the early to mid-twentieth century. As the rural peasantry died or emigrated in large numbers after the Famine struck in 1845, their unorthodox folk Catholicism came to be replaced by centralized control, Roman devotions, regular practice, sexual abstinence, and intense clerical supervision.[2] This was facilitated by the rapid development of Church infrastructure and clerical discipline over the course of the nineteenth century. Spearheading this "devotional revolution"[3] was Paul Cullen, archbishop first of Armagh and then of Dublin and finally Ireland's first cardinal. He was also the principal architect of the dogma of papal infallibility. Cullen's mission from the Vatican was to bring popular Irish Catholicism in line with Roman best practice under one of the

Church's most conservative pontificates—indeed, to make Ireland an example of an ideal Catholic society. Between 1850 and 1870, under Cullen's watchful eye and steady hand, Ireland's ratio of priests to people went from 1:3,300 to 1:1,100, and the number of nuns increased from 1,500 to 3,700.[4] National identity was intertwined with an iteration of Catholicism that bore the authoritarian and reactionary stamp of Cullen's master, Pope Pius IX, who sought to consolidate the power of the papacy in reaction to the threat posed by the spread of secular liberalism.

Under this influence, Irish Catholicism developed a particularly clericalist bent. Drawn largely from an emergent Catholic middle class deeply concerned with issues of social respectability, sexual control, and self-abnegation, the clergy were deferred to on all ethical and social considerations, forming a kind of austere public conscience. Post-independence, this culture was institutionally and politically reinforced. The state was born without resources and left the healthcare and education systems to the Church and its legions. Strictly speaking, Ireland was never a theocracy, but Irish political elites were socialized within a totalizing Catholic system, guaranteeing profound ecclesiastical influence (though also permitting a Protestant cultural and religious space for a small minority). The country's underdevelopment and isolation were viewed by bishops and religiously inclined politicians as an opportunity to preserve national sanctity in the face of the secularizing trends that were sweeping across Western Europe in the aftermath of World War II. Ireland's leaders sought to construct an isolationist Catholic state, immune to the licentiousness of modern Europe (and Britain in particular). The signature preoccupation of the religious hierarchy was unlicensed sexual activity, an object of fixation and disgust that threatened the chaste image of the Irish nation. Nor was this ethos limited to the clergy alone. People often use the phrase "Catholic guilt" to suggest a distinctive psychological state of inner torment, but in the Irish case it was joined and eclipsed by "Catholic shame": the judgment leveled at those who publicly failed to live up to the unifying national ideal of exemplary Catholic purity. At the same time, the orthodox Catholic supernatural world provided a potent source of meaning and religious experience for many people. God was real; fear of his judgment drove people to the confessionals in great numbers, where they waited in long queues to unburden themselves. Mary, to whom the faithful prayed for "intercession," was more merciful and offered succor in times of trial. And then there were the saints, approachable and modest demigods with special domains of interest; pious individuals could turn to them for any number of life's problems and could cultivate a particular "devotion" to them. Irish religion was profoundly performative and public, but in many cases it also stretched deep into the intimate sphere of the family and into the mental life of the individual. It is impossible to disentangle all the motivations of midcentury Irish piety today. Both devout belief and social coercion were involved, as were the need for some sense of control over life's challenges, instrumentally motivated social participation, and simple conformity.

The result was that Catholicism touched everything. People deeply, inalienably *were* Catholics. Narratives around the historical suppression of Catholicism were amplified after independence, often in the educational sphere, where they were expounded with particular zeal by the Christian Brothers, a lay order committed both to educating the next generation and to infusing them with an unshakeable Catholic nationalism. Jeremiads about the long "800 years of oppression," propounded again and again in the classroom and elsewhere, fused the people to the faith even more. And fused they were. Recently, scholars have suggested that there may be at least two distinct types of group consciousness: group identity, which is based on shared symbolic behaviors indicating belonging;[5] and fusion, where experiences of shared adversity manifest in a visceral feeling of common essence with co-sufferers.[6] Both factors bound Irish identity to Catholicism. The daily rituals of Catholic obeisance built up a strong group identity through the constant projection of symbolic Catholic behaviors indicating one's status as "a good Irish person." Broadly, "good Irish people" were those who went to Mass every week or more, who lined up in front of confessionals, who doffed hats when passing churches, who took the ashes on Ash Wednesday without fail, who had a Sacred Heart hanging at home to watch them and also to be seen watching them, and who peppered their speech with phatic religious language. Alongside this, economic hardship and the direct experience of colonial humiliation—subsequently experienced vicariously in Irish historical narratives perpetuated in the education system and elsewhere—increased the sense of fusion, of a fate bound by persecution to a shared essence as Irish Catholic. Both channels of collective consciousness flowed into one another, congealing into a dense compound of ethnoreligious identity: "Irish and Catholic." No matter how one felt about Catholicism as it manifested in daily life, Catholic was what one was—even if one resented it. Cords woven of suffering, whether experienced directly or vicariously, cannot easily be cut. Even though the political, and indeed religious, ethos changed—and by the late 1960s the country was beginning to open up somewhat economically and culturally—most of the population would remain solidly Catholic for another three decades, at least outwardly so.

To the untrained eye, the foundations laid by Cullen under Pius seemed to hold strong deep into the latter half of the twentieth century. By 1977 Ireland was sufficiently resistant to secularization that Pope Paul VI praised it as the "last Catholic country" after Italy, France, and Spain all decriminalized contraception in quick succession.[7] The economically stagnant 1980s even marked a period of religious retrenchment. Irish Catholicism was strategically reinforced by the Vatican right at the cusp of that decade. In 1979 Paul VI's almost immediate successor, John Paul II, rewarded "the last Catholic country" with its first pontifical visit. It is impossible to overstate the euphoria that the visit generated. Film footage that could have been directed by Leni Riefenstahl shows John Paul II's plane detouring over Dublin's Phoenix Park to whet the appetite of the largest crowd ever to gather on Irish soil.[8] The rapturous welcome the pope received exemplified Ireland's outlier status in Western Europe, the most godless part of the "free world." When the pope dismounted from the "St. Patrick" (the Aer Lingus Boeing 747 commissioned to carry him), he kissed the runway at Dublin Airport. In return, he was greeted with a speech in Irish that included the words, "We are all very happy that this honor has been bestowed on our country during our lifetime." In the Phoenix Park the pontiff celebrated Mass to a congregation of no fewer than 1.25 million people—fully 37% of the population.

This sense of ethnoreligious cohesion, so anomalous in a late-twentieth-century Western European society yet manifested with such ecstasy by the crowds gathering to cheer John Paul II, was not to last. Greeted by a national roar of euphoric abasement, the papal visit was the final hurrah of Holy Catholic Ireland. Though spectacular, it perhaps inevitably served as the precursor not to a permanent reinvigoration of Irish faith and obedience but to a profound religious anticlimax. After the papal euphoria died down, the Catholic comedown commenced. In the coming decades religion would retract from its central position in the lives of the majority, and, as their interest waned, the Church would begin to lose its institutional and legal toeholds. Today, unifying collective effervescence of the kind that greeted the pope is still possible, but mostly in the domains of sport and entertainment, not religion. Religious conviction is now optional, and it is often a private matter (school "faith formation" notwithstanding). Furthermore, whether and how one ought to relate to the Church and Catholic tradition have become topics of critique and debate. Irish Catholic conformity has crumbled, increasingly replaced by the imperative to form a more personalized identity based on one's own attributes, values, or tastes and to build this persona with less emphasis on relationships and background.[9] This "individualism" is often associated with the complex and academically contested process known as secularization.[10] Although there are broad patterns in how societies secularize, each society also does so in response to its own set of historical and social idiosyncrasies, and Ireland is no exception here.

Irish Secularization

In his doleful elegy *Dover Beach*, the Victorian poet Matthew Arnold describes the disenchantment of England as the "sea of faith" recedes. Historian Callum Brown, in his highly influential book *The Death of Christian Britain*, moved the dial forward some hundred years. British religious attendance had been in decline since the late nineteenth century, but it was only with the sweeping socially liberalizing changes of the 1960s that Christianity truly began to lose its place in forming attitudes and worldviews. Arnold's poem was preemptive: It was the Pill, not the theory of evolution, that caused faith to expire "on the naked shingles of the world." But many of the social changes of which Callum Brown writes were held at bay just across the Irish Sea: Contraceptives were made fully available only in 1992, and divorce remained illegal until 1995 (and remained more difficult to obtain than elsewhere in Western Europe until further changes were instituted through another referendum in 2019). Nor was this legislation simply a matter of top-down diktat. Through public referenda, the electorate voted *against* divorce in 1986 and formalized the ban on abortion in 1983. According to many secularization theorists, Ireland clung to conservative religiosity for decades as Europe secularized around it. For instance, sociologist Steve Bruce saw Ireland as an anomaly, a place where religion remained necessary as a result of its role "as a guarantor of national identity and integrity."[11]

Specialists in Irish religious change describe a trajectory that is longer and more nuanced than this. Tom Inglis, Gladys Ganiel, Louise Fuller, and a number of others point out that a network of factors has acted for decades to undermine the devout obeisance of pre-Conciliar Holy Catholic Ireland. These include the expansion of tertiary education[12] and shifts in government policy toward economic productivity over the preservation of traditional Catholic values;[13] changing gender norms and their influence on domestic religious socialization (once chiefly the province of the traditional Irish mother, who supported the moral control of the priests in the domestic sphere and encouraged religious vocations in her children);[14] the relativization of Irish worldviews through such technologies as television, affordable travel, and, later, the internet; the new, more uncontrollable social commentators ushered in by these technologies; the demystifying changes wrought internally by Vatican II;[15] a decades-long, simmering resentment of the Church's authoritarianism and the brutality of some of its servants, in particular, the Christian Brothers;[16] and, perhaps most important, the tension generated between a gradually liberalizing society and a religious institution generally opposed to social change. As both Gladys Ganiel and Callum Brown note, this last item was perhaps most powerfully exemplified in the growth of a fairly marginal but impassioned feminism that arose in response to the restrictive implications for women of church-state influence. The greater independence that had been granted to women through economic and social developments was still constrained by laws concerning reproductive technologies, such as access to contraception, something with a greater influence on women's lives than on men's.[17] Galvanized by objection to the Church's continued resistance to contraception and abortion as put forth in the papal encyclical *Humanae Vitae*, the 1970s thus saw the emergence of protests against Catholic influence on state policy and the first real emergence of female anti-clericalism.[18] Although society generally remained outwardly conservative[19]—with religious belief, identification, and practice almost universal and with far tighter social control and greater deference to authority and conformity than found elsewhere in Western Europe—a suggestion of underlying discord, of a crevasse forming between the laity and the Church, was breaking through the external image of Irish Catholic obedience. Callum Brown sees this as a critical moment for what was to come, noting that, although "little outwardly changed in the 1960s or even the 1970s, liberalizing ideologies like feminism took root[20] . . . the change was initially highly localized to Dublin, but leaked out in the 1980s and early 1990s into a slow nationwide decline in Mass attendance that accelerated in the latter 1990s and 2000s."[21]

Other observers emphasize less obvious changes taking place during the 1970s. They suggest that ongoing high Mass attendance statistics concealed a shift toward a less anxiety-ridden but also perhaps less all-consuming form of religious participation. Louise Fuller, for instance, notes that the changes instituted by Vatican II meant that the "stern taskmaster" was replaced by a "loving, understanding God, who was not out to catch people if they made a mistake," meaning that the "kind of dread that filled people's minds at the idea that they might have committed a mortal sin—and not be in a 'state of grace'—no longer had the same urgency."[22]

The psychological cost of the Church's effort to harmonize with the new liberalizing climate was a loss of attentional space for its once-terrifying mental representations. This newer and more lenient God concept could safely be shifted from the front of the mind to the back. One acute observer, journalist Malachi O'Doherty, noted how, as far back as the 1970s, the awkward interaction between *Humanae Vitae* and Vatican II's overall ethos, whereby violations were codified more rigorously but their implications were diluted, encouraged a confused, laissez-faire attitude.

> At the moment at which it chose to try to police our sexual conduct more rigorously, by formalising its ban on contraception, it threw away the whip in its own hand and stopped preaching about Hell and damnation. We were told that it was a sin to use a condom—in Dublin, they were called "frenchies" then—but we were no longer told that sins had painful consequences for us, apart from making God a wee bit unhappy.[23]

As the 1970s and 1980s progressed and as continued high Mass attendance coincided with public conceptions of moral behavior that increasingly diverged from those still being advocated from the pulpit (albeit in less stentorian tones), the socially compulsory dimension of Mass attendance became awkwardly obvious—the historian Diarmaid Ferriter uses playwright John B. Keane's term "practising lapsed Catholics."[24] And though it is true that many babies born in 1980 were christened John Paul in honor of the pontiff's spectacular visit, the economist David McWilliams suggests that a not-inconsiderable number were conceived out of wedlock in the campsite that serviced pilgrims to the papal Mass; the atmosphere there was, by some accounts, not dissimilar to what one might find at a rock festival.[25] A duality was emerging: For growing numbers Catholicism was retracting into something that did not really structure daily life. Despite John Paul II's public relations triumph in 1979, the 1970s was also the decade when the outline of a more disengaged and more openly habitual version of Irish Catholicism began to take shape: "Being Catholic" remained obligatory, but at the same time it became quarantinable to Sunday Mass, funerals, First Communions, and census forms.

After what some see as a secularization hiatus or at least a deceleration in the economically stagnant 1980s,[26] the 1990s was another critical decade. Callum Brown considers Ireland perhaps the only country to have been "secularized by scandal," but this picture is complicated by the fact that scandal coincided with explosive economic growth. Ireland has one of the highest per capita GDPs in the world.[27] It has transformed itself into a globalized neoliberal hub offering low taxes to international corporations, and Dublin—its narrow streets now clogged with SUVs—has become one of the world's most expensive cities to live in. This transformation went into overdrive during the "Celtic Tiger" economic boom, which lasted from the mid-1990s to the late 2000s. As described by one commentator, this was a time of "hagiographic" discourse around conceptions of a modernized "new Ireland" where "capitalists are lionised for their enterprise," where the "elementary pursuit of profit" is translated "into a rather higher moral calling," where trade books and popular media articles seek "to identify the talent and zeal of those who have accumulated personal fortunes in a time of boom in a country that, until recently, was scarcely associated with business acumen."[28] The spoils of the boom were far from evenly distributed, but they did create a substantial increase in the middle classes. Although there was some tutting from the sidelines, the Celtic Tiger years were full of a sense of pride at the idea that Ireland, once an oppressed backwater, could become a model of praiseworthy cosmopolitanism and the economic envy of its neighbors. Irish confidence and prosperity were viewed as an escape from the "backwards" "theocratic" past, a past that was better sealed away. Fuller noted a "change in people's perceptions of themselves, their lifestyles, morale, confidence and sense of independence."[29] It became more normal for people to think of themselves as individuals defined by their choices in a free and open market of glossy products and liberated ideas. Economic immigration also meant that Ireland became a much more diverse society. Even when the Celtic Tiger era ended and the 2008 recession began, the fortunes of institutional religion were not revived.

Ireland fits a global pattern here. Wealth is critical to secularization. In a wide-ranging cross-cultural study, US scholars Pippa Norris and Ronald Inglehart identify levels of existential security—freedom from such factors as disease, high mortality, hunger, poverty, inequality, conflict, lack of social security, and natural disasters—as a key factor in determining levels of orthodox religiosity.[30] Thus, for example, the Scandinavian countries are exceptionally secular, whereas African and Middle Eastern nations are highly religious. The United States' outlier status as an unusually religious nation—which is changing[31]—is due in part to its relatively poor social security net despite the country's exceptional wealth. Within societies and between them, the poor are almost universally more religious than the rich. The main fault line between the secularizing West and the religious "rest" seems to be one of morality; more religious nations cleave to conservative, religiously inflected values. In the words of one group of scholars, this may be because commitment is required for obtaining such goods as "communal mutual support, charitable services for those in need, and supernatural beliefs that help to 'explain' pain and suffering."[32] Because of the way that the world's major religious traditions have developed, these same values also tend to involve strongly pronatalist sexual norms. Thus, though there are now more nonreligious individuals than ever before in the West and a growing number of other enclaves, overall they are increasingly outnumbered as a fraction of the global population, thanks in large part to the more fecund and faithful global South. In the mid- to late twentieth century, Ireland continued to be the economic "sick man" of Western Europe, distinguished by economic emigration up to the end of the 1980s and shadowed by the Troubles across the border in Northern Ireland. The country's sexual and gender norms (and birthrate) remained defiantly traditional compared with the rest of Western Europe. Yet by 2005 it was possible for one economist to declare that "Ireland has arrived. We are richer than any of us imagined possible ten years ago."[33] The era of grinding existential insecurity was over, and so too was the era of Irish religious exceptionalism. Ireland's wealth, growing nonreligious population, and slowing birthrate are bringing it into harmony with the rest of the shrinking West.

In most respects, Ireland today is secularizing in a fairly typical way. Some secularization theorists emphasize that the concept ought to be broken down into a number of distinct and interlocking processes, each of which applies well in the Irish case. Charles Taylor, for instance, describes the secularization of "Latin Christendom" as consisting of three components: Secularization 1, the expulsion of religion from the public sphere; Secularization 2, the decline of religious belief and practice; and Secularization 3, the replacement of transcendent religious values with "secular humanism," a long-gestating this-worldly moral ethic based on the maximization of human flourishing.[34] Ireland is secularizing in all three of Taylor's senses: Religion is being explicitly expelled from the public sphere through secularizing referenda; religious belief is declining in importance, and practice is declining in frequency; and as recent referenda reflect, moral worldviews are formed with reference to "self-evident" humanistic values such as "rights" and "equality" rather than religious doctrine reflecting the will of a transcendent deity. When societies "secularize" in this manner, the broad but by no means certain tendency is for the results to be greater intellectual and social autonomy, a loosening of traditional in-group bonds and ideologies, and the fragmentation and personalization of the religious field into an expanse of more self-expressive worldviews.[35]

Ethno-Catholic Divergence and the Emergence of Irish Nonreligion

Despite all these changes, in statistical terms Ireland can still appear to be a staunchly pious outlier by Western European standards. In the last national census (2016), 78% of the population in general (and 84% of the native-born population) identified as Catholic. Even in the more nuanced European Social Survey (ESS) data, the figure for Catholics is still 69%.[36] And this is not simply a matter of labeling. Among Catholic European countries, Irish weekly self-reported Mass attendance, which the ESS reports as standing at 34%, is second only to Poland (51%) and is higher than Portugal (29%), Spain (14%), and Austria (14%). Self-reports of theism and prayer are also higher than most European peers. One observer noted that "if you compare Ireland to any other modern Western country, it's astonishingly religious," adding that "to have got this far into the twenty-first century with economic growth . . . and still be so religious is remarkable."[37]

But what does "religious" mean exactly? The statistics just presented are drawn from a country that was once unusually integralist and theocratic by the standards of twentieth-century Western Europe—one that has even been compared to a Catholic equivalent of the East German regime in one particularly thought-provoking book.[38] Although this is no longer the case, a residue may well have been left behind. Irish Mass attendance statistics, and possibly measures of religious belief, could well be distorted by socially desirable responses of an almost unconscious nature resulting from deeply ingrained associations between being "religious" and being "a good Irish person" in a country where the Catholic Church controls more than 90% of primary education. Large distortions in Mass attendance figures are well attested in other societies where religion is socially normative.[39] And Irish religious attendance was certainly not always motivated by deep spiritual conviction, at least not in the past. John McGahern, for instance, describes how, under de Valera's regime,[40] "faith and obedience were demanded, mostly taking the form of empty outward observances and a busy interest that other people do likewise, which cannot be described as anything other than coercive."[41]

And though the numbers may always have concealed a great deal of ambiguity, Ireland's astonishing level of religious attendance is now also in steep decline, perhaps in part because it is simply less socially obligatory, although this may also mean that what remains is more authentically devout in motivation. The 34% weekly reported Mass attendance in 2017 may look high, but it was 85% in 1990 and 65% in 2002.[42] The Church's moral stances have also become objects of widespread rejection. As long ago as 2012, 87% of Catholics believed that priests should be allowed to get married, 75% believed that Catholic teachings on sex were irrelevant, and 61% disagreed with the Church's stance on homosexuality. In 2017, shortly after the census, the Archbishop of Dublin opined that only 20% of the Irish Catholic "78%" were "true believers."[43]

But just as we cannot say that the widespread religious attendance of the past, or ticks in survey boxes today, always equate to actual piety, we also cannot say that all contemporary *non*attenders have rejected God and Catholicism, even when they appear also to disagree with the Church's moral positions or theological formulations. Instead, as the Church's power wanes, many may be reappropriating and redefining Catholicism into something that better suits them. Based on ESS data from 1981 to 2008, the sociologists Ó Féich and O'Connell note that "high levels of belief and identification as a religious person, coupled with the decreases in attendance and confidence in the Catholic Church, indicate that, for Catholics in Ireland, religion [is] becoming private and personal."[44] They interpret the ongoing prevalence of Catholic rites of passage among those who no longer practice as evidence of large numbers "who have distanced themselves from the Church but continue to identify as Catholic, identify with other Catholics, [and] place great importance on shared Catholic heritage."[45] They take the maintenance of high levels of religious identification with growing rejection of conservative Catholic moral positions to indicate the emergence of "liberal Catholicism" as the new majority position.

Qualitative sociology further complicates this picture, suggesting a scene of greater fragmentation. As early as the 1990s, Tom Inglis, in his seminal work *Moral Monopoly*, described how Irish Catholics were changing as the Church lost its ability to dictate what made a "good Irish person."[46] He divided the Irish Catholics of this time into three distinct ideal types: orthodox, creative, and cultural. "Orthodox" is self-explanatory. "Creative" refers to those who blend their Catholicism with other spiritual and religious influences, such as New Age beliefs and practices. "Cultural" refers to those who do not really believe in Catholic doctrine or feel that they are part of the Church but who nevertheless maintain certain links, such as rites of passage. More recently, Gladys Ganiel has advanced the concept of extra-institutional religion. Based on interviews with committed believers, Ganiel describes a subsection of practicing Catholics who are both very religious and highly critical of the institutional Church. Her informants tended to unfavorably juxtapose the Church as a whole with smaller groups or figures who they felt did not share the tarnished status of the establishment. Some, for instance, "demarcated their parish and their 'good' priests from the 'institutional' church of the Irish bishops and the Vatican."[47] Being devout is no longer as homogeneous as it once was, and believers may sample from a newly emerging spiritual marketplace while also retaining the status of practicing, if critical, Catholics.

For many of those not motivated to seek out such extra-institutional buttresses, Catholicism is further fading in relevance. Inglis followed up 1998's *Moral Monopoly* with another book in 2014, in which he interviewed a representative sample of 93 Catholics about a range of aspects of their lives.[48] He found that only 28 could be described as religiously "convinced." For many of his interviewees, Catholicism was something peripheral, barely even an object of interest next to careers, love lives, sport, and other more pressing concerns. Inglis's interviews also suggest greater hesitancy around endorsing religion among the orthodox. When talking about basic Catholic theological concepts such as God or heaven, some testimony contains a striking preponderance of vacillating terminology, such as "I'd love to think" or "I'd like to believe." Perhaps most significant, Inglis also added a fourth "disenchanted" type to his original three Catholic categories. The disenchanted consist of "a good number who have become distanced, disenchanted and alienated from Catholicism and the institutional Church." Inglis found that such individuals were "willing and often anxious to dispose of the legacies of the Catholic Church in the way they understood themselves and approached life."[49] A sizable portion of his interviewees (21 of 93) fit this new category.

This outright rejection of Irish Catholicism is growing rapidly. The number of those claiming "no religion" has increased dramatically in recent years, from 4% in 2002 to 10% in 2016 in the national census[50] and from 14% in 2004 to 26.3% in 2016 and then to 32% in 2018 in the European Social Survey.[51] As with most Western nations, the nonreligious category is also more pronounced among the young. The 2014 ESS data reveal that 6% of those age 75–84 were "nones," but 40% of those age 15–24 were; the 2016 census found that 54% of 16–29-year-olds did not identify with a religious denomination.[52] Theism, too, is in decline, and it is not being replaced by apathy alone. In 2012 Ireland had the eighth highest global percentage of those claiming to be a "convinced atheist" according to WIN/Gallup (10% of the population), coming just after Germany and the Netherlands, tying with Australia, Iceland, and Austria, outstripping the United Kingdom, the United States, and the Scandinavian countries, and growing faster than anywhere else in the world barring Vietnam.[53] Other research suggests that the nonreligious in Ireland are the most antireligious in Western Europe,[54] and as we have seen, the nonreligious are also the country's fastest growing "religious" demographic. Catholicism has not only fragmented; it has become a matter of choice—and of controversy.

A burgeoning international academic literature illustrates the variety in the cumbersome "nonreligious" label and how the nonreligious differ from society to society.[55] In many other parts of the secularized world, stances toward religion can be siloed off from the public realm thanks to their relative social irrelevance. "Not being religious" may barely even be a component of one's sense of self. In some countries de facto atheists may retain religious affiliations without really thinking about them. In other countries the nonreligious are not particularly antireligious. These are usually places where religion has become largely cultural and plays no embedded role in the functioning of state institutions. Religion offers no threat to the secular order here, and as such it fails to drive up secular hostility. Phil Zuckermann's work on Denmark provides an example of an often purely cultural religious institution (Danish Lutheranism), and nontheistic Danes are rarely highly antireligious and are frequently happy to be on-paper Lutherans.[56] The growth in British nonreligion has been described as the "triumph of indifference."[57] There are also places with highly secularized institutions but where a powerful and vocal conservative religious lobby seems to threaten the secular order. This is the case, for instance, in the United States, where the rapidly growing nonreligious population primarily disaffiliate because they disapprove of the conservative politics associated with their natal denominations and the manner in which the religious right threatens to roll back secular freedoms.[58]

The Irish case is somewhat different. Because of the state's quasi-theocratic development after independence, Ireland is a rapidly secularizing society where a single dominant religious institution has nevertheless retained institutional influence. The Catholic Church remains powerful in the education system, and, until recently, the Irish Constitution reflected Catholic thought in a number of ways (most significantly in terms of abortion legislation). As we will see later, this lingering influence is integral to driving up the antireligious charge of Irish nonreligion, promoting tension between not only the conservatively religious and the nonreligious but between the nonreligious and the culturally religious.

Are Irish ethno-Catholics losing religion, or is their religion simply changing?[59] Both are happening. Catholicism has been pulled into conscious scrutiny, and the ethno-Catholic majority is now subject to a complex refractory process of deinstitutionalization, disengagement, disenchantment, critical reappropriation, apathy, and outright disaffiliation. In an increasingly individualized, secularized environment such as this, the events of the social world play a crucial role in influencing people's choices about what they want to be aligned with. Here, finally, we must talk about the moral contamination of the Church.

The Scandals: The Expanding Circle of Catholic Contamination

The scandals began with revelations in the media about a small number of high-profile clerics who had violated their vows of chastity. However, these accounts swiftly progressed to the disclosure of decades of clerical child sexual abuse and religious-run institutional abuse on a nationwide scale. From there the Church's long-standing culture of self-interested cover-ups could no longer be concealed. It soon came to seem that Irish Catholic culture itself was pathological, and "scandal" came to refer not to any single, isolated phenomenon but, darkly and somewhat vaguely, to any and all of the moral failings linked to the dominant role of Catholicism in twentieth-century Irish society.

The first public scandal took place in the early 1990s and involved two of Ireland's most high-profile clerics, who had together served as the warm-up act for Pope John Paul II's Galway audience in 1979. In 1992 the charismatic and influential Bishop of Galway, Eamonn Casey, was revealed to have secretly fathered a teenage son with an American divorcée and to have misappropriated more than IR£70,000 from diocesan funds to support him.[60] Then, in January 1994 the story broke that the recently deceased Father Michael Cleary, known popularly as "the singing priest," had conducted a secret 26-year relationship with his live-in housekeeper, producing at least two children. In an Ireland where citizens' own private lives were rigidly constrained by pervading Catholic moral codes (divorce and abortion were prohibited; contraception and homosexuality were only just being legalized; Magdalene laundries and mother and baby homes still operated; the Ann Lovett and Kerry babies cases had taken place less than a decade before[61]), the disgrace and hypocrisy tied to these revelations, when not met with willful denial, were felt with especial bitterness.[62]

As the 1990s wore on, however, these feelings would be dwarfed by the horror, disgust, and outrage that the gathering tidal wave of clerical child sexual abuse scandals was to unleash.[63] In September 1994 the UTV documentary *Suffer the Little Children* reported the case of Father Brendan Smyth, who had been sentenced for child sexual abuse in Northern Ireland but fled to the Republic of Ireland. The program revealed that the Irish government had received a warrant for Smyth's extradition to the north months earlier and had failed to act on it. In November 1994 it emerged that a previous extradition request for another priest had been handled in a similar way and, as a result of its mismanagement of these issues, the Irish coalition government collapsed.[64] Soon the full extent of the republic's own ruinous secret of clerical child sexual abuse was uncovered, one terrible revelation after another. The first Irish victim to go public was Andrew Madden, a former Dublin altar boy who shared his story in the Irish media in 1995. Madden had received an out-of-court settlement from his abuser, Father Ivan Payne, two years earlier, which was soon revealed to have been borrowed from the diocesan coffers with the assent of the Archbishop of Dublin, Desmond Connell.[65]

Turn by turn, Ireland's "pedophile priests" came to light and were charged and sentenced for the abuse of hundreds of children over the course of decades.[66] These criminal reckonings were widely reported, as was the suicide in 1999 of one of the most notorious abusers, Father Seán Fortune of Ferns, County Wexford, while he was awaiting trial for the rape of 29 boys. The 2002 BBC documentary *Suing the Pope* drew attention to the fact that Fortune's crimes had been facilitated by the Church's policy of concealing abuse allegations and moving suspected abusers from parish to parish in an attempt to avoid scandal.[67] Within two weeks of the broadcast, the Bishop of Ferns, Brendan Comiskey, resigned. Later the same year, another high-profile investigative program, RTÉ's *Primetime: Cardinal Secrets*, exposed the prevalence of clerical abuse in the Archdiocese of Dublin and unearthed further evidence of the Church's cover-ups of such cases. In a pattern that would become well established in the years to follow, the Fortune case and the public outcry it caused led directly to the commissioning of a government investigation. The resulting Ferns Report, published in 2006, revealed that successive bishops had failed to report sexual abuse allegations to the Gardaí, who had additionally neglected to properly investigate complaints received from lay citizens. The report demonstrated that, for the Church, child abuse was considered a moral rather than a criminal issue and offending priests were transferred as a matter of course when abuse was uncovered or suspected, allowing them to continue abusing even more children elsewhere.

Cardinal Secrets also led to the establishment of a major commission of investigation, which resulted in the publication of the 720-page Murphy Report in 2009. The Murphy Report made clear that, in dealing with clerical child sexual abuse, the Church had repeatedly and systemically failed to comply with both the law of the state and its own canon law and that it had consistently prioritized its reputation above the protection of children. The report described how prelates from John Charles McQuaid onward had concealed scandals and had used canon law to shield abusers at the expense of their victims. Although representatives of the Dublin archdiocese claimed to the Murphy commission that it had been naive (or "on a learning curve" to use the exact phrase) with respect to the issue of child sexual abuse, it had in fact been careful to take out insurance as far back as 1987 in anticipation of precisely such legal liabilities. On foot of the Murphy Report, another report was published in 2011 that focused on allegations surrounding the Diocese of Cloyne. The Cloyne Report was unique in revealing that the Vatican had, in secret correspondence, dismissed as a "study document" the guidelines drawn up by Irish bishops in 1996 for dealing with clerical abuse in a legally responsible manner, pronouncing that these need not be taken as a set of binding rules. Significant controversy flared up over the fact that the Holy See had sought to interfere in Irish domestic affairs and had directly undermined the Irish Church's own efforts to deal lawfully with clerical child sexual abuse. In the ensuing spat, Taoiseach Enda Kenny made a speech describing how the report "excavates the dysfunction, disconnection, elitism . . . the narcissism that dominate the culture of the Vatican to this day." He added that the "rape and torture of children were downplayed or 'managed' to uphold instead the primacy of the institution, its power, standing and 'reputation.'"[68]

Tom Inglis remembers that, when he was a child, priests were "dark, distant, unapproachable figures" who had "direct access to sacredness." In *Moral Monopoly* he describes how they "would open the tabernacle and raise the host and I would kneel before them and receive Our Lord. I felt so pure and holy then."[69] Much has changed since. Today, the symbol of the priest is charged with the diabolical as much as the divine. As the grim ubiquity of the phrase "pedo priest" demonstrates, the Irish association between the Church and pedophilia is deeply entrenched. According to one survey (by a conservative Catholic think tank), the average population estimate of the number of clergy who are pedophiles is an astonishing 28%, with 42% of the population advancing estimates in excess of 21%.[70]

Ireland's economic transformation and social individualization thus coincided with the Church's desacralization, the result of a sustained period of revelations of extreme moral violations in their own right, violations that carried the added charge of being profoundly hypocritical. *Hypocrisy* has been defined as "publicly upholding moral norms, especially for others to follow, but personally violating them in private."[71] Human beings are extremely sensitive to fairness, and few things provoke more bitterness than being deceived and cheated. It is difficult for a culprit guilty of exploiting somebody's confidence to reclaim their trust afterward. In their 2003 study on Irish public responses to the clerical abuse scandals, Goode and colleagues write that the public was "horrified" not only "because people abhor child sexual abuse *per se*" but also because abuse constituted an abuse of power by people taken to "embody the divine"; abuse constituted "the polar opposite of what priests and religious are meant to be doing."[72] And it is not only that priests embody the divine; they are also the ones who set the oppressive rules of moral conduct in Holy Catholic Ireland. The scandals generated a potently compounded moral outrage. As one Cork housewife interviewed for a seminal longitudinal study by the sociologist Betty Hilliard pithily said of the clergy, "They were laying down the law to you and I, but they were having their own fun afterwards."[73] One expert has unpacked in more detail the causes and repercussions of this exact sentiment.

> The gap between preaching water while drinking wine, between the rhetoric of love and the reality of abuse, between the presumption of celibacy and the reality of sexual violations, have brought the trust that once existed between the all-powerful clergy and the all-believing Catholic laity

into sharp decline. The Church's handling of abuse complaints and the position of the Vatican *vis-à-vis* its role in this situation have contributed further to the breakdown in relations, leading some commentators to refer to a "crisis of credibility" in the Catholic Church that has not been experienced since the Reformation.[74]

Speculation has always abounded regarding what effect exactly these scandals have had on Irish Catholicism, whether that be at the level of practice, belief, or affiliation. Confidence in the Church, Mass attendance, and prayer all halved in the period 1991–1998.[75] Donnelly and Inglis found that trust in the Church and Mass attendance declined much more rapidly over the 1990s in Ireland than in other European Catholic societies but that belief in God appeared to remain relatively stable.[76] In a 2003 survey of 1,000 members of the public, Goode and colleagues also found that belief in God was high among their respondents, with most people reporting some kind of personal relationship with God, although just under half said that their religious practices had been affected as a result of clerical child sexual abuse.[77] This led them to conclude that, although trust in the Church had been damaged, faith in God had not been. This conclusion is also supported by a large-scale quantitative study carried out in the United States[78] that found that, if there had been an incident of clerical abuse in a parish, on average attendance dropped by 12.2%, affiliation dropped by 14%,[79] and charitable giving declined by 13.3%, whereas belief in God, heaven, and hell remained largely unaffected. Furthermore, Ganiel found that, although many devout Catholics were outraged and turned against the official institution, many resolved to stay with Catholicism and accomplished this by harnessing extra-institutional forms of spiritual support. The limitations of these studies, though, may be their demographics. The Irish research primarily documents the reactions of people who were raised in more devout times and who often have memories of and have experienced intense socialization under Holy Catholic Ireland at its zenith. The effects may have been quite different on those coming of age in a more disengaged, culturally Catholic environment. And any effects of clerical abuse scandals specifically are also difficult to disaggregate from the institutional revelations that were similarly emerging during the same period.

As the clerical abuse scandals were developing, Ireland's Church-run carceral institutions similarly became an object of public scrutiny. These revelations followed a similar pattern to the clerical abuse scandals: television documentaries or media reports, followed by public outcry, followed in turn by damning government reports. Ireland had become notably dependent on such institutions as a means of poverty alleviation, crime prevention, budgetary disbursement, and social control since gaining independence.[80] The vast "architecture of containment" included a considerable infrastructure of industrial schools, Magdalene laundries, and mother and baby homes run by Catholic religious orders with state support.[81] Impoverished, inexperienced, and intent on a policy of isolationism, the newly independent Ireland had effectively established the Catholic Church as an unanswerable and autonomous entity within the state,[82] granting it primary responsibility for public services such as education and health.

Operated almost exclusively by Catholic religious congregations,[83] the industrial schools were intended as residential institutions for "neglected, orphaned and abandoned children"[84] where they could train in practical skills while being lodged, fed, and educated. In reality, the schools were places of incarceration characterized by privation and cruelty where children suffered systemic physical, emotional, and sexual abuse, received minimal education or care, and were often exploited as a source of free labor. Child inmates were committed for minor juvenile offenses, destitution, truancy, and the perceived risk of criminality, but the principal reason given by the courts for removing children to industrial schools was that their families were unable to care for them, usually because of poverty. Between the 1930s and 1970s—when the industrial school system was finally abolished in Ireland—more than 42,000 children were incarcerated in over 60 institutions, some from infancy.[85] Increasing social welfare payments to poor families would have been considerably more economical than the industrial school system,[86] but alternatives such as universal social welfare, a single mothers allowance, regulated adoption, and the legalization of contraceptives and abortion would have constituted a threat to Church control over such matters and were anathema to the Catholic moral ethos enshrined in the Irish Constitution. The system was also of material benefit to the presiding religious congregations, who received maintenance costs from the Department of Education on a capitation (head-counting) basis. Although ostensibly subject to oversight and inspection by the Department of Education, in practice the department showed a "very significant deference" to the religious congregations.[87] This inevitably compromised its ability to monitor and regulate the schools. Several major reviews of the system left it largely unchanged,[88] and not until the 1967–1970 Kennedy Report was it finally decided that the schools should be closed down in accordance with the report's findings that they were unfit for their purpose.

Although the industrial schools ceased to operate after the 1970s, the experience and legacy for the thousands of children who had been detained at them remained a largely unexamined open secret for decades longer.[89] As with clerical abuse, media documentaries were once again key to bringing the internal culture of these institutions into the light. In 1996 RTÉ screened *Dear Daughter*, a dramatized documentary that told Dubliner Christine Buckley's story of the physical and emotional abuse she had suffered as a child in an industrial school. Public interest began to build, and when journalist Mary Raftery's three-part documentary series *States of Fear* was broadcast on RTÉ in 1999, the impact was momentous. Whereas *Dear Daughter* told one woman's story of a single institution, making it liable to claims of exceptionalism, Raftery and her team had compiled the accounts of literally hundreds of individuals throughout the country, pulling together a body of evidence that was so compelling it could not be denied or dismissed.[90] The significance of the program was such that, before the broadcast of the final episode, Taoiseach Bertie Ahern formally apologized on behalf of the Irish people to those who had spent their childhoods in residential institutions run by religious congregations. He also set up a commission of investigation that would go on to produce the Ryan Report and established the Redress Board to manage a compensation process for those who had suffered abuse in the industrial school system.

The 2,600-page Ryan Report took nine years to complete and was published just months ahead of the Murphy Report in 2009. It described how thousands of Irish children had been subjected to a brutal regime of fear, starvation, sexual and physical abuse, humiliation, and degradation in Church-run residential institutions. The testimony of over 2,000 interviewees demonstrated beyond doubt that "the entire system had treated children more like prison inmates and slaves than people with legal rights and human potential."[91] Children were frequently cold, hungry, and poorly clothed; food was inadequate or inedible; children were usually referred to by a number instead of by their name; the standard of education was abysmal and the purported "training" was tantamount to slave labor more of profit to the schools than to the children; there was sustained verbal and emotional abuse, and children were constantly humiliated and denigrated and told they were worthless; they endured a climate of perpetual fear created by frequent, severe, and often arbitrary beatings, forcing them to live in "daily terror" with nowhere to seek comfort; sexual abuse was "a chronic problem" and "endemic in boys' institutions," particularly those run by the Christian Brothers, with abuse ranging from improper touching to violent rape. Some of the conduct documented in the report is so cruel and degrading that it beggars belief. One child told of being "stripped naked and whipped by four nuns to 'get the devil out of you'" after telling them about being molested by an ambulance driver; another boy described being "tied to a cross and raped whilst others masturbated at the side." Overall, the Ryan Report documents the actions of 800 abusers in 200 Catholic institutions over a period of 35 years. Once again it was found that the Church had been aware that long-term sex offenders were repeatedly abusing children, but religious officials had shielded the abusers amid a "culture of self-serving secrecy." The Vatican also repeatedly refused to share its files with Irish investigatory commissions.[92] Although it was originally intended that abusers would be publicly named in the report,[93] the Christian Brothers had successfully sued the commission in 2004 to prevent it from identifying any of its members, dead or alive. Consequently, despite the details of abuse in its pages, the report does not call for the prosecution or sanction of any of the parties involved and cannot be used for criminal proceedings.

The Magdalene laundries were another Church-run corrective institution that came under scrutiny during this time. Dedicated to the concealment, punishment, and exploitation of so-called fallen women, the laundries had eighteenth-century Protestant origins but came to be operated by congregations of Roman Catholic nuns.[94] Under the purview and moral codes of Holy Catholic Ireland, their mandate included any women deemed to challenge or transgress conservative Irish Catholic morality, with inmates commonly including unmarried mothers, abused and neglected girls, petty criminals, women with disabilities, orphans, and those simply deemed "at risk of moral danger."[95] Women continued to be incarcerated in these institutions almost to the end of the twentieth century, when the last laundry closed in Dublin in 1996. Quietly supported by the Irish state,[96] the laundries developed into an oppressive system of shame, penal servitude, and indefinite incarceration by which such women were made to literally disappear from Irish society. Once inside the convents, their names were often changed, their hair was cut, and their clothes were taken away and replaced with coarse uniforms. Imprisoned behind locked doors and subjected to a rule of silence, the women were typically given no indication of when or if they would be released. Some stayed in the institutions for the rest of their lives. As penance for their "fallen" status and to sustain the institutions' self-supporting economic models, inmates were required to work long hours without pay, primarily doing laundry and needlework. They were routinely brutalized and humiliated, enduring abject living conditions and severe physical and psychological maltreatment. Although the inner workings of these institutions were shrouded in secrecy and willfully overlooked, their competitive laundry services were widely availed of by Irish society and state alike and they developed into considerable commercial enterprises.[97] During the post-independence period alone, at least 10,000 women and girls are estimated to have been enslaved in the laundries, the profits of their labor being retained by the religious orders in charge.[98]

In 1993 the press reported that the remains of 155 women had recently been exhumed from a mass grave at a former Magdalene laundry in north Dublin and then quietly cremated and re-interred elsewhere to facilitate the sale of the lands for development.[99] Despite it being a criminal offense not to report a death, death certificates had been obtained for only 75 of the women. The remains of 22 unaccounted-for women had additionally been discovered during the exhumation process.[100] Following these revelations, public interest in the laundries began to build, sustained by television and film treatments of the subject. These included Channel 4's *Sex in a Cold Climate*, broadcast in 1998, which necessitated the setting-up of help lines "to cope with the hundreds of calls received from former inmates . . . still suffering the effects of their incarceration."[101] Although a redress scheme had been established in 2002 to compensate those who had suffered abuse in industrial schools and other residential institutions, the Irish government markedly excluded the Magdalene women from any reparations. Thus it was not until the UN Committee Against Torture formally criticized the Irish government's handling of the issue in 2011 and recommended that it "issue prompt, independent, and thorough investigation into all allegations . . . prosecute and punish the perpetrators . . . and ensure that all victims obtain redress" that a public inquiry was established into the Magdalene laundries.[102] This eventually led to the publication of the McAleese Report in 2013, together with a compensation scheme and a formal state apology from Taoiseach Enda Kenny. Once again, no prosecutions or sanctions were brought against the perpetrators of abuse.

The revelations have not ended. As noted in the Introduction, outrage at the Holy Catholic past flared up again with disclosures surrounding the Tuam affair in 2014 and 2017 and with the subsequent publication of the Mother and Baby Homes Report in January 2021. This additionally reignited debate around issues of redress for those who had suffered abuse.[103] In the years since the reevaluation of the Holy Catholic past began, religious orders have been strongly criticized for failing to adequately contribute to the cost of compensating and supporting survivors of abuse. Blame for this has largely been leveled at the state for hastily agreeing to a controversial backroom deal with religious congregations in 2002 during the time of the Ryan commission investigations. Under the deal the congregations agreed to pay €128 million in cash and property to the state in return for indemnity against all future actions by those who had suffered child abuse in Church-run reformatories, industrial schools, and orphanages. As the costs of redress grew, this resulted in the state taking on a significantly greater share of the required outlay, despite the culpability and wealth of the Church. After the Ryan Report revealed the full horror of what had happened to children at these institutions, the congregations made modest increases in their commitments, but this did little to bring the total contributions up to an equal share of what would become €1.5 billion in costs. There have also been lengthy delays in the handover of Church assets, and the actual value of contributions that have been received from the religious orders to date remains far below the levels agreed.[104] Beyond this, the religious congregations responsible for running Ireland's Magdalene laundries all refused to make any financial contribution to the restitution fund set up for survivors by the government. At the time of this writing, the state is still in negotiations with Church leaders regarding potential contributions to a redress scheme for survivors of mother and baby homes. It has been estimated that costs could reach €1 billion, which would be in addition to the costs of other church redress schemes so far.[105]

As this discussion indicates, the moral crisis of Irish Catholicism goes far beyond the phenomenon of clerical pedophilia. Whether in reality or merely in rhetoric, clerical child abuse can be pinned on pathological individuals and unscrupulous institutional leaders; it is also something that has dogged the Church all over the world. Ireland was different: Alongside clerical abuse, it had a punitive and brutalizing religious ideology that was widely accepted by the public of the time and was enforced by a considerable infrastructure of carceral institutions. Pride in the newly independent but postcolonially humiliated nation had to come from integralist Church and state purity—a closer connection to the world to come, the world that really mattered, not the world that *they*, the English, had dominated. It was a religious system that encapsulated Christian *ressentiment* as outlined by Nietzsche in *The Genealogy of Morality*: The sickly disparage the world to deny victory to the vigorous who thrive in it. Britain may be strong, but Ireland would be pure. As such, individuals deemed tainted by sin in post-independence Ireland were national stains and were removed from view when possible. In 2012 Eoin O'Sullivan and Ian O'Donnell suggested that, if the extrajudicial systems of "coercive confinement" run by both Church and state were taken into account, post-independence Ireland would have incarcerated a larger proportion of its population than did Stalin's USSR.[106] To an even greater extent than clerical pedophilia, the scale and visibility of the "shame-industrial complex"[107] raises inevitable questions about public complicity and knowledge, questions that scholars have yet to resolve even as they come to feature ritualistically in political rhetoric. Television, film, literature, and drama have responded more quickly to such revelations, offering vivid depictions of the religious past as a place of suffocating theocratic conformity, religious hypocrisy, barely concealed child abuse, and institutionalized cruelty. A new public representation has formed in which Holy Catholic Ireland itself has taken on the mien of a sadistic and perverse totalitarian regime: Purity and obedience were everything, and cruelty seemed barely a concept.

Viewed through modern eyes, Holy Catholic Ireland can seem offensively and incomprehensibly alien in its moral priorities. Some light can possibly be shed on how priorities such as these could have ever existed by considering what psychologists have to say about moral cultures. According to Jonathan Haidt and Craig Joseph, all human societies construct their moral systems by drawing on emotional intuitions produced by a suite of so-called "moral foundations."[108] These foundations are split into two categories: individualizing and binding. Individualizing foundations encourage protection of individuals within the group, whereas binding foundations serve to maintain the coherence of the group, even at the expense of some individuals within it. The individualizing foundations are care/harm (producing intuitions around protection of kin and, by inadvertent extension, the vulnerable more generally), fairness/cheating (the phobia of cheaters and those who free-ride on others), and liberty/oppression (the desire for autonomy). The binding foundations are loyalty/betrayal (intuitions encouraging tribalistic in-group prioritization), authority/subversion (intuitions encouraging hierarchical obedience), and purity/sanctity (intuitions of disgust toward those who violate norms, in particular, norms relating to the body).[109] Different moral cultures blend these elements in different ways, producing their own moral cuisines as it were—and producing populations with utterly irreconcilable notions of the good. Haidt and Graham, for instance, have found that liberals in the United States tend to build their moral systems around the individualizing foundations alone (in particular, care and fairness), whereas conservatives emphasize all the moral foundations equally (i.e., they are just as concerned with obedience, in-group loyalty, and sexual purity as with care and fairness).[110] Holy Catholic Ireland seems to have had its own, quite distinct moral cuisine: a culture so preoccupied with unblemished purity and so utterly deferent to authority that it lost sight of harm. As the sociologist Gordon Lynch has observed of children who have endured "immoral" family settings and then suffered harrowing sadism in the industrial schools:

> Children's subjection to sexual abuse in family or institutional settings was commonly thought about, in terms not of psychological harm to the child, but of moral taint, and sexually abused children might find themselves further punished for their (albeit unwilling) involvement in polluting behaviour. In this context, children exposed to "immoral" family settings could be perceived as "moral dirt," fundamentally stained and at risk of extending moral pollution if not subjected to firm moral correction.[111]

In addition to considering abused children as "moral dirt," uncaring attitudes were pervasive in Irish society toward the categories of children most vulnerable to suffering abuse, which included those who were working class, illegitimate, or orphaned. Not only were these children more likely to be condemned to the industrial schools but, as one clerical informant disclosed, abusers were most commonly transferred to working-class communities when misdeeds were suspected or discovered. Evidence indicates that many people at all levels of society had various degrees of knowledge of the abuse of children, particularly in the industrial schools. Mary Raftery and Eoin O'Sullivan have reported that, across Ireland, communities living adjacent to industrial schools were aware of their regime of abuse and frequently heard the screams of child inmates from the institutions at night.[112] Knowledge and discussion of the abuse sometimes surfaced in the press, usually voiced by outsiders.[113] In 1946 the issue of institutional abuse was widely debated in the Irish papers when Roscommon-born US citizen Father Edward Flanagan, the famous founder of the Boys Town schools for orphans and delinquents in the United States, toured Ireland's industrial schools and publicly described them as "a disgrace to the nation." The government denied the accusation, and no public pressure was brought upon the state to address the issue.[114] In 1963 photographs of eight girls whose heads had been brutally shorn after attempting to escape from an industrial school in Bundoran, County Donegal, were published on the front page of a British tabloid newspaper (circulated in Ireland) with the headline "Orphanage Horror." Instead of prompting public concern and calls for intervention, the term "Bundoran haircut" was callously coined to be used as a threat of punishment for mischievous children.[115]

Decades later, in a profoundly and rapidly altered cultural climate, the Irish Catholic Church's fall from grace was facilitated by the investigations and disseminations of the media, the nation's new moral mouthpiece according to Tom Inglis.[116] The public proved far more receptive to critical stories about the Church than they had been previously. From the Church's perspective, clerical malfeasance, institutional revelations, and cover-ups have emerged in the worst possible environment: a social universe that is increasingly populated by individualized people who have weak "culturally Catholic" religious socialization and who are more predisposed to conceive of religious affiliation as a choice rather than as an ethnic given. They are also unrelentingly wired into the most powerful technology to have ever existed for transmitting information that might influence that choice. The amplification of the scandals through modern communications technology and the reappraised image of the past combine with another factor: moral warfare.[117] In Ireland tensions between individuals adopting contrasting positions are amplified by church and state holdovers from the Holy Catholic past. This situation of stalled secularization propels scandal further into the atmosphere as an affordance in efforts to combat rival positions and win over vacillating third parties. And at a more everyday level, scandal soaks into scenes of small-scale interaction, as individuals jostle for moral status. Verbal statements of outrage or disgust are not mere statements of fact; they are also actions expected to cause a certain effect in the minds of others—for instance, to establish moral status or to distance oneself from a transgressor. These kinds of public and private interpersonal dynamics in a semi-secularized society powerfully boost an already extremely strong signal of religious hypocrisy and immorality.

By the late 2000s, the popular image of the priest was widely inverted, and the freshly exposed moral culture of Holy Catholic Ireland—only a few decades out of date—had come to seem almost incomprehensible. The late 2000s was also when people who came of age in the "era of scandal" began filling in their own census forms and when the emergence and rapid growth of outright religious rejection began. It may be the case that younger generations, who have been raised by more religiously disengaged parents and who already may have preexisting objections to what they perceive as the Church's antiprogressive social influence, have relatively little motivation to stay affiliated. To see how this connection can be eroded from one generation to the next, let us look at how clerical abuse scandals and the reappraisal of Holy Catholic Ireland's moral system arrived into a religious tradition that may still have appeared outwardly hegemonic but had in fact quietly become threadbare. Like a colony of termites set loose on a dying tree, the scandals exacerbated the collapse of the hollowed-out Irish religious system.

CRED Depletion: Religious Hypocrisy Beneath a Threadbare Catholic Canopy

Scholars of religion have never been able to agree about what the term *religion* actually means. Some claim the word picks out a parochial Western historical construct, a category invented when Europeans sought to conceptualize the worldviews of those they conquered.[118] Others argue that the term remains useful, but only as a convenient shorthand for phenomena that are often found together but do not necessarily entail one another.[119] On this second understanding, religion must be "fractionated" before it can be understood: One can analyze the psychology and social dynamics of rituals, or sympathetic magic, or group bonding, or belief in supernatural beings, or collective identities, but not the whole package. Other theories are more integrative and aim to describe how such elements work together to support an imagined metaphysical order imbued with such strong social support that it is simply experienced as reality.[120] One classic example is sociologist Peter Berger's idea of the "plausibility structure."[121] By this, Berger means the dense network of social practices and institutions that can act to make a religious world seem self-evident to those embedded within it, even if the senses can provide no direct proof of the existence of the gods.[122] For Berger, the plausibility structure produces a "sacred canopy," an all-encompassing horizon of religious "enchantment" that overlays the mundane world.

"Sacred canopy" and "enchantment" might seem like peculiarly romantic terms to apply to the Irish Catholic religious system as it developed after Cullen's reforms, but Berger's metaphor is in fact quite applicable. Catholic concerns were intertwined in all areas of life, from education to politics to mundane daily turns of phrase, creating a totalizing Catholic universe into which children were socialized. Public Catholic ritual went far beyond simple Mass attendance. One scholar describes the trappings of Irish Catholicism at the height of the "long nineteenth century," the period following Cullen's "devotional revolution," as follows:

> Confession and communion . . . became much more frequent. Pastoral gains . . . were consolidated by the introduction of a whole series of devotional exercises designed not only to encourage more frequent participation in the sacraments but to instill veneration by an appreciation of their ritual beauty and intrinsic mystery. . . . The new devotions were mainly of Roman origin and included the rosary, forty hours, perpetual adoration, novenas, blessed altars, Via Crucis, benediction, vespers, devotion to the Sacred Heart and to the Immaculate Conception, jubilees, triduums, pilgrimages, shrines, processions, and retreats.[123]

Religious inflection did not disappear outside its many ritual expressions. Large numbers of individuals were organized into lay religious guilds known as sodalities. Members of these sodalities would have dedicated themselves variously to "spiritual works of mercy," such as admonishing sinners, policing local morality, encouraging religious participation, combatting disbelief, and praying for living and deceased individuals. Others pursued "corporal works of mercy," which mostly consisted of charitable activities. Sodalities provided an extensive network of worthy and demonstratively Catholic individuals whose mission it was to model ideal Catholic citizenship and encourage correct Catholic behavior in others through informal pressure.

In addition, large-scale social institutions, such as the education and health systems, were dominated by the Church and woven into the plausibility structure. Almost without exception, children were taught in schools with a Catholic ethos. Religion was not limited to particular moments of the school day—it was expected to inform all pedagogical and instructional approaches at some level. Government discourse was often saturated with expressions of deference to the Church and was regularly heightened by the shadow of threats posed to Irish devout purity.[124] Fulmination in the Dáil Éireann about moral slippage, Godless communism, and the need to maintain public (Catholic) decency was commonplace. And the minutiae of daily behavior on the street wove further tiny threads into the sacred canopy. Nuns, priests, and religious brothers were not a common sight on the street—they were a completely mundane one. People blessed themselves and hats were doffed religiously as churches were passed. Even outside obligatory ritual moments, public behavior radiated religious concern. A heightened consciousness of sexual sin meant that the prick of desire could instantly trigger religious worries. Confessional unburdening was almost a recreational activity, like going to the cinema—or perhaps it was more like taking an anxiolytic drug. A frightening God has more cognitive potency than a benevolent one: As social creatures incurably concerned with our reputations, it is easier to believe that we are being watched and judged than to believe that we are unconditionally loved. The rather merciless Holy Catholic God instilled a restless unease in many, and in myriad small ways this uneasiness would signal itself, telegraphing belief.

Louise Fuller says that these sinners were driven to the confessionals by their own consciences, though we must also wonder to what degree they were driven by their families. The domestic sphere was often no respite from a public realm dominated by the reinforcement of Catholicism. Collective prayer and the rosary were common pastimes in the evenings. According to some observers, women—denied agency elsewhere in society—often took to the role of domestic religious enforcer. Only by going into alliance with the priests to supervise the morality of their husband and family could women obtain some kind of power in a deeply patriarchal society. Inglis describes the role of the idealized Irish mother in bringing the plausibility structure into the home as follows:

> She brought the family to prayer and enforced the Church's code of morality. She was the Church's representative in the home who supervised the moral conduct of her husband and children. She became the living embodiment of Our Lady—humble, pious, celibate and yet fecund. She gave herself to the Church, and in each succeeding generation produced the religious vocations that sustained the Church. Her moral power in the home was sanctioned by the priests, nuns and brothers that she bore.[125]

In the face of this culture, Inglis suggests that social capital and advancement depended on possession of a Catholic "habitus" consisting of a web of opinions, verbal platitudes, private and public pieties, and assiduous practices that served to project the sense that the individual was a good Catholic and thus a reliable, morally trustworthy person.[126] Of course, not everyone really bought in to the plausibility structure, but this did not mean that skeptics could openly express their skepticism or drop out of religious practice. Some Irish people behaved religiously because they believed fervently, others because they were in an environment where this was expected. Either way, all this outward obeisance would have fed back into the system at the level of intergenerational religious socialization. Recently, cognitive anthropologists have tied *behavioral* reinforcement specifically to the intergenerational transmission of religious belief. A particularly influential formulation of this view has been the idea of the credibility-enhancing display, or CRED, an acronym coined by the anthropologist Joseph Henrich.[127] CREDs are behaviors that give some indication that people believe what they say they do, because they are costly to perform or hard to fake: costly ritual, self-abnegation, sitting through Mass, sacrificing kin to religiously inspired brutalization, all the way to martyrdom and clerical celibacy. The idea behind the importance of prominently practicing what is preached is that human beings have evolved to be particularly cautious around the possibility of being deceived. Language makes deception pitifully easy, allowing cheap Machiavellian manipulation to run riot. One way of combatting this is by evolving a particularly keen sensitivity to behavior and whether it corroborates what somebody says they believe or rather draws that professed belief into suspicion. Religious systems, which make claims about the world that cannot be verified by everyday experience, are particularly vulnerable to suspicion, but they are also well positioned to reinforce themselves by making costly demands of their adherents. Religious CREDs are a culturally evolved psychological hack: The most successful religious systems are built on the backs of innumerable acts of faith that telegraph the conviction of their adherents. It may just be a coincidence, but the symbol of the world's most populous religion, a man dying on the cross for his beliefs, is itself a CRED.[128]

Through its religiously run social institutions, its zealously deferent political class, its abundant Roman rituals, its networks of religious worthies in the sodalities, its acute focus on regular public practice, its culture of denial and self-abnegation, the domestic reinforcement of religious indoctrination at the hands of the Irish mother, its culture of shame avoidance at all costs, and its hallowed clerical caste of austere and unquestionable moral specialists, Irish Catholicism was once a particularly CRED-rich religious tradition. There were reasons that this religious system required such copious infrastructure to sustain conviction. Many observers, such as the theologian Vincent Twomey and, more recently, the journalist Derek Scally, have observed that, because of its clericalist and hierarchical culture, the version of Catholicism that came into being with Cullen's devotional revolution was distinctive for its lack of reflectiveness or theological sophistication. The dogmatic style of religious belief that characterized Irish Catholicism relied on the sheer weight of surrounding social proof and a vigilant defense against outside influence to keep it safely beyond question. Maynooth trained zealous dogmatists who believed wholeheartedly in clerical authority, and they ministered to a largely uneducated and impoverished populace. The results were almost medieval, with dogma dictated by a sanctified elite and accepted from below as truth, plain and simple. This way of believing is ill-suited to a more culturally open, questioning, and educated environment. For this reason, the expansion of secondary and tertiary education in the latter half of the twentieth century was particularly corrosive to the style of belief encouraged by the Irish Church.[129]

As this architecture of CREDs began to crumble, because of the influence of the various secularizing forces, the unquestioning belief mandated by the Irish Catholic system began to become unsustainable. By the 1990s it was still generally normative to "be Catholic," but in an increasingly phoned-in way that did not really entail much behaviorally. The journalist Malachi O'Doherty observed that by the 2000s Irish Catholicism had largely morphed into "spirituality" requiring neither explicit definition nor "sacrifices in acknowledgement of it."[130] The "simple faith" of Catholic Ireland had long faded, relegated to the preserve of those old enough to remember the intense religious conditioning of their upbringing, and the Church had not devised a compelling alternative. Lip service and inertial Sunday Mass replaced the totalizing Catholic canopy of the past and, as priests in pulpits across the country were frequently to warn, consumerism was the new god of the nation. Few heeded what they had to say. The priesthood is in such precipitous decline that Ireland is now considered a country of mission by the Church.

As Irish society became more comfortable and as the Church lost its harsh pre–Vatican II power, religious performance began to slide. We could call this a process of CRED depletion. The cognitive anthropologist Jonathan Lanman has tied secularization to the idea of CREDs in a way that is relevant to the Irish case.[131] As we have seen, existential security is closely tied to secularization: The safer people feel, the less they turn to God. But what mechanism connects the easing of the existential struggle to the decline of belief? According to Lanman, as life becomes easier, people are less likely to turn to God to give them a sense of control over their precarious lives, and they are less likely to behave religiously in an instrumental fashion to ensure the support of their co-religionists. Although they may not actually stop believing, both these forces ensure that they no longer telegraph this belief with the same intensity. For those growing up in the resulting social environment, religious beliefs and identities become wraithlike heirlooms, social memories rather than present realities.[132] Belief and affiliation peel apart. Some people keep up the connection to a natal religious affiliation in a low-cost way, as a form of cultural marker—what the sociologist David Voas calls "fuzzy fidelity."[133] It is much easier to let go of this than to leave devout obeisance to a terrifying God coupled to a powerful sense of one's place in a sacred ethnoreligious community. It was into this hegemonic but increasingly shallow religious culture that the scandals arrived. For many relatively disengaged Irish Catholics who had not directly suffered abuse, religious hypocrisy settled into a secularization process that was already well under way. Into the haze of a majority "fuzzy" connection to an ethnocultural tradition that seemed vaguely obligatory but personally irrelevant intruded a sudden, sharp image of gross moral malfeasance. Ripping through the media, these images built on one another to create a picture that was far starker in its reality than the watery memories of a fading tradition.

But there are still those who believe. Turning from the disengaged and the disaffected to the devout and from the intergenerational to the personal, CRED theory provides a new perspective on the effects of why, exactly, religious hypocrisy should also matter to the true believer. After all, why should one religious person's certainty be disturbed if another is a hypocrite? To answer this, we must consider what happens when religious paragons in particular very much look as though they *don't* really believe in what they are preaching. If the specialists of a religion that vilifies sexual intercourse without the intent to reproduce are themselves violating sexual mores in the most extreme manner imaginable and if the institution they represent is at the same time covering up for these errant individuals, this may undermine the confidence of witnesses that the Catholic hierarchy truly believes in the omniscient and morally interested God it publicly endorses. This may be corrosive not only for the intergenerational transmission of religious belief but also for its sustenance in the individual. If there are CREDs, there may also be "CRUDs": credibility-*undermining* displays.

Does extreme religious hypocrisy actually prompt believers to question religion in this way? The evidence is mixed, and a wide variety of reactions are possible. Many victims of clerical abuse certainly recount a violent ripping-aside of the veil. In his fieldwork in a survivors group in Chicago, the religious scholar Robert Orsi describes a kind of extreme "ontological dissonance" experienced by the abused, noting that for many, "to be abused by a priest, the *alter Christus* in Catholic theology, the other Christ, was to be abused at one remove from God." As a result, survivors have "seen the machinery of false authority, the predators working the levers of the theology of the *alter Christus*." One of his informants, Frank, used the metaphor of the curtain being pulled back in *The Wizard of Oz*. Another said, "I just can't make myself believe in what I see as smoke and mirrors. . . . The effect of this loss is like watching the Technicolor go out of something."[134] At the same time, sociological literature has demonstrated that institutionally critical devout Catholic stances have also proliferated in the wake of clerical abuse scandals. But some further evidence suggests that scandal causes the devout to withdraw from participation, most likely from feelings of complicity and shame.[135] Even if they remain theistic and Catholic, albeit in a more tortured way as they are tugged between loyalty and outrage, their religion becomes more invisible. There is no one way the devout respond to extreme religious hypocrisy on the part of their paragons. But when such acts of hypocrisy involve grotesque and disgust-inducing extremes of violation and harm, they do often dampen believers' enthusiasm to be seen to affiliate with and endorse the institution. They are a privatization accelerant and thus an additional secondary source of CRED depletion.

Today, the Catholic sacred canopy is tattered, stained, and shrunken. Behavioral evidence of Catholic commitment is minimal compared with what it was in the past. Catholicism has entered a strange and ambiguous place in Ireland, anchored variously to the sacred nationalism of the past, to the mundane rites of belonging and community, and to a compound image of hypocrisy, repression, self-interest, and corruption. This is the background against which the more individualized and existentially secure ethno-Catholic population of a freshly globalized society choose whether or not to remain affiliated. In the next chapter I present quantitative data that show just how prevalent the outright rejection of Catholicism is among the baptized ethno-Catholic majority and what we can know for certain about its background conditions and motivations.

CHAPTER 2

"HOSTAGES OF CATHOLICISM"
QUANTIFYING THE NATURE AND SCALE OF THE REJECTION OF THE CHURCH

In this chapter I present quantitative data that help to illustrate the background causes of disaffiliation and the worldviews of the disaffiliated, things we will examine in more intimate detail in the subsequent ethnographic chapters. Although the survey, being correlational in nature, cannot establish causality, the data do show the degree to which the Church is perceived as morally unpalatable, especially by those who have disaffiliated. They suggest that atheism and outright disbelief in the propositions espoused by the Church especially may be more widespread than previously recorded. In terms of religious socialization and its associated behavioral costs (discussed as credibility-enhancing displays [CREDs] in the previous chapter), the results demonstrate how superficial and thus easy to shake off much (but by no means all) Irish Catholicism has become. The survey results also suggest that cultural Catholicism may be skin-deep: When given the opportunity to think about the Church before being asked how they identify, many Irish people stop calling themselves Catholic and register instead as something else. This implies that the choice between ex-Catholicism and cultural Catholicism may rest on something of a knife edge.

After presenting the quantitative data, I set the scene for the rest of the book with an ethnographic vignette: the papal visit of 2018, a stark contrast to that of 1979. I describe the papal visit of 2018 in some detail, as it offers a prismatic view of the tensions between some of contrasting orientations toward Catholicism evident in the data. The reception of Pope Francis illustrates not only how the influence of the Church has waned, but also how the institution has become a source of endless controversy. It demonstrates how clerical abuse and other revelations about the Catholic past have formed a canker that poisons attitudes toward the Church and creates a powerful urge to disconnect from Catholic identity. Against the backdrop of this widespread feeling, Catholic moral positions and lingering institutional influence serve as foci for social division. The papal visit also highlights the increased visibility of the openly nonreligious in Irish society, many of whom have *chosen* not to be Catholic. At the same time it reveals that, alongside open defiance of the Church and the fragmentation of consensus around religion, there runs a deep countercurrent of relative indifference, often on the part of nominal, "cultural" Catholics.

Survey Data Overview

I ran the survey in 2017 using the Qualtrics Panels participant recruitment service. The sample comprised 229 Irish individuals of at least 18 years of age who had been baptized Catholic. This sample was acquired through a market research company and was nationally representative for age (collected in categorical tranches: 18–24, 25–34, 35–44, 45–54, 55–64, 65+), gender, and socioeconomic status (as represented by standardized categories regarding the occupation of the chief income earner in the household). The survey also contained quite a representative mix of urban and rural respondents (26% described themselves as living in a city, 13% a suburb, 25% a town, 12% a village, and 24% the countryside—a fairly even breakdown of Irish habitation), though, surprisingly, this variable rarely proved significant. The survey was run online and had a high response rate: 45% of those approached completed it.

The survey examines some of the differences in background and worldview between those who do and those who do not consider themselves Catholic anymore. The survey used alternative question structures to those found in such measures as the census and the European Social Survey (ESS) to delve a little further into the desacralization of the Church and the relationship between this and Irish Catholic disaffiliation. *Disaffiliation* here means baptized individuals' self-categorization as non-Catholic (the Church's position is that once you have been baptized, you are Catholic and therefore a Christian forever). *Desacralization* means the replacement or contestation of the Church's prior high moral and spiritual status by a new set of associations revolving around various forms of immorality or moral unpalatability. The survey allowed me to build a more representative picture of disaffiliation and the extent of critical attitudes toward the Church than would have been possible had I relied on my field sites alone. It was also deemed necessary because disaffiliation is relatively underexamined in existing accounts of Irish religious change, which tend to focus on the fragmentation of Irish Catholicism into a range of different and more bespoke forms (including orthodox Catholics, deinstitutionalized Catholics, liberal Catholics, cultural Catholics, and so forth).[1] Although the data have some limitations,[2] they establish a base from which to contextualize the experiences described in more detail in later chapters.

Because of the enormous amount of data recovered by the survey, not all of it can be included here. Instead, I focus on the following key topics: (1) Catholic identity, (2) the relationship between distrust in the Church and disaffiliation, (3) how the associations and representations of the Church differ between Catholics and ex-Catholics, (4) why ex-Catholics have rejected the Church and how this differs from those who retain a Catholic affiliation while rejecting the institution, (5) the degree to which ex-Catholics are skeptical of religious beliefs (both theistic beliefs in general and Catholic doctrines specifically), (6) the strong relationship between childhood exposure to Catholic CREDs and the retention of Catholic belief and identity in the present, and (7) the degree to which the moral contamination of the Church has made some people more unwilling to perform CRED-type behaviors indicating their Catholicism to others.

Who Is (Still) a Catholic?

In statistical data Ireland looks very religious by Western European standards on a number of measures.[3] But religious affiliation can be so flexible and contextual that different measures will give different counts. The 2018 census, for instance, reported that 78% of the Irish population was Catholic, whereas later the same year, the ESS reported the figure as 69%. The 2016 census reported that 10% of the Irish population was nonreligious, whereas the 2018 ESS data put the figure more than three times higher, at 32%. There are also reasons to think that survey response habits might differ in Ireland from elsewhere in Western Europe. Ireland, until recent decades, had many of the characteristics of a de facto theocracy (one of the few twentieth-century Western European societies of which this can be said). The vast majority of the population was, and still is, educated in Catholic schools. There, Irishness and Catholicism are deeply and implicitly linked together. Where the fusion of religious and ethnic identity runs so deep, unconscious and social pressures might be guiding that pen or mouse, almost like the planchette of a Ouija board, toward the "Roman Catholic" box. This does not mean that this kind of reflex identification is invalid or uninteresting, but it does raise the possibility that it may be more contextual, more superficial, and less stable than it is sometimes taken to be. Reports of religious belief and prayer can also be influenced by socially desirable responding in a country where religion has long been deeply socially normative.

In particular, many existing survey instruments are limited in how they deal with what sociologist Abby Day has called *natal nominalism*: people reporting what they were baptized as, not what they think of themselves as now.[4] In a society where so many people describe themselves as "born Catholic," this is a problem. It could be the case that a significant number of respondents, having been baptized, put themselves down as Catholics habitually or even reluctantly, "as though honoring some strange sense of conscription," as one field informant phrased it. Furthermore, existing questions, such as those in the ESS, feature only a rather blunt nonreligious option: the "none" category. By virtue of its negative form, "none" may carry associations of something lacking that other people have, no matter the degree to which "nones" may hold personally important political, metaphysical, or moral beliefs. Overall, it is likely that the number of baptized Irish Catholics who no longer think of themselves as Catholic in everyday life is underrepresented in current measures and would be higher if different questions addressing these issues were asked.[5] To this end, the survey reported here uses an alternative question setup devised to reduce natalism and provide more nonreligious options. It was expected that this would offer a different view of the relative extent of three categories: Catholics (i.e., orthodox believers who are obedient to the Church), liminal Catholics (i.e., the broad category of those who, for varying reasons and with varying levels of religious belief and commitment, qualify their relationship to Catholicism by rejecting the institution of the Church while retaining Catholic affiliation), and ex-Catholics (i.e., the disaffiliated, those who claim to no longer think of themselves as Catholic in any way).

Respondents were first asked whether they were baptized Catholics ("Have you been baptised as a Catholic?"). The hypothesis was that, by discreetly affording participants the chance to say that they had been "made Catholic" at one point in their lives, this would forestall default natalist responding later on. The survey then adopted an alternative two-step approach to measuring the current commitment of an individual to Catholicism, based on self-description (i.e., identity) and self-perceived acceptance of doctrine (i.e., belief). First, participants were asked how they currently described themselves: "Would you describe yourself as any of the these? Please select all that apply—you may choose more than one if you wish: Agnostic; Atheist; Catholic; Christian—no denomination; Member of a non-Christian religion; Protestant Christian—any denomination; Spiritual but not religious; None of these."

After this, participants were asked whether they rejected the "official" doctrines and teachings of the Catholic Church: "Overall, would you say you personally have or have not rejected the official beliefs, doctrines and teachings of the Catholic Church as guidelines for your life?" This allowed the rejection of Catholicism to be characterized with respect to two components: the rejection of a Catholic identity (e.g., disaffiliation) and the rejection of Catholic teachings (disbelief in institutional orthodoxies). It is possible to reject either, both, or neither. This leaves the three larger groups mentioned earlier: Catholics, liminal Catholics and ex-Catholics.[6] Catholics were operationalized as those who identify as Catholic and do not reject the teachings of the Church, liminal Catholics as those who identify as Catholic but reject the teachings of the Church, and ex-Catholics as those who reject both a Catholic identity and the teachings of the Church. Overall, this yielded 88 Catholics (38.4%), 56 liminal Catholics (24.5%), and 85 ex-Catholics (37.2%).

TABLE 2.1 Number of Respondents Identifying as Catholic, Liminal Catholic, and Ex-Catholic by Age

Age	Catholic	Liminal Catholic	Ex-Catholic
18–24	6 (18.2%)	9 (27.3%)	18 (54.5%)
25–34	9 (21.4%)	11 (26.2%)	12 (52.4%)
35–44	14 (33.3%)	10 (23.8%)	18 (42.9%)
45–54	26 (57.8%)	10 (22.2%)	9 (20%)
55–64	6 (44.1%)	9 (38.2%)	19 (17.6%)
65+	27 (62.8%)	7 (16.3%)	9 (20.9%)

Source: Author's 2017 Qualtrics Panels survey data.

The breakdown by age group (the strongest demographic predictor) can be seen in Table 2.1.

Because of the small sample size, the results of the survey should be interpreted as broadly indicative. To gain more insight into variation within the categories, descriptive data on how the members of these three categories currently identified were also compiled. For simplicity's sake, responses adopting multiple identifications were combined into one of two categories: hyphenated Catholic (if they included Catholicism) and hyphenated nonreligious (if they did not).

The ex-Catholic category is composed of self-identified atheists (30%), agnostics (29%), the spiritual but not religious (23%), "nones" (9.5%), and hyphenated nonreligious (8.5%). Descriptive statistics indicated a trend toward atheists being younger and more often male, whereas the spiritual but not religious were older and more often female, but the sample was too small to establish statistical significance. The number of hyphenated Catholics (those choosing a "dual identity," typically either "spiritual but not religious" or "Christian—no denomination" alongside Catholicism) was significantly more pronounced in the liminal Catholic group (42% "hyphenated" to 58% "pure") than in the Catholic group (19% "hyphenated" to 81% "pure").[7] Last, no one in the sample had converted to any other religious tradition. Although these things do happen among baptized Irish Catholics, they are relatively rare. According to some observers, it is much more common to drop out entirely or to attempt to construct some kind of personal theism that nestles, often invisibly, within an outward Catholic identity.[8]

Two things need to be addressed about these results. First, there are proportionately a lot more disaffiliated respondents here than are found in the census, Pew's 2018 religion in Europe data, or even the ESS. Existing interpretations of Irish religious change suggest that the liminal Catholic category should be bigger than either the ex-Catholic or the orthodox categories, because it stands to reason that it should encompass all those gradated stances that fall between the two extremes of outright disaffiliation and devout obedience; this is where we would naturally expect to find all the cultural Catholics (i.e., those who have a link to a Catholic identity but no real religious interest in Catholicism), all the liberal Catholics (those who remain dedicated believers in Catholic theology but reject Church morality), deinstitutionalized Catholics (those who remain committed to Catholicism but have rejected the institutional Church), and so forth. In the 2018 Pew data, for instance, 34% of Irish respondents were "church-attending Christians" (roughly analogous to my Catholic category), 15% were "religiously unaffiliated" (roughly analogous to my ex-Catholic category and, furthermore, including all those who were never Catholic at all), and 46% were "non-attending Christians" (roughly analogous to my liminal Catholic category). It could be that the results presented here relate to an ex-Catholic skew in the admittedly small sample.[9] This is unlikely, though, because the number of orthodox Catholics was also high. The survey appeared to be generating polarized responses rather than attracting more individuals of one persuasion than the other. Why the difference?

One possibility is that the survey attracted responses from those at either end of the spectrum who were more involved in the topic of Catholicism, and therefore disengaged cultural Catholics were underrepresented. Another likely answer lies in the structure of the survey itself. For a start, people had the opportunity to say they had been baptized before they were asked how they would identify now. Their ethno-Catholic origins were thereby registered and did not need to be affirmed by proxy later using the religion question. Furthermore, at the beginning of the survey, participants were asked to fill in an associational list of what came to mind when they thought of the term "Irish Catholic Church" (the striking results are shown later in this chapter in the section "How Do

Catholics and Ex-Catholics See the Church"). It is likely that the increased cognitive salience of the Church in the present study—and thus of Catholicism as a religious rather than a cultural or ethnic marker—caused those with a negative view of the Church to repudiate an already tenuous Catholic identification. This would likely have meant that the more disengaged cultural Catholics who might otherwise have ended up in the liminal category were hoovered up by the ex-Catholic category in this survey (in Pew's data, many would likely have ended up in the nonattending rather than the unaffiliated category). This is not to say that the present survey data are correct and that Pew's data are wrong, but the difference has some interesting implications. The primary one is that some Irish Catholic identification is sufficiently shallow that thinking about the Church makes these individuals less inclined to call themselves Catholic.[10] Merely by responding to a different set of questions that brings Church and religion forward while taking natal origins out of the equation, many cultural Catholics seem to percolate through into the ex-Catholic category, leaving the liminal category to a more concentrated residue of committed, but perhaps, as will be seen, somewhat institutionally conflicted, theists.

Finally, the data on this residue of liminal Catholics reveal that they are more likely to claim multiple hyphenated identities than either Catholics or ex-Catholics. This could reflect what Irish sociologists have designated as creative Catholicism, namely, those who comfortably combine elements of Catholicism with other influences in a kind of individualized spiritual bricolage.[11] It could also indicate that many of these people are deinstitutionalized but still committed; that is, although they have rejected the authority of the Church, Christianity and Catholic identity remain important aspects of their lives. Later, we will see that this group also has a lot of highly salient negative moral associations with the Church and that they tend to reject official Catholicism for moral reasons. In light of this, selecting a hyphenated Catholic identity may reflect not a freewheeling spiritual creativity so much as a troubled compromise generated by moral tensions around institutional Catholicism. Through an act of nuanced self-positioning, the hyphenated Catholic could be cleaving to a deeply personal social identity, perhaps one linked to family and memory, while also dissociating from negative moral associations with the Church as an institution. They are Catholic, but their Catholicism is *different*.[12] If this interpretation is correct—that, in response to their own or others' moral disapproval, the more committed of the liminal Catholics must hedge their commitment to Catholicism by reaching for qualifying disclaimers—then it also places a question mark over the future stability of this kind of qualified Catholicism as an intergenerationally transmissible form of religiosity. Are people really willing to go on affiliating with a religious tradition if even their own parents seem conflicted over their connection to it?

Is Distrust Related to Disaffiliation?

Overall declines in clerical trust linked to Catholic scandals have been quantified by a number of observers.[13] However, many of these observers maintain that this decline in trust has not seriously affected theistic belief and Catholic identification. Instead, it has primarily spurred the rejection of the institution. Questions remain about this, though. Scandal has not abated but has rather persisted and consolidated since the data analyzed in many of these studies were collected. The institution has become more deeply implicated in the events themselves and in further efforts to evade their consequences, and all of this has been, and continues to be, widely publicized. Furthermore, the data analyzed by these scholars tend to date to the 1990s and early 2000s, when there were few Irish Catholic apostates; no existing work treats them as a separate category or even acknowledges their existence. Now, there are far more, so there is the opportunity to inspect whether a lack of clerical trust does in fact relate to the outright rejection of ties to Catholicism.

In the current survey, clerical trust was measured by using a list-dragging task to calculate how well priests and bishops are trusted compared with other social categories. Respondents were asked, "If you had to generalise, which of the following groups would you trust the most, and which the least? Please rank the following in order of how much you would trust them by dragging the items up or down (most trustworthy at the top)," before being presented with the following randomized list: atheists, bankers, bishops, builders, criminals, police, politicians, priests, shop workers, teachers. Mean rankings were interpreted as a "trustworthiness score," with scores closer to 1 indicating greater reported trustworthiness and scores closer to 10 indicating greater reported untrustworthiness. Presumably, those who have rejected Catholicism would be more distrustful of clergy than those who have not.

Overall, mean (M) scores ranged from 2.7 for the most trusted category (teachers; standard deviation [SD] = 1.92) to 8.5 for the least trusted (criminals; SD = 2.01). Collapsing across all three groups (Catholic, liminal Catholic, and ex-Catholic), the results indicated that priests (M = 5.15, SD = 2.69) and atheists (M = 5.11, SD = 2.45) had around the same trust ranking (both coming in the middle of the range). Bishops (M = 6.16, SD = 2.47) were trusted less than atheists and priests but more than bankers (M = 7.37, SD = 2.00), politicians (M = 7.83, SD = 1.99), and criminals (M = 8.5, SD = 2.08). Importantly, these results differed by category. There were no significant differences between groups for any of the seven "religiously irrelevant" categories, but highly significant results were found for atheist trust rankings ($F(2, 236) = 28.64, p < .001$), priest trust rankings ($F(2, 236) = 56.041, p < .001$), and bishop trust rankings ($F(2, 236) = 48.033, p < .001$). Between-group differences in trust rankings are presented in Table 2.2. Post-hoc tests revealed that all these differences were significant at the $p < .001$ level with the exception of liminal Catholic and Catholic rankings of atheists, where there was no significant difference ($p = .063$).

Results can be inspected visually in the box plots in Figure 2.1. For readers unfamiliar with this means of illustrating data, the median is the black line in the center of the box. The box itself contains the central 50% of the data. The top section of the box represents the quarter of the data above the median, and the bottom of the box represents the quarter

TABLE 2.2. Catholic, Liminal Catholic, and Ex-Catholic Differences in Trust Rankings for Atheists, Priests, and Bishops (Mean and Standard Deviation)

	Atheists	*Priests*	*Bishops*
Catholic	M = 6.16, SD = 2.12	M = 3.39, SD = 2.21	M = 4.66, SD = 2.40
Liminal Catholic	M = 5.32, SD = 2.29	M = 5.35, SD = 2.51	M = 6.37, SD = 1.91
Ex-Catholic	M = 3.66, SD = 2.28	M = 6.88, SD = 1.95	M = 7.72, SD = 1.74

Source: Author's 2017 Qualtrics Panels survey data.

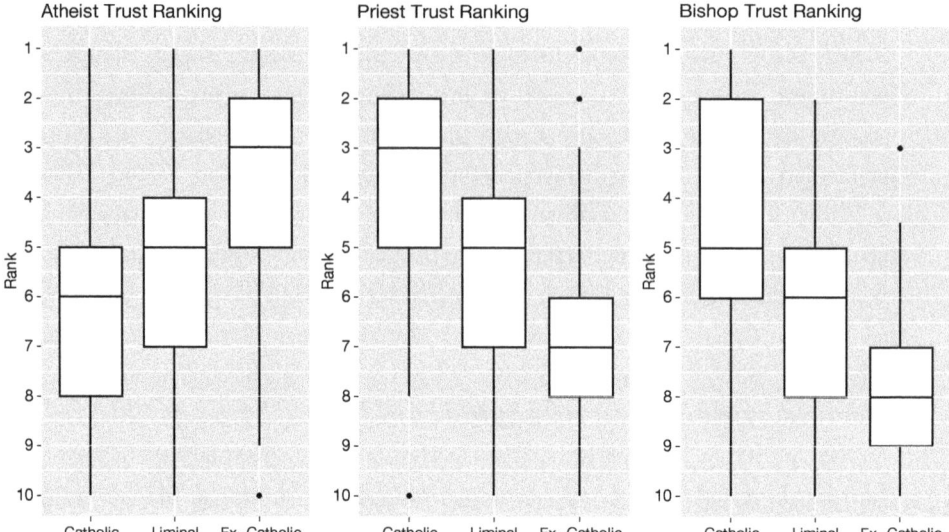

FIGURE 2.1. Ex-Catholics show extreme distrust of priests and bishops. Catholics retain their trust of priests and, to a lesser extent, bishops. Both Catholics and liminal Catholics are statistically equally distrustful of atheists. Source: 2017 Qualtrics Panels survey data.

of the data below it. The "whiskers" above and below the box represent the distribution of the 25% of data above and the 25% of data below the central box. This way of plotting data allows us to compare the entire distribution of responses between groups more easily than a conventional bar chart. For instance, looking at ex-Catholic responses for bishop trust rankings on the far right of Figure 2.1, we can see that the median is very low (8), and three-quarters of ex-Catholic respondents gave bishops a 7 or lower in the trust-ranking task.

The trust rankings demonstrate the degree to which clergy have lost their status as trustworthy in the explicit evaluation of many members of the public; overall (at least in self-reported data), they come out the same as or, in the case of bishops, worse than atheists—a category that the cross-cultural literature tells us is treated as inherently untrustworthy.[14] This tells us that in Ireland one can encounter both a tendency toward mild suspicion of religious rejecters *and* a tendency toward suspicion of religious specialists. Examining the data further shows that this is due to a stark division in the allocation of trust by Catholics and ex-Catholics. Those who retain Catholic belief and affiliation remain more trustful of clergy. On the other hand, although the data cannot say whether this distrust actually causes rejection, the majority of ex-Catholics are deeply, profoundly distrustful of the Church's representatives. For ex-Catholics, bishops are second only to criminals in untrustworthiness, and priests are separated from them only by the nationally reviled category of bankers (generally held responsible for Ireland's severe recession after the 2008 global financial crash). The elevated distrust of bishops also suggests that the institutional Church is trusted even less than individual priests. Finally, the results may reveal something about those in the liminal category: Although they are quite distrustful of priests and very distrustful of bishops, the data suggest that they also share more traditional Catholics' suspicions toward atheists. It is possible that, in an environment where theism and Catholicism are so often conflated, declaring disaffiliation might be seen as a marker of unbelief, with all the amorality this is so often assumed to entail, and is avoided as such. The retention of a Catholic label alongside the rejection of official Catholic doctrines may in part function as a socially legible declaration of trustworthy if nebulous theism alongside rejection of the contaminated institution.

It is impossible to determine whether distrust stems directly from clerical abuse scandals, but existing work suggests that the perception of the Church and its emissaries as untrustworthy is deeply connected to the status of the scandals as highly salient, sustained acts of hypocrisy.[15] Overall, these data are compatible with the claim that a collapse in trust has contributed to disaffiliation, but a causal claim cannot be established here. It is also likely that those who have already disaffiliated would trust clergy less anyway. Nevertheless, the low levels of ex-Catholic clerical trust are striking and at the least suggest that clerical status is not viewed in a neutral manner by ex-Catholics. The perceptions that lie behind this trust are examined in more detail in the next section.

How Do Catholics and Ex-Catholics See the Church?

Although it is likely that Catholics and ex-Catholics do indeed view the Church in a different light, currently there is no quantitative proof that this is so, nor is there any structured data on how their views differ. To establish some initial rough insight into this, respondents were asked whether, on the whole, they considered the Catholic Church to have been more of a positive, neutral, or negative force in Irish society, or whether they simply did not know. This allows us to see the degree to which negative appraisals of the Church are distributed between Catholics and ex-Catholics. This also provides a rough overview of the degree of consensus in these groups regarding evaluations of the Church's role in Irish society, giving us some sense of where the most cohesive and powerful ideology is to be found. The response frequencies differed significantly according to categorical status (Catholic, liminal Catholic, or ex-Catholic),[16] with ex-Catholics selecting "negative" the most frequently and Catholics selecting "positive." Liminal Catholics were in-between. Results are displayed in Figure 2.2.

The question on overall appraisals of the Church as a force for good or ill revealed the focused moral consensus of the contemporary ex-Catholic position: They nearly unanimously disapprove of the Church's

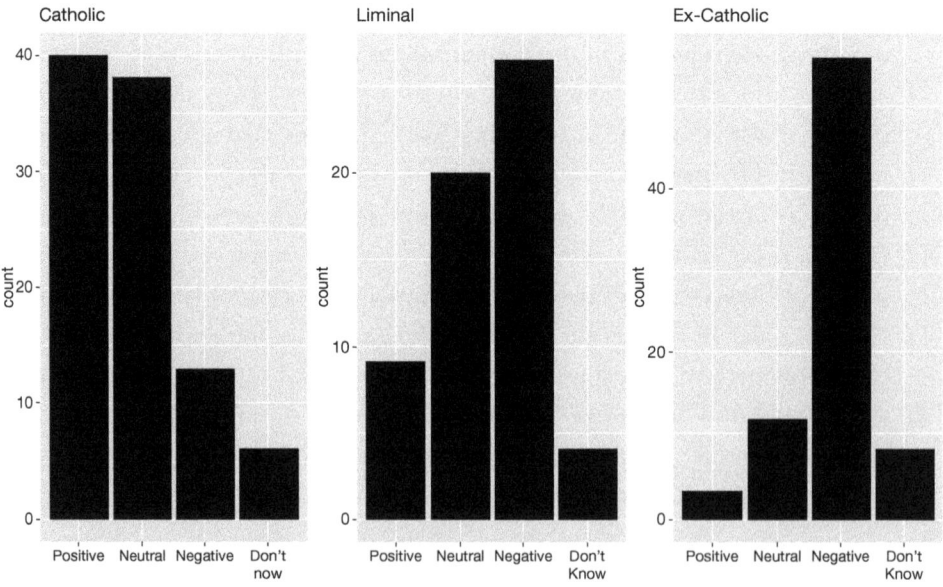

FIGURE 2.2. Evaluations by group of the Catholic Church as a force in Irish society. Source: Author's 2017 Qualtrics Panels survey data.

influence. Collapsing across all three groups, "bad" was the most popular choice. Therefore, although it may be correct that there is a larger pro-religious majority in Ireland than anywhere else in Western Europe, this should not be confused for a large pro–Catholic Church majority. Even though "religion" is widely normative, a critical orientation toward the central religious institution that one would consider more typical of the antireligious is in fact widely distributed across Irish society, including among a sizable minority of Catholics. Even the obedient Catholic category seems somewhat ambivalent, given that "neutral" and "bad" together outweigh "good," a profound about-face compared with the deferential attitudes of the clericalist past. Given the younger age profile of ex-Catholics, the data also suggest that this negative evaluation is not gradually evaporating with time. Instead, it appears to be consolidating as the majority opinion among younger cohorts. Cross-tabulations between age and evaluation of the Church showed that the percentage who viewed the Church as a positive force in Irish society increased with age, being lowest in the youngest age group (18–24), where only 6.1% chose "good." In the oldest age group, 46.5% chose "good."

To gain a richer perspective on how people view the Church, at the beginning of the survey participants also filled in a free list for the term "Irish Catholic Church." The traditional objective of a free list is to elicit the contents of a particular category of shared cultural knowledge, known as a domain. Free lists have been used extensively by early cognitive anthropologists to denote the contents of tightly defined domains ("animals," "traditional medicines," "kin terms," and so forth),[17] but they can also be used to contribute to a picture of conceptual variation between populations of interest on more abstract concepts (e.g., differing perceptions of "romantic love"[18]).

When given a free list, participants are asked to list everything that comes to mind when they are presented with a certain term, and they are generally probed in a number of ways in order to exhaust ensuing associations. One of the primary methods of analyzing free list data is to organize the resulting associations in terms of Smith's *S*, a measure of what is known as salience. This is computed from the frequency of items across lists and the order within lists.[19] The greater the frequency of an item across lists and the closer to the start it tends to be within lists, the greater its salience and the more central the association in question is to the mental model that the population of interest may have of the domain in question. Participants in the current study were asked to list everything that came to mind when they read the term "Irish Catholic Church."[20] The top 20 associations per group in terms of salience are depicted in Table 2.3, giving some idea of how the Catholic Church is conceptualized by the Catholic, liminal Catholic, and ex-Catholic groups.

The free lists provide a clear and detailed picture of what lies behind the negative evaluation of the Irish Church. Perhaps the most striking feature of the lists is the salience of negative *moral* associations among ex-Catholics and, to a lesser extent, liminal Catholics. Ex-Catholics appear deeply opposed to the Church on almost exclusively moral grounds, based on multiple negative associations. Ex-Catholics associate the Church with extreme moral transgressions (pedophilia, their most salient association); they consider it to violate bonds of social trust (it is deemed dishonest and corrupt), and they disapprove of what they perceive to be the Church's own version of morality (it is conservative and authoritarian). There are really two broad dimensions of negative moral association for ex-Catholics then: the association between the Church and failure to adhere to basic universal moral standards (it causes harm and is dishonest); and the association between the Church and the imposition of a set of norms that are immoral from the ex-Catholic point of view (conservativism, authoritarianism).

Ultimately, the fact that abuse/pedophilia is the top association in the free list for ex-Catholics belies the view that clerical abuse has already done its damage and that people are no longer preoccupied with it. They may be moving on from the time when such revelations shook them, but they are not moving *back* toward a pre-scandal relationship with the Church and allowing clerical abuse to slide from their minds. Instead, it seems to be a deeply habituated association. Even if people are no longer actively shocked by clerical abuse, for many all it takes is reflection on the Catholic Church for it to spring to mind. Behind this, for some, associations of deceit and self-interest swiftly follow. Ireland may be a post-Catholic society in some respects, but these results suggest that it should

TABLE 2.3. Free List Associations with the Term "Irish Catholic Church" Ordered by Salience (Smith's S)

Rank	CATHOLIC Association	Salience	LIMINAL CATHOLIC Association	Salience	EX-CATHOLIC Association	Salience
1	Clergy	0.54	Clergy	0.44	Abuse/pedophilia	0.43
2	Mass	0.43	Sacraments/rites of passage	0.39	Clergy	0.39
3	Sacraments/rites of passage	0.39	Mass	0.32	Corrupt/materialistic	0.31
4	Communion	0.37	Communion	0.28	Outdated/conservative	0.30
5	Churches/buildings	0.32	Corrupt/materialistic	0.26	Authoritarian/dominant	0.26
6	Pope	0.28	Abuse/pedophilia	0.25	Mass	0.22
7	God	0.20	Outdated/conservative	0.18	Education system	0.22
8	Abuse/pedophilia	0.19	Authoritarian/dominant	0.17	Dishonest/untrustworthy	0.18
9	Jesus	0.18	Confession	0.17	Communion	0.18
10	Confession	0.17	Religion	0.16	Sacraments/rites of passage	0.17
11	Good/holy	0.16	Education system	0.16	Pope	0.17
12	Religion	0.15	God	0.15	Churches/buildings	0.16
13	Prayer	0.14	Churches/buildings	0.15	Nonsense/fiction	0.16
14	Tradition	0.13	Jesus	0.15	Nuns	0.15
15	Vatican/organization	0.13	Belief/faith	0.14	Declining	0.14
16	Community	0.13	Prayer	013	Patriarchal/misogynist	0.14
17	Comforting/caring	0.13	Dishonest/untrustworthy	0.12	Old people	0.14
18	Christmas/other religious occasion	0.11	Pope	0.11	Religion	0.14
19	Nuns	0.11	Nonsense/fiction	0.11	Hypocrisy	0.13
20	Scandal	0.10	Religious artifacts	0.11	Vatican/organization	0.12

Source: Author's 2017 Qualtrics Panels survey data.

also be viewed as a post-clerical-abuse society, culturally habituated to the idea of a morally tainted Church. Indeed, when asked to estimate what percentage of priests had abused children, the ex-Catholic data yielded a mean of 39%, with a median of 32% and a mode of 20%.[21] Liminal Catholics were if anything even more extreme in their evaluations, giving a mean, median, and mode of 36%, 30%, and 30%, respectively. Despite their high regard for priests, even obedient Catholics greatly overestimated the likely prevalence of clerical pedophiles, giving figures of 20%, 15%, and 10%, respectively.[22] Any understanding of current Irish secularization must come to grips with this issue of the moral desacralization of the central religious institution and account for the role it plays in ongoing moral conflicts about the role of Catholicism—and when, whether, and with what caveats one ought to still call oneself a Catholic.

Given the prevalence of clerical pedophilia in the popular imagination, it is worth asking how people in our three rough categories feel about it and whether there are any differences in their moral-emotional responses that may have some significance for the analysis of the social status of religious affiliation in a context of institutional desacralization. To attain a quick quantitative overview of this, survey participants were asked to rank 10 randomized emotional reactions (disgust, anger, sadness, shame, shock, contempt, disbelief, vindication, apathy, amusement) from 1 to 10, where 1 is that which best described their reaction on first learning about clerical abuse and 10 being that which was least representative.

In order from most endorsed to least, mean rankings on the 10 emotional responses to clerical abuse across all groups were as follows: disgust (M = 2.6, SD = 1.832), anger (M = 3.45, SD = 2.037), sadness (M = 4, SD = 2), shame (M = 4.69, SD = 2.92), shock (M = 4.71, SD = 2.298), contempt (M = 5.34, SD = 2.379), disbelief (M = 5.94, SD = 2.169), vindication (M = 6.71, SD = 2.597), apathy (M = 8.62, SD = 1.573), amusement (M = 8.92, SD = 1.518). Disgust and anger, therefore, were the two most highly ranked responses in relation to clerical abuse. In their respective ways, both these emotions encourage punishment: anger by eliciting the desire to approach and confront, and disgust by eliciting the desire to withdraw and ostracize. At the other end of the scale, people virtually unanimously rejected apathy and amusement. If the result pertaining to disgust is combined with the free list finding that pedophilia is the most salient association ex-Catholics have with the Irish Catholic Church, it is reasonable to infer that many ex-Catholics feel a sense of moral disgust just by thinking about the institutional Church.

But the points of divergence, though not enormous, are also of interest. Significant between-group differences existed for anger, contempt, vindication, shame, and shock. Ex-Catholics ranked anger ($p = .015$), contempt ($p < .001$), and vindication ($p < .001$) significantly higher than Catholics. Catholics ranked sadness ($p = .018$), shame ($p = .003$), and shock ($p < .001$) significantly higher than ex-Catholics. Despite the fact that many ex-Catholics strongly endorse clerical abuse as a factor in the rejection of Catholicism, the group ranks shock significantly lower than Catholics. This could suggest that many already had a dim view of the Church before finding out about abuse, rendering its transgressions less surprising. Abuse may have been the straw that broke the camel's back. Alternatively the ranking of shock may reflect the younger age profile; more of them grew up in the era of scandal. It could also suggest that the Church was less important to many ex-Catholics, so its fall from grace simply came as less of a blow. On the other hand, high Catholic rankings of shock may serve to project an innocent status with respect to knowledge of "what was going on" and to ward off the threat posed by accusations of past mass public complicity in and willful blindness to clerical abuse. Ex-Catholics are also significantly more likely to endorse vindication. It is unlikely that Catholics would have ranked this factor highly, but it suggests nevertheless that for at least some ex-Catholics, the scandals confirmed their prior negative evaluation. Also of interest are the differences around shame and contempt. Ex-Catholics are significantly less likely to feel shame and significantly more likely to feel contempt. Catholics likely rank shame higher because of a feeling of contamination or complicity connected to abuse, given that they still construe themselves as loyal to the institution from which the perpetrators originated. Psychologists suggest that shame entails the urge to shrink from sight and withdraw, often also accompanied by feelings of anger and victimization.[23] These indeed are emotions I was subsequently to encounter in the field among some of the devout. Contempt, on the other hand, entails a sense of moral superiority or greater moral status,[24] suggesting that, although the scandals may have weakened the moral self-certainty of the devout, they have elevated the self-perceived moral status of those who reject Catholicism. This, too, was something I encountered during my fieldwork.

But the free list also shows us that pedophilia and the disgust it elicits is far from the only moral factor that springs to mind when ex-Catholics think of the Church. Also of note is the presence of other forms of moral disagreement, in particular, the evident focus on conservativism and authoritarianism. This is despite the fact that ex-Catholics are by and large younger than Catholics, meaning that they are in fact less likely to have grown up while the Church was at the zenith of its power and are less likely to have personally experienced the full brunt of the conservative social mores of Holy Catholic Ireland. This focus on conservativism and authoritarianism suggests that Irish ex-Catholics may also have similar moral motivations to the nonreligious in the United States, who disaffiliate largely because they are political progressives who dislike the association between their natal denominations and political conservativism.[25] By contrast, among Catholics—many more of whom belong to the generation that did actually experience the Church at what might be considered its most oppressive—we can see a wide range of positive associations, such as tradition, community, and comfort. This disparity could be taken to suggest that the withdrawal of the Irish Catholic sacred canopy and the rise of increasingly habitual and practice-free Catholicism in more recent decades means that many ex-Catholics lack the kind of deep and sustained personal experiences that might cause them to opt instead for a liminal Catholic compromise. The Catholic Church is not only immoral for many ex-Catholics but also might be something of an evil abstraction.

Together with ex-Catholics' evident moral progressivism,[26] this poses questions about the relationship between clerical abuse scandals and disaffiliation. To what degree is abuse simply more salient because ex-Catholics lack more positive associations with religion, or more inalienable experiences of it, perhaps because of a lower degree of religious socialization growing up? Could it be that abuse's salience is partly due to its weaponized potency in anti-Church moral discourse surrounding a rejection primarily motivated by other factors, such as opposition to Catholic conservativism, which is seen as standing in the way of progressive causes? The lists may even be best read as the output of moralistic social minds pitched against one another in a conflicted social arena, where what is salient is often what is most useful for moral combat, whether that is within one's family (e.g., resisting pressure from older and more pious relatives) or in society more broadly (e.g., resisting Catholic antagonists in various facets of the secularization debate).

Differences in Liminal and Ex-Catholic Rejection of the Church

Clerical abuse and Catholic conservativism may be highly salient for ex-Catholics, but we do not know from the data discussed so far whether they were actually causal in the decision to reject Catholicism. Nor do we know how ex-Catholics differ from the liminal category in this respect. To assess the overall subjective importance of various factors cited as reasons for rejecting the Church, participants were asked to rank a series of 11 reasons for perceived importance in their own processes of rejecting Catholic teachings. These rejection factors were based on the apostasy factors described by Zuckerman in his work on the nonreligious[27] and on more culturally contingent factors that appeared prominently in my initial fieldwork, interviews, and open-ended pilot survey data. All items were rated on Likert scales, where 0 = not at all important and 6 = extremely important. The factors were irrational beliefs, conservative moral values, religious hypocrisy encountered among everyday Catholics, clerical sexual abuse scandals, Church oppressiveness/authoritarianism, personal irrelevance of Catholicism, influence of secularist or atheist thought, boredom with religious services, knowledge of other religious or spiritual beliefs, perception that the surrounding Catholicism was primarily a matter of habit or pressure, and knowledge of science.

Once all participant scores were aggregated, they provided a representative picture of what baptized Catholics who have rejected Church teachings perceive to be the most and least important factors in this outcome. Descriptive data on these rankings are in Table 2.4.

In addition to these rankings, the rejection data were broken down into the two rejecting groups (liminal Catholics and ex-Catholics) to

TABLE 2.4. Rejection Factors for All Church-Rejecting Participants Combined (Liminal Catholics and Ex-Catholics), Ranked from Most to Least Important

Rank	Rejection Factor	Mean and SD
1	Moral conservatism	M = 4.8, SD = 1.54
2	Clerical abuse	M = 4.69, SD = 1.7
3	Authoritarianism	M = 4.45, SD = 1.67
4	Everyday hypocrisy	M = 4.22, SD = 1.72
5	Irrational beliefs	M = 3.9, SD = 1.79
6	Inauthentic practice	M = 3.75, SD = 1.82
7	Personal irrelevance	M = 3.53, SD = 1.957
8	Boredom with services	M = 3.5, SD = 1.993
9	Scientific knowledge	M = 3.12, SD = 2.04
10	Secularist/atheist intellectual influence	M = 2.59, SD = 2.06
11	Knowledge of other religions	M = 2.58, SD = 1.98

Source: Author's 2017 Qualtrics Panels survey data.

TABLE 2.5. Differing Rejection Emphases Between Liminal Catholics and Ex-Catholics

Rejection Factor	Liminal Catholic	Ex-Catholic	Significance
Personal irrelevance	M = 2.63, SD = 1.85	M = 4.21, SD = 1.77	$t(140)$ = 5.137, $p < .001$
Irrational beliefs	M = 3.27, SD = 1.78	M = 4.37, SD = 1.67	$t(140)$ = 3.757, $p < .001$
Scientific knowledge	M = 2.42, SD = 2.01	M = 3.63, SD = 1.92	$t(140)$ = 2.203, $p < .001$
Conservatism	M = 4.42, SD = 1.66	M = 5.06, SD = 1.4	$t(140)$ = 2.504, $p = .013$
Authoritarianism	M = 4.08, SD = 1.63	M = 4.72, SD = 1.66	$t(140)$ = 2.270, $p = .025$
Inauthentic practice	M = 3.37, SD = 1.75	M = 4.04, SD = 1.84	$t(140)$ = 2.193, $p = .029$
Secularist influence	M = 2.2, SD = 1.95	M = 2.9, SD = 2.1	$t(140)$ = 2.203, $p = .045$

Source: Author's 2017 Qualtrics Panels survey data.

explore the motivational differences between those who reject Church teachings but not a Catholic affiliation and those who disaffiliate outright. Significant differences existed between liminal and ex-Catholics on seven of the rejection factors, with ex-Catholics rating the following factors significantly higher than liminal Catholics: personal irrelevance, irrational beliefs, scientific knowledge, conservatism, authoritarianism, inauthentic practice, secularist influence (Table 2.5).

Two different patterns emerge from these comparative data on rejection factors. The first and most obvious is a common trend, the second a divergence. The common trend is, again, an overall focus on what might be termed moral factors in the rejection of Catholicism. Across both rejection groups (liminal Catholics and ex-Catholics), the perceived conservativism of the Church and sexual abuse scandals are the highest ranked factors in the rejection of Catholicism, with authoritarianism and everyday Catholic hypocrisy not far behind. Ex-Catholics are even more emphatic than liminal Catholics here; they rank some moral factors (i.e., conservativism and authoritarianism) significantly higher—indeed the results show extraordinarily strong consensus on ex-Catholic opposition to Catholic conservativism as a factor in their rejection of Catholicism. The divergence is the tendency for ex-Catholics to significantly differ from liminal Catholics by also giving high ratings to what might be termed intellectual factors (the irrationality of belief, scientific knowledge) and Catholicism's personal irrelevance. It is tempting to conclude from this divergence that for many ex-Catholics, Catholicism never really caught on in the first place. Liminal Catholics, on the other hand, despite their moral reservations, cleave to Catholicism as an identifier, perhaps because they are less likely to find Catholic doctrine irrational or irrelevant, even if they may disagree on the details. Given their slightly older age profile (see Table 2.1), this may relate to stronger prior religious socialization.

Are Ex-Catholics "Unbelievers"? Unbelievers in What?

Just under one-third of ex-Catholics in the data actually identified as atheists, but identity and belief are separable: There may be many more "unbelievers" than those who are willing to elevate this perspective to the status of identity marker. Theism in general remains widely normative cross-culturally, and atheism carries much cross-cultural stigma ("extreme prejudice," as a recent study phrased it)[28] based on the intuitive assumption that people need religious beliefs to be moral, something that likely prevents some skeptics from overtly identifying as atheists.[29] In Ireland this intuitive link between religion and morality is also reinforced in the Catholic education system. In later chapters we will see that in Ireland atheists are also frequently stigmatized as intolerant or aggressive; it is not unusual to see Irish atheism portrayed as the mirror image of Catholic totalitarianism, something that tends to drive some Irish nontheists away from the atheist label.[30] There is also the question of "unbelief" in *what*: Catholic beliefs in particular or belief in God generally? Catholics, liminal Catholics, and ex-Catholics were thus compared on their levels of Catholic belief specifically and theistic belief more generally.

Commitment to Catholic religious beliefs was assessed using an orthodox Catholic belief scale (Figure 2.3a).[31] Possible scores ranged from a minimum of 7 to a maximum of 42. Catholics had a mean score of 31.05 (SD = 10.183), liminal Catholics had a mean score of 22.08 (SD = 8.481), and ex-Catholics had a mean score of 8.72 (SD = 5.102). In other words, when it comes to signature Catholic beliefs (transubstantiation, the virgin birth, and so forth), ex-Catholics have almost flatlined. The groups were then compared on their level of general nonspecific theism (Figure 2.3b). Possible scores on the theistic certainty measure ranged from a minimum of 1 to a maximum of 7. Catholics had a mean score of 5.92 (SD = 1.426), liminal Catholics had a mean score of 5.53 (SD = 1.186), and ex-Catholics had a mean score of 2.72 (SD = 1.8).[32]

Ex-Catholics are much more atheistic than the other categories but are still quite varied in their attitudes toward the idea of *some* kind of God existing, with the top quarter of the data showing a fair amount of general theism. This likely relates to the "spiritual but not religious," who are far more likely to endorse this possibility, whereas self-identified atheists are far less likely to do so. What all subcategories of ex-Catholics do evidently coalesce around is a flat-out rejection of specifically Catholic religious representations. By contrast, liminal Catholics are markedly equivocal about the signature tenets of Catholic orthodoxy. We can see that the box plot in Figure 2.3a stretches evenly across the whole range of possible scores. This probably reflects the great variety within the liminal category. Some of these people may be quite devout and religiously engaged liberalized or deinstitutionalized Catholics who retain a strong connection to Catholic theology while rejecting the institution, whereas others might be much closer to the disengaged, culturally Catholic position. In contrast to ex-Catholics, though, they are just as strongly theistic in a general sense as the obedient Catholic group.

This could suggest that for the more narrowly distributed, minority-status liminal Catholicism found in this survey, theism really is important

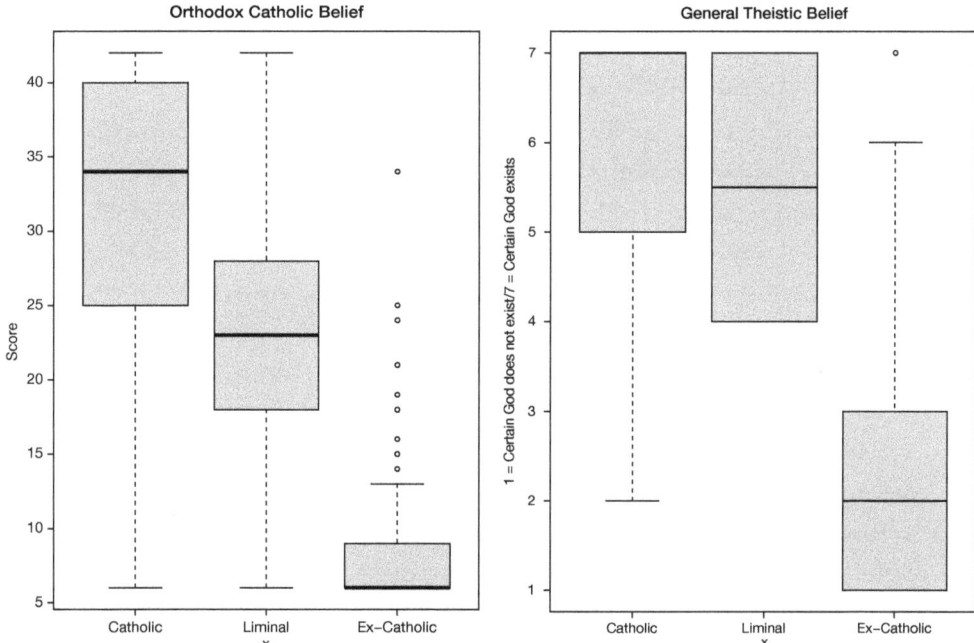

FIGURE 2.3. All groups differ highly significantly in their acceptance of Catholic doctrine, but there is no significant difference between Catholics and liminal Catholics in certainty about God's existence. Source: Author's 2017 Qualtrics Panels survey data.

rather than being purely a matter of religious fuzziness. In fact, Figure 2.3 shows that it is not uncommon to be a fairly atheistic or at least strongly agnostic orthodox Catholic, but all liminal Catholics are pretty convinced theists. The liminal Catholics are perhaps caught in a bind. Given that they believe that about 30% of priests are pedophiles, many may reject the contaminated shibboleths of clericalist orthodoxy while clinging to the Catholic label as a signal that they do still believe in something. Ex-Catholicism, by contrast, is a rejection of this ambiguous option: It could be seen as a resuturing of belief and identity. As we will see in subsequent chapters, this consonance is often performed as a brave, uncompromising stance of *authenticity*. However, the ease with which individuals can adopt this stance may also vary according to the degree to which they have been socialized as religious in the first place.

How Do CREDs Relate to the Retention of a Contaminated Affiliation?

In Chapter 1, I discussed CREDs, namely, the idea that religions (and other worldviews grounded in empirically unverifiable propositions) are transmitted most effectively when people witness those close to them behaving as though they very much believe in what they say they do. Ritual, practice, and personal sacrifice for the faith are all forms of such costly proof. From this, I postulated that, like any other religious tradition, CRED exposure is an important component in the transmission of Irish Catholic belief and identity and that, compared with the grand extremes of Holy Catholic Ireland, CRED exposure has been declining over time because of what sociologists have described as the fragmentation of Catholic consensus, the decline of mandatory devout obeisance, and the widespread transition to low-cost cultural Catholicism. Data supporting these two hypotheses are shown in what follows.[33]

A multiple linear regression was calculated to predict the effects of age, gender, urban or rural habitation, and the extent to which one was exposed to CREDs from one's parents, on the strength of Catholic belief (Figure 2.4).[34] CRED scale scores were the strongest predictor, followed by age and being female.[35] Similar statistics were obtained for Catholic social identity. Age lost a large amount of predictive power once CREDs were included in the model, suggesting that the high CRED exposure of older Irish Catholics in part drives their religiosity.[36]

As can be seen from Figure 2.4, those scoring low on the CRED scale almost never report strong Catholic beliefs: the top left-hand corner of the chart is conspicuously empty. Across the generations, visible devotion on the part of caregivers breeds devotion in turn. Overall, Catholic beliefs and "being Catholic" are of little importance to those who have not been subjected to a devout upbringing—and the reasons that they should be not just irrelevant but in many cases objectionable enough to warrant their rejection are suggested by the moral associations depicted previously.

Another part of the argument is that as Holy Catholic Ireland receded and as Catholicism became more of a cultural matter limited to

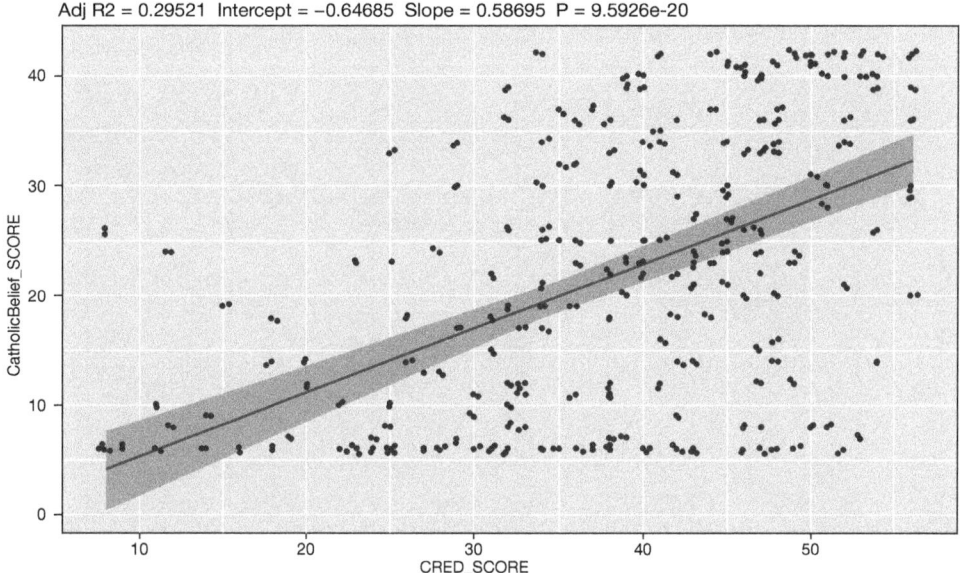

FIGURE 2.4. There is a strong linear relationship between domestic Catholic CRED exposure and acceptance of orthodox Catholic Christian beliefs. Source: Author's 2017 Qualtrics Panels survey data.

quarantined occasions rather than an all-pervasive force, CRED-type behaviors came to be depleted and the transmission of strong Catholic belief and identification also began to break down. Assessing this process of CRED depletion was more problematic, as the data were not longitudinal. Given that the CRED scale ought to measure recall of concrete experiences rather than purely subjective current phenomena that may change over time (such as strength of Catholic identification or belief), it was judged acceptable in this instance to use age cohorts as a proxy in the absence of longitudinal data, though such data would of course be more desirable. To this end, a second multiple linear regression was calculated to predict the effects of age, gender, and urban or rural habitation on the CRED scores themselves (Figure 2.5).[37] It was found that age was the only significant predictor of CRED scores.[38]

Although not without their limitations,[39] these age data suggest that, overall, each generation perceives its parents to be less motivated in their actions by religious beliefs than the one before. As I show in the next

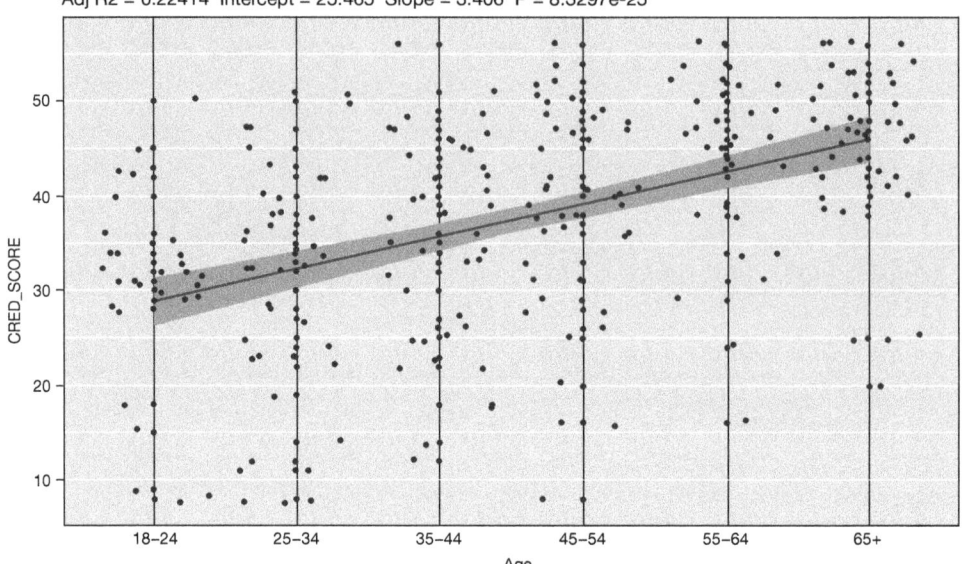

FIGURE 2.5. Domestic Catholic CRED exposure decreases as age decreases, suggesting that Catholic CRED performance is declining over time. Source: Author's 2017 Qualtrics Panels survey data.

chapter, the acceptability of the inference that CREDs are important to belief—and that CREDs are fast fading—was reinforced by qualitative data collected in the field. The proposition that CREDs have declined over time is consonant with the historical and sociological records, which depict devout embodied Catholicism coming to be replaced by what is increasingly a fuzzy and tenuous laissez-faire connection. This is a purely (and rarely even) verbal stance, offering little to no behavioral evidence of commitment. Children's rites of passage and church weddings are not good CREDs; they involve getting something, not sacrificing something. Being culturally Catholic may transmit across the generations but at present only as a shallow connection rather than as a state of deep commitment and perhaps only insofar as it confers certain advantages or incurs no major costs. Being culturally Catholic is likely vulnerable to a powerful counter-ideology with CREDs of its own, as it can be quite easily disowned. It is likely also vulnerable to CRUDs (credibility-undermining displays, as discussed in Chapter 1) within the religious tradition—and there have been many of those. Why cling to a religious tradition of only peripheral importance to you and whose paragons you associate primarily with hypocrisy? As I show in subsequent chapters, there are in fact reasons to do so, but they primarily revolve around social pragmatism rather than any kind of deep personal commitment to a religious worldview or identity.

Has Scandal Driven Down CRED Performance?

On top of preexisting secularizing processes, it is also possible that the scandals have caused further CRED depletion by driving down people's willingness to be seen to affiliate with a contaminated institution. In an attempt to quantify the degree to which CRED depletion may have been accelerated by the scandals, thinning out the sacred canopy even more, survey participants were provided with a list of potential CRED behaviors[40] in random order and asked the following question:

> Were you less likely to do any of the following things after the Catholic Church sexual abuse scandals emerged? Please select any that apply. (Note: Only tick things that you did less or were less likely to do as a result of the sexual abuse scandals, not things you would not have done in the first place or stopped doing/did less often for other reasons.)

The results of the scandal-related CRED depletion question are contained in Table 2.6. The percentages indicate the proportion of respondents who said that they were less likely to engage in the activity in question as a direct result of Catholic Church sexual abuse scandals.

The results show that there is particularly strong resistance to Mass, confession, and donation, the most traditionally common Irish Catholic CREDs. Confession evokes particular rejection, likely because people are unwilling to present themselves to a morally tainted institution as sinners seeking forgiveness. Even obedient Catholics evince a strong reaction against confession. We can also see that in each case liminal Catholics evince the highest reaction, providing further evidence that institutional rejection is a method used by some theistic Catholics to distance themselves from the Church. The category that least constitutes a convincing CRED—namely, rites of passage, which are enjoyable social occasions rather than onerous sacrifices—is also the least affected by the scandals.

TABLE 2.6. Degree to Which People Reported Being Less Likely to Perform Various CREDs Because of the Scandals

CRED Type	Catholic (% Less Likely to Do)	Liminal Catholic (% Less Likely to Do)	Ex-Catholic (% Less Likely to Do)	Total (% Less Likely to Do)
Mass	26.3	46.2	36.0	35.3
Confession	47.5	50.9	37.8	45.0
Donation	31.1	54.4	49.3	44.1
Candles	17.8	16.4	20.5	18.4
Ashes	21.3	20.0	31.5	24.6
Public prayer	25.7	10.7	18.1	18.8
Rites of passage	14.1	3.7	23.7	14.9
Bless oneself	15.5	27.3	28.8	23.6
Lent	20.8	27.3	21.9	22.9
Confront blasphemer	20.3	7.4	11.0	13.4
Hide skepticism	5.6	9.3	11.0	8.5

Source: Author's 2017 Qualtrics Panels survey data.

It also seems that behaviors that identify the individual as a devout Catholic have undergone substantial declines. A quarter of obedient Catholics say that they are less likely to pray in public, and a fifth say that they are less likely to receive ashes or confront those whom they perceive to be disrespectful to Catholicism. This suggests a fairly substantial trend toward not wanting to stand out as religiously Catholic.

Although there is something to be gleaned from these data, it must be mentioned that, in retrospect, the CRED depletion question contains a number of limitations. Principally, the data provide no indication of how often respondents performed these various actions before the scandals emerged. For instance, although 36% of ex-Catholics said they were less likely to go to Mass, this may have been a reduction from once a year to never, hardly a significant dent in ambient CREDs for whatever cultural learners might be to hand. Furthermore, the wording of the question effectively conflates "did less" with "were less likely to do." "Did less" is concrete, but "were less likely to do" can refer to an entirely hypothetical potential state. In other words, it is possible that many of the respondents would not have performed the particular action anyway but became more adamant that they would not perform it as a result of the scandals—it seems unlikely, for instance, that 49% of ex-Catholics would have been donating money to the Church if it had not been for the scandals. Finally, the possibility remains that, when given the opportunity, people will either consciously or unconsciously simply exploit the scandals as a morally praiseworthy justification for renouncing various onerous social obligations. As a result of these limitations, the results are at best viewed as evidence of an increase in unwillingness to perform various CREDs rather than as a concrete measure of actual CRED depletion.

Overview: Religious Attenuation, Distrust, and Moral Antipathy

Ex-Catholics are no monolith, and in a larger, more nuanced sample it would be possible to draw out a huge range of distinct subgroups—perhaps as many as there are individuals. Nevertheless, it can be said that ex-Catholics almost unanimously share a flat-out rejection of Catholic beliefs and a stance of deep moral opposition to the Church based on the two issues of abuse and conservativism. Here, I bring together some of the data outlined in this chapter to give some idea of what background variables best predict this stance of moralized ex-Catholicism. Two multiple linear regression models were run on the acceptance of Catholic beliefs and the strength of Catholic social identification using the following independent variables: age, gender, urban or rural habitation, CRED exposure, clerical trust, and moral progressivism.[41] Clerical trust was operationalized as a continuous variable using the priest trust rankings (see Figure 2.1). The dependent variables were the Catholic belief scale (Figure 2.3), and a measure of social identification with Catholicism.[42] The significance of each independent variable in predicting the acceptance of Catholic beliefs can be seen in Table 2.7.

In descending order, then, clerical distrust, low CREDs, and high progressivism are the three strongest predictors of low Catholic belief and identity. There is doubtless reverse causality and lateral influence here: Low religious socialization likely entails less experience with positive religious exemplars who might push back against the taint. This would raise distrust. Lack of religious exposure would also obviously prevent the adoption of a more conservative, Church-inspired moral worldview. However, the sheer potency of distrust and low CREDs in predicting Catholic

TABLE 2.7. Significance of Clerical Trust, CRED Exposure, Moral Progressivism, Gender, Age, and Rural Habitation on the Acceptance of Catholic Beliefs

Variable	β	$t(193)$	p
Clerical trust	−0.462	−8.537	< .001
CRED score	0.269	4.503	< .001
Progressivism	−0.138	−2.709	.007
Gender	0.127	2.512	.013
Age	0.122	2.163	.032
Urban/rural	−0.10	−0.196	.845

Source: Author's 2017 Qualtrics Panels survey data.

rejection suggest that both the scandals and the rise of disengaged cultural Catholicism have, in some interconnected way that we will attempt to tease out in the field, weakened the foundations of Irish Catholic religious belief and identity. When a second regression model was calculated using Catholic social identity as the dependent variable, the statistical results were almost identical. This would indicate that if signature Catholic beliefs are not very important to people, then "being Catholic" is also not very important to their sense of who they are. The idea of a committedly cultural Catholic may be oxymoronic.

Taken together, the data presented throughout this chapter suggest that Ireland could be understood as entering a state of moral polarization and religious fragmentation defined by acute moral tensions about the subject of Catholicism and its ongoing influence. On the one hand, a substantial portion of the population continues to be quite orthodox, cleaving to doctrinal beliefs and trusting clerical authorities. They tend to be older and are now outnumbered by those with a highly negative evaluation of the Church. Tensions in particular appear to revolve around moral issues, namely, growing perceptions of the Church's moral stance as being too conservative and the ongoing salience of clerical abuse and other signature acts of immorality in which the Church has been implicated. Ex-Catholics tend to be younger, are more progressive than Catholics, and are far more distrusting of clerical personnel. Clerical abuse is the most salient association that ex-Catholics have with the Church, and the dominant emotion all people report feeling about this phenomenon is disgust, leading to the possibility that Catholicism itself, and certainly the Church as an institution, may elicit moral disgust for ex-Catholics.

In terms of predictive variables, CREDs seem to be a particularly important component in determining who does and does not reject Catholicism, as high parental CRED exposure strongly predicts the retention of Catholic beliefs and social identity. However, each age group reports lower CRED exposure, suggesting that CRED depletion is taking place, as hypothesized previously. Furthermore, the survey found somewhat ambiguous descriptive evidence that CRED performance has been further reduced by the scandals. Although the data here must be treated with caution because of the outlined limitations, including small sample size, they do serve to provide an alternative, and more conflicted, picture to existing measures. They suggest that cultural Catholicism is threatened by the withdrawal of CRED performance, the growth of moral progressivism, and the moral tainting of the Church. For the children of disengaged cultural Catholics, the Church is primarily associated with media-relayed CRUDs and the obstruction of progressive causes.

The current data suggest that the contribution of clerical abuse scandals in particular has been underestimated in some (primarily theological) literature on Irish secularization.[43] The scandals have continued to occupy a prominent status in the media for over two decades and new scandals consistently come to light and reactivate these associations.[44] The issue has not causally evaporated, and it continues to have implications for Catholic affiliation, perhaps more so now than ever before. As the CRED data could be taken to depict, domestic immersion in Catholic ritual and behavior is in steep decline; on the other hand, as the free lists could be taken to suggest, scandals are widely salient. Essentially, new generations are born into a "Church of scandal," as one religious field contact put it, and this likely militates against the acquisition of strong orthodox Catholic belief and identity, especially in the absence of strong CREDs. As some have suggested, the abuse scandals appear to have had a critical role not just in the rejection of institutional authority but also in spreading and normalizing an antireligious worldview and must be recognized as a crucial component in the emergence of Irish irreligion.[45]

They may not have been the only factor that set things in motion, but they have provided the meat for a new way of being stridently, proudly, and above all *morally* nonreligious. This new stance was prominently visible when Ireland once again received a pontifical visitor in 2018.

The Return of the Pope

In 2018 Pope Francis was scheduled to follow in the formidable footsteps of Pope John Paul II, visiting as part of a global Catholic event titled the World Meeting of Families. He too would speak in Dublin's Phoenix Park and was expected to draw an audience of at least 500,000. But the visit did not come off as many had expected. In no sense was it a repeat of John Paul II's victory lap. Francis found himself in a very different country—one where the Church's reputation, for many, had been turned on its head. In the weeks before the pope's arrival, media coverage had been dominated by critical coverage of the Church's handling of clerical abuse claims.[46] The recent harrowing discoveries at the Tuam mother and baby home were also fresh in many Irish people's minds. As a result, Pope Francis's visit was more a fraught balancing act than a triumphant state occasion, and it was handled as such by the political establishment. It was important to the Irish government that the visit come off in a way that would, on the one hand, allow the state to demonstrate its progressive leaps toward moral independence from the Vatican and, on the other, reassure traditional Catholic Ireland that the Church was not under attack.

The taoiseach, Leo Varadkar, ritualistically spoke of "stains on our State, our society and also the Catholic church," of "cries for help that went unheard," but he also emphasized that these "mistakes" were shared.[47] Everyone, and no one, was to blame. It was time to leave the miasma of the past behind. Even though the Church was no longer at the center of Irish society, a "new covenant" was possible. This equivocal keening is often performed by Irish politicians when unpalatable aspects of the Holy Catholic past are triggered in public consciousness and they must be seen to react. It reflects the fact that the relationship between politics and religion in Ireland, once one of subservience, must now reflect the attitudes of a polity that is much more divided on religious matters.

Politicians must appear to give concessions to the Church's critics while also retaining the votes of religious conservatives and traditionalists.

This involves particularly deft maneuvering at times when grassroots pressure to dismantle lingering religious influence in the Constitution is growing, because this sets up zero-sum moral confrontations between elements of the Irish population with diametrically opposed visions. Thankfully for the politicians, the Irish Constitution provides a mechanism for resolving such issues that saves them from committing themselves too deeply to one side or the other: decision by public referendum. Such plebiscites have been a prominent feature of legislative secularization in recent years. As the intensity of Catholicism has unwound, Fine Gael, one half of Ireland's oscillating (and historically currently co-ruling) governing duopoly of the political center right, has courted the growing liberal sections of the electorate by dismantling various forms of church-state intertwinement in a series of "social upheavals," such as the marriage equality referendum in 2015 and the abortion referendum of 2018.[48] But even if these referenda exculpate centrist politicians from directly making controversial decisions and provide them with a patina of social liberalism, they can still find themselves blamed by conservative critics for calling them in the first place or for endorsing the results with too much enthusiasm. The twin "civil war" parties (Fine Gael and Fianna Fáil) that have dominated Irish politics since independence must still placate the conservative elements of their bases, even as they appear to betray them on moral issues. Enter Pope Francis.

When the pope came to visit, one-third of the electorate was freshly hurting from defeat in the abortion referendum. Although it was widely acknowledged that the new pope would have to face the music in what has been described as "the Ground Zero of Catholic clerical sexual abuse,"[49] hopes were high that he might even manage to do this in a cathartic way and that Francis, often considered a liberal pope with wider appeal beyond just the devout, might also provide the country with something of a healing or unifying experience. This may be why Varadkar became so animated when he caught wind of trouble brewing. A mysterious cadre of secularists had been organizing an online campaign called "Say Nope to the Pope." As plotted, this campaign would involve the mass acquisition of free tickets, sometimes even entire coachloads worth of them, to reduce the pope's Phoenix Park audience as a form of protest, forcing him to sermonize to empty allotments symbolizing the disgust people felt at the Church's handling of abuse claims. Varadkar described the campaign as "wrong, petty, and mean-spirited"; in his view it was not "legitimate protest." He was echoed by the leader of the opposition, Micheál Martin of Fianna Fáil, who said that the campaign was "petty, intolerant, and certainly the opposite of progressive."[50]

As a surprisingly divisive visitor, the pope chose to cut a far humbler figure than his almighty predecessor. A private meeting with a group of eight abuse survivors was swiftly organized, and he expressed shock about the stories they told him. He referred to abusers and their enablers as *caca*—roughly translated as "shit." At the Phoenix Park Mass, he apologized for the abuses perpetrated by and in the name of the Church and begged for forgiveness. I was there and could tell from the devout reactions around me—gasps and sighs—that this display of humility moved many of those who were present. It did not move the other side, though. As Colm O'Gorman of Amnesty International, himself a prominent abuse survivor and one of the organizers of a large protest timed to coincide with the papal Mass, said, "He could have talked to the people of Ireland, beyond just those who might identity as faithful Catholics. He could have talked to us all in a way that was blunt, that was clear, that was frank, that was human and that was accessible. He refused clearly to do so and that's a huge shame."[51] The pope's efforts were interpreted by secularists—some of whom I have heard refer to him as the "PR pope"—as one more instance of ecclesiastical wind. He held back from giving any details as to how the Church would actually recompense the abused or penalize their abusers, and this vagueness caused considerable further outcry from these sectors in the weeks after the visit.

Those who objected to the visit seemed much more strident and confident than the pope. A protest march in Dublin city center went from the Garden of Remembrance to Seán MacDermott Street, the site of the last Magdalene laundry to be closed. There a moment of silence was held for the victims of the Holy Catholic past, those who had been

FIGURE 2.6. Protestors objecting to the Pope's visit in 2018. The central placard depicts singer Sinéad O'Connor tearing up a picture of Pope John Paul II on air on NBC's *Saturday Night Live* in 1992. Vilified after the act, for many, O'Connor now appears vindicated. Source: Author's photograph.

incarcerated in the "shame-industrial complex." The march drew protestors demanding restitution for the abused and punishment for their abusers, with many also condemning the Church as a misogynistic and homophobic institution—accusations that would have been nearly inexpressible in public in 1979. The march projected the kind of indignant but optimistic confidence that comes with believing that one is on the right side of history but unjustly blocked from achieving one's aims. The protestors included survivors' groups, secularist organizations, LGBTQ support groups, liberal Catholic splinter factions, and lone individuals sympathetic to the cause (see Figure 2.6). They asked that the Magdalene site be preserved as a memorial.

Despite the relatively diffuse nature of the gathering, there were some figureheads. In an interview with an RTÉ journalist, one of the main organizers, Lisa Breslin, stated that the pope needed "to be accountable for all of the undeniable abundance of abuse cases." But she also went on to broaden the topic: "This is not just about abuse cases. We need, in

Ireland, a complete separation between church and state. And we think every human has the right for freedom of conscience and belief in a religion for both religious people and nonreligious people." These critical and secularizing stances were not the preserve of nonreligious people alone. They were also shared by a substantial minority of devout Catholics. In the run-up to the papal visit and in its aftermath, influential liberal Catholic figures such as former president Mary McAleese and abuse survivor Marie Collins had mounted sustained criticism of the Church's handling of abuse claims, of Francis's perceived inaction on the matter, and of issues such as the Church's opposition to abortion alongside its perceived misogyny and homophobia.[52] McAleese even went so far as to reveal that she had voted to repeal the Eighth Amendment and liberalize Irish abortion laws.

But beyond considerations of ecclesiastical complicity in and failure to redress abuses and beyond even the issue of lingering Church influence in social institutions, an extra layer of antipathy was evident in some of the nonreligious. When Lisa Breslin was reminded by the journalist interviewing her of recent liberalizing victories for her side in referenda on same-sex marriage, divorce, and abortion, she revealed a deeper strand to her objection to the pope's visit. It was not just a matter of unraveling the last knots linking church and state, an ambition shared by a considerable number of liberal secularist Catholics as well. She simply was not Catholic and was sick of being claimed as such: "This is how I've felt from a very young age, and a lot of people in Ireland feel the same. They feel like they're hostages of a religion they don't want to be part of. And I'm one of those people."[53] Breslin and others like her did not perceive Catholicism as an integral and near-unconscious component of their Irishness. Nor did they seek to redeem or reclaim Catholicism from the hierarchy, as per a figure such as McAleese. They claimed to feel no bond to Catholicism whatsoever. Baptism was not a fait accompli to be blithely accepted; it was a stain, a culturally sanctioned imposition.

However, another looser but larger and perhaps more representative group made themselves felt by their very absence. The most significant outcome of the day was not the protest but rather the low turnout for the Mass, which the Office of Public Works placed at just under 152,000.[54]

Dashing back and forth, I had managed to attend both the march and the papal Mass. In Phoenix Park Pope Francis shuttled about in the popemobile between half-full holding pens, waving and blessing as he went, like a pontifical Pac-Man. After a while, people started to disperse. On the way out, I overheard street vendors cursing that it was all "no use" as they stuffed fistfuls of unsold yellow Vatican flags into refuse bins.[55] After the visit, sociologist Gladys Ganiel conducted a representative national survey. Thirty percent of her respondents said that they did not attend any events because they disagreed with how the Catholic Church had handled sexual abuse claims. Fifty-one percent said they did not attend because they were simply not interested.[56]

What the "Say Nope to the Pope" campaign had failed to realize was that it had never really been necessary to artificially drive down the number of attendees. While some had said nope, a larger number had already decided "meh." The pope was an exciting visitor perhaps, but no more so than previous guests Queen Elizabeth II or Barack Obama. It also rained too much that day. As one informant told me, "The Church are a bunch of pricks but the current lad seems all right." He was not motivated to go out, given the rain, but despite his apathy at the prospect of glimpsing "the current lad," he was still Catholic—after all, he had been "born Catholic," a common and telling phrase showing just how deeply Irish Catholicism is implicitly thought of as an inalienable ethnicity, even if it is not something the individual would bother thinking about very much.

In addition to its good and evil resonances, Catholicism has also come to embody a kind of unobjectionable and near-invisible banality for a wide swath of the population: You get your broadband from Vodafone, your Corolla from Toyota, and your kids' rites of passage from a national service provider called the Catholic Church. To act otherwise is to upset the fabric of intergenerational and social relations. And many large corporations (Toyota, for instance) have had scandals. Since the moral humbling of its institutions, Catholicism in Ireland can be experienced—if "experienced" is even the right term—as a kind of innocuous cultural wallpaper as much as a source of holiness or horror. Self-assertive Irish nonreligion exists in a symbiotic relationship with this aspect of Catholicism and here verges more toward antipathy than apathy; the religiously apathetic in Ireland tend not to bother dropping the "Catholic" label. Much Irish nonreligion should therefore be understood as a deliberate rejection of wallpaper Catholicism—of what those in Breslin's position perceive as religious indifference overlaid with a complicit Catholic label. A fault line thus arises between those who choose overt rejection and those who are content to maintain vestigial ties. This tension is frequently suppressed (for it cuts across generations and within families) and does not so much constitute a polarized tug-of-war between conservatives and secularists as create a sharp friction between near neighbors: those who say nope and those who say meh.

Irish Catholicism: What was once unimpeachable and then gradually more and more habitual has now become impure, desacralized, and openly questionable. New, non-Catholic identities are being born, and the rejection of religious belief is no longer something that needs to be hidden. It is instead part of a burgeoning, highly moralized social stance. Before examining in a more detailed and qualitative way how the Church's moral contamination has enhanced the motivation and viability of this stance, I consider the degree to which Irish Catholicism was becoming "thinner" and less commanding even before the scandals emerged, creating a version of Catholicism that was much easier to shake off. For many people, the decision to be or not to be Catholic now presents itself as an option—and the choice rests on something of a knife edge. Yet at the same time, the thinner nominal link to Catholicism can persist not despite but *because of* its limited relevance. Sometimes it is easier just to let things be, especially if they are not particularly demanding and also carry certain advantages.

CHAPTER 3

"FOR EMERGENCY USE ONLY"
THE WANING OF RELIGIOUS SOCIALIZATION

When Grandma Prays, Does Anyone Hear Her?

> We are an *intentional Catholic family*: We go to Mass on a Sunday and on holy days. We pray together. We don't waste things. We say the rosary. We protect our children from the evil of alcohol, drugs and internet addiction. We do our best to give a good example. We have prominent religious symbols in our home and we refer to them. We do penance every Friday, we go to Confession *together*, we fast for Lent and we abstain on Ash Wednesday and Good Friday because we're *Catholic*. We visit the sick, look after elderly and sick relatives and pray for them. We forgive one another for family quarrels *because we're an intentional Catholic family*. We contribute to the parish both financially and by participating in the liturgy and parish groups. We gather with other, like-minded families. We help the poor and the marginalized at home and abroad *because we are an intentional Catholic family*.

This praiseworthy CRED-leavened litany did not issue from the mouth of a real member of the laity. It was an ideal—and a reprimand— forcefully expounded by Eamon Martin, Archbishop of Armagh and Primate of All Ireland, in his opening speech at an event co-organized by the Iona Institute and *The Irish Catholic* newspaper to drum up enthusiasm for the 2015 Synod of Bishops on the Family. The meeting was also held, so it was whispered among some of those present, to reinforce local zeal to oppose further moves against Church influence that might be coming in the wake of the marriage equality referendum, which had passed earlier that year. At least a few hundred people attended the synod, and the atmosphere during tea breaks and lunch was animated. The message to all present was more serious, though: Act like you mean it. Like a frog slowly boiling to death, Ireland was immersed in an ever more vapid version of Catholicism and risked losing sight of God completely. Soon, even abortion laws might be challenged. Something had to be done to reverse this downward slide, and it had to be done within families, the primordial site of socialization. Without the cooperation of families, faith formation would fail. This basic theme articulated by the archbishop in the litany, that the true Catholics of Ireland need to live their faith more so that it might better transmit, was repeatedly endorsed throughout the day. The Catholic journalist Breda O'Brien talked about how it should be "normal for Catholics to be more enthusiastic," "knowledgeable," and "expressive" about their faith, before going on to describe much Irish Catholicism today as "for emergency use only" and "semi-detached," eliciting mirth from the crowd when she described seeing young people at a funeral googling how to say a rosary. Another speaker complained how there was no religion at home these days, and parents just "put their kids through the ritual motions" of various sacraments, palpably without any religious motive. He added that the scandals had delivered a blow to Catholic confidence, inhibiting open endorsement, and that Catholics needed to recover from this. The audience murmured in agreement with this pep talk and nodded along in unison as its major points were delivered. Each time, it was like watching a gentle wave passing over a gray and white sea. It was markedly ironic that the speakers were preaching to those who were well beyond the age of rearing children to whom they might pass on the faith. As I circulated among the crowd during the break, curious glances followed me. Falling into conversation, a woman told me how good it was to see a young person present (I would turn 35 later that year).

The issue of Catholic aging was also vividly expressed in most of the churches I visited for Sunday Mass, where most of the congregants were over 60. There would always be some young people, of course, and a number of faithful families with children in tow. But sometimes there was a strange sense of fuss over the presence of children; they would be especially singled out in a positive manner by the priest. In one service I attended, some toddlers were running up and down the aisles, screeching loudly, one swinging from the handle of a confessional. An elderly woman hissed a reprimand at them. The priest gently rebuked her, saying that the children were praising God in their own way. It was as though their presence was something fragile and miraculous, to be nurtured at all costs—even if they drowned out the homily.

A Jumbo Jet Running on One Engine

It is no secret that religious practice in Ireland has declined rapidly since the 1990s. Religious people, both from the clergy and the laity, often presented this to me not just as a consequence but also as a cause of declines in the strength of Catholic commitment. It was not that parents were antipathetic to God—they just did nothing to encourage him in their children. Although children still encountered religion in school, the domestic engine of Catholicism had sputtered to a standstill. As one parish priest said, "The kids at school are clueless. They just . . . their parents don't go to church regularly anymore." The educational sphere alone was judged inadequate to transmit commitment to Catholic doctrine effectively when "the vast majority of children come in from homes where they would have no kind of concept about religious things or ideas, and what the school is doing is putting a kind of theory on nonexistent values," as another priest described it. His colleague maintained that "even if they [rites of passage] are taken seriously as religious events, they are *school* religious events. So, when school ends, religion ends."

Once, teaching had been known as the "second priesthood," and the first priesthood made sure it was stocked exclusively by those who were "religious in observance, obedient and conventional,"[1] but this backup layer of institutionalized religious socialization was portrayed to me as well on its way to breaking down too. According to religious informants, the intergenerational decline in domestic religiosity is now sufficiently entrenched that the younger generation of teachers recruited to transmit religious messages in the Catholic school system lack the background to do it convincingly.[2] Instead, they treat religious material as though it simply consisted of moralistic fables; as one parish priest said, teachers were "not expressing their faith. They're teaching it and they're doing a great job, but I don't know, maybe they don't practice themselves. It's just stories." The proportion of pious individuals in the education system has indeed dropped; for instance, between 1970 and 1990 the proportion of teachers belonging to religious orders declined from a third to a tenth.[3] Even among nonreligious parents worrying online about the indoctrination of their children at school, I quite frequently saw displays of reassurance from parents of older children that outsourced religion alone was insufficient to make true believers of offspring without domestic reinforcement. Some cultural Catholic discourse contained a comparable stream of secularist condemnation based on the principle that Catholic education is impotent and that anyone of any sense should know this. Anyone who wants to can shrug it off as they mature, and to object too strenuously amounts to being a "snowflake" intent on rocking the boat.

Although by no means a deterministic guarantor, much academic evidence from elsewhere corroborates this focus on parental religious behavior as the weak link in the transmission of Irish Catholicism. For example, in their comprehensive study of the factors that predispose American Catholic youth to retaining a high degree of Catholic religiosity, Christian Smith and colleagues repeatedly emphasize the importance of highly religious parents and other religious adults of influence. Smith and colleagues primarily attribute the importance of this factor to what they describe as "religious socialization," which involves "parents or other adults training young people how to be religious," not so much through explicit teaching as "through modelling (by the adults) and imitation (by the youth)," making teens "more likely to accept the religious worldview of their parents . . . and embody a similar set of priorities that leads to a continuation of religious behaviors"—a highly CRED-like definition.[4] In the United States, Bengston and colleagues[5] and Sherkat[6] also reached similar conclusions. Something or things had made Irish parents stop presenting as religious: The domestic CRED production engine had broken down. The transmission of Catholicism was guttering out as a result.

Orthodox Beliefs as Psychological Sectarian Tattoos

This transmission problem has implications for any religious tradition because, in a general sense, explicitly articulated belief in orthodox points of doctrine, perhaps especially very particular and "absurd" ones,[7] are a signal of commitment.[8] They are performances of cognitive self-tuning that maintain the boundaries between groups and keep people in, cutting them off from those who do not share the psychological shibboleth. The doctrine of transubstantiation—that humble bread, despite all sensory evidence to the contrary, is somehow transformed into the body of Christ—provides a typical example, and I sometimes encountered it being used to justify "staying in." During one interview, for instance, an older Mass-going Catholic woman in her 70s reached across the table and clasped my wrist as she expressed deep disgust to me about the clerical abuse scandals, saying she "nearly walked out the door." She then used her belief in transubstantiation to justify not doing so.

> This is my Church. This is the Church I was born into. This is what is expected of me. . . . Where would I go? I would go most obviously to [the] Church of Ireland . . . but then I did believe in the real presence [of Christ in the Eucharist]. I really believed. There was no denying it . . . so it would be cutting my nose off to go there and have nearly everything the same . . . but it couldn't be the same. It couldn't.

The woman's emotional language palpably relates to belonging and the fear of its loss: The Church is family, something one is "born into," and any exit would be needlessly self-destructive. This fear of exodus—"Where would I go?"—leads her to reach out for an anchoring doctrinal belief so she can make a powerful statement of loyalty. Her acceptance of this belief is an indisputable psychological fact, and it prevents her from stepping beyond the boundary of the Church. Through the expedient of fetishizing an early-thirteenth-century theological standardization edict, having "nearly everything the same" elsewhere is simply not good enough. There can be no replacement for the one true Church, no matter how rotten: Transubstantiation cuts off the possibility of moving. Its power lies in its unthinkable violation of one of the most basic laws of thought, the law of identity: The bread is itself and yet not. It is unthinkable. Accepting it acts as a psychological tattoo, signaling to others of the faith through displays of awed incomprehension before the sheer sacred mystery of the Host's contradiction.

In a complementary way, I found that one discursive practice used by members of liberal Catholic splinter groups who wished to wrest control from the hierarchy and establish their own purified identity as "true" Catholics was pruning beliefs tied too closely to the authority of the Church: Papal infallibility, the virgin birth, and other metaphysical postulates (including even transubstantiation) were discarded, and Jesus was referred to as "the Man from Nazareth" and portrayed almost as a Che Guevarra–style revolutionary, the son of God only in the most metaphorical of senses. For these breakaway heretics, precisely targeted statements of selective unbelief, styled as the repudiation of warping superstitions, allowed for the creation of distance from the contaminated institution. But although they had reinvented the Reformation on a smaller scale, they had been basted in Irish religion growing up and could not leave the body of the Universal Church. Instead they contested ownership of the term *Catholic*, thereby preventing absolute exit and the charge of Protestantism. They went to great effort constructing and defending this critical half-in, half-out position, layering it with sophisticated theological and historical justification.

I found it difficult to imagine the same effort being poured into the defense of a low-cost identity revolving around the sporadic arrival of census forms and rites of passage. If majority Catholicism is becoming a spectrum of loose cultural ties—entailing also that it is representationally amorphous and less standardized between individuals—then its content may lack the level of specificity needed to act as a psychological anchor to a shared social identity. At the same time, this gives it massive flexibility: Anyone, no matter what they think, can claim cultural Catholic status. The cost of this enormous elasticity is that it also becomes vaporous.

Disengagement from Onerous Duties: The Decline of Domestic CREDs

By contrast, for people raised in the CRED-enriched environs of pre-Conciliar Holy Catholic Ireland, even if one's Catholicism is resented, it can still be impossible to relinquish. This troubled, divided relationship to religion of many in the generation coming into adulthood in the

1950s and 1960s set the stage for greater breaches to come, but many never exactly pulled free themselves. For instance, Roberta, a woman in her 70s, had a profoundly ambiguous relationship to Catholicism. Her early years were spent in Mayo before moving to Dublin as a child, and she describes a domestic life that would have gladdened the heart of the Primate of All Ireland: "We were Catholics. We went to mass on Sunday. We said the rosary every night, upended kneeling over our chairs, with our backsides in the air." School, a convent boarding school in western Ireland, was an even more religious environment. The days were punctuated by rites, prayers, and the vigilant policing of the nuns. At night, nuns steamed open letters to censor them or spy on their contents. The looming threat of regular confession meant that religious concerns were ever on the mind.

> You got up at 6:50 a.m. and went to Mass. Mass every day, communion every day—that was before you had breakfast or anything. Then in the evening there was rosary. Oh yes, we had rosary there, at six o'clock as far as I remember. I think there was a prayer every day, possibly before each class. Every nun that came in said a prayer. There was a lot of praying, yes: grace before meals, grace after meals. There was confession every week if you wanted to go, or every two weeks, I can't remember, and you'd be sort of searching your mind for sins to confess a lot of the time.

Despite this strong foundation, Roberta became a "lapsed Catholic" during her 20s because she found the Church repressive and domineering. However, she could not bring herself to disaffiliate or fully relinquish the sense of the reality of the Catholic supernatural that had been instilled in her. She says she does not believe in God, though she sometimes wishes that what is dictated by her "logical mind" weren't true. However, she retains "a certain predilection for saints because they're sort of concrete people. There's a history there. They're real," and she lights candles in the Church when she feels she needs their help with something. God, by contrast, connotes disapproving surveillance, and for that reason she does not want to believe in him; yet at an intuitive, almost somatic level, he has sunk in so deeply that he goes on causing her to feel "uneasy" even when she knows she shouldn't. Despite, or rather because of, this unwanted divine baggage, she identifies as Catholic on the census. She is aware of the ambiguity of her own position.

> I don't really believe and I don't practice and, yes, I call myself a Catholic, and that's a bit of a dichotomy, I suppose, but it's what I was brought up as. It's a sort of heritage thing almost. It's a sort of cultural thing really. But I must say, if you had the sort of upbringing that I had, which was quite rigid, brought up in the fifties and sixties when you know it was thumbs down on everything from the Church—it's very hard to shake all that, very hard. I suppose it leaves you with a sort of vague, residual guilt about everything, which is not very nice. Guilt about things that you think or were told were wrong, sins or whatever, which is complete nonsense, but it does leave you with a sort of residual uneasy feeling.

This could be termed reluctant Catholicism, and it is an underanalyzed quantity in current descriptions of Irish Catholicism. It is a state of resignation. You cannot do anything about having been made Catholic: The signature guilt is there.

This entrenched, implicit sense of oneself as inalienably Catholicized can provide an anchor drawing back people who attempt to exit, especially when a more benevolent Catholic spiritual product is on offer, something that will let you keep the tradition but shed the guilt. A former schoolmate of Roberta's, Máire, described a similar trajectory of moral rejection. Máire distanced herself from the Church during the 1960s and 1970s because it was oppressive and incompatible with the new way people around her were beginning to behave. Later, in the 1990s, she rejected Catholicism outright because of the issue of clerical abuse, and she stopped attending Mass completely. At the same time, around the "era when all that stuff was coming out," she still felt the need for spiritual succor. She began "a journey" "about eight or nine years ago," when she started "going along to this Hindu-related meditation group. And the meditation was absolutely lovely. The people were absolutely lovely. I went along for two years and I loved it." Nevertheless, she "felt that there was something missing": "I just couldn't tune in to a lot of their beliefs about the kind of gods they had and all this sort of thing. I always felt a bit of a hypocrite. In my heart I couldn't. I just couldn't." She links this inability to accept non-Catholic religious beliefs in part to her parents (in particular, her mother) who "were religious. They were religious and my mother had two nuns in her family. So, she came from that culture, and they seemed to have had great faith in that they didn't question things." Now she has come back to Catholic belief, albeit on her own terms and in a more individualized, deinstitutionalized fashion, largely consisting of attendance at private Catholicism-inflected spiritual self-help courses organized by a Jesuit group who constitute an alternative religious authority stamped with the Catholic imprimatur but detached from the institutional moral taint.[9]

Rooted in a time of transition and tension, religious ambiguity results in reduced CRED exposure for the subsequent generation. Máire and Roberta both described scaled-down institutional involvement during the initial wave of social liberalization in the 1970s after religious childhoods. Roberta described "a puritanical attitude to relations between men and women, and that largely would have been the reason why I ceased to want to be part of it." Similarly, Máire described "a very patriarchal Church" that "didn't fit with her" and a dissonant time period when hypocrisy was tacitly accepted by a laity who lived a dual life "outside of it." This sense of dissonance affected the degree to which she was willing to expose her own children to Catholicism.

> So it was more about feeling I can't, I can't be that nun-like person. You know, there was more sexual freedom, all that sort of thing. Oh yes, the Pill was banned for women here, you know, and contraception wasn't allowed by either the Church or the state. So it was a very strange time, but you just tried to live outside it. Do your best, but I couldn't. Well of course now I am a bit of a hypocrite because at the same time I always did believe in God. I always felt there was something more. Yeah, the girls [her daughters] were baptized and so on, and they received the sacraments, but I couldn't convey the religion that was conveyed to me to them because I felt that was hypocritical. So, I left the poor things just floundering out there.

This exemplifies one common pattern in Irish religiosity. The all-encompassing, totalizing experience of Holy Catholic Ireland implants robust Catholic identification and belief, but the institution itself begins to look unpalatable because of shifting moral norms. Its intrusive fanaticism on the subject of sex in particular breeds resentment and leads to a sense of a life unjustly cramped. Catholicism is retained as an identity, but participation is dialed down to the obligatory minimum but not entirely eliminated, and belief is privatized and individualized, with its transmission becoming less of a priority—each is on their own path. Máire's privatized interpretive "takeover" from the Church resolves her own personal dissonance between having a Catholic identity and theistic beliefs linked to her cherished upbringing and concurrently disagreeing with the Church about everything else. It allows a vision of progressive modernity to be embraced *and* Catholicism retained, albeit relatively unexpressed, because it is understood as a relativistic, personal source of meaning or comfort that it is not one's duty to transmit. It is secularized Catholicism, Catholicism as personalized therapeutic option,[10] certainly not Catholicism as a missionaristic religion of conversion and the sole repository of absolute truth. Crucially, it is free of obligations; it does not need to be actively performed in any manner, and, in its sheer mild pleasantness (a little meditation, country hikes with the "lovely Jesuit"), it is CRED-poor. It is the retirement home of a tradition.

Roberta's account of her children's religious exposure is even more distinct from her own. It reveals an attitude toward religious transmission defined by gerontocratic placation and the avoidance of social conflict. Belief is nowhere in the picture, and the possibility of religious rejection by offspring is treated in a sanguine, almost blithe manner, with the buck being passed to the next generation to choose whether or not to undertake the social costs of Catholic renunciation.

> We had Grandma of course. That would be one reason for doing it. We didn't talk about it that much, or think about it that much. It was expected, I suppose; we just followed the expected thing. The background was Catholic, but we didn't particularly raise them as Catholics, but they did have it in school. Would I not do it now if I was starting over again? I don't know. I think I'd probably still do it. Maybe we felt we'd give them the option of rejecting it themselves, or accepting it themselves. It

was probably easier to do it [that] way, do all the stuff and then accept it or not.

Roberta's children have since opted for rejection, and this does not seem all that surprising. In such a regimen, Mass itself may have been as much a CRUD as a CRED, accompanied by expressions of reluctance, both verbal and embodied, transmitting the clear impression that religion is a matter of keeping other people, not God, happy: It must be respected in public, but it does not need to be followed in private. Nor are its motivations durable: Grandma will only stay around so long.

When CREDs Are CRUDs and CRUDs Are CREDs

Can CREDs work if they are cheapened by coercion? The Irish Church was so dominant and saturated the society so totally with its power that it may actually have been undermining belief by fostering a constant obsequious veneer of transparently forced or calculated piety. Martin, a 48-year-old nonreligious man from Kildare who moved to Dublin in his 20s, described a religious upbringing distorted by power and hypocrisy. He claims to have "always been secular," despite—or perhaps because of—his experiences of religion while at Catholic boarding school and at home. In school one of the Christian Brothers would grope boys as they walked up the aisle to hand in their homework—it was a kind of gauntlet that had to be run, presented almost as a game. This was so normalized that the class would laugh and mock those lacking the swiftness to escape one of these fondlings. This was never mentioned at home, where both of Martin's parents were outwardly devout, but in a way that seemed linked to various projects of reputational enhancement. In particular, Martin believed his father's public piety and involvement in a sodality were sociopathic means of social climbing. Early on, this disjunction unsettled his sense of Catholicism as something that might be true. It is still a topic that he wrestles with: "I really don't understand Ireland's connection with faith. I've tried to work it out for years. I really don't get the connection. Does it come from a paralyzing fear because of the power of the Church?" He vividly recounted the coercive nature of Catholicism in the town where he grew up, recalling that observance had no "spiritual element . . . it was more to do with fear. There was a naming and shaming thing where if you didn't put a certain amount of money into the envelope each month . . . in the back of our church in County Kildare there was a list of people that didn't pay." He described how local people, while remaining publicly deferential, would devise their own systems for resisting intrusive clerical authority, such as sending their children over the terrace back wall and up and down the lanes to warn neighbors when the bishop was doing his rounds of the parish, so that they would know not to answer the door. These practices were never a matter of outward confrontation; this would have been impossible. But, as Peter Mulholland has shown in his recent book, resentment of religious hubris and abuse was festering beneath the surface, even if it was inarticulable or shouted down by the outraged counterattacks of Dáil conservatives or local worthies.[11] As the current Archbishop of Dublin, Diarmuid Martin, has noted, the "conformist Ireland of the Archbishop McQuaid era changed rapidly and with few tears," something that may have been "an indication that the conformism was covering an emptiness and a faith built on a faulty structure to which people no longer really ascribed."[12] In various forms, this "emptiness" features in more devout religious criticism of the Irish Catholic religious system[13] and in atheist descriptions, such as the following from a man in his 60s:

> I was brought up strictly Catholic, but even as a child I knew instinctively it was all bollocks. It's a tribal thing. A belonging to the group. I go to Mass occasionally, funerals. I look around and no one is listening to the mad shit that's being read from a Stone Age book full of contradictory out-of-date waffle. They genuinely don't hear it. They're there because they were born into it. Nothing more. No thinking for themselves. They bring their kids as well. All dressed up and they don't really believe it any more than me. Irish people never really believed to an unacknowledged extent. It was being seen to belong and conform. Heaven help you if you stood out from the crowd back in the day.

Some remember silent stands against this coercion: religious CRUDs or quiet atheist CREDs, depending on how you choose to interpret them. A good example was provided by Catriona, a member of Atheist Ireland's executive committee who was in her late 40s when I interviewed her. Catriona attributes her atheism to encounters with New Atheist writers such as Richard Dawkins and Christopher Hitchens after a sojourn through various forms of what she describes as spiritual "woo"[14] in her early 20s, but her overt rejection of Catholicism stretched back further than this to her late teens and was predicated on the perception that Catholic doctrine was morally repressive and inhibited the development of progressive social values. However, her description of her family background suggests that a root factor may have been that her father's skepticism was evident to her from a much younger age, even though this was something he did not verbally express until many years later.

> He used to stand at the door. Like he'd put on a suit and just stand outside. I remember asking mum when I was a little girl how come dad doesn't go into church, and I remember mum saying that's because he smokes. He just stands outside and listens from the door. He couldn't believe what other people found so easy to believe. So, I think maybe somewhere along the line some of that brushed off, or rubbed off, despite the indoctrination and everything.

Fading Habits

As people get younger still, the breach becomes even more explicit. The "paralyzing fear" and silent forms of protest recede, replaced by a perception of completely Sunday-quarantined conformity. In the words of Diane, an agnostic informant in her 30s, Mass (and it is always Mass alone, as a social obligation with nothing else around it to suggest an ulterior doxastic motive) "was so boring and seen as a chore and an inconvenience. However, it was not a big part of our lives and was not enforced any more than any other banal expectation parents have of their children." Religion, for many, was clearly seen early on as a fairly trivial once-a-week social obligation. This was sometimes vindicated by later experience of parents dropping out as social pressure eased. As Diane related further, "When we grew up, they didn't have to bring their children to Mass anymore (which seemed to be a requirement of parenting at the time), and this gave them freedom to only go when they felt like it themselves." This sense of transparent conformity was sometimes accompanied by perceptions of conflict and resentment on the part of religious models. One man in his 30s said that today, his "ma has no time for it [the Church], while my dad would be a little more indifferent." Despite regular attendance as a child, he believes his mother was already alienated from the Church because of "all the shit that went on . . . holding back a lot of stuff in the country, sort of repressive stuff," but at some moment he cannot pinpoint or explain (tellingly, the subject was simply not important enough to have been reliably memorized), it became acceptable to act on these preexisting reservations; at that point, "we all dropped out." I dated this with the man, and it would have taken place roughly in the mid-1990s.

It was not that I did not hear stories of younger people who had rebelled against the CRED-rich religiosity of their devout parents and families; I did (in online ex-Catholic groups, they sometimes referred to themselves as black sheep). It was just that these seemed to be unusual stories, and there was some evidence that they made religious belief harder to shake off, in a way that harkened back to the experiences of older informants. For instance, Aisling, an explicitly atheistic woman in her 30s, describes how her father had a "very strong personal faith" that manifested in emotional displays that would have been hard to fake.

> He'd pray a lot and then sometimes . . . He had a bit of a breakdown when I was a child, and I'd hear him at night praying really quite desperately and in a way that scared me maybe. I think it made me more religious, or more fearful . . . and then my father and myself would often talk about God a lot. From about, I'd say I was about eight or nine we used to have proper, quite serious, you know, long conversations about God, and he used to bring me to prayer meetings.

Unlike most of the public, Aisling's father was a member of a charismatic Catholic sect, and this involved a number of profound, intense experiences during childhood that have stayed with her, such as the sect members "simultaneously kind of singing, chanting, making whatever noise it is. Sometimes you'd go and some people would be blessed at some point maybe after Mass and whatever and people would collapse. It kind of freaked me out, I suppose." These public experiences were complemented by further domestic experiences. For instance, Aisling encountered "tapes that my dad used to listen to . . . of this woman who said she used to be visited by Jesus and said she'd met the devil . . . and ah, I listened to them and they scared me so much. She seemed to believe it, so I was, like, it must be real. The Devil must actually exist."

Aisling is now adamant that she is not a Catholic, but she believes these early influences led to her rejecting Catholicism later than she would otherwise have done, based on the experiences of her peer group, most of whom shook off belief fairly easily during their early teenage years and have now settled into a range of stances from outright ex-Catholic atheism to more blasé cultural Catholicism. For Aisling, however, the threat of Hell and the Devil remained real for much longer, even after she explicitly repudiated Catholicism: "I think it probably wasn't until I was about in my early twenties that I actually just kind of went [shrugs]. It wasn't sudden. It was a slow realization that I was just, like, this is bullshit." Like a number of others, she described this lingering unease using the term "Catholic guilt."

Contrary to all this, I encountered almost no devout Catholics with CRED-poor Catholic upbringings. They all reported that religious belief was an important part of their parents' lives and played a role in determining their behavior on a day-to-day basis. This was particularly obvious in the case of the priests. For instance, one recalled that, although much of the usual domestic devotional paraphernalia was lacking in his upbringing (pictures of the Sacred Heart, Infants of Prague, and so on), his parents' behavior projected a strong impression of faith. His mother cultivated a personal devotion to Francis Xavier, and religion was woven into how both his parents lived their lives. Both were actively involved in religious charities, and the sacrifice of self-interest was understood to flow directly from religious motivations; he noted how "they would have been very Catholic in their ethos, in their understanding of life and doing the right thing . . . corporal works of charity, all the rest of that."

This leads me to believe that, though it is far from unusual for people whose parents performed many CREDs to nevertheless reject Catholic belief, it is quite unusual for someone with low parental CRED exposure to go on to be a committed Catholic believer. Younger people were generally only religious if their parents had been unusually devout by the standards of their generation. The one exception was Roger, a sui generis gay traditionalist in his late 20s, but his orthodoxy appeared strongly influenced by his devout grandparents rather than his own parents, from whom he seemed somewhat alienated. I ruminated at length on Roger's relationship to clerical stigma. He deliberately dressed like a 1950s Catholic priest in everything but the collar, projecting an intense aura of pre-Conciliar Catholicism that was almost jarring to see on a contemporary Dublin street. In other words, he intentionally, almost provocatively, took on a visual identity that he knew to be socially tainted, especially in some of the places he socialized—gay bars, for instance, where the Church is frequently associated with homophobia. From our conversations, I believe that his early life had been hard, marking him out as unusual and making him a target for bullying. Perhaps, in adopting a cloak of stigma, there was some solace in converting personal outsiderhood into socially categorical outsiderhood. In a way, the fact that this unusual informant was able to use a potent layer of Catholic signifiers as a means of holding others at bay by creating a kind of repellent cocoon around himself is testament to the transformation of Irish attitudes toward Catholicism. Although priests were always a caste apart, they were never exactly seeking pariahdom.

For his age, Roger was certainly unusual. Catholicism as a transcendent worldview based on a coherent body of doctrine is in steep decline, and the Church is rarely considered a legitimate source of moral guidance by most of those younger than their 70s. But although a tight connection to the Church is increasingly seen as odd in those below retirement age, the looser cultural link to Catholicism remains widely normative. There is no one single defining characteristic of this cultural Catholicism. The term is a broad one, and it can refer to a number of different things that may be done and felt to different degrees by different people. One is the maintenance of Catholic practices for social reasons. These may be undertaken in pursuit of instrumental goals; they may relate to the conscious preservation of intergenerational harmony; or they may simply be matters of expedience, enjoyment, or custom. Another is the feeling of having been Catholicized in some way by one's upbringing or environment. This creates a feeling of commonality with others whose experience of the world is similarly inflected by Irish Catholicism, even if Catholicism as a religion is rejected. This can manifest in shared humor or, at a more private level, in unexpected feelings and subjective experiences. Last, cultural Catholicism can be experienced as a matter of essence: Much as a person may disagree with everything the Church stands for, and even if "being Catholic" is not personally important, people may still feel that they just "are" Catholic. It is an ethnocultural fact that cannot be denied or renounced. Compromised as it is, the education system—the last remaining pillar of Catholic socialization—is one of the main sites where this attenuated but tenacious complex of culturally Catholic links is reproduced.

The Education System and the Reproduction of Cultural Catholicism

Today, primary schools—more than 90% of which are under Church patronage—are tasked with the business of Catholicizing children in Ireland. Although there may be little evidence or reinforcement of Catholicism at home, through sacramental preparation and religious and historical instruction at school, many Irish children learn that they have in fact been Catholics all along.[15] The collective rituals and generational curricula also create a sense of shared identity connected to Catholicism. The resulting deep associations with school and childhood may account for the nostalgic sheen that Catholicism maintains for many of those who retain no great commitment to the Church. This nostalgic and quasi-ethnic sense of group membership can persist even in the total absence of interest in the doctrinal or moral dimensions of Catholicism.

The link between cultural Catholicism and education might be said to begin even before a child starts school. As will be touched on in more detail in the case of Peter later in this chapter, pragmatic concerns entirely divided from spiritual matters can motivate some to maintain ostensible Catholic links in the presumed interest of a child's education, with baptism widely perceived to unlock more favorable scholastic and therefore social and professional prospects.[16] This motivation is particularly strong in middle-class contexts. The arrangement of outsourcing Catholic rites of passage to schools also ensures that parents are not dissuaded from baptism or enrollment in Catholic education by any onerous responsibilities for religious instruction, with little more required than occasional financial outlay for sacraments, such as First Holy Communion, which come with their own social and material incentives. The undemanding nature of participation in this system means that there is no expectation of zealotry or even much commitment, and the advantages to be gained from struggling against it are negligible. This promotes a majority compliance that both normalizes and perpetuates the seemingly passive cooperation and identification characteristic of much cultural Catholicism.

This majority compliance brings its own sense of belonging and social inclusion that is often cited by cultural Catholics as a key motivational factor for participating in rites such as First Holy Communion and Confirmation—often in spite of "not believing." For many, these occasions are more explicitly social than sacramental and are chiefly experienced (and remembered) as exciting festivals celebrated with family and peers. Their social import is such that many parents cite the fear of social exclusion as a factor in deciding whether their child should be "opted out" of religious education. All of this is to say nothing of the material bonanza that has become synonymous with First Holy Communion, which typically includes extravagant outfits, lavish gifts, and a generous cash bounty. The windfall has become so notorious that a widely shared 2020 article on the satirical website *Waterford Whispers* reported that children who had been "scheduled to make their First Holy Communion and rake in up to €1,000 each over the last few months" were applying to the government for a COVID-19 bailout.[17] I found a further example of this kind of satirical intent at the end-of-year fashion textile show at the National College of Art and Design in 2019. A number of T-shirts displayed artwork lampooning culturally Catholic practices. One depicted First Holy Communion as "First Holy Casino" and featured pious-looking children, hands clasped in prayer, beside the phrase, "How much did you get?" Cultural Catholics themselves also participate in satirizing the materialism of their own cultural practices, and some also bind this subverted religious ritual to notions of ethnonational belonging, excluding those who do not take part. For instance, I saw a meme "from a culturally Catholic acquaintance" being circulated among secularists online, where it generated a considerable degree of low-level exasperation. The meme depicted various First Communion tropes (an inflatable bouncy castle, euro notes changing hands, balloons, little "wedding dresses," chintzy congratulation cards, and, in a final concession, a bowl of the Host) beneath the banner "If this wasn't your weekend, are you even Irish?"

Religion classes also play a role in perpetuating cultural Catholicism in the education system, but in a different way. Although outsourcing religious instruction to schools has proved ineffective at reproducing orthodoxy, this does not mean that there has been no effect whatsoever. Instead of focusing on doctrine, the pedagogical approach in religion classes since the 1980s tacitly elides Catholicism with an amorphous haze of positive and prosocial feelings (with some softly drawn conservative positions on various signature issues slipped in), helping to establish an almost Pavlovian link between the vaguer terms *religion* and *morality*. In this approach, school curricula conjoin "ethics" and "belief" as though belief were necessary and sufficient for ethics. This may partly account for the fact that, despite estimating as many as one-third of priests to be pedophiles and frequently considering the Church to have been a negative influence on Irish society (see Chapter 2), many Irish people will go on to link "religion" to "morals" and "structure" for the rest of their lives, without being able to clearly define what these signifiers refer to, nor why they are interdependent. In some cases, "religion" becomes so elided with "morality" that it comes to be understood as a code word for a kind of general prosocial housebreaking. Indeed, some nonreligious parents report soft pressure from school authorities along exactly these lines when they seek to opt their children out of religious instruction: "Sure it's not really *religion*. It's just about how to be a good person and be kind. Are you *sure* you'll opt him out?" To resist religious education within this slippery semantic framework, then, becomes antisocial. This is bolstered by the secularized and softened post–Vatican II framing of religion in the education system, which makes something of a mantra of 1 John 4:8—"God is Love." Notwithstanding its professed benevolence, this emphasis risks characterizing those who seek to exempt their children from religious education in schools as misanthropes and cranks, as rejecters of love and kindness. Absent the past rigorous and punitive focus on the memorization of doctrine and any kind of intellectual or spiritual content, school Catholicism has been reinvented as the very heart of compassion and care, a soft pink core of harmless feel-good pablum that only the doggedly perverse would renounce. This outcome is probably not deliberate so much as the result of an awkward effort by post–Vatican II educationalists to make religious instruction "relevant" by purging the taxing doctrinal content and reframing the leftovers in a sort of out-of-touch, quasi-secularized guise.[18] Through this religious education link, religion becomes a good thing, but good in a fairly platitudinous way. This unchallenging framing may preserve links to Catholicism, but it does so by infantilizing it and reducing it to a set of moral training wheels that can be abandoned once adulthood is attained.

Beyond religious instruction, some of the broader areas of school curricula also feed into the reproduction of cultural Catholicism, particularly when it comes to representations of historic national identity. Being Catholic, even if only nominally, continues to give Irish people a sense of themselves as a distinct and, especially, non-British community. At school this invariably arises in connection with cultural objects of study about which all Irish schoolchildren are instructed to be proud, from the myth of St. Patrick to the poetry of Seamus Heaney, from Celtic crosses and illuminated manuscripts to the stained-glass windows of Harry Clarke. It is reinforced most markedly in history class, where students learn of Ireland's venerable reputation as "the land of saints and scholars" that kept the embers of learning aglow in its monasteries during the Dark Ages before suffering "800 years of oppression," and where they learn that this long victimhood was predicated on their status as Catholics. In addition to framing Catholicism as an ancient, authentic, and integral part of Irishness, the further implication here is that disaffiliation may bear the dishonorable associations of treason.

All this persists against a wider backdrop of religious scandal, creating two streams of divergent associations. Many have thereby learned to hold contrasting associations with the term *Catholicism*, rendering it a loose, multivocal symbol with different latent meanings that can be activated at different times. For many cultural Catholics, "school Catholicism" is just the local variant of something called "religion," which is itself simply a code word for "morality" or "being a good person" or even "being a good Irish person." We can equally speak of "news Catholicism," a variant of the recent historical past unearthed in repeated scandalous revelations, associated with puritanism, immorality, authoritarianism, hypocrisy, and child abuse. Cultural Catholics can oscillate between these contrasting representations depending on the context. Many voted to repeal the Eighth Amendment to the Irish Constitution or condemned institutional perfidy around child sexual abuse while simultaneously presenting their infants at the baptismal font.[19] This ability of cultural Catholics to quarantine the moral taint associated with the Church is often decried as baffling and infuriating by those who have explicitly severed ties with Catholicism. As one exasperated online Irish atheist expressed it, "WHAT THE ACTUAL FUCK GOES THROUGH THEIR HEADS??"

Fear of Missing Out: The Case of Peter

Let us try to answer this by looking in more detail at a case study. Much cultural Catholic reluctance to explicitly disaffiliate is best understood as a mixture of pragmatism and somewhat nebulous fears of ostracism. These considerations push back against the taint associated with news Catholicism. At the same time, cultural Catholicism is sustained in part because "being Catholic" has become undemanding. Because the Church has become widely viewed as morally spurious, its injunctions and demands do not need to be taken seriously. The perceived advantages of remaining affiliated or perpetuating affiliation in the next generation by baptizing children outweigh the perceived costs. Cultural Catholicism is also frequently experienced as a relatively trivial dilemma. Religious concerns or their absence are peripheral to one's sense of self and attract attention only in those odd moments when they are made salient. Cultural Catholics may be "born Catholic" but are not *really* Catholics if they do not believe in God, but they also are not *really* outright atheists. Like a quantum particle, their religious status may exist in a kind of noncommittal, flexible, and advantageous superposition. Peter, a middle-class IT specialist and the parent of Keith, a young boy of 5, exemplified this dynamic, so we will examine his case in a little more detail.

When I asked Peter to provide me with a free list of 10 words for the term "Irish Catholic Church," he began as follows: "Repressive, domineering, old people (that counts as one word), you can't not put child abuse in there somewhere." Then he found himself stuck for a moment. He began to go in a positive direction ("There's an element of community"), but after that one association, he came to a halt, saying, "Most of my thoughts are negative." The list started to rattle on again after a pause: "Controlling, "guilty," and "unapologetic" all followed each other in short order before, finally, "There's a bit of evil comes in there. I nearly want to call it that. Was that ten?" It was eight, so I held out for two more. After much humming and hawing, Peter said "fear," and then couldn't come up with a tenth. His associations seemed to have hit a brick wall.

Peter says he "was born Catholic" but, as he told me, "I wouldn't say I was raised Catholic." His father was quite religious during his early years, bringing him to Mass regularly as a child, but this tailed off during his early teens, and Peter now describes his father as "anti-Catholic." At around age 12, once the school boxes had all been ticked, the Mass rigmarole was allowed to slide: "After my confirmation, it was basically, you know, [do] whatever you like." By contrast his mother, who used to be quite apathetic about religion while he was growing up, has become more enthusiastic about the topic now, a transformation Peter attributes to fear. Sometimes, even now that Peter is a father himself and has reached the age of 38, she chides him for not going to Mass at Christmas, something he finds insufferable: "I just find that so bizarre, like, why should I make an effort for a thing once a year that I don't make any other time, you know?" Peter also follows a man on Twitter who talks at length about his experiences of brutalization in industrial schools. Despite this stance of disapproval for inauthentic religious involvement and a keen sense of past religious abuses, Peter has baptized his son Keith into the Catholic Church. I found this all the more surprising because he had done it shortly after his own humanist wedding ceremony. He appeared to have broken away but still felt the need to make a Catholic of his child. I wanted to understand this seeming contradiction.

Peter does not consistently think of himself as a Catholic, but nor does he think of himself as a humanist. Humanism is a "nice philosophy" but not one he "particularly believes in." Instead, he was attracted to the fact that the humanists (i.e., the HAI, or Humanist Association of Ireland) had been approved by the state as marriage solemnizers and were making significant gains in the market of marrying those disaffected by the Church. The HAI offered something that would not be an anticlimax, something more special than a civil ceremony in the registry office. It would have the pomp and appearance of tradition without the baggage. This choice of wedding celebrant precipitated a little concern when the day for Keith's Catholic baptism drew near: "We had to ring the . . . the local parish to apply for it. And . . . we were worried about would they ask us about our wedding. And I had a whole spin story I was going to give for that, of 'well we lost our faith but we don't want our son to be so unlucky and, you know, we want to raise him Catholic and blah blah blah blah blah.'" But thankfully, "It didn't come to that."

Early in our interview, Peter had described himself as atheist. Later, after our discussion about Keith's baptism, he wasn't so sure: "I don't think I'm a Catholic but I don't think I'm an atheist. I hate the label of atheist because you're like, 'no, down with the Church!' I just don't care, you know. But I don't think I'm agnostic. I just, I don't believe and everyone let's go about their own business, you know. That's kind of my view." As so often, a de facto doxastic atheist was put off from self-labeling as atheist by perceptions of the crude and dogmatic stridency of contemporary New Atheism and the risk such an ascription might carry for social relations. Peter would rather remain in a malleable superposition where affiliation can be worn or cast off in a pragmatic manner, as befits certain moments and circumstances: What need is there for him to be nailed down? But despite this ambiguity, Peter does have some traits that he feels are more stable. He describes himself as "scientificy-slash-businessy-minded," and if something "gives him an edge," he will take it. The reason he had Keith baptized was so straightforward he took pleasure in answering in a single, clipped syllable: "Schools."

The word was delivered with a terse conviction quite different from the rest of his account. Peter felt it was an unimpeachable justification. School applications are "all very stressful and you kind of want every advantage you can get." Baptism is one of them, and Peter's choice to baptize Keith was thus portrayed as a rational calculation pursued in the interests of his child. This is because Irish education operates according to a patronage system. Ninety percent of primary schools in Ireland, including most of those paid for by the state, are run by the Catholic Church, and 6% are run by Protestant churches. Secondary education is also largely Catholic. The state provides the funding to run many schools, but the reins are handed to the "patron," in most cases a religious body, who will then determine its "ethos." Places in nondenominational schools are decidedly limited. Crucially for somebody from Peter's background, the most prestigious private schools are also Catholic in ethos. Although since 2019 schools are not supposed to choose pupils based on religious background, Peter believes that they actually still do this: "Even though they may not word it like 'We're a Catholic school' or 'We want religious people,' they . . . they do kind of want people who come from a religious background." Eventually Peter secured a place for Keith in a Gaelscoil[20] that he described as "agnostic." Nonetheless, Peter ticked both "Catholic" and "No religion" on the entry forms, just to be sure. But this will offer just a few years of respite. Peter worries that he will have to resume the charade in the future, when Keith must go to a secondary school.

I asked him how he would have felt had Keith been subjected to Catholic religious instruction. Although Peter reiterated that he was "pretty atheist," he went on to say, "I don't think learning, like being raised Catholic, did me any harm. Em, and maybe in ways I haven't comprehended it did me some good, like the whole community thing. I, I'll never know, you know, I, em, I, I am who I am." The idea that religious instruction "did not do me any harm" and that it is somehow linked to some ineffable good—"the whole community thing" in this case, "morals and structure" in others—are commonly deployed by culturally Catholic unbelievers to justify compliant participation in the religious education system.

It also "all comes down to a fear of will his education suffer if he doesn't play the game," with Peter worrying that Keith might face not only ostracism but slimmer chances of getting into the best schools if he is not communed or confirmed. Peter sees these kinds of motives reflected widely among his peers and, as he put it, "The impression I got from anybody I talked to was that it was tactical." Peter seemed to view the religious inauthenticity of his decision that Keith should participate in Catholic rites of passage as morally praiseworthy. It was evidence that he and his family had been coerced by circumstances and that he had no real love of the Church, only concern for his child. By being willing to submit to these rituals despite what he actually thinks of the Church and despite his lack of belief, inauthentic participation is transmuted into a type of altruistic sacrifice. Soon, the issue of further sacraments would raise its head.

> We need to think about communion. Because neither of us are religious and this is a bit hypocritical, but for me a little bit of peer pressure comes in as well, like, I don't want him to be the only kid in the class who doesn't make his communion, or the only one who doesn't come in saying, like, I got a thousand euro yesterday or whatever, you know. And that's, that's more of a, a peer thing than a, a belief in religion, you know. It's sort of, it, it, I nearly see it more as a rite of passage than a, a spiritual event, you know.

Unlike the imaginary family conjured up in Archbishop Eamonn Martin's speech at the outset of this chapter, Keith will not be part of an "intentional Catholic family." Instead he will be given the opportunity to "choose his own way in life, emmm . . . and sort of go from there." Peter is not completely averse to Catholicism, and often, when pressured to respond to why he involves his son in Catholicism, will have recourse to vague statements linking Catholicism to community and morality, even though his swiftest associations with the Church are of moral contamination and even though he does not participate in his local Catholic community. The Church is something that can be held at arm's length, brought closer when it is useful, held away from the body when there is a risk of moral contamination. His sense of what the word *community* entails is also ambivalent. At first he seems to use it to mean something positive, such as "belonging" or "support," but when he turns to think of his experiences more explicitly, the word *fear* comes up again, and it becomes clear that it is the fear of ostracism, not from the Church but from society, that weighs the heaviest.

> I don't want Keith to be the only kid who doesn't make his communion, confirmation or get the, you know, huge bonanza of cash or whatever, like . . . to me it's nearly a peer pressure thing more than anything or, a, a schooling pressure like, it's all . . . it's all the fear of either, of, I suppose it's the fear of being left out, em, but not by the Church, by . . . everything else, you know.

Peter is not afraid of God; he is afraid of the consequences of not playing the game. Keith is a growing boy, and he will start to notice and understand the social rules around him as he gets older. I asked Peter whether he will ever tell Keith that he does not believe in the religious aspects of such rites as First Communion or confession. Like Roberta, the buck got passed: "I'd like to think I'll give him the choice and he'll decide." Peter closes by saying, "I will definitely tell him when he's older, but if he's doing the thing and believes it, I'll encourage it. Like Santa." Despite this relaxed attitude, Peter is well aware that his choices are opposed both by the religious, who expect him to cultivate religious beliefs in his offspring because he (sometimes) claims to be a Catholic, and by secular purists, who expect him to fight the institutionalization of religion in Irish society because he is an unbeliever. This disapproval from two fronts is something he must grapple with.

> A lot of people said to me early on, like, it's, you know, kind of jokingly, but like jokingly aggressively, like "it's people like you that allow them have that hold," and I agree with that, but I didn't want to be a martyr. I didn't want my son to have to go to like the worst school in the country because . . . em, my principles were too strong. I, I read a thing a couple of years back, of I think it was the Archbishop of Dublin saying people who get their children baptized to get into school are abusing the sacrament, and I was like, I can't abuse a thing I don't believe in, you know.

Father Ted, Patron Saint of Cultural Catholics

As Peter's case demonstrates, cultural Catholics can sometimes feel a vague sense of disapproval from various quarters. The Church's reputation has darkened, and cultural Catholics can find themselves criticized by more rigorous secularists for maintaining links to it. At the same time, religious conservatives and personnel may be critical of them for their laissez-faire attitudes toward "their religion." Most seriously of all, cultural Catholics themselves are aware of all the contradictions that exist in their ambiguous, detached relationships to Catholicism but nevertheless feel some need to maintain that link, a link whose nature they sometimes find difficult to articulate or defend. Although cultural Catholicism is often self-conscious, its contradictions can never be fully reconciled or worked out. Sometimes this results in accepting one's status as a hypocrite in the eyes of purists while implying that those same purists have a simplified, intolerant view of the complexity of human reality. For instance, in a glossy magazine interview, Dublin-born UK television presenter Laura Whitmore describes a typical Irish childhood of habitual Mass attendance fading gradually into irrelevance as she left her teens, followed by a more acute breach resulting from "the feeling of betrayal when allegations of sexual abuse of children in Ireland emerged." Nevertheless, as she goes on to say:

> I can't give it up completely. In fact, I still classify myself as Catholic, but it's more to do with cultural heritage than what I actually believe. I like the comfort and belonging and nostalgia but don't want to sign up for the whole shebang. Does that make me a hypocrite? Maybe. But open my kitchen cupboard and you'll find a bottle of holy water.[21]

Like many others, Whitmore enjoys belonging to an Irish Catholic cultural background and associates it with comfort and nostalgia, but she does not adhere to the doctrines and the demands of the Church, and she is keenly aware of the Church's history of scandal and abuse. By displaying awareness that she might be seen as a hypocrite for this combination, she appears to be anticipating and attempting to ward off criticism. Simply describing one's connection to Catholicism as cultural in the way that Whitmore does is another way of warding off disapproval from more fastidious others; the link is a matter of gut reactions that result from deeply layered experiences. It is not, and cannot be, chosen. As a deep and enculturated nest of associations and feelings, it does not need to be coherent and it is unreasonable for others to expect this. Another way of dealing with the impasse of cultural Catholic contradiction is simply to revel in it through humor. In this way, cultural Catholics can create a sense of shared commonality based on deep cultural familiarity with the Church in the total absence of respect for it: Everyone, together, is in on the joke of Irish Catholicism.

In this way, dated representations of pious Catholicism are sometimes consumed for their amusement value. In particular, the cultural products of the softer, post–Vatican II era and its awkward efforts to integrate Church teaching with more liberal social attitudes can be tapped as a source of cringe-inducing yet endearing amusement. Catholic school sex education videos from the 1980s are a good example, especially those featuring "Catholic sex guru" Angela MacNamara. One of her videos (*Sex Education for Girls*) has been watched (ironically) more than 100,000 times on YouTube (Figure 3.1).[22] These unthreatening videos gently encourage abstention and chastity before marriage and were shown in

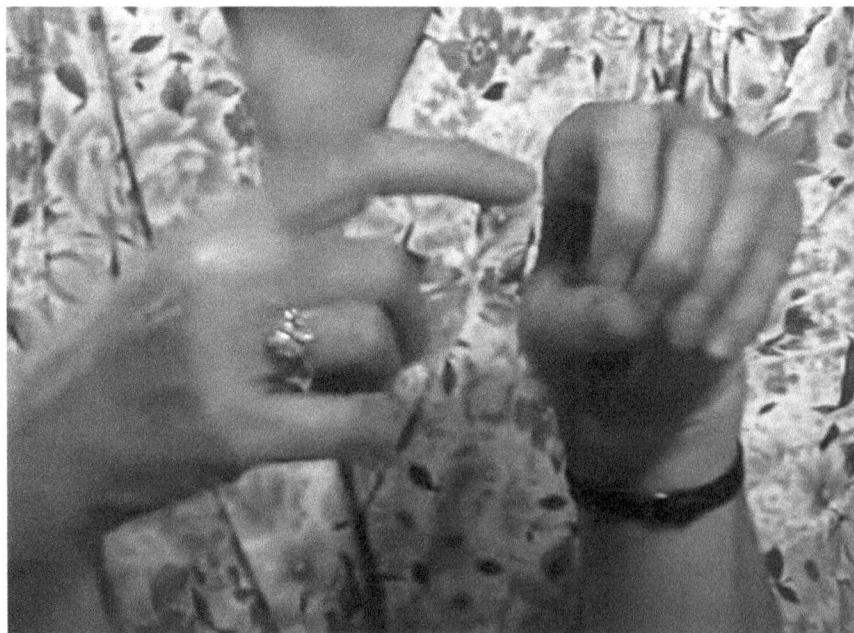

FIGURE 3.1. Still from *Sex Education for Girls*. The film begins with a lengthy prayer to God, followed by an ode to marriage, before Angela gets down to the details. Source: https://www.youtube.com/watch?v=RD8i4GICuyw. Credit: Angela McNamara.

classrooms at a time when Magdalene laundries still operated. The implications of this, however, did not factor into responses when the videos resurfaced and went viral on social media decades later. Instead, the outdated purity-focused moral system they represented was consumed with no little nostalgia as a harmless, absurd in-joke. Angela's videos allowed viewers of a certain age to enjoy their Catholic heritage while also ridiculing the moral system that once underpinned it.

Perhaps the best example of this complex equilibrium between nostalgic fondness and outright ridicule is the much-loved *Father Ted* sitcom. *Father Ted* first aired in 1995, right as the age of scandal was dawning and just a year before the last Magdalene laundry closed its doors. But though *Ted* pokes numerous transgressive fingers in the Church's eye, it seems to take place in a nostalgic idyll. The dark questions pouring forth from the freshly unearthed mass grave at High Park in Drumcondra never threaten to reach Craggy Island, the fictional outpost where *Ted* follows the irreverent antics of three lovable clerical buffoons. Instead, most episodes foreground the absurdity of Catholic doctrines and feature the trio's daft interactions with cynical, inept, or corrupt members of the higher clergy. Episodes sport artlessly irreverent titles such as "Kicking Bishop Brennan up the Arse" and feature over-the-top scenarios such as heavily perspiring priests creeping stealthily about the lingerie section of a department store as though it were the jungles of wartime Vietnam, a priest with a secret Nazi memorabilia horde,[23] and cardinals enjoying a bawdy discothèque in the Vatican.[24] *Ted* looks quite tame now, though it caused consternation in its time and had to be produced and screened by the UK's Channel 4, as the national broadcaster Raidió Teilifís Éireann was too timid to touch it (though they have played reruns religiously in the years since its success).

Ted has gone largely unacknowledged for the degree to which it contributed to a form of national awakening: It allowed large swaths of the population to openly communicate their less than serious attitudes toward Catholicism using a repertoire of sayings and images from the program and to recognize this more openly in one another. One of the meta-gags of the series is that even its priests have arrived at a point of cultural Catholicism themselves, with interests, ambitions, challenges, and foibles that are conspicuously secular rather than spiritual. No longer domineering and unassailable bastions of divinely endorsed moral rectitude, the priests in *Father Ted* themselves draw awkward attention to the questionable power that the clergy wielded in Irish society: "I'm not a fascist, I'm a priest. Fascists dress in black and go around telling people what to do, whereas . . . priests . . . [changes the subject]"

Ted may in fact have tacitly re-endeared people to the Church just as the scandals were getting properly underway, and whether *Ted* played a greater role in preserving or undermining links to the Church is difficult to determine. *Father Ted* coexisted with famous pedophile priests such as Brendan Smyth and Seán Fortune in the public realm, and its comic take may well have leavened horrors, inoculating against increasingly demonic public representations of clergy with the weekly administration of a down-home, lovably incompetent alternative. Rather than tapping into the "pedo priest" trope (something that would probably have been commercially and socially impossible at the time), *Ted's* most confrontational character—the anarchic and wrathful Father Jack—channels the far more venerable and ambiguous archetype of the drunken priest, a folkloric figure of uneasy respect.[25] Drunkenly leering at Playboy centerfolds of fully grown women, the scabrous Father Jack may have been an improbable public relations salve for the Church during a time when the pedophilic predations of various actual priests increasingly dominated the news.

Decades later, "*Ted*-talk" remains a recognizable component of everyday Irish conversation, and snippets of the mildly anti-clerical sitcom are commonly exchanged much in the way that myriad audiences rehash moments from *Friends* or *The Simpsons*. These snippets form a kind of ironically detached yet nostalgic commentary on Irish Catholic cultural heritage and are so pervasive that even the Irish national postal service (An Post) has gotten in on the act, issuing postage stamps in 2020 that feature popular quotations from the program (Figure 3.2). One stamp bears the catchphrase "That money was just resting in my account," which indicates that even the show's hero, Father Ted himself, is (ineptly and thus endearingly) corrupt. With its connotations of quaint and farcical incompetence and cack-handed self-interest, *Ted*-talk cannot but be

FIGURE 3.2. *Father Ted* postage stamps, celebrating the 25th anniversary of the popular sitcom. Reproduced by kind permission of An Post ©.

deployed with a gentle inflection, even if this is somewhat inadvertent. Consequently, the practice would seem to have a dual effect: Its manifest ridicule undermines the Church's monolithic authority, but its many fond overtones also chart those aspects of Catholicism that Irish people continue to cherish as part of their idea of themselves—this time on their own terms. Here, the post-*Ted* Church becomes a source of quaintly ludicrous symbols by which Irish people can enact cultural difference from out-groups such as the British while indulging in nostalgia (or imagined nostalgia) for a simpler age that they might oddly miss but never actually wish to restore.

The underlying ethos of *Ted*-talk thus seems to be that Catholicism is all a bit absurd, but it is *our* absurdity.[26] Today, you can even attend Tedfest, a cosplay and traditional music event held annually on the Aran Islands. *Father Ted* may well act like a restrained televised equivalent of the medieval Feast of Fools, a bawdy celebration that involved inverting the status of the clergy and laity for a day and parodying ecclesiastical rituals and liturgical language. Anthropologists have long argued that such rites act as a pressure valve, preserving the status quo by allowing people to confront and subvert authority in a controlled and limited way. In the role it has come to play in contemporary Irish society, then, *Ted* both parodies and preserves the bond to Catholicism, and perhaps unsurprisingly it is indulged by clergy in some cases. At the ostensibly Catholic funeral of one fairly agnostic man, for instance, I saw a mourner place a *Father Ted* DVD box set on the coffin. Aware that he was being observed, the priest gave an awkward smile—the only viable strategy.

Father Ted was produced early in the age of scandal, when Ireland was considerably more deferent than it is now, and by today's standards it is tame. Comedy has long since moved on, and the jokes, both in everyday talk and on television, have grown much darker. Picture the scene: a Dublin City Council housing estate in the year 2010—a year after the publication of the government's Murphy Report into clerical abuse and cover-ups. In evident distress, a young woman rushes from her pebble-dashed two-up two-down home toward a waiting ambulance, clutching her baby to her breast. Her mother is sick, and she calls out in desperation to two onlookers that she needs someone to mind her child while she goes to the hospital. One, a curly-haired and earnest young priest with an open and caring face, volunteers his help immediately. Beside him, a man in a tracksuit sways on the spot for a few moments, sweating, pallid, eyes half-closed in an intoxicated stupor while a can of budget cider dangles from his hand, before slurring, "Here . . . I'm brilliant wit childereren" in the wheedling but tranquilized drone associated with Dublin heroin addicts. The woman glares for an instant at the priest, her face contorted in outrage and disgust, before handing her child to the addict. This comedy sketch was broadcast on *The Savage Eye* on RTÉ in 2010—the very same channel that refused to produce the lightly anti-clerical farce *Father Ted* in 1993. Another *Savage Eye* sketch, filmed in grainy black and white, features a priest being reprimanded by his superior for beating a schoolboy with a cricket bat. After this dressing down, the priest's superior gives him a far more patriotic hurling stick to beat the child with, telling him to "use this instead."

These sketches worked not because of their shock value but because of the opposite. The archetypes and scenarios they portrayed were comically familiar. Even ten years ago, they channeled a compound and calcified image of hypocrisy, perversity, harm, and oppression, illustrating just how acclimatized Irish people had become to that darkened Catholic image and how much of a stereotype it had become. But the joke was not simply a matter of laughing at the Church. It also contained a deeper level, commenting on the audience itself. All the complex and systemic abuses of the past, and the society that permitted them to happen, had become bottled up in the simplistic, lurid symbol of the pedophile priest. The *Savage Eye* ridiculed the limits of this malevolent but cartoonish collective representation. For their insensitivity the sketches elicited a number of complaints from more devout viewers, but nevertheless the vast majority of the audience who would have laughed at them in 2010 (when nonreligion in Ireland was below 5% according to the census) would still have been "born Catholic," would have baptized their children, and would have sent those same children to Catholic schools. They would have thought of themselves as Catholics (albeit likely of a disengaged variety), and they would have been united in a culturally specific form of empowering schadenfreude at the reputational collapse of those who would once have considered themselves their moral betters.

Tailbones of Religious Experience

Aside from the maintenance of Catholic practices for social reasons and the various means of justifying or legitimizing peripheral Catholic links in the face of mixed feelings, moral disapproval, and external criticism, cultural Catholicism can still evidence itself in unexpected subjective experiences and reflexes. At this affective level, cultural Catholicism connotes legacies of Catholicism in the subjectivity of people who consider themselves otherwise secularized. Such holdovers may be patterns of thought or emotion, such as feeling inexplicably guilty about sex or experiencing vague twinges before holy images. These are understood by the uncommitted-but-baptized to be quintessentially Catholic yet somehow at odds with what they perceive to be their modern, secularized worldviews. They are sometimes framed almost as the mental or cultural equivalents to vestigial appendixes and tailbones. As aspects of consciousness, these experiences cannot be denied: They exist because they are felt. Someone can be made aware of this inward cultural Catholicism suddenly and unexpectedly, like an unsought interior locution.[27] Consider the following description from Sally Rooney's bestselling novel *Conversations with Friends*. The young protagonist, a quintessentially progressive millennial, sick and wandering the streets of present-day Dublin in a state of near delirium, has inadvertently stumbled into a church off Thomas Street that smells of "dry incense and stale air."

> The pain kicked against my spine, radiating up into my skull and making my eyes water. I'm praying, I thought. I'm actually sitting here praying for God to help me. I was. Please help me, I thought. Please. I knew that there were rules about this, that you had to believe in a divine ordering principle before you could appeal to it for anything, and I didn't believe. But I make an effort, I thought. I love my fellow human beings. Or do I?[28]

As the character finds herself—to her own incredulity—*praying*, she simultaneously analyzes the sheer absurdity of what she is trying to do. The encounter with the dusty church exposes a nest of unsorted associations and paradoxical thoughts, scattering about like insects disturbed by the lifting of a stone. For a moment, the environment of the church seems to trigger the elision between "being good" and "believing" that is put in place by school Catholicism, before it fades away again. This is a mind inhabited at the fringes by Catholicism, but it is not a mind structured around an explicitly formulated Catholic worldview. It is what is left over when Catholicism has receded. Should they prompt further reflection, depending on people's stances in life, such experiences might be treated as evidence of cultural belonging or as echoing impositions from a reviled past. Either way, there is something spectral about this kind of residual Catholic experience. For a moment, some confluence of breezes sends a shred of the tattered old sacred canopy fluttering overhead, and then it is gone.

Those in the generations who reached middle age before Rooney's protagonist was even born, who grew up under the aegis of Holy Catholic Ireland and were exposed to a highly CRED-rich environment, were largely imparted with a strong sense of the immediacy and reality of the Catholic supernatural world and of their own identity and affinity as Catholics within a distinctly Catholic society. In time, profound social changes led many to dissociate from the institutional Church's demands, but rejecting Catholic belief and identity was more difficult. The preference, generally, was to redefine and maintain it in a looser, more permissive incarnation. Consequently, for many of those raised in subsequent decades, the reality of Catholic belief and belonging was somewhat thinner and less commanding, despite its seeming pervasiveness. During their upbringing, CREDs had waned and Catholicism had become something tangential, vague, and largely defunct—for the most part irrelevant but still demanding occasional homage, such as during rites of passage or, if they grew up immediately pre-scandal, phoned-in Sunday Mass attendance during childhood.

The result is that in many cases, God, at least in explicitly Catholic form, seems increasingly analogous to the Tooth Fairy: an empirically unverifiable proposition with a limited shelf life resulting from a lack of adult endorsement, accepted during a brief window when children have yet to discern fact from fable. For large numbers, Catholicism as religion is perceived to be a maturational stage, but one that does no harm. It is at its most active in school, where individuals finds themselves suspended, for a while, in a kind of Catholic amniotic gel, a pleasant protective casing that they will wriggle out of in their own good time. Then they go off into the secular world, returning to the shallow waters of religion to repeat the cycle once the time comes to spawn. Subsequently they may drop by again to celebrate their nuptials[29] and/or various key stages of juvenile development with their offspring. At the end, almost all will be buried Catholic, though the priest may find himself needing a lot of guidance from family members for his homily about the deceased.

This light and socially enjoyable cultural Catholicism is freely acknowledged and celebrated, and its contradictions are widely tolerated. In many ways, it represents a sort of strategic triumph of the laity over the Church. Since the Church's desacralization and its loss of authority, many people are free to involve themselves in Catholicism only as far as it suits them and to craft disengaged relationships to religious tradition that salvage expedient aspects while jettisoning costly practice, exacting moral codes, and the cultivation of oppressive beliefs. But even though the Church has lost its power to command obedience, the expectations of extended family and the local community can still bind people critical of the Church and uninterested in religion to a Catholic identity. In places where such relational bonds are particularly commanding, cultural Catholicism is less a matter of expedience. Instead, people may feel that disaffiliation is impossible or that it may simply be unthinkable. In these contexts, quietly privatized stances of stoic religious skepticism and anti-clericalism have long since developed beneath the outward screen of an unquestionable ethno-Catholic identity. Irish religious skepticism may be more widespread and more long established than surveys suggest, but, as we will consider in the next chapter, these older subcultures of closeted Catholic unbelief might also be an underappreciated impediment to the further statistical growth of disaffiliation and nonreligion.

CHAPTER 4

"A LOAD OF SHITE"
HIDDEN CULTURES OF CATHOLIC UNBELIEF

Finbarr's Dilemma

"Am I a Catholic? Pssssshhh . . . I don't know! Of course I am! What? Do I believe? Jesus, Mary, the Holy Ghost, and the lot of it? No, not a bit of it. Am I, what did you call it, one of those atheists then? Fine, have it your way! But no, no, sure I can't be that. I go to Mass now and then. It's what you were born into. You can't just pull it out of yourself. But it's not religion, not like the Muslims or those American holy rollers. It's social. Irish Catholicism is . . . it's a social thing, and that's the whole point of it. I was raised in it, basted in it. So I'm Catholic because what else would I be? But am I an atheist too?"

At this point Finbarr, a former schoolteacher in his 60s, put his head in his hands and let out a particularly deep harrumph. The A-word seemed to disturb him—he could feel it was somehow true of him in a formal sense but not something he wanted to apply to himself. The notion "that Jesus died for our sins and all that" was laughable. An admission of atheism among friends was acceptable (in the sense of an absence of a belief in God or skepticism about Catholic religious propositions in particular), but atheism as an identity was another matter altogether. "Being atheist" seemed incompatible with "being Catholic," something Finbarr felt to be an inalienable part of himself. Finbarr was a cultural Catholic, but his cultural Catholicism was not just a matter of pragmatism. It was a deeper link than what we saw with Peter in the previous chapter. Finbarr was *always* Catholic; he could not flit between stances in the way that Peter seemed to do. Catholic was something that he just was, something that could not be "pulled out of him." At the same time, like Peter, Finbarr was equivocal about Catholicism. It was not necessarily something he particularly liked, or at least not all the time. It was an essence bequeathed to him by his upbringing. It was not a matter of choice. He had been baptized, or, rather, he had been *born* Catholic. He had also been raised in a deeply Catholic environment in rural Cork. All his peers were Catholics—some devout, some social. Out of duty to this heritage and also because it allowed him to get away from the family for an hour or so of peace, he always went to Mass at Christmas.

In everyday life Finbarr kept Catholicism at arm's length but he could not let it go completely. This stance was one of comfort and passivity most of the time, but it contained contradictions that caused him to experience a sense of dissonance on those occasions when these were made explicit. He could find himself rendered wordless and exasperated by demands to explain himself. This was most likely to occur when he was drawn into debate with his daughters, both of whom were baptized but now reject a Catholic identity. They sometimes cited the Church's lack of moral credibility and questioned outright Finbarr's need to maintain an ongoing link to Catholicism, especially because he seemed to take little pleasure in the connection. But in his turn, Finbarr raises an important point: To what degree can someone who has been born and raised in a society where religious and ethnonational identity are so intertwined really choose not to be Catholic?

As observed briefly in Chapters 1 and 2 and as we will examine in more depth in Chapter 6, defining oneself as ex-Catholic in Ireland involves resisting "conscription" and constructing a social position that is felt to be consonant with what one takes to be one's individually determined or "authentic" moral values, attributes, and beliefs. It is the local manifestation of a long, complex historical shift away from ascribed or relational identification and toward individualistic self-assertion. Going deep into historical time, this is a process that may have been unintentionally initiated by the Church itself and that accelerated further during various milestones in the development of modern Western notions of the ideal self. The Reformation, the Enlightenment, Romanticism, industrialization, the counterculture of the 1960s, globalization, and more have all been connected at one time or another to the development of the idea that our religious labels, or lack thereof, ought to reflect some inner aspect of who we are as individuals and not just the social groups into which we were born. Cultural Catholicism at the deep level exhibited by Finbarr is different and arguably draws on something much more ancient. It is a form of relational identification—identification based on tribe, kin, and family. Although it is not a zero-sum game and although most individuals will think of themselves in both individualistic and relational terms, the weighting between the two may vary considerably from place to place. Where relational identities run strong, local commitments and relationships are prioritized above social identities based on inner states or concerns with authenticity. Beliefs, in fact, can be somewhat irrelevant, so long as they are prevented from interfering with the group. At the same time, deep cultural Catholicism of this sort also rejects the hierarchical obeisance that is more typical of conservatives and traditionalists. As with Peter's position in Chapter 3, this kind of cultural Catholicism is partly sustained today because it has become increasingly viable not to take surrounding religious Catholicism or the imprecations of the Church too seriously. But it is also sustained by something that very much must be taken seriously: one's ethnic heritage, one's family, and one's community. Here, religious identity is ascribed at birth. To reject this identity risks casting oneself adrift and disturbing other community members and weakening the bonds of solidarity. Catholic affiliation cannot be shed, and beliefs that run counter to it must be privatized. As a result, such beliefs can become a kind of dangerous secret insight, aspects of a private self that are shared in a low voice and only with the like-minded, if at all.

Quiet Subcultures of Catholic Disenchantment

Some data, such as the European Social Survey, suggest that Irish nonreligious identification is more common in wealthier socioeconomic brackets and in urban rather than rural areas.[1] This does not necessarily mean that skepticism about Catholic religious doctrine is absent in other communities (i.e., among poorer socioeconomic or rural groups). It may mean that other motivations and considerations cause skeptical people to retain a Catholic affiliation in these contexts and that something of a taboo hangs over expressing religious disbelief where community bonds may be tighter and more important than they are in relatively anonymous urban environments or in middle-class milieus oriented around the competitive pursuit of professional and material status. In working-class and rural communities, different types of moral concern may push back against overt disaffiliation. Although many people from these backgrounds have disowned the Church, older and quieter ways of being a skeptic might also be nestled within outward Catholic compliance.

Such dualities have long featured in Irish literature and were certainly the experience of the author John McGahern. His early novel, *The Dark*, was banned by the Irish Censorship Board, and McGahern was forced to move to England after being dismissed from his job as a teacher on the orders of Archbishop John Charles McQuaid. According to McGahern himself, his dismissal was a result not only of the book but also of an intolerant reaction to the unacceptable fact of his marriage to a foreign Protestant. Unsurprisingly, his work often depicts lives lived against the backdrop of a society suffocated by conformity. At the same time, it also offers glimpses of suppressed anti-clerical undercurrents. For instance, in his novel *The Leavetaking*, the protagonist—a thinly veiled version of the author—takes a room in the house of an elderly couple. To his surprise, once they come to know him well enough to feel more comfortable in his presence, they reveal themselves as rabidly antireligious. After McGahern returned from his exile in England, he took up life as a small farmer in his native County Leitrim. In his essays he reflects at length on the power of the Church, his personal faith, and the Irish relationship to religion. In a particularly noteworthy passage, he describes the following conversation with his neighbor:

> "Why don't you go to Mass, John?" I was asked by a dear friend and neighbour once.
> "I'd like to but I'd feel a hypocrite."
> "Why would you feel that?"
> "Because I don't believe."
> "But, sure, none of us believe."
> "Why do *you* go then?"

"We go for the old performance. To see the girls, to see the whole show." He was completely unfazed by my question, even mimicking the pious prancing of a fashionable woman as she approached and left the communion rail, and laughed out loud: "We go to see all the other hypocrites!"[2]

Skeptical but obligatory participation alongside unquestionable identification as Catholic can be found in the Ireland of today as well, including in its capital city. Many long-established working-class Dublin communities were dislocated to newly built estates during the middle decades of the twentieth century—but not all. Those that remain have often maintained strong links to the Catholic nationalist past. They are home to local cultures and collective memories that middle-class areas rarely share because their populations tend to be more transient and less interconnected. These working-class communities are also places where Catholicism has often provided hard-pressed people with a much-needed salve and a sense of meaning. At the same time, over the course of the twentieth century, many such places bore the brunt of Holy Catholic brutality.

Although many are loath to acknowledge it, Ireland is a society with rigid class distinctions, and in Holy Catholic Ireland class position was critical in determining a person's experiences of religious authority. Although corporal punishment was commonplace for students from all walks of life, children from less prosperous backgrounds in particular were chronically exposed to excessive beatings and humiliation. Class-based poverty was the strongest indicator of a child's likelihood to be interned in an industrial school, where abuse was at its worst, and even outside the institutions socially sanctioned and religiously justified violence was a regular feature of school life. In his book *Love's Betrayal: The Decline of Catholicism and the Rise of New Religions in Ireland*, anthropologist Peter Mulholland describes how a punitive pedagogical culture, influenced by St. Augustine's doctrine of original sin and his justification of religious coercion, took hold in the realm of Irish education. According to Mulholland, this oppressive culture "reproduced itself through recruiting religious aspirants from the large pool of self-estranged, relationally incompetent and psycho-sexually immature people that it helped to create," and the "less able and less stable" were "dispatched or demoted to less prestigious parishes and institutions."[3] In these lower-status places, young, damaged, and inexperienced teachers, who had been recruited and trained by the religious orders, meted out the violence that they in turn had suffered and that they believed was necessary to purify their sinful wards.

Class distinctions were also reflected in the ranking of which religious orders taught which children. The Jesuits, for instance, were more typically tasked with educating wealthy students than were the Christian Brothers (though this was not exclusively the case). Undoubtedly both benign and violent individuals were present in every teaching order, but the Christian Brothers in particular became synonymous with classroom brutality. According to Mulholland and others, the middle classes were able to turn a blind eye to the violence inflicted on poorer children by justifying it to themselves as a kind of tough love that the religious orders were necessarily providing to those in need of discipline, incontrovertibly for their own good. This willful obliviousness could never be sustained completely, though. Drawing extensively on newspaper archives, Mulholland describes how the issue of physical abuse led to the emergence of a critical discourse of religious discontent stretching back decades before the sexual abuse scandals came to light in the 1990s. In the 1950s and 1960s, for instance, reform-minded liberals launched a number of campaigns for change in the Dáil. Their efforts came to naught and were interpreted with outrage as "anti-Catholic" or "communist" by zealous political rivals incapable of countenancing any criticism of the Church.

Today, Catholicism continues to act as a source of community bonds and collective identity in many working-class societies, but the era of Church control has left damage and resentment in its wake. Feelings about Catholicism draw on this complex legacy and can be divided. Even with the added contamination of the scandals, outright renunciation can still be difficult or undesirable. In Chapter 3 we saw that Peter was afraid of losing out if he did not baptize his child, but he was also confident that his atheistic, instrumentally motivated cultural Catholicism was so widely shared among his middle-class peers that he was comfortable—and perhaps even eager—to confess to his Catholic inauthenticity. His willingness to endure this religious inauthenticity proved he was a good middle-class father willing to make sacrifices for his family's social and professional advancement. But there can be other reasons to cling fast to a contaminated religious tradition, even in the absence of belief or moral endorsement. These reasons may be less baldly instrumental than Peter's. The fear of clerical authority has evaporated, but the expectations of family and community persist—be they real or imagined. This inertial pressure can create a sense of concern that binds individuals into delicate social compromises just short of absolute exit. In the single microcosmic example to follow, I outline a cultural Catholic social strategy involving the maintenance of vestigial Catholic identity and ritual behavior to preserve social harmony at the expense of individualistic self-expression. This case study illustrates how local ties can act to put the brakes on disaffiliation, even for the deeply uncommitted and critical.

Kilbreagh: Social Harmony and Stoic Skepticism

One of my field sites, Kilbreagh, proved particularly instructive as a lesson in the elasticity of this deeper kind of cultural Catholicism, and so it will be our focus. Kilbreagh yielded a group of people who identified as Catholic but disparaged the Church for its moral failings and who frequently reported an outright lack of religious belief and general contempt for religious practice. In a way, they represented cultural Catholicism in its most extreme form. The tendency among some committed secularists is to view cultural Catholics of this sort as unconscious, sheeplike, contradictory, or self-interestedly cynical. They are portrayed as being in a state of inauthentic dissonance from which they must be awakened. Yet despite such characterizations, Kilbreagh's unbelieving cultural Catholics were perfectly aware of the tensions and contradictions in their commitments and of the nonreligious arguments against them. They simply operated according to a different ethic: Social bonds were more important than the issue of belief.

Kilbreagh is an old, traditional working-class inner suburb of Dublin city, once home to a thriving dockworker community. It prides itself on its sense of community, with many families going back several generations.

There is also a strong tradition of Irish nationalism in the area, with the 1916 Easter Rising leaders, particularly Patrick Pearse and James Connolly, greatly venerated. Newer working-class areas, such as those in West Dublin, are often noted for having seen a particularly steep decline in Mass attendance,[4] but Kilbreagh piety has not suffered to quite the same degree, though it could not be described as healthy. The area does boast an institution called the Catholic Men and Women's Society, but this primarily functions as a bingo hall. Nevertheless, geographically and culturally, St. Teresa's, a nineteenth-century Catholic church from whose steeple stare four huge clock faces, is the focal point; it towers above the neighboring council flats, projecting a strangely appropriate maritime form, like a gigantic gray squid suspended by its mantle along the steep banks of the Turrow River. Next to the church is an old stone bridge, a choke point on one of the main arteries into Dublin city center. When someone of local significance dies in Kilbreagh, it is tradition to shoulder their coffin over this narrow old bridge and into St. Teresa's, unrepentantly obstructing traffic until the ritual has concluded.

Inside the church there is an annex, the Chapel of Remembrance, that contains three walls with hundreds of tiny bronze plaques, each inscribed with the name of a deceased worker from a local factory, once a main source of employment in the area. The church notably contains a statue of St. Anne with a prayer against suicide pinned to her and a devotional area dedicated to the Venerable Matt Talbot, a Dublin manual laborer who was renowned for his self-mortification and who is considered a patron for those struggling with alcoholism.[5] Mass attendance on Sunday is generally confined to the elderly. This is also the case on particular feast days or holy days. For example, on the Feast of the Baptism of Our Lord (that year, January 10) the pews were about half-full and, as usual, skewed toward the elderly. Some children were also present, and much was made of them through an innovation that saw the priest summon them to the altar and then disperse them up and down the aisles to shake hands when time came for the congregation to make the sign of peace. The priest delivered a sermon on the power of oratory to sway individuals for good or ill and on how people were often diverted toward the wrong answers to their problems, such as drugs, drink, or material possessions. The right answer was, of course, Jesus, who reminds us that we are special even when we feel worthless. When I spoke with some congregants, the general consensus was that religion "gives you a bit of hope" and "helps you to be a good person." An expression that I heard used by older Kilbreagh residents when they met later on Sundays, perhaps in the pub, was "Did you get Mass?" as though it were a meal (which it is in a sense)—basic sustenance required to keep one going through the week.

The local church, however, is plainly not the natural habitat in which to seek those with an attenuated relationship to religion. The area is well supplied with pubs—Connolly's, The Docker, The Tall Ship, and others. I got to know the barman of one of the bars, Eamon, and a group of five regulars there (all male, all in their late 30s and early 40s, an age range where hostility toward the Church is often thought to be at its zenith).[6] I generally visited Kilbreagh once a week or sometimes once a fortnight, and sometimes others of the group's acquaintance would join and I would have the opportunity to talk to them also. Although I was always an outsider and my obsession with religion was clearly vexing at times, it was also a subject on which the men were often more than happy to hold forth.

These men all evinced varying degrees of skepticism about the Church, with the common verdict being that Catholic doctrine was "a load of shite," a frequently recurring phrase. A view often articulated close behind this observation was that the Church basically operated in its own self-interest. For example, an older man who joined the group one night stimulated much agreement when he expressed the view that the Catholic Church had deliberately kept people ignorant in order to sell its "shite" to them and thereby control them for its own ends. It was rare for the Catholic Church at an institutional level to be treated as anything other than hypocritical and duplicitous. Despite this, the men would discuss the role of religion in ordinary people's lives with a large degree of fluidity and ambiguity. At times the view was expressed that religion was needed by some people, in particular the elderly, as a form of support. Sometimes it was suggested that people in general (or, at other times, weak people specifically) needed some kind of external moral structure, and religion, including the Church, provided this. And when asked whether or not they were Catholic, the men would either affirm that they were or would deliver a qualified answer, saying that they had been raised Catholic or baptized Catholic. All identified as Catholic on the census. None, not even the most considered unbelievers among them, wanted to drop the term completely.

Similarly, no one was willing to go so far as to identify as an atheist, even those who made the most strident professions of religious disbelief. Eamon, for example, claimed to have seen through the charade of religion as early as 4 or 5 years of age, an awakening he attributed to early experiences of Mass-goer hypocrisy (specifically the manner in which people maliciously gossiped on the way out the church door despite their displays of devotion and piety within) and his own prepubescent musings on the problem of theodicy. His current ontological views were as follows:

> I'd like to think that there is some sort of a release of this energy or electricity from a dead corpse into the . . . into oblivion or the universe or whatever, and then maybe we are just re-entered, like a data bank or thrown back into the star-making machine that turns out all these stars in the center of the galaxy, but it's unfortunate to believe that we are just food for crows. That's the way it is.

The concepts of believing and belonging were pretty firmly separated among these Kilbreagh Catholics, and views such as Eamon's coexisted quite comfortably with a sense of oneself as inalienably Catholic. For instance, a young man called Georgie was adamant that he was a Catholic—and could scarcely believe he was being asked this question—despite dismissing belief in concepts such as God, Jesus, and heaven as "a load of shite." Belief, specifically, was also noteworthy for its unfixed nature. The men were perhaps best glossed as flexible, fluctuating agnostics. Metaphysical propositions entertained by speakers shifted regularly during conversations and were deployed or concealed in a context-dependent way. All beliefs were fair game for speculation and critique, though not necessarily in all situations. For instance, a local man called Mark was particularly prone to oscillating backward and forward within the bounds of a few remarks. He described how he had lost any theistic certainty after his father died, because if anyone would have come back from beyond to tell him not to worry about death, his father would have.[7] However, Mark then went on to say that he did go to Mass occasionally, such as at Christmas, and enjoyed the way it made him feel, gingerly concluding from this that he "must believe a little bit" before shifting to a sociological defense of religion based on the proposition that it helps people to behave well and that without it we would have chaos. On the subject of Church scandals, he did not really have a ready answer, producing the hesitant compromise that "they're not all like that" but also conceding that religion does not necessarily make you good. His ultimate conclusion: "Maybe it is all a load of shite then. I don't know."

The relationship to Catholic performance, however, remained somewhat more rigid. Mass attendance was generally viewed as a fusty and obsolete mark of weakness, but certain Catholic rituals, notably baptisms and church funerals, were obligatory in the area, even though others, such as marriage, had declined.[8] Georgie was a new father, and he had recently had his child baptized despite his views of the Church as a "cult" and a "money-maker." He remarked that he would have had to put up with a lot of "moaning" from the child's grandparents if he had not had his daughter baptized (this was a common complaint), but concluded on a more conciliatory note that the Church was a "safety net for olds, and that's OK," adding that "maybe we all have our own higher power." This move—where contempt for the institution and concern for social relations collide and are then reconciled by back-stepping to a position of tolerant but vague agnosticism—was a common one. However, despite the softer tone engendered by considerations of Catholicism's therapeutic possibilities, there was a definite feeling that the Church did not live up to its billing as an institution of love. It compared unfavorably with other options. Georgie and another man who had joined us talked about this new arrival's mother, who was described as a "spiritualist," which seemed to indicate an involvement with the New Age. Although this was viewed as a somewhat absurd worldview, both agreed that she had "so much more love than a Christian."

Inevitably, the men were well aware of Catholic sex scandals and cover-ups. They rarely attributed their own skeptical attitudes directly to these revelations, but it was commonly held that they had produced more of an impact on older people, or sometimes, more broadly, on other people in general. For instance, John, a 40-year-old electrician who had stopped going to Mass around the age of 16, did not hold any religious beliefs and attributed this to a rational awakening regarding the improbability of Catholic doctrine. He described how his mother had been very religious, acting as a Eucharistic minister and attending Mass daily. However, he noted that, during his early teenage years, she and others greatly scaled down their attendance. Eventually he realized why when a friend described a personal story of abuse to him.[9] John's main memory relating to clerical abuse from this time was successfully using it to resist his mother's efforts to get him to go to Mass. This was the first time that he was able to stay home on a Sunday: "There I was locked in the bathroom with my Ma banging on door, and I says to her, I says, 'Why the fuck should I go there and listen to that bunch of fucking pedophile priests and the pedophile nuns that protect them?'"

There were also cases where it was not atheism, agnosticism, or resistance to religious practice that was vindicated with reference to clerical abuse scandals, so much as one's right to decide for oneself what God was and what he wanted. Paradoxically, the pedophile priest trope could even be instrumentalized to legitimize *staying* theistically Catholic while rejecting all Church claims to authority on doctrine. It justified liberation from subordination to the theological hierarchy, affording an opportunity to insert a self-tailored moral therapeutic deism[10] into the socially approved external husk of ethnic Catholic affiliation. Craig, a young self-identified Catholic theist in his early 20s, provided a good example of this. Craig adopted a generally scornful view of religious practice, maintaining that it was primarily an opportunity for old busybodies to get together and gossip vindictively about other people in their absence: "Did you see Mary wasn't at Mass today? Isn't that terrible?" Nevertheless, Craig made it plain that he himself was a Catholic and that he believed in God because it was important to believe in something. He professed—or rather gave the impression of producing in an ad hoc manner—a belief that God was a form of voluntary reincarnation where the soul chooses its next incarnation based on a need to develop tolerance by experiencing life from different perspectives. The incompatibility of his view with

Church dogma was defended by his observation, "Well, they're against everything really—except for molesting little boys!"

In general, the concept of clerical authority was treated as risible, in large part because the clergy were viewed as sexually dubious. This sexualized picture of the clergy attached itself to the present incumbent of St. Teresa's. This priest, who had delivered the sermon on drink and drugs, would sometimes drink in the pub frequented by the other men and was referred to by some as "Father Carlsberg." Although the priest was described as competent and charismatic, commanding the respect of his congregation, he was also seen as somewhat overbearing, especially when socializing in the pub. Incidents of misogynistic behavior (disparaging women drinkers as "sluts" or "whores") were recounted, and there was a perception that he had little time or understanding for the issues that local people faced. One man's negative evaluation in particular may have stemmed from a personal conflict centering around an argument in which he had loudly challenged "Father Carlsberg" on the plausibility of Catholic doctrine and his sincerity in professing it. This incident was framed as an example of crossing the line, but it was also evaluated as necessary to put the priest back in his place. At this point, another of the group chimed in to intimate that the priest was conducting a covert sexual liaison with a young Filipino man. The drinkers were thus a fairly anti-clerical group, though not obsessively so—only when the matter was raised. Priests were viewed with suspicion and definitely as sexual misfits,[11] something that Eamon explicitly linked to their religiosity.

> There are some very slippery people who end up in the priesthood. A lot of the more gentle race who tend to find solace there, safety maybe behind the veil of religion, because of the lack of physicality . . . or the lack of . . . em . . . being able to satisfy their sexual need elsewhere. I think they definitely turned to God for an answer to the questions they needed answering about the way they were feeling and who they were attracted to and who they felt closest to. I think as you're growing up you know very young whether or not boobies turn you on or is it guys that turn you on. It's really fuckin' strange . . . so maybe in their darkest hour and they're thinking, "Jesus what's wrong with me?" and they turn to Jesus and he

says, "I'm calling you to the priesthood—spread my word." I'm not sure really. People get deluded in all sorts of ways.

If the Church was depicted as a hotbed of sublimated sinful desire, it was also viewed as hypocritical in a more straightforwardly self-interested way. A theme frequently introduced by the men, and one that may well have drawn on their own experiences of subordination within a capitalist system, was the notion of the Church as an exploitative business enterprise. It was often discussed in an almost anticapitalistic way, as a cynical entrepreneurial corporation that cultivated and then fed on fear and ignorance in pursuit of this-worldly profit. According to one informant, the Church had "sold the business of spirituality to the human race and they've done it very well." Eamon in particular painted a picture of a kind of abusive relationship, whereby the needy and the weak come to church for some kind of comfort fix, almost as though it were a drug; he described Kilbreagh as a dependent place where people need something to get through life, whether it be drink, drugs, or, in the case of the elderly, religion. However, despite these insights, or perhaps because of them, there is a tendency to keep this disbelief in check in situations where it might lead to conflict.

> It's not like being a Liverpool supporter and having a chat about our newest winger, or whatever. It's just always been a personal thing that, eh . . . I've often felt the need to say to people could you not cop on, are you serious, do you seriously believe that we're all going to Heaven and we're all going to meet again in Heaven, this paradise in the sky? I've often felt like shaking people and saying, "Do you really believe this?" But I'm not . . . I tend more, when I do hear how people feel about these things . . . I tend to find myself shutting up and listening to the conversation and trying to understand their point of view, rather than trying to throttle them with mine.

Eamon also describes a kind of early stalemate, a pivotal moment reached between the believing world and the individual skeptic at some defining point in the past that makes their mutual intractability known to one another and brings an end to debate on religious matters (though, tellingly, the unbeliever in his description is still a Catholic).

> Well, the Catholic who has been educated by the Catholic school system, reared in the Catholic way by a Catholic family, who says, "No, I'm sorry, I'm not going to believe in all this. I'm not going to Mass. I don't want to participate and I don't want to send my kids to a Catholic school" and all that . . . it's almost like a virus, a cancer really. As much as they tried to indoctrinate you to make you believe in their unwavering beliefs in their god, we still sit back cynically and argue our point and they can't beat us and we can't beat them, so you come to loggerheads without there being violence, without there being too much of a debate.

"Virus" here is ambiguous, initially redolent perhaps of the New Atheist virus of faith. The context, however, seems rather to suggest that disbelief is a virus on Catholicism—and, ultimately, something incurable and metastasizing, given its comparison here to cancer. It is almost as though Eamon views his own position as an impediment to the canopy of agreement that would bind the local community together more effectively without such as himself. He views his atheism-that-dare-not-speak-its-name as a social danger to some degree. This element of loggerheads is important. It portrays an intractable ideological division that must be suppressed for the more important business of living together to continue, producing a functionally restricted form of personal skepticism. Both sides recognize its presence. But even though this loggerheads might look like a kind of victory for the unbelieving underdog, it is actually a tacit compromise. Religious skepticism is not something to be proselytized; rather, it is constructed as an insight that has been rebelliously won through personal reflection and confrontation against an overarching society that leans on—that *needs*—the crutch of religion. It may even confer a certain status, telegraphing intellectual autonomy as well as moral and mental strength and is permissible to bring to bear in moments of argumentative conflict.[12] If you perform well in these, you will be left alone on the matter afterward. But notably, once the status of being religiously unswayable has been conferred, the unbeliever effectively rests with their trophy and it is up to others to earn the same insight themselves, if they can.

Crucially, how far personal religious skepticism can be permitted to influence social action has its limits. Capitulation to these social forces is reflected in the fact that, despite his long-standing personal rejection, Eamon, like Georgie, had both his children baptized to avoid

> Holy war, a jihad, a holy war . . . not by the Catholic priests, but I mean the woman I was married to at the time. If I tried to argue my point, said, "Listen, maybe we should wait till the child is of the age that she can decide for herself, then she can get herself baptized if she wants to in the Catholic Church, get herself communed and confirmed when she's eighteen or sixteen—maybe we should leave them to make their own choice." There is no arguing with these people. It's a tradition that is expected and has to be respected, you have no argument against that.

For many in Kilbreagh, strong social pressure seemed to leave no choice but to engage in Catholic rites of passage, and this certainly catalyzed a certain amount of resentment. With the idea of his wife and extended family waging Catholic "jihad" on him for his defiance, Eamon displays the concept common among New Atheists of religion entailing a dangerous fanaticism that destroys the possibility of reason or compromise. Unlike with New Atheism, though, this irrationality is tolerated in a stoical manner, because it is linked not only to the power of tradition but also to an underlying condition of psychological vulnerability in the religious relative. This pressure was often framed as a matter of maintaining the peace by capitulating to concerned nagging, in particular by older female relatives, who were invariably portrayed as fragile and anxious. Earned unbelief was therefore not permitted to affect the operation of certain basic obligations such as baptism, which make Catholicism a component in community membership—"It's a tradition that is expected and has to be respected. You have no argument against that." But capitulation is not cowardice. It is concern, even love. Should the pressure exerted by family members' emotional distress at seeing tradition violated fail as a means of justification, a second layer of more pragmatic concern can be leveraged. This layer of argumentation often focuses on institutional obstacles, such as the potential ostracism of the child during later rites of passage, and on the issue of securing a convenient (or, in the middle-class case, strategic) school place. Indeed, we saw how Peter refused to "martyr" his child by not baptizing him, and, in another context, refusing to baptize a child was described as "sacrificing your child to your ideology."

Overall then, the Kilbreagh men's relationship to Catholicism involved a number of factors that combined to preserve the delicate equilibrium of their skeptical, stoical, and flexible cultural Catholic agnosticism. For a start, religious Catholicism was almost always portrayed as inherently hypocritical at the levels of both the institution and the laity: Refusing to get involved too deeply was a mark of moral integrity. All the Kilbreagh drinkers were perfectly aware of the Church's past abuses and agreed on the dark picture of its historical role. The Church was viewed as a cynical institution focused on its own gain at the expense of ordinary people. A popular image that arose from all this was the picture of the Church as an avaricious and duplicitous business enterprise, a capitalist exploiter. It was also seen as being staffed by pathological individuals at war with their own sexual natures. In addition to this, when not portrayed as the result of weakness or obligation, religious participation by the laity was at times construed as hypocritical: Believers professed a love of their neighbor, but they went to Mass specifically to engage in gratifying calumny as soon as they were out the door. All of this justified personal detachment. Taking up this dark, compound picture of a Church defined by avarice, exploitation, illegitimate claims to judgment, and underlying psychological perversity was associated with maturity and mental strength; devotion by contrast was the mark of soft-headedness, of the hoodwinked dupe or the weakling. One can imagine this as a series of three concentric circles with moral weakness deepening as one progresses inward. The firm, stoical, and independent agnostic is on the outside; the fragile and irrational religious relative is a ring closer to the center; the warped and manipulative clergy are at the very heart. Yet the structure holds up. It is impossible to ascertain the degree to which this perception of a religion enmeshed with hypocrisy and weakness led to the rejection of Catholic beliefs and behaviors or whether that perception was itself a product of rejection and the need to defend against theistic antagonists. The tactic of emphasizing Church hypocrisy, including the scandals, also seemed at times to function as a weapon of last resort when the effort of maintaining independence and resisting traditionalist Catholic pressure became too arduous. Distance from that clerical center was proportionate to purity, but the structure still had to be preserved.

This raises the question of why one would acquiesce to this corrupt system rather than try to abolish or reform it. Practically speaking, all these men experienced strong levels of religious socialization from their families growing up. This, perhaps, contributed to their unwillingness to say or feel that they were not Catholic at all. Another factor is likely the high degree to which Catholicism is bound up with aspects of the area's culture, such as the ritual of carrying the coffin over the bridge, an activity that was only ever spoken of with respect. To defect completely from Catholicism in this context might signify a form of betrayal or even treason, a factor possibly enhanced by strong ties to the nationalism of the past. Strong social pressure, most notably from anxious older female relatives, to maintain Catholic traditions such as baptism were a further powerful component in Kilbreagh cultural Catholicism. But these factors do not simply drive brute impulses that operate under the cover of unconscious darkness; they are also topics of explicit reflection. In Kilbreagh one's cultural Catholicism was often constructed as a self-aware process of enchainment and sacrifice for the common good rather than as a condition of passive acceptance. This ethic of harmony requires a kind of private/public dichotomy, and it exists because social relations are considered of greater importance among the Kilbreagh cultural Catholics than the pursuit of ideological consonance in all matters of public behavior. Aligning oneself with this harmonizing ethic (often expressed among the Kilbreagh group with a reproachful plea not to be a "pain in the hole" about something) involves the complex, rationalized prioritization of one ethical obligation concerning the maintenance of smooth social relations above another that pertains to individual freedom and the responsibility of acting fully in concert with one's individual values or sentiments. It does not necessarily entail an absence of ethical awareness or blind conformity, yet it could equally be seen as a force preserving the status quo. To what degree capitulation to pressure about such issues as baptism was genuinely a self-effacing peacekeeping obligation and a matter of mercy toward the religious anxieties of others, or whether this praiseworthy interpretation was, as many ex-Catholics might maintain, a dissonance-reducing gambit that acquitted them for adopting the path of least resistance, is open to interpretation.

Another component in this stasis was that religion could be swiftly recoded as a benevolent force: Despite the dark image, its status was not fixed. Just as Catholic pressure produced detachment, strong arguments for disaffiliation could backfire and draw the interlocutor closer to the fringes of the Church. It was often emphasized in such moments that Catholicism seemed to serve some positive comforting function for others in the community. By virtue of being a member of the category "religion," it was also sometimes held to be a positive force in ensuring public morality. Such considerations would temporarily detoxify the Church by transmogrifying it into a locally contingent service provider fulfilling an intrinsic need for metaphysical consolation and an underlying social need for a source of objective moral guidance, though neither need seemed to apply to the men themselves. The Church may not have been the most desirable provider for such needs, but it was a provider nonetheless. Like an underwhelming Eircom rural broadband package, it was a bit subpar but it was the only service to which ordinary people had access. This interpretation was in unresolved tension with the idea of the Church as a ruthless brainwashing corporation, and the men seemed to oscillate between the two valences according to the requirements of their position in a given conversation.

The capstone of this ambiguous worldview consisted in the way atheism (note that the word itself was almost never used to describe unbelief and seemed to be a taboo) was constructed in Kilbreagh. Unbelief was presented as a personal achievement, something that one earned by a kind of stoical "seeing through the veil" and a recognition that socially advocated beliefs enforced by local traditions are, in fact, "a load of shite." This was presented as an individual and rational accomplishment, even though it was widely shared in a broadly similar form among the nine or ten men I talked to from the Kilbreagh drinking group. But though there was no special need to hide it, there was also no imperative to promote it or expect it of others. It was something about which one ought to be reserved. It was personal and conferred a different, deeper perspective on the world. Most people were simply depicted as not having the capacity for that kind of awareness, and it was conjectured that if something were to replace whatever was left of Kilbreagh Catholicism in time, it would most likely be apathy. This construction of unbelief as a stoical personal achievement that most people did not have the strength for also allowed it to coexist with the maintenance of seemingly incompatible social practices, such as baptism, which were portrayed as indicative of a desire to keep up good relations and to minimize upset for others.

Essentially, Kilbreagh is a fiercely local area. Being a Kilbreagher is more important than being part of some larger abstract struggle around such notions as secularism, and Catholic traditions are part of that Kilbreagh identity. As the center of its own world, Kilbreagh seemed like it would go on as it always had, and on a practical day-to-day level, for these men at least, religious Catholicism was more of an occasional mild but irritating inconvenience than an omnipresent oppressive force, being elevated to the latter status only in conversation when there was a point to be made or an imposition to be resisted. Kilbreagh's Catholicism seemed to be tentatively pinioned between immemorial practices, such as the coffin ritual, and the growing lack of religious interest among younger Catholics, who might produce ad hoc "Catholic" beliefs, such as Craig's reincarnationist hybrid, or alternatively assume the forbearing cultural Catholic unbelief of the Kilbreagh drinkers. The religious pressure brought to bear by older relatives is something likely to diminish with time; given the superficiality and, some might say, hypocrisy of the Kilbreagh men's own relationship to Catholicism, their children may in turn be less motivated to bring the Kilbreaghers' grandchildren to be baptized one day. Most important, the Kilbreagh men existed in a kind of moral tension between an obligation to ensure social harmony and an ethic of authenticity. The conception of atheism and agnosticism as personal dark insights and the construction of others as not only fragile but also volatile in defense of this fragility acted as conceptual or rhetorical mechanisms for reconciling this tension, allowing them to save face and avoid social conflict. The form of religious skepticism that emerges in this context thus effectively suppresses its outright expression in order to prioritize the cohesion of the local community. On the one hand, this demonstrates how closely cultural Catholicism and ex-Catholicism can overlap and how an individual might shift from one to the other depending on the circumstances.[13] On the other hand, however, when one considers how many such local cultures of compromising unbelief might exist and that the effectiveness of their conciliatory solution arguably renders them self-perpetuating, one must concede they could pose a substantial challenge to any social actors seeking to encourage disaffiliation among religiously disengaged ethno-Catholics. It is difficult to imagine how entrenched cultural Catholics such as the Kilbreagh unbelievers could be convinced to put local matters to one side, be "a pain in the hole" and "stand up for what they believe in," when they are already cognizant of the controversies surrounding Catholicism, along with the compromises and advantages that their loose relationship to it involves. And then there is the issue of nationalism.

In what was to be one of my final visits to Kilbreagh, I accompanied the men on a night out that eventually took us to the local GAA (Gaelic Athletic Association) club. The club had a large hall that served the role of nightclub on weekends. Unlike the more fashionable nightlife venues to be found in Dublin city center, the GAA club drew a notably intergenerational crowd, one that skewed a little bit more toward men than women. It also seemed that everyone knew one another. People moved freely among tables and standing groups, joking and bantering, buying one another drinks. As the night wore on and the drinks kept flowing, things became increasingly boisterous. Then, with jarring abruptness, the grim hour of 2:30 a.m. arrived. This is when Irish bars must close in accordance with the country's strict licensing laws. As is customary, the venue lights were unceremoniously flicked on, a practice intended to encourage patrons to finish their drinks and depart as promptly as possible. The ritual that followed, while not unknown to me, was one I had not thought to anticipate. The DJ played one final tune: "Amhrán na bhFiann" (The Soldier's Song), Ireland's national anthem. First written as a rebel song in 1910 by the Irish republican Peader Kearney, by 1928 "Amhrán na bhFiann" had gradually come to be accepted as the anthem of the new Irish Free State. Everyone in the harshly lit hall—even those I had thought the most inebriated—managed to gather themselves together and stand to attention with hands on their hearts. They sang along and knew every word. The old spirit of revolutionary nationalism in Kilbreagh ran deep.

The staying power of Irish Catholic affiliation amid the rapid drain of actual religious interest relates to how deeply it is amalgamated into various unquestionable levels of relational identity. It is bound up with the family, with local tradition and belonging, with school, and, intrinsic to all this, with nationalism. Even for the utterly religiously disengaged and critical, actual exit from affiliation can feel like ethno-apostasy. But though Catholicism can seem so deeply intertwined with Irishness as to be inextricable, the crucible of moral conflict can shake up historical narratives and reassemble them in potent and unexpected new ways. Since 2015, a series of crucial national centenaries all came into view at once: It was soon to be 100 years since the 1916 Rising, and after that the Civil War, and then independence. As we will see in the next chapter, during this time, moral battles around secularization reignited with particular intensity. Several flashpoints came at once: the referendum on marriage equality, the 2016 census, and, most important, the highly symbolic referendum on the legalization of abortion, the result of decades-long grass-roots activism to reverse the clause that had been inserted into the Irish Constitution in 1983. The 2014–2018 period marked a kind of culture war over what direction Ireland should be going and how Catholic it really wanted to be. It was far from the first time that such divisive issues had reared their heads—the decision in 1983 to insert the Eighth Amendment and effectively prohibit all access to abortion had itself been highly divisive. The culture war of 2014–2018, however, was waged not only after decades of profound social change but also after the Church's image had been thoroughly inverted. The relative power of dedicated actors at opposite poles to sway the culturally Catholic middle was different. In the heated public rhetoric of the period, the moral contamination of the Church cross-pollinated with a vision of it as an authoritarian interloper that had diverted and then continued to derail the true progressive spirit of Irish independence. Over the course of the culture war, this new narrative, drawing on the romantic revolutionary tropes of the 1916 period—but switching in the Vatican in place of London—became visible in marches and in the rhetoric of advocates for a number of secularizing causes. It remains to be seen whether this is a transient reflection of turbulent times or a stable collective representation of the past capable of challenging the Catholic version of nationalism.

CHAPTER 5

"THIS IS OUR RISING"
SECULARIZATION AS A SECOND STRUGGLE FOR "IRISH FREEDOM"

Mustering the Troops

On September 24, 2016, *The Irish Times* ran the following headline: "Thousands Taking Part in Pro-Choice Rally in Dublin."[1] About 20,000 people were reported to have attended the March for Choice that day, which shut down much of the city center. The aim of the protestors was to lobby for the repeal of the Eighth Amendment to the Irish Constitution, which guaranteed equal rights to life for "the unborn and the mother," thereby preventing access to abortion. Riding on the coattails of a surprisingly liberal decision by the Citizens' Assembly,[2] the marchers wanted an urgent referendum to be held on the Eighth Amendment because "the Irish people are pro-choice" and "ready for change."[3] As one of the organizers put it:

> In 1916 people dreamed of a better Ireland, one of self-determination and the right to choose their own destiny. A hundred years later, we're still fighting for that right; there can be no freedom without bodily autonomy.... Enough blood has been spilled, enough women have died. No more shame, no more silence, no more stigma. This is our Rising.[4]

In broad terms the moral focus of the march concerned issues of individual freedom and the reduction of harm to a traditionally disempowered group: women. Yet the slogan of the march, "Rise and Repeal," borne aloft in campaign imagery by a figure evoking the feminine avatar of Irish nationalism, Kathleen Ní Houlihan, cannily fused the struggle for abortion rights with national loyalty and sacrifice by linking it to the 1916 Rising in the year of its much-hyped centenary. The 1916 Rising is synonymous with patriotism and the struggle for national self-determination. By implication, to be pro-choice—and, by extension, probably anti-Church—was certainly not to be anti-Irish. Rather, it was to complete the Irish struggle for freedom, extending it to all the population. To oppose abortion was to oppose the extension of freedom to fellow members of the national community. It was unpatriotic.

The indignation of the crowd was evident in the placards carried by the marchers: "Get your rosaries off my ovaries." "Pro-life, that's a lie, you don't care if women die." Organizers maintained that the protestors were drawn from all walks of life, and this was true, though the crowd seemed to skew toward the younger end of the spectrum and their appearance suggested a decidedly urban and liberal disposition. Despite the focus on self-determination, equality, and bodily autonomy, a number of toddlers were unknowingly recruited to the cause and clad in jerseys proclaiming their superior status: "I was a chosen child." There was much ire and indignation among the marchers, who, as many I spoke to put it, protested their subordination to a controlling conservative elite and cowardly state in thrall to a patriarchal Catholic Church. But there was also a palpable sense that this was a cathartic moment. The oppressed were rising up and striking out in numbers that could no longer be ignored. A young man remarked to me that superstition and a submissive fear of the Church—a fear so extreme that people had stood by and allowed "it" to *rape children*—would no longer impede the way of progress. He explained further how his generation, the millennials, was the first truly moral generation because they were willing to sacrifice their self-interest for their beliefs and values. In this protester's view, they alone had broken free of "brainwashing." The scale of the march, which took place just over a year after the 2015 referendum legalizing marriage equality, seemed to indicate that this time the goal was in sight and that a liberalized majority supported the aims of the protestors. For this cohort, it represented the birth pangs of a freedom that had been denied half the children of the Irish nation. In 2016 the end of a protracted century-long labor was at hand.

On July 1, 2017, *The Irish Times* ran another headline: "Thousands March in Dublin in Support of Eighth Amendment."[5] In the national media, 20,000 people were reported to have attended the Rally for Life (though the supporters' website claimed 80,000), which also shut down much of the city center. The rally was a response to political rumblings of an incoming abortion referendum tentatively penciled in for 2017 or 2018 in the wake of the Citizens' Assembly's recommendation. Speaking at the rally, Níamh Uí Bhriain of the Life Institute proclaimed it the "real Citizens' Assembly," adding that "the pro-life majority has arisen and will work night and day to Save the 8th."[6] Accompanied by loudspeaker-amplified speeches, the unexpected pounding of bawdy 1990s Eurodance,[7] and marchers carrying placards with the slogan "Abortion Stops a Beating Heart," the rally eventually culminated in Merrion Square.

Like the previous year's march, the rally was a cathartic event, an awakening. From all four provinces (including the six counties of Northern Ireland), Ireland's pro-lifers had come to make their voices heard, and together they would stand up to the machinations of a politically correct elite hell-bent on pushing through a "culture of death" that denied the rights of "preborn children." County banners—Kerry, Mayo, Leitrim—were raised in the air like battle standards, proclaiming the nationwide reach of the crusade and its adherents. Foreign groups also flew in to lend their people and financial support to the cause. Yet, despite the majoritarian claims of the speakers and the diverse and youthful participants marshaled to carry "Save the 8th" banners at the front of the crowd, this assemblage did not quite look representative either. The protestors appeared to be older overall than those at the March for Choice and also more rural. Many of the young people participating were there as members of niche Catholic youth groups, such as Youth 2000, rather than as unaffiliated sympathizers, and others were there as part of family groups.

A notable number of religious individuals were in attendance. A particularly large banner bore an image of the Shroud of Turin with the slogan, "The Holy Face of Jesus Christ." By today's standards, nuns were greatly overrepresented, and a number of priests wearing full cassocks circulated conspicuously through the crowd.[8] But although the presence of devout individuals at the rally was highly visible, although everyone I approached identified as a believing Catholic, and although certain conservative Catholic tropes lay buried in the day's rhetoric,[9] a striking feature of the *official* symbolism and language used—both at the rally and in subsequent coverage on the websites of the trinity of organizing bodies (The Life Institute, Youth Defence, and Precious Life)—was the almost complete absence of overtly Catholic or even religious themes and references. Pro-life stances are typically reinforced with the Catholic tradition's rich religious imagery and theology, but these resources had been scrupulously avoided by organizers.

Instead, the rally and the organizations behind it almost exclusively leveraged secular moral rhetoric regarding the prevention of harm and the protection of equal rights (in this case, the equal right to life of what was invariably referred to as the "preborn child" and the mother). Some of the marchers carried signs with the slogan "Every Life Matters"— clearly a tactical effort to tap into the youthful social justice credentials of the Black Lives Matter movement.[10] These themes were couched in signage, imagery, and colors that stylistically would not have looked out of place on a corporate or social media webpage, suggesting a sort of cosmopolitan modernity. This approach was amplified online, where the organizing bodies' three websites offered scientific facts questioning pro-choice narratives about suicide risks and unwanted pregnancies or used medical interpretation to challenge clinical review report findings concerning the case of Savita Halappanavar, a woman who was refused an abortion and subsequently died of septicemia.[11] Online images showed smiling freckled Irish children under the heading "Human." The photographs on all three sites were populated by young people brandishing dynamic T-shirt slogans and smiling behind "Save the 8th" banners. Where the image of the environment could be fully controlled, faith, God, and the elderly were absent from the picture in favor of reason, youth, and social justice. It was as though the rally I saw had been turned on its head and was trying its best to speak the language of the secular.

The Ideological Tug of War over the Ambiguous Middle

Both the pro-choice march and the pro-life rally claimed to represent a majority of "the people of Ireland," but the way the organizers framed and promoted these two events suggested something else. The guiding value of the March for Choice was surely individual freedom, and it wore its confrontation with the Catholic Church on its sleeve, but it had conjured up the specter of heroic nationalism to supplement its individuating ethics and anti-clericalism with an appeal to group loyalty and the fulfillment of national destiny. On the other hand, the Rally for Life was clearly underpinned by the religiously motivated moral sentiments of an older generation, but religion was excised from the official imagery and rhetoric wherever possible and replaced with social justice style sloganeering. Online, the campaign was cosmetically tailored to appeal to its least representative demographic, the young.[12] The effort poured into these aspects of both events undermined their majoritarian claims and was a testament to the perceived presence of a substantial number of people yet to be convinced by either side.

The difference between the pro-choice march and the pro-life rally was that the march was able to play up its historical dimensions by drawing on a prevailing narrative in Irish society around oppression and liberation in which Catholicism is deeply negatively implicated.[13] The marchers could borrow from the past to create a kind of highly symbolic revolutionary pantomime, whereas the rally attendees strove to conceal their connections to history in a mirage of contemporary-seeming language and innocuous corporate imagery. In other words, the rally had a lot of tainted recent history to hide. The irony, of course, is that the group whose aim and values look to the future and largely revile the ideologies of the past can call on the symbols of history, whereas the side endeavoring to preserve traditional morality must block the past from view. This is a manifestation of the fact that, even though one of the starkest divisions in Ireland today is between conservative Catholics and liberal secularists, what really matters is the broad middle ground, people who ascribe fully to neither position. Over time, this middle group has drifted further and further away from the conservative sphere of influence, and more and more of them look askance at Church doctrines and indeed the Church itself. As the former Archbishop of Dublin Diarmuid Martin, has noted, there are now "few votes to be won through being closely linked with church issues."[14] At an address in Würzburg on the future of the Irish Church, he went further, describing increasing numbers of "vocal supporters of a much more hostile relationship" between church and state and noting that "alongside hostility to the Church one can identify integralist elements within the Church who see a Christian presence in a more pluralist culture purely in terms of a negative culture war."[15]

The Irish "culture war" entered a particularly heightened phase in the period from 2014 to 2018 and centered on tensions around the marriage equality and abortion referendums, alongside the Tuam affair revelations. These tensions manifested in an information and propaganda battle fought by opposing ends of the spectrum to influence the intricately graded center. Both sides claimed to represent silenced majorities. Structurally, the conflict was not quite the same as contemporaneous socially divisive struggles such as Leavers versus Remainers in the United Kingdom after the Brexit referendum or pro-Trump and anti-Trump camps in the United States. Irish society was not riven so clearly down the middle into two fiery, opposing camps. In interviews and fieldwork outside of rallies and marches, I noticed a considerable amount of reticence to disclose positions. Sometimes this was the product of genuine anguish and personal conflict, and sometimes it seemed more like a social screen that had been cultivated for the sake of collective harmony. Dedicated actors were attempting to cause this delicate ambiguity to collapse into one of two definite positions, hoping to either catalyze or forestall the secularization of the nominally, "culturally" Catholic.[16] The secularist side lured with a story of light overcoming darkness, whereas the conservative Catholics threatened with a story of darkness eclipsing light. Despite the compelling narratives offered by both sides, the battle was to reveal that secularists had utterly overtaken conservative Catholics in terms of public viability. What the sociologist Joseph Ruane in 1998 described as a fringe stance of "secular revisionism"—the view that the Holy Catholic past was a dark place indeed and that its institutional legacies should be overcome rather than preserved—is now burgeoning and mainstream.[17] This is resisted primarily by an aging minority of traditionalists whose views are shepherded by small cadres of reactionaries described decades ago by Ruane as "Catholic neo-conservatives."

At a basic level, both secular revisionism and Catholic neo-conservativism seek to limit harm, but their conceptions of how to achieve this, and of what constitutes harm, are diametrically opposed. In typical humanist style the secularist narrative seeks to expand the freedoms available to the individual and focuses on self-determination and individual conscience. It projects away from what it portrays as the dour gray past of Holy Catholic Ireland and looks toward the future with impatient optimism, observing the present with angry but confident frustration. Change is viewed as progress rather than degeneration, and institutionalized Catholicism is considered a repressive and controlling force that belongs in history. As one woman in her late 50s who has rejected Catholicism put it:

> The country grew up in a shadow of fear of the Catholic Church. The abuse suffered at the hands of Catholic leaders was horrific. Unmarried mothers were tortured and emotionally scarred for life because of religion. The division between north and south is based on religion. The Church offers nothing in return to people who commit themselves.

Although perhaps tolerable in privatized form, from this perspective Catholicism acts as an impediment to moral evolution; in particular, its continued institutional influence in domains such as health and education is perceived to hold Irish society back.

By contrast, the neo-conservative narrative is built on notions of unevenly distributed moral expertise and obedience to superior moral authority. Neo-conservatives are a collection of pressure groups who adhere to an anti-relativistic philosophy inspired by Pope John Paul II and later Pope Benedict XVI.[18] Neo-conservatism is a form of what is known as integralism, namely, the view that the Church should guide state policy on moral issues. The Iona Institute is a good current example of such a group. It primarily attempts to exert influence by appealing to a large aging bloc of traditional Catholics who can be "mobilized to try to block changes of which it disapproves."[19] The master trope promulgated by the Iona Institute and other neo-conservatives is that the freedom of the individual must be curtailed for what is perceived to be the greater good of the group, and this can be discerned only by the Church, because it is God's instrument. Neo-conservative ideology projects backward in time and sees Church influence as a guarantor of moral order and the past as a place of harmony and belonging; it regards the abuses of the time as exaggerated in contemporary discourse and unfairly overshadowing all the good that the Church has done. Unlike integralist movements elsewhere, neo-conservativism here must be retractionist: Catholic influence cannot be expanded in Ireland at the current historical moment, so neo-conservativism looks to the present instead, steeling itself to keep the faith pure and secure and to cling to the last bastions of influence. This perspective emphasizes obedience to the Church to protect absolute moral truths in the face of unchecked self-interested behavior that is perceived as stemming from a growth in amoral relativism, which is usually equated with secularism. By obeying the objective moral expertise of the Church, selfish inclinations are overcome and the collective good is preserved. Here is a stark example taken from *Alive!*, a conservative Catholic newspaper that sometimes arrives unsolicited in domestic letterboxes and that can also be found among the literature on offer in many churches:

> As a result not only secularists but vast numbers of Catholics now believe that "choice," "what I want," is the ultimate moral principle. You don't need to worship God. It's your choice. . . . You want sex without marriage, to "marry" someone of the same sex, to vote for a politician with harmful policies, to end your senile mother's life, or your own? All are your choice. . . . This leaves the way open for members putting their individual self-interest ahead of the community's shared good.[20]

Scandal as a Secularization Affordance

The principal driving force behind this antagonism is the institutional influence of the Church in Irish life. These are the structures left from the time when the relationship between church and state in Ireland really was an integralist one. One side wishes to maintain this influence, whereas the other wishes to do away with it. There are a few main forms of influence. One is the prevalence of a Catholic ethos in the state-funded education system, which means that most Irish children undergo some degree of religious socialization. Even though Catholic schools can no longer give entry preference to Catholic pupils (the "baptism barrier" was revoked in 2019), the process of opting out of religion classes in these schools is generally not considered an adequate compromise by many secularists. I have also heard rumors, in nonreligious parent groups and elsewhere, that loopholes exist by which schools can still discriminate on entry. Allegedly, methods for sabotaging parents' efforts to avoid their children's religious indoctrination (or at least rumors of such practices) also exist, and Atheist Ireland has reported that, in some respects, Catholic schools and religious instruction are actually more evangelical than they once were, contravening protections that are guaranteed in the Irish Constitution.[21] Another important source of Catholic influence is religious patronage in the healthcare system; religious voices on hospital ethics committees are seen as contributing to restricted access to procedures viewed as contrary to a Catholic ethos. As depicted at the outset of this chapter, perhaps the most divisive example of church-state influence was the legal restriction on reproductive rights enshrined in the Constitution in 1983.[22] And finally, these major entanglements are accompanied by secondary issues of a more symbolic nature that generate less heated controversy, such as blasphemy laws (quietly repealed by another referendum in 2018)[23] and the existence of an obligatory Christian prayer in Dáil Éireann, the Irish legislature. One by one, these battles have been lost by religious conservatives, but secular victory is not yet absolute. The primary focus of hostilities is currently the Catholic education system, and this is probably the most intractable and complex of all the Irish church-state intertwinements, given that the Church owns the lands on which its schools are built. As we have seen in the case of Peter, this is also an issue that cultural Catholics are less easily inflamed by. For now, the issue of lingering institutional influence looks set to continue, along with the stark, polarized hostilities it generates at the ideological fringes—though fringe positions can rapidly spread to become new orthodoxies.

In 1998 Joseph Ruane was of the view that if secular revisionists tried to achieve institutional secularization, they would face an insuperable backlash from a coalition formed by the neo-conservatives, their traditionalist backers, and the cultural Catholic middle ground. Today, the relative strength of secular revisionist and neo-conservative ideological influences has flipped, and this has a lot of implications for which way cultural Catholics might lean. But this change really required something else to take off properly: the emergence and proliferation of religious scandal and the manner in which this scandal can be linked to both the issue of lingering influence and the moral legitimacy of disengaged cultural Catholicism.

In the opinion of Archbishop Diarmuid Martin, the Church has a "credibility deficit,"[24] yet it maintains institutional control in certain key areas. Neo-conservativism must address this and explain it, whereas secularism can leverage it. This leads to secularist rhetoric that foregrounds the scandals and elicits powerful emotions of disgust, anger, and outrage at hypocrisy, conjoining these to contemporary institutional influence and creating an atmosphere in which it is difficult to defend neo-conservative positions. This, for example, was palpable in a typical 2017 post on the subject of the Tuam scandal on the PSS Facebook page (the PSS, discussed in Chapter 6, is a group of nonreligious parents seeking advice on navigating the Catholic education system).

> I really wish that I was shocked. I really wish that this was not our nation's history. I am sickened, disgusted and angered—as I was about the child sex abuse scandals too. . . . How this organisation can still claim to have any moral high ground is beyond me. . . . We owe it to ourselves to tell this bunch of hypocrites to keep their damn noses out of our Constitution (given the Pope wants to come here to advocate for the 8th Amendment. . . . Fuck off with that, your organisation has no moral ground left to stand on).

This rhetoric now produces almost instantaneous counterclaims of victimhood from some Catholic quarters when a new scandal comes to light. One bishop (Bishop Leo O'Reilly of Ferns), for instance, described the Ireland of 2016 as a culture "hostile to faith" and the Church as persecuted, adding, "There is denigration of religious beliefs, practices and institutions on radio, television and on social and other media. There is often a focus on bad news about the Church to the almost total exclusion of any good news."[25] In the article "Church-Bashing Is the New Brit-Bashing," David Quinn, founder of the Iona Institute, asks, "Why the continuous negativity about the Catholic Church? Why are we presented only with its misdeeds while the good it has done over the long centuries is kept hidden from our view?" He answers his own rhetorical question:

"Because that makes it all the easier to whip up public support for removing all significant public traces of it from national law and life."[26]

The production of rejoinders promotes further polarization. Rival victimhood claimants express outrage on seeing their legitimacy questioned. In terms of venues for confrontation, the internet plays a key role in heightening rhetoric and consolidating polarized positions; from war in the comments sections beneath articles, to Twitter screeds, to the production of online groups where ideological positions are competitively reinforced, the problems of geographic dispersal are overcome and the social risks of open stances are sidestepped. The flames are then fanned further, as articles oriented toward allies of either side or the petitioning of the undecided are shared on opposing online groups. For instance, Quinn's church-bashing article was shared among a secularist group I was monitoring (the PSS) and prompted such typical responses as the following: "So these fuckers want to claim Ireland for themselves once again. This shows how far out of touch they are. So, what does 'Catholic Ireland' stand for? Child abuse, hiding perverts, silence, trampling of women's rights??????? The list is endless." Bishop O'Reilly elicited similar comments.

> Persecution?? From the mouth of the bishop of fucking Ferns[27] of all places! He should look up the dictionary definition of persecution and take a long hard look at his own institution, in his own back yard in the very recent past before passing judgement on people legitimately criticising religion in the public sphere. The lack of self-awareness in these people is extraordinary.

When I was in the field, the Tuam affair brought home the degree to which scandal has enhanced the potency and efficacy of secular stances. Public outcry and media commentary were ignited when it was reported in 2014 and confirmed in 2017 that possibly hundreds of infants had been improperly buried in a defunct sewage system at the former mother and baby home run by the Bon Secours nuns in Tuam, County Galway. Rhetoric adopted the pattern described: secularists leveraging the issue to push for separation of church and state, and religious commentators diverting attention to the historical context and deflecting blame onto society as a whole, or portraying the nuns as victims of a hate campaign.

The situation was exacerbated when the minister for health subsequently announced that Ireland's new National Maternity Hospital (NMH) would be 100% owned by the Religious Sisters of Charity, an order that was involved in the running of Magdalene laundries and in the brokering of illegal adoptions in the past and that had failed to deliver its full commitments to the redress for institutional survivors. Concerns were promptly raised that the new hospital would be operated according to the order's Catholic ethos, and the plans were perceived by substantial numbers both as a continuing attempt by the Church to control women's fertility and as the product of unscrupulous backroom dealings between a craven state and a greedy, controlling Church. Protests ensued, and a petition to block ownership by the nuns was signed by 104,600 people.[28] The former master of the NMH, Peter Boylan, joined with other health professionals in strongly urging a total separation of the nuns from the NMH; he subsequently resigned after coming into conflict with colleagues on the board, further heightening tensions. In response, the nuns announced their intention to withdraw their involvement completely by transferring their shareholding to a private charity, and that "upon completion of this proposed transaction . . . [the] Ethical Code will be amended and replaced," implying that Catholic ethos would not impact women's reproductive healthcare at the new hospital.[29] After this apparent resolution, a high-profile member of the Sisters decried media representations of the nuns as "power-grabbing," alleging, "In another context, this would come under elder abuse"[30]—seemingly an effort to conjure up a kind of mirror image of the abuse of vulnerable people so often associated with the Church. This is but one small example of the way in which the word *abuse* activates when the Church is in mind, as swiftly as *priest*, *pew*, or *steeple*. It simply proffers itself.

Scandal is the moral herpes simplex from which the Irish Catholic Church suffers, breaking out constantly and blighting its efforts to push back against institutional secularization. On an issue-by-issue basis the constant emergence of horrors such as the Tuam affair allow the production of powerfully intuitive, clear challenges to moral stances linked to the Church. These do not require elaborate arguments or rhetoric and can be simply portrayed in pithy statements and images that can be instantly understood by anybody and transmitted with ease through word of mouth and electronic media. Tuam, for instance, was firmly yoked to the smoldering abortion issue, as evinced in a cartoon disseminated on the popular news website Journal.ie, which depicts a priest condemning a pro-choice activist from atop a mound of children's skulls (Figure 5.1). The image is rich but instantly digestible. It orients the characters in space to indicate hierarchical status in a way that is understood without much need for thought ("high" is up, "low" is down),[31] before swiftly subverting this with the details on closer scrutiny: the pyramid of children's skulls, a depressingly accurate rendering of the drab gates of the Tuam site. The pro-choice protester is depicted as calm under attack, the epitome of besieged forbearance: She is utterly rational and endlessly patient. The protestor is also in the foreground and her antagonist in the background, suggesting the present rolling its eyes at the past. The cleric

FIGURE 5.1. A post-Tuam pro-choice image published on Journal.ie. Source: Atheist Cartoons (https://atheistcartoons.tumblr.com/post/158200689064).

himself is shrill and hysterical, shrieking accusations from his insecure perch atop a mound of charnel. It is a powerful image of frantically defended, ill-gotten status and the profound moral hypocrisy that so often accompanies it. This is an example of Archbishop Martin's "credibility deficit," whereby the moral stances of institutions implicated in abuse are instantly and easily rendered suspect.

Public Rhetoric and the Question of Blame

Fissures do exist in secular revisionism, and the deepest ones relate to the question of blame. The most divisive issue revolves around how large-scale public complicity in the abuses and oppressive machinery of Holy Catholic Ireland ought to be addressed in the present. As Derek Scally has noted, unlike a country such as Germany, Ireland has not come to terms with the oppressive aspects of its history. Memorials remain vague plans; there are no permanent museum exhibitions; and school history textbooks do not describe institutional or clerical abuses or the features of Irish society that allowed them to happen. Politicians frequently blame society without acknowledging that society is composed of human individuals with varying levels of culpability who can be held to account for crimes. Despite numerous government reports, prosecutions for institutional abuses have been avoided. Survivors have described the processes for redress as antagonistic and retraumatizing. Much of the Irish population at large appear to feel disconnected from the abuses of the Holy Catholic past, as though they were something that happened in another country or something that has already been fully resolved. Amid this murk, half-formed accounts of the past circulate and are put to work in moral rhetoric. In particular, the opacity and complexity of the past allow rival interpretations to be leveled against one another in a process of irreconcilable blame attribution. Different public narratives can be used either to deflect blame away from the Church, by emphasizing people's support and complicity stemming from the puritanical attitudes of Irish society at the time, or to concentrate blame on the Church, either by maintaining that people were not complicit so much as coerced through fear of the Church's power or by claiming that their puritanical attitudes were the product of the Church's "brainwashing" influence.

Some commentators argue that one popular public conception is that the legacies of Holy Catholic Ireland have been triumphantly overcome. The past serves as a clerically dominated and unfree backdrop against which the globalized and liberalized present is contrasted. One of Ireland's foremost cultural commentators, Fintan O'Toole, describes this as "a way of thinking about the Ireland we inhabit that divides its consciousness into two states: a dark past and a bright future."[32] In 2011 cultural critic Emilie Pine described a growing "anti-nostalgia" in representations of the Irish past.

> We have seen so many allegations in recent years that we no longer question the meaning or consequence of melodramatic representations of one-dimensional sadistic religious figures. The implication of this is, of course, that not only are religious communities becoming identified with abuse, but that the past is also being held up as a scapegoat. The Irish past is, like the representatives of these institutions, being identified as a site of trauma.[33]

These types of "Celtic noir" representations are prominent in the sphere of mass media, which lends itself to stark representations of good and evil. Although the film *The Magdalene Sisters* (2002) is a sensitive and earnest treatment of Magdalene laundries, its trailer provides an interesting example of the type. The film is set in 1964 and tells a story of abuse at the hands of nuns in one such institution for "fallen" women. In the laundry of the film, the women are dehumanized and subjected to indentured servitude. The sequence of images in the trailer portrays cruel abuse and brave resistance, evoking empathy, outrage, and a feeling of ennoblement generated by being in the right alongside the unjustly treated. The trailer culminates with words that are a fusion of manifesto and historical retrospective: "Miramax films proudly presents the triumphant true story of three extraordinary women who found the courage to defy a century of injustice and inspire a nation." The subtext here suggests a hidden quasi-Christian rebirth, insinuating that the suffering of the Magdalene Sisters brought about an Irish transfiguration, that the trauma of the past was cathartic and necessary, and that it has been overcome. Such representations, particularly common during the Celtic Tiger boom, undergird a version of national identity that emphasizes pride in how thoroughly and swiftly modern Ireland has overturned and banished Holy Catholic nationalism. As Derek Scally describes, Magdalene survivors today can find themselves feted as heroes of the new, reformed Ireland, but it is not clear who really benefits from such celebrations, and these events may have the counterproductive effect of exculpating the state and society from further reflection.

A contrasting representation tends to focus on past public complicity and the gaps in present understanding, suggesting the necessity for greater examination of Ireland's history. For instance, around the time of the Tuam discoveries, Fintan O'Toole described acquiescence to injustice in pathogen-like terms as something that still "lurks in our bloodstream."

> In Ireland, we don't live in the past—but the past lives in us. The abusive relationship between church, State and society may, like the dead babies that have haunted us in recent weeks, be buried beneath the surface of our postmodern globalised reality. But its consequences still lurk in our bloodstream and until we understand them, the past will be our present and our future too.[34]

In its left-leaning format, this understanding draws on ongoing failures to bring adequate restitution to Holy Catholic Ireland's victims, a lack of clarity around issues of culpability, and the capacity of perpetrators to escape direct consequences. Politicians have shown themselves adept at making speeches and commissioning reports, but the consequences of this confrontation with the past are less clear-cut. The indemnification deal that the state made with religious congregations in 2002 has, according to victims' advocate Colm O'Gorman, allowed the Church to escape "much financial liability and all moral responsibility while still being allowed the power to challenge or dispute cases."[35] Relatively few clerical abusers have actually been punished, and most have been allowed to remain anonymous. The state also made extended efforts to minimize its responsibility for Magdalene laundries and, despite the recommendations of the UN Committee Against Torture in 2011, the religious orders directly responsible for running the institutions have avoided any financial contribution to the redress fund and have evaded the risk of their members being prosecuted for harms done. Ireland's post-independence identity as an enclave of morally pure Catholicism required infrastructure and institutions for suppressing those designated "impure." But there is political reluctance to view post-independence Ireland as a systemically abusive society requiring a broader process of redress. Aside from the involvement of church and state, widespread public complicity in and perhaps even enthusiastic approval of the oppressive systems and ideologies of the past may receive conspicuous reference in political handwringing, but this complicity fundamentally remains an unresolved and perhaps unresolvable issue. As Scally observed in one newspaper article:

> Oppressive regimes survive through compliance, both active and passive. . . . Our narrative to date has one major blind spot: it consistently misses the wood for the trees. It ignores "us" to focus on "them." That is because it remains a taboo to suggest that it wasn't just the priests or the politicians who kept Catholic Ireland alive for so long. It was also us, the Irish people.[36]

Scally goes on to make a number of interesting comparisons between Catholic Ireland and the East German regime, noting that Germans have today come to terms with their past, as evidenced by the DDR Museum and the Stasi Museum in Berlin, but that no similar institutions exist in Ireland, suggesting that it is time that such a monument to national complicity be built. The article concluded with an anonymous "Confession Box" phone service and email address that allowed troubled readers to call in and confess to instances of Catholic oppression and abuse that they had witnessed. As distinct from Celtic noir, we might call this stance of compound responsibility between church, state, and populace for a quasi-totalitarian system "mass complicity."

Mass complicity has found a cultural place on stage, including at Ireland's national theater, the Abbey Theatre. Emilie Pine, for instance, discusses "The Darkest Corner," a series of three works of documentary theater dealing with institutional abuse and its consequences, which was staged at the Abbey in 2010. One of the pieces, *No Escape* by Mary Raftery, is distilled from testimony included in the Ryan Report, and it compels its audience to directly confront the collective denial that allowed abuses to happen. In 2018 the Abbey staged *On Raftery's Hill* by Marina Carr, which uses the harrowing metaphor of incest to address Ireland's capacity to turn a blind eye to sexual abuse perpetrated by those in power. The same year, on its smaller Peacock stage, the Abbey premiered *Come on Home* by Philip McMahon, which revolves around a troubled small town family and the devastating effects exerted by their past toleration of an abusive cleric. Most recently, in March 2021 the Abbey produced *Home: Part One*, a curated series of readings from survivor testimonies included in the Mother and Baby Homes Report. Performed online because of the COVID-19 pandemic, the timing of *Home* deliberately coincided with Saint Patrick's Day; as the Abbey website proclaimed, "A day where we celebrate our identity should also be a day for us to reflect on Ireland's history and on the experiences of its citizens."

Perhaps the most extreme example was 2019's premiere of *Pasolini's Salò Redubbed* by Dylan Tighe.[37] Presented on the Peacock stage, this work consisted of a live redubbing of Pier Paulo Pasolini's 1975 film *Salò, or The 120 Days of Sodom*, itself loosely based on the Marquis de Sade novel.[38] Overdubbed live onstage by Irish actors, the film's context was transposed to real institutional abuses perpetrated in Holy Catholic Ireland. It opened with a speech by Tighe foregrounding the degree to which sadistic regimes exist because they are permitted to exist by those who turn a blind eye. Later, scenes of extreme violation, such as a powerful man forcing a helpless young woman to eat his excrement, were overdubbed with actual depositions from victims who had suffered similar treatment in Irish institutions, such as a boy forced to lick excrement off the ground by a Christian Brother. Watching *Pasolini's Salò Redubbed* was a deeply disturbing experience, and the uncanny fit between the footage and the archival Irish dialogue was undeniable. Toward the end, Tighe also deployed depositions from current asylum seekers, many of whom languish in a state of limbo in the country's Direct Provision Centres—frequently likened in left-leaning media discourse to a contemporary version of Ireland's dehumanizing midcentury systems of coercive confinement. He thereby created an extended version of mass complicity that reached into the present to absorb contemporary issues, asserting that Ireland today cannot distance itself from all such power relations and injustices by relegating them to "another time." One flustered critic asserted that "traumatising your audience is not art, it is an abuse of power."[39] But for all its ire, the reach of a production like *Pasolini's Salò Redubbed* is limited to a self-selecting liberal bohemian urban audience who largely already agree with its moral standpoint—and who perhaps even feel vindicated by it. Powerful as it can be, theater, with its narrow audience demographic, may lack the potential to bring about a large-scale reckoning. Indeed, theatrical productions and works of literature have long sought to incite public conversation on institutional abuses, sometimes decades before the era of scandal, such as Richard Johnson's play *The Evidence I Shall Give* (1961), Gerard Mannix Flynn's novel *Nothing to Say* (1983), or Paddy Doyle's memoir *The God Squad* (1988).

As deployed in public rhetoric, mass complicity contains substantial dangers. It must be handled carefully by all involved. It is potentially divisive for secularists, because it destabilizes and dilutes the hitherto powerfully cohesive and simple Celtic noir narrative and flirts with the arguments of the enemy. This has led to a discernible moral schism between secularist stances regarding systemic oppression. In the following example, the left-wing politician Luke "Ming" Flanagan attacks the mass complicity stance, summoning up a vintage Celtic noir vista of an entire population living in cowed terror (in overcrowded houses with barely enough to eat).

> When I hear the line that society was complicit in the latest church atrocity to be exposed, I get angry. Who are we on about here? People living in overcrowded houses with barely enough to eat. They were expected to speak out? Do I really need to write this? Do I really need to spell it out for those bullshit academics? Does one really have to say—But they too would have been incarcerated if they spoke out—Is this not obvious? Well it is obvious. But accepting this obvious truth can't be allowed. You see if we don't take the blame then the Church will need to. Sure we couldn't have that. Especially after all they've done for us.[40]

More dangerously for secularists, mass complicity can be deployed across the political and moral spectrums in pursuit of different agendas.

It is, for instance, the favored stance of tactical centrist politicians who wish to placate all sides while avoiding direct condemnation of extant institutions. Former taoiseach Enda Kenny, for instance, fulminated in a skillfully ambiguous manner after the 2017 Tuam revelations: "No nuns broke into our homes to kidnap our children. . . . We gave them up to spare them the savagery of gossip, the wink-and-elbow language of delight in which the 'holier than thou' were particularly fluent."[41] In other words, the "holier than thou" forced a generalized "we" to give up our children. The speech delivered by current taoiseach Micheál Martin after the publication of the Mother and Baby Homes Report in January 2021 closely followed Kenny's template but drew criticism from many quarters for an overemphasis on the collective culpability of the Irish public rather than of those in power. In such constructions as Kenny's and Martin's, mass complicity is used to anonymize and diffuse blame across all society: Institutions and individuals directly involved can rest easy, and the actual structures and social relationships that facilitated abuses can be simultaneously condemned and unexamined.

Worse still from a secularist perspective, arguments about public complicity can also be turned around and used by secularism's outright antagonists. Just as it carries the affordance of tying contemporary cultural Catholicism to abuse, mass complicity is also regularly exploited by Church apologists, who can argue that the Church, staffed by and catering to people who were of the time, had a public mandate to run oppressive institutions, which only reflected general social values rather than attitudes nurtured by religious authorities. By this reckoning, the Church is a completely different entity now and should not be held to task for past instances of oppression, nor should these past instances be instrumentally deployed in service of secularizing agendas. The volatile moral affordance of mass complicity is thus either hotly condemned by those who wish to keep blame tightly assigned to the Church or eagerly seized on by those who want to expand it.

Developments in Organized Secularism

In addition to having greater rhetorical resources, Irish secularism has developed a more solid organizational structure. In 1998 there was only one small pressure group, the Campaign to Separate Church and State. Today, an enormous range of dedicated groups are confronting individual causes that intersect with secularist concerns,[42] and the internet allows for geographically dispersed individuals with a strong commitment to secularist goals to form communities and self-organize in a way that was not possible before. Although they were a fairly peripheral presence in the Repeal the Eighth campaign because of the wealth of grassroots organizations more directly committed to the issue, one group—Atheist Ireland[43]—is deeply involved in efforts to secure further church-state decoupling, particularly around the education system. Atheist Ireland is quite numerically small and acts much like a mirror image of such neo-conservatives as the Iona Institute, in attempting to organize disparate interest groups to promote the further separation of church and state.

Atheist Ireland's motto makes its role clear: "Promoting atheism, reason and an ethical, secular state." Atheist Ireland began in 2006 as an online group aiming to combat anti-atheist prejudice, but today it functions as the country's most high-profile secularist lobby group. The group's members have addressed the United Nations, met with government ministers, and regularly act as foils for religious Catholics in television and radio debates.[44] Unlike some nonreligious organizations, Atheist Ireland is not particularly concerned with filling in the communitarian void left behind when religion withdraws; it does not provide services such as "Sunday Assemblies" or alternative secularized rituals for rites of passage (this duty falls more to the Humanist Association of Ireland). It is, essentially, a lobby group that advocates for the rights of atheists and other nonreligious individuals and for the secularization of Irish institutions more generally. One Atheist Ireland committee member told me that if Catholic institutional influence were fully overcome, then the group would have achieved its purpose and could be wound down. The mantle that Atheist Ireland has assumed has caused it to become more outwardly pragmatic and ecumenical than many New Atheist organizations in the United Kingdom or the United States. For instance, Atheist Ireland has formed an alliance of convenience with evangelical Christians and Ahmadiyya Muslims in pursuit of educational secularization and must now moderate its official language around religion accordingly. Overall, then, Atheist

Ireland acts primarily, and effectively, as an organizing centripetal force within the broader context of Irish secularization initiatives, campaigning alongside nonatheist secularists and minority religions to reduce Catholic influence.[45] Along with this shift in organizational power, Irish secularism as an ideology has also broadened its focus from combatting institutional influence and discrimination against non-Catholic minorities to actually getting people to question their status as Catholic in the first place. Cultural Catholicism, the prior default, is now in play.

The Obstacle of Cultural Catholicism

The true cultural obstacle for secularists is often seen to lie in the tendency of a broad swath of Irish people to go on affiliating as Catholic even though they sustain no obvious commitment to Catholicism in doxastic or moral terms.[46] This looser form of attachment is seen as being a relatively recent secularizing development (progressing from the 1970s and accelerating post-1990s), but it is not a particularly unusual characteristic for a contemporary Catholic society more generally. It is often understood that people will have varying degrees of proximity, including the most attenuated, to the Church while still remaining Catholics, and anthropologists of Catholicism have noted that in most Catholic cultures, "lapsed," "ethnic," or "cultural" variants are generally still considered Catholic by the rest of society, and many Catholic populations happily defy and disregard the moral precepts of the hierarchy when it suits them.[47] Why, then, does Catholic identity matter if it is so easily separable from commitment to the Church and its goals?

One aspect is that it is unpleasant for some people to note that, in the Church's view, having been baptized means that they have "become" Catholic ontologically and irreversibly,[48] whatever their current metaphysical views or stance toward the Church may be—an "anthropological link" that the Church believes leaves the door open for future re-evangelization.[49] Thus, if people who do not really adhere to Catholicism nevertheless choose to baptize their children for reasons of social expediency, they will then produce more ontological Catholics for the Church to claim.[50] Much more important, however, a self-defined Catholic of whatever stripe is a full-blown Catholic on paper so far as the national census is concerned.[51]

The number of "on paper" Catholics is then used to defend or challenge the continuing religious patronage of schools and hospitals and to make general claims about what it is Irish people collectively believe and want. The larger the group that can be claimed, the greater the power of ideological actors to influence the shape of social institutions, causing them to reflect their values. For this reason, Atheist Ireland has expended great effort in getting the census religion question changed to a format that does not encourage habitual affiliation. These moves have been successful, and the 2022 Irish census (deferred from 2021 because of the COVID-19 pandemic) will be designed to incorporate a slightly modified question structure that is likely to reduce Catholic numbers somewhat.

How people describe themselves on the census is thus of enormous interest to secularists and neo-conservatives, and census results are endlessly used to defend opposite agendas. Secularists emphasize the growth of nonreligion and the problematic nature of the census's religion question to claim that nonreligious people are both burgeoning and underrepresented, especially in the education system.[52] Religious conservatives regularly cite that the majority of the population is Catholic to claim that any moves toward institutional secularization, such as the reform of abortion laws, are being forced on an unwilling public. Leaders of ideological groups confront one another across the media, projecting these issues into popular consciousness. In one radio debate, for instance, Michael Nugent, head of Atheist Ireland, noted that census forms are often filled in by "heads of households," meaning that younger nonreligious household members are often entered as Catholic. He noted that the question itself assumes a religion and thereby encourages high levels of natalist religious responding among people who neither practice nor believe ("What is your religion?" rather than "Do you have a religion?"). He cited that "8% of Irish Catholics said that they don't believe in God, which would be a low hurdle for Catholics."[53] His antagonist, David Quinn of the Iona Institute, executed a more sophisticated rearguard defense than the usual gesturing toward the Catholic census majority. He accepted that Catholicism had declined and that Catholic census identification may not mean full support for a neo-conservative agenda, but he quoted European Values Study statistics on self-reported theism among Irish "nones" to argue that the "fact that so many 'nones' believe in God and even pray daily means they cannot simply be claimed by atheist organizations for themselves, and cannot be simplistically used as part of the campaign against church-run schools."[54] Here, Atheist Ireland's exclusive legacy name was tacitly used to undermine its broader secularist agenda.

For secularists, although religious conservativism may be the source of the ideologies they abhor and although institutional Catholic entrenchment may be the proximate cause of their perceived oppression, a primary force to be reckoned with is the power of cultural Catholic inertia that they believe sustains Church power. Cultural Catholic tendencies risk that the goals of absolute religious privatization will be interminably deferred, that the number of Irish Catholics will continue unabated, and that Irish schoolchildren will go on having their "faith formed" forever. Even though much of the secularist effort goes into directly fighting church-state influence, another important aim is to get potential census "swing voters" to observe the dissonance between their reported status as Catholics and their rejection of beliefs and, more especially, moral values disseminated by the Church. It is hoped that this will lead them to "awaken" and shed their inertial identity, thereby curtailing production of further ontological and bureaucratic Irish Catholics through the practices of baptism and box checking. The scandals once again enter the picture at this juncture.

Moral Contamination as Disaffiliation Incentive

In an op-ed in *The Irish Times*, the popular film critic and cultural commentator Donald Clarke lamented that, even though the Tuam story "buzzed furiously about social media" and even though the minister for children and youth affairs had branded it "a shocking reminder of a darker past in Ireland when our children were not cherished like they should be," it still had not conjured up the appropriate levels of disgusted withdrawal. Irish Catholics, and in particular cultural Catholics, still had not realized their complicity.

> Last month the streets teemed with dolled-up children making their way to and from First Communions. The average couple still gets married in

church. The vast majority of newborn babies are baptised. Even secular cremations tend to take place in grey rooms decorated with stone crosses and images of the suffering Christ. . . . After all that has been revealed, the time has surely come to raise eyebrows at the agnostics, atheists and the loosely committed who go through the rituals because they "like the tradition" or don't want to upset older relatives. Many non-believers of my generation convinced themselves they were the last heathens who, terrified of fanged, rosary-swinging aunts, would feel compelled to marry in church. It still goes on.[55]

This is an object of frustration for Atheist Ireland as well as for Donald Clarke. Atheist Ireland leaders appeared to be cautious around the blunt deployment of religious hypocrisy. One woman, the moderator of Atheist Ireland's online Facebook group, told me that clerical abuse is a difficult topic to deal with; some posters to the group, in particular older men whom she suspects have been damaged by experience, would inveigh against the Church in no uncertain terms. She permitted this, but was evidently somewhat conflicted about it, lest the organization be accused of simply being anti-Catholic.

However, in 2016, Atheist Ireland launched an online campaign, "Time to Tick No," to encourage Catholic disaffiliation on the upcoming census. One strand of the campaign was focused on belief, encouraging those with no doxastic commitment to Catholic doctrine, such as those interested in spirituality or the New Age, to disaffiliate. Another strand made tactical use of Catholic immorality, as in Figure 5.2, which includes references to three forms of scandal alongside the issue of continued educational dominance. The perception here is clear that emphasizing harm and oppression is a key ingredient in getting complacent cultural Catholics to drop a tainted affiliation. The color choices in the original image are also noteworthy: the use of nationalist green for the text denoting the merits of a future post-Catholic (and apparently unified) Ireland, juxtaposed against a drab institutional gray for the list describing the unsecularized present.

The acceptability of making such connections waxes and wanes according to the degree to which scandal is present in the environment at

FIGURE 5.2. Propaganda for the "Time to Tick No" campaign. Source: "Time to Tick No" campaign page, Facebook, 2016.

any given time. When scandal is in the air, cultural Catholicism is more frequently portrayed as outright complicity rather than mere obliviousness, both in the media and in secularist discourse. This underlying theme became far more overt, even in this official outlet, in the wake of the Tuam affair, when the Atheist Ireland Facebook moderator posted a series of images and statements explicitly linking cultural Catholic affiliation to complicity in Church abuses, such as the image in Figure 5.3, which was accompanied by the following statement: "If you want a school place, demand one from your politicians and the Department of Education. Don't submit to fake Catholicism. Every single baptised child in Ireland is a fresh vote to retain the insidious, hateful organisation known as the 'Catholic Church.' We, as free Irish people need to make this change."

Another post elaborated on the theme in more detail.

> Dear People of Ireland, what exactly will it take for you to disassociate yourselves from this disgusting organisation which hides dead babies, hides paedophiles (y'know . . . child rapists) and then doesn't even

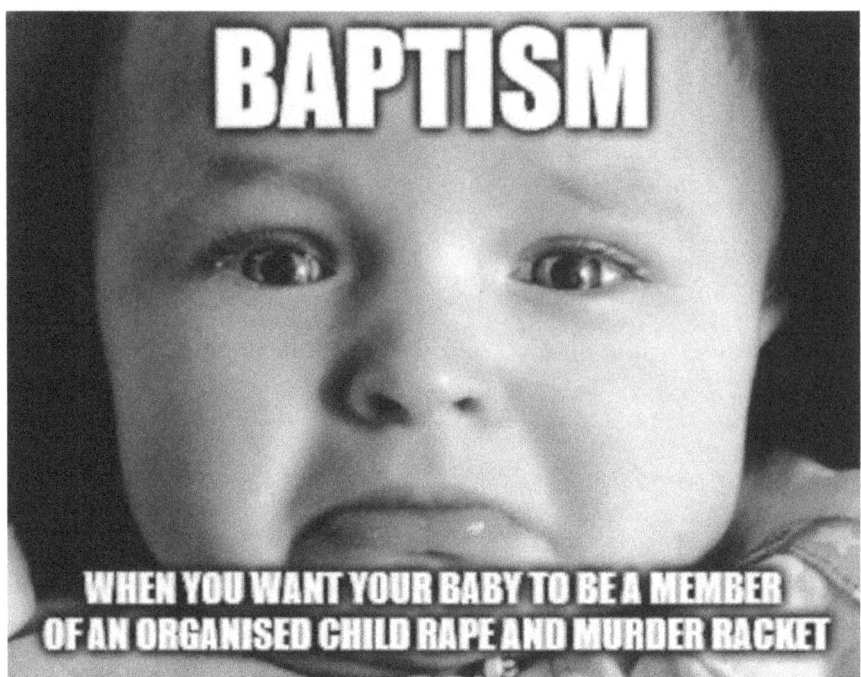

FIGURE 5.3. Image posted on "Time to Tick No" Facebook page in the aftermath of the Tuam affair.

bother to pay in full the redress scheme for survivors and then has the sheer fucking audacity to lecture us on the value of life? You sell yourselves and your identity for a "church wedding" and fake baptise your children for a school place and have a communion or confirmation for a piss up. Where were your ashes on Wednesday? When was the last time you were at mass? Do you even know what transubstantiation means, never mind believe it? Our republic can never be free until you free yourself from your group Stockholm Syndrome with the Catholic Church. #TimetoTickNo#Repealthe8th[56]

The address to the "People of Ireland" solidly foregrounds institutional complicity in harm-causing behavior, bypassing potential "bad apple" style arguments, and connects the contaminated ("disgusting") institution's abuses to contemporary policies (opposition to abortion), rendering them hypocritical. Cultural practices are then portrayed as a form of complicity in the vilest crimes. Worse still, these cultural practices are also exposed as inauthentic, in that they are not motivated by Catholic belief; cultural Catholics have no excuse, not even indoctrination—they are at best in thrall to a psychological malady (Stockholm syndrome). The meme (Figure 5.3) operates by "exposing" the true cost of the moral compromises involved in cultural Catholicism.

These materials also raise questions. Who were they for, exactly? The official propaganda material itself in Figure 5.2 could be precisely demographically targeted. The more extreme slogans and images such as Figure 5.3 existed in private groups and would in effect have been preaching to the converted. They could be best understood as infusing preexisting sympathizers with a sense of purpose around upcoming conflicts and encouraging the zeal necessary for further proselytization. Such is the aggression of these statements that, if they had been shared by group members on their own pages, it is difficult to see how they would have swung cultural Catholic acquaintances rather than merely alienating them. Images and statements such as these certainly indicate the extent to which the outright rejection of Catholicism can be easily constructed as a moral virtue, something that owes a lot to the scandals. But they also demonstrate another factor: frustration. The scandals have not had the full disaffiliating effect that some believe they should. If Ireland is more secular than it pretends, it is also more comfortable with this pretense than many purist secularists would like.

The 2018 Abortion Referendum and the Unmasking of the Ambiguous Middle

On May 26, 2018, the Irish public voted to repeal the Eighth Amendment to the Irish Constitution, paving the way for the liberalization of Irish abortion laws, then among the strictest in the world. In the run-up to the referendum, there was near universal consensus that the vote would be tight. By legal obligation, ideologically balanced national media debates created an impression of two equally well-supported positions. Surveys suggested a great deal of uncertainty among the public on which way they would vote, and there was much talk of misleading polls concealing a "shy no" to the liberalization of abortion laws, especially in the wake of such unpredictable international phenomena as Brexit and the election of Donald Trump.

The pro-life side benefited from extensive international funding, and it opened its campaign first. Within days, Ireland's lampposts and billboards were trimmed with posters that foregrounded imagery of children, babies, fetuses, and ultrasound scans. The campaign used a sophisticated and multifaceted assortment of emotive tropes. The most visible pro-life group, Love Both, called from door to door in distinctive pink high-visibility vests and spoke with pedestrians on the streets in towns and cities across Ireland, carefully calibrating their messaging to express the campaign's loving concern for both the unwanted unborns *and* the anguished pregnant women who carried them (hence the group's name). This also came across in their caring slogan: "There is *always* a better option." The pro-life campaign tools included materials personifying the fetus ("Mammy, what colour eyes will I have?"), testimony from supportive medical professionals, "slippery slope" arguments regarding extreme potential outcomes, and populist misgivings about untrustworthy politicians who should not be given free rein to implement abortion legislation. Beyond this, billboards and posters tapped latent Anglophobia with bleak statistics from the old enemy: "In England, 1 in 5 babies are aborted—don't bring this to Ireland." At conservative rallies, populist rhetoricians channeled nationalism by summoning up implicit schemas of plucky Irish resistance to unjust power, and posters urged everyman voters to "Join the Rebellion" against the Dublin political elite's liberalizing ambitions. Overt religious motivation was generally refrained from by the main organizing groups.

The pro-choice side (or Repeal the Eighth campaign) seemed to be on the back foot at first, entering the public fray belatedly and saddled with a more complex and perhaps less poster-friendly case. Repeal's campaign was no less emotive than Love Both's, channeling as it did issues of women's personal autonomy and equality, the tragedy of fatal fetal abnormalities and other health risks, the extent to which Irish women were already procuring abortions in the United Kingdom and elsewhere, and the past mistreatment of women and children in Church-run institutions such as Magdalene laundries and mother and baby homes. Toward the end though, it was telling that the word *abortion* was notable by its absence in prominent campaign materials, many of which consisted of a simple "Yes!" against a background of bright colors. This was an apparent attempt to tap into the feel-good factor associated with the 2015 "Tá" (Irish for "yes") campaign for the legalization of marriage equality, a diversionary tactic that did not imply confidence in the ability to win based on the facts of the issue at hand.

When it ultimately came to pass, then, the emphatic nature of the Repeal victory was greeted with widespread surprise: 66.4% of voters were in favor, with 33.6% against. This was an even more resounding secularist victory than the marriage equality referendum, which had passed with a majority of 62%. In Dublin Castle, Repeal revelers gathered in jubilation, much as many had done in response to the legalization of same-sex marriage. Some cried in disbelief, such was their relief at the result. Some had been campaigning for most of their lives, ever since the Eighth Amendment had first been instituted in 1983. Others spoke of suddenly feeling like they belonged, that society was catching up and molding itself to what they viewed as their own, more contemporary values. Media commentators framed the event as a kind of moral and political maturity, particularly in an era when other nations—notably England and the United States—seemed to be backsliding into reactionary politics. Much was made of the fact that the shy no turned out to be a shy yes. Internationally, Ireland cemented its position as a moderate centrist darling, the result making headlines and approving editorials in the *New York Times*, the *Washington Post*, and elsewhere. Toward the end of 2018, popular economist and columnist David McWilliams published a book on the new Ireland and the "million little mutinies" that had brought it to fruition. He called his book *Renaissance Nation*. But despite this proud image of an unexpected frontrunner nation in the international leagues of progressivism, realities were more complex. Anthropologists Ella Drażkiewicz and Tom Strong raise the plausible point that a powerful component in the Repeal victory was not a highly progressive liberal majority but the encouragement of the Repeal side to get women who had procured abortions abroad (all 200,000 of them) to discuss their experiences with friends and families. As a result, "When the symbolic war escalated in the last few weeks before the vote, the overwhelming majority of 'Middle Ireland' did not hear the abstract phrase 'abortion = murder,' but you are calling *my* wife, daughter, cousin and/or aunt a murderer."[57]

The result was a bitter disappointment for the pro-life side. One consequence of the vote was that right-wing ideological conservatives could no longer claim to represent a silenced moral majority. Some swiftly turned wrathful. The celebrations in Dublin Castle were portrayed in some quarters almost as a kind of near-orgiastic, secularist bacchanalia: Two-thirds of Ireland's electorate had been deluded into sacrificing the nation's "preborn babies" out of vanity and conformity, eager to be at the vanguard of trends in international progressivism. They were the unwitting dupes of a neoliberal, corporation-friendly elite waging a "phony war" on "Taliban Ireland" to hide their own socioeconomic selfishness.[58] Some international rhetoric, for example, in *The Spectator*, argued that Ireland's liberalizing populace was as submissive and dogmatic as they had ever been under the crozier. Enraged by their unforeseen betrayal, some more vocal conservative religious commentators turned on the nominally Catholic populace, decrying the result as exposing "rank hypocrisy" among the Catholic "78%" as declared in the census. A handful of outspoken conservative clerics threatened to withhold such omnipresent social rites of passage as First Communion from the children of those who had betrayed the wishes of their Church. The referendum result was blamed on factors ranging from the reluctance of prominent clergy to step up and provide vocal leadership to biased meddling in online advertising by Google and Facebook. Pro-life leaders promised to fight oncoming legislation every inch of the way. In a certain sense, the hammer blow of the referendum may even have re-energized some conservative Catholic voices, who could reposition themselves as rebel outsiders fighting the good fight against a brainwashed, baby-killing population. A few fell back on the power of prayer. *Alive!*, the free conservative Catholic newspaper, carried an advertisement exhorting believers to place their hands on a "blessed map of Ireland EVERY DAY" to "block abortion by prayer" because the "battle is not over!"

Most religious observers, however, seemed more crestfallen than reinvigorated. Archbishops and bishops, unusually silent during the campaign for fear of doing damage to their cause, did not know what to say afterward. Their fighter's optimism that the momentum of Irish secularization would stall at this final, critical obstacle suddenly looked misplaced. In retrospect, the outcome was unsurprising. The referendum was not the birth of a new moral order so much as its long-delayed baptism. It revealed just how far the population had shaken off orthodox Catholic obeisance, high levels of sacramental participation and Catholic census affiliation notwithstanding. These facets of Irish life could no longer be used to claim widespread endorsement of the Church and its values. The frequently deployed conservative trope of a cowed, devout majority silenced by media-elite secularists became unsupportable.

But even when they were unmasked in this way, the middle continued to prove ambiguous in other respects. They had no interest in the moral advice of the Church, but they strongly preferred that RTÉ Radio should keep playing the *Angelus*, a daily Christian devotion broadcast for one minute at noon as a "moment for reflection" signaled by the repeated sounding of a church bell.[59] They were pro-choice, but they seemed happy for the Catholic Church to "form faith" and dictate the contents of moral education in schools. Tensions regarding secularization are not as high as they once were, but they have entered a new and perhaps more enduring phase.

The Continuing Struggle for Irish Freedom (from the Church)

Church scandals are global, but they play out in local contexts. In Ireland this context has involved a high level of church-state influence in the past, a background of social liberalization, the relegation of religion to a much more quarantined sphere, the emergence of a new default of low-cost cultural Catholicism, and a present where the Church nevertheless retains lingering influence in certain social institutions and legal frameworks. This creates tensions, as state institutions are seen by some to be less secularized than the population at large. Under these circumstances, lingering influence is sometimes understood by dedicated secularists as persisting because of the intersection of a cowardly state, a cunning Church, and a complacent populace.

In his book *Ethical Life: Its Natural and Social Histories,* anthropologist Webb Keane describes the social world as "saturated with the ongoing business of establishing one's ethical worth in the eyes, or ears, of others."[60] Ireland is no different. Here as elsewhere, people draw on available moral affordances—the events thrown up by historical circumstance—to formulate and promulgate their stances in more effective ways, or to undermine the arguments of their opponents. In this febrile environment, clerical abuse combines with past systems of oppression to summon up powerful and, some would argue, pan-human moral intuitions of anger at the sheer unfairness of the hypocrisy involved, the harm done to individual lives, and the restriction of liberty and freedom of thought and deed, not to mention the sense of disgust elicited by many of the violations themselves. These intuitions then find themselves bound up in a potent narrative, and the past itself comes to be viewed as an inverted empire of perversion and oppression. The pursuit of secularization becomes a kind of moral mission of national cleansing. If those of previous generations wore pins or medallions indicating membership of a religious sodality, today some display badges signaling their secular credentials with equal pride (Figure 5.4). Irish secularism relates to an anxious hunger to be as modern as possible, but it keeps a cautious eye on the past as well.

This worldview is potentially rendered even more compelling because of the way it maps onto existing schemas of Irishness. Although it runs afoul of the traditional fusion of Irish ethnic and religious identity, it can be conceptualized by those embedded in it as the continuing struggle for "Irish freedom." As a result—and somewhat like a church built on the ruins of a pagan temple—this stance maps perfectly, and often quite explicitly, onto the age-old Irish schema of oppression-induced solidarity through resistance to an occupying force of greater power. For some, it forms the latest iteration of how Irish people have learned to view themselves as a collective historical entity for generations, a view based in colonial suffering and refreshed each generation in the school history classroom. Emilie Pine is right about the Irish past being reconstructed as a site of trauma, but the Irish past has been viewed as a site of

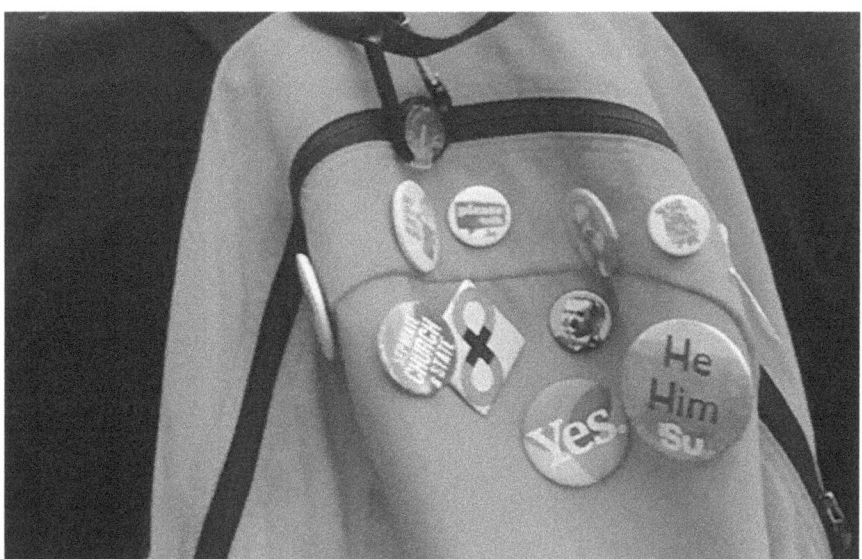

FIGURE 5.4. The symbols on these badges represent a kind of hybrid liberal nationalism: the fight to free Ireland from the Vatican and make it an exemplar of progressive modernity. Note the presence of 1916 nationalist martyr James Connolly alongside a rainbow-colored "separate church and state" and Repeal-related symbols. As a socialist, Connolly is a useful secular bridge to the Easter Rising, providing secularists with an excellent alternative to Catholic nationalists such as Patrick Pearse or Éamon de Valera. Source: Author's photograph.

trauma for a long time—it is from trauma that Irish identity is derived.[61] The primary architect of that trauma for secularists is the Vatican, not London, and it is the cultural Catholic who is the new home ruler. Catholic nationalist tropes of endurance under oppression, plucky resistance to power, martyrs for the cause, and the dream of long-deferred freedom have been successfully reformulated to fit the Irish secularization struggle. To a great many "likes," this was summed up on Facebook as follows by one pro-choice supporter in the wake of the referendum decision to repeal the Eighth Amendment and legislate for abortion:

> We've been colonised by Vikings, Normans and English, but the worst offenders have been the Roman Catholic Church. They beat and raped and killed our children, enslaved and silenced our women and told us we'd go to hell for questioning them. Today, the church is hanging on

by its fingertips and we just took a hammer to their hands. The future is ours!

As a result of this potent new moral stance, rather than something to be hidden, avoided, or denied, Catholic disaffiliation can be publicly enacted as an expression of personal moral integrity and civic concern. As we will see in the next chapter, the disaffiliated often conceptualize themselves as a kind of awakened moral vanguard of an idealized future Ireland.

CHAPTER 6

"AWAKENING FROM CONSCRIPTION"
EX-CATHOLICISM AS ANTI-NOSTALGIC MORALIZED AUTHENTICITY

The Moral Rejection of Catholicism

Ex-Catholic is a catch-all term used here to describe all those who were baptized but who would no longer claim the label "Catholic" in any way. Few would explicitly reach for the term unprompted; rather, they would almost always give a firm no if asked whether they were Catholic. Although certain demographic variables (notably, youth) are strong predictors, ex-Catholics are dispersed throughout society, congregating only in a minority of instances as an ideological community and, even then, generally doing so in the virtual world. Furthermore, this gathering is usually in response to particular topics of concern rather than a result of a shared identity based on religious rejection. Being ex-Catholic hovers just at the brink of being an explicitly held collective identity, although there are a great many ex-Catholics. Because the Church has grown weaker and its foot soldiers are fewer and less zealous, it could be that being ex-Catholic is only really salient at certain key moments and in response to a particular set of battleground issues. When the Church must be faced down or its influence broken, ex-Catholicism is activated. Under these antagonizing conditions, disaffiliation can become more closely and more consciously tied to the ex-Catholic's self-conception. In such moments, boundaries are robustly erected around what one is *not*: One is not allied with the perceived prudishness and authoritarianism of conservative Catholicism, but, perhaps even more important, one is also not a docile cultural Catholic blithely preserving the last theocratic dregs of the status quo.

Even though many ex-Catholics could be described as atheist, not all are; and those who do fall into this category by virtue of their lack of belief in a God or gods do not necessarily subscribe to a doctrinaire New Atheist worldview or even identify with the term *atheist* in the first place. In this chapter my primary concern is with the broad majority of ex-Catholics who might be defined more generally as nonreligious. Whether they see themselves as atheistic, humanistic, spiritual, or agnostic or have even given little or no thought to the matter, they have not aligned themselves with some other religious tradition after rejecting Catholicism. (This kind of affiliative switching, famously common in the United States because of its consumerist marketplace of sects, is rarer in Ireland.) What comes closest to binding this large and highly varied group of people—and allows them, for these purposes, to be treated as a category—is their explicit, self-conscious, and generally *moral* rejection of Catholic affiliation.

Ireland's "nones" are bound by a moral cord. Few are motivated to disaffiliate by apathy or indifference alone. Religious indifference tends to result in cultural Catholicism of the various types described previously. In contrast, the nonreligious often perceive themselves to be taking a stance against conformity, ease, and fecklessness. As the survey in Chapter 2 suggested, again and again, such factors as conservatism, abuse, the hypocrisy of the Church, the hypocrisy of other Catholics (especially cultural Catholics), and onerous social pressure are key markers in the trajectory toward ex-Catholicism. And when the nonreligious think of the Catholic Church, the image that springs instantly to mind is the negative one consisting of historical abuses and current conservativism. A more explicitly atheistic subgroup (usually male) often also asserts the rational rejection of implausible ontological content as the root cause of their disaffiliation, but even in these instances moral factors often simmer beneath the cool analytical façade. The picture that emerges overall is that the growth in Irish nonreligion should be understood to exist not only as a heightened moral opposition to the Church—especially when it is seen to encroach on the business of the state—but also, and perhaps even more so, as a rejection and condemnation of habitual, "cultural" affiliation.

What follows is a particularly comprehensive, articulate, and prototypical account of moral disaffiliation, related by Diane, a 32-year-old professional from a suburb in North Dublin. This is a woman's narrative, and its focus resides squarely on the Church's moral failings, in particular, the troubling effects it is perceived to have had on women's lives.

> It has created a lot of guilt and oppression for generations. It has been used to control and punish people and has slowed down the country's intellectual and economic development. It has particularly had a negative effect on women's rights and helped to establish the view that all women are seen either as virgins, mothers, or whores and that they do not hold the rights to their own bodies, either in terms of sex or reproduction (which are two separate things). It held such a choke hold on the country that it was able to, for years, facilitate the physical, sexual, and psychological abuse of children by hypocritical authoritarian priests who preached one thing and did another and whose offenses were routinely covered up as a matter of course in a society where laypeople feared speaking out against the regime of the Catholic Church. Sorry, I've gone on a bit of a rant and can't even remember the question.

Oppression, violation, hypocrisy, and the moral straitjacket placed on women are the central themes provided here. In order, Diane's free list associations with the term "Irish Catholic Church" were old, priest, Mass, school, oppressive, grannies, self-righteous, stranglehold, dreary, dead, sex abuse scandals, cover-up, power, history. Not surprisingly, Diane no longer considers herself Catholic. In a number of conversations held on the topics of religion and other social issues, she generally held liberal views. In terms of theism, at times Diane would espouse a stridently atheist position. This was framed not so much in a humanistic idiom so much as a stark anti-natalist one: Life is pain, we should never have been born. She once quoted the character Pozzo's grim summary of the human experience from Samuel Beckett's *Waiting for Godot*: "They give birth astride a grave, the light gleams an instant, then it's night once more."[1] At other moments she veered more optimistically toward the agnostic. This seemed to depend on her mood at the time, with dark moments triggering lapses into a kind of bleak antihumanistic materialism, whereas lighter moods would prompt her to rejoice in the beauty of the natural world around her and in her relationships with other people. When she discussed Catholic belief, she sometimes used metaphors pertaining to madness and schizophrenia—organized religion was a kind of sanctioned insanity, a sort of mass control achieved through the cultivation of delusion. Diane's own positions on matters ontological and spiritual were thus in a constant state of self-reflective exploration. Some years later I carried out a follow-up interview and, while she could probably still be best described as atheist or agnostic in a strict sense, the antihumanistic element appeared to have gone, replaced by a Spinoza-like emphasis on the profound interconnection of all being. Her views on Catholicism remained basically the same: Although Catholicism was tolerable at a personal level as a source of spiritual comfort for others, it was philosophically stunted and morally warped. At a public level the Church was a negative influence to be opposed.

Both of Diane's parents still consider themselves Catholic, but she primarily remembers her exposure to Catholicism while growing up in terms of habit and pressure. She reported the feeling that, though her parents brought her to Mass regularly as a child, it was a "chore" and an "inconvenience" that was "not enforced any more than any other banal expectation parents have of their children." Mass attendance was allowed to slide once it became more socially acceptable to do so. Despite this, what domestic religiosity there was, was accompanied by self-righteous disapproval. Her father would at times refer to her as a "heretic" in a "quasi-abusive fashion" if she expressed disbelief: "What *do* you believe in, then? Nothing, I suppose?" This was despite what Diane described as her father's signature inactivity on matters religious: He did the bare socially obligatory minimum, that is, Sunday Mass. Some members of her father's extended family were more devout, but Diane associated this with narrowness; as she said of a pious aunt, "It seemed to make her life smaller somehow." Nevertheless, Diane warmed to religion classes in school, not so much because she was enticed by the message itself but rather because it "was an easy subject" involving songs, stories, and the "comforting aspects of religion." She noted that "Holy Communion and Confirmation were exciting events associated with rewards and status" but that "outside of when we were 'doing religion,' it wasn't really part of school life."

This experience of Catholicism—little more than an inauthentic and enforced habit at home and a quarantined "fairy tale" reprieve from routine in school—was shared by many informants. Yet, though Diane reported drifting away from any kind of religious belief during the 1990s at about 16 years of age, like many she continued to passively identify as a Catholic for much longer, up to 2011.

> After the 2011 census, when I entered myself as Catholic and subsequently realized that I had just put this down because I felt I had to, as though honoring some strange sense of conscription, I considered that this sort of response was possibly hugely falsely inflating the numbers of Catholics that the Church was able to claim were extant in the country, which they can then use to wield power and lobby the government on issues such as abortion and marriage equality. I don't want to be a number in their favor that can be employed in service of agendas I vehemently disagree with. And I'm really not a Catholic.

Somehow, reflecting on filling out that census form in 2011 produced a kind of awakening: She had never really believed; she disagreed completely on a moral level, so next time around she would no longer call herself Catholic. Catholicism as an oppressive, immoral force had become more salient than her own pallid and ambiguous lived experiences of it. She became aware of her passive complicity, and she cast off an uncherished identity marker of which she had barely really been aware. "Catholic" shifted from dutiful irrelevance to moral stain as it became connected in her mind with the Church's past abuses of power and its ongoing social influence.

Diane's case offers a complete example of the rejection of Catholicism. Childhood religion was simultaneously dull and oppressive, a shell of sanctimonious conformity. Despite this, religion was sustained to some degree in the school environment but also deeply associated with it, thereby infantilizing it. As Diane got older, she became more aware of how the Catholic Church supported a suite of conservative moral values that she opposed and that, far more in the case of women than men, affected her personally. In her view the Church's era of control in the past, where it enforced these values, was marked by harm and oppression. Furthermore, the Church itself, in addition to some of its operatives, was hypocritical and the most profound violator of basic human values, including those it claimed to endorse. To cap it all, despite its outrages, it continued to collude with the state to maintain some measure of control and influence, retarding moral progress. By maintaining a Catholic identity, Diane supported this—thus a Catholic identity in itself was seen as wrong. Finally, she realized that she never really believed in the dogma anyway.

Ex-Catholicism, more than anything, is about casting off the paper-thin chrysalis of an identity connected to an institution and set of values judged as immoral. Naturally other trajectories and forms exist, but from my interviews and ethnographic fieldwork, this appeared to be the dominant one. One corollary of this is that ex-Catholicism is an explicit repudiation of cultural Catholicism as much as religious Catholicism. At times, it is even more explicitly anti–cultural Catholic than anti–believing Catholic (the latter have excuses—brainwashing, weakness, and so on), though the Church, generally, is the cardinal evil. Despite the fact that men are more likely to identify as atheist and to join groups such as Atheist Ireland, ex-Catholicism often seems more impassioned among women. This is almost definitely because women, though many may also have been the Church's domestic enforcers, were greater victims of Holy Catholic Ireland, thanks to such factors as the Magdalene laundries, the mother and baby homes, domestic relations in a patriarchal society where a man could not be convicted of raping his wife until 1990, and the legislation against abortion that was only recently repealed in 2018. It is women who feel that their rights remain the most infringed, thanks to what many describe as the misogynistic streak that runs through Irish Catholicism, even though it is also women who remain most likely to cleave to the faith.

This trajectory was prominent in open-ended survey responses from women in Atheist Ireland. Women were more likely to tie their rejection specifically to moral factors than men, who were more likely to lead with colder claims of rational repudiation. A respondent in her 30s provided a typical account, describing how, "as a woman, I couldn't understand why my parents were supporters of a religious organization which discriminates against women." She described further how she began to feel "very uncomfortable at the Catholic Church's attitude towards survivors of clerical abuse, and their attitude towards LGBTQIA people." At first, this led her "to leave the Catholic Church, and to find a different religion which meshed better with my values. Then I realized that in fact, I didn't believe in the existence of any higher power at all." A young woman in her 20s described how she "just found the Catholic Church to be so hypocritical. I couldn't make my peace with a church that would systematically abuse the most vulnerable in our society and then cover it up. I began to find some of the teachings and beliefs absolutely ridiculous. I started to read more about science and watched documentaries by Richard Dawkins. I found the Church's response to the Repeal the Eighth movement in Ireland abhorrent, and I just decided I'd had enough of all religion." Here, moral antipathy leads to the discovery of rational rejection, something that emerged as a common pattern.

In interviews with ex-Catholics outside of Atheist Ireland, a number of instances were reported where a person's departure from Catholicism had been set in motion by the Church's conservativism, but no one explicitly tied their rejection to clerical abuse as the first cause. These topics were extremely *salient* but not necessarily causal in some direct way. They did not generate many sudden atheist epiphanies that banished prior orthodox Catholic theism. Instead, they contributed by drawing previously existing but somewhat latent reservations into conscious awareness. By providing a sense of motivation and story of collective obligation, they marked an exit route from an unconscious limbo of disengaged cultural Catholicism. Diane described just such an awakening: Seeing herself and the world around her through a new narrative lens, she found a way to make sense of what had previously been ambiguous and inarticulable.[2] This new moral narrative made her objections explicit by tying them to a larger story and a grander struggle, and this promoted the outright rejection of Catholicism. She came to inhabit a new world with new aims (liberation from Church influence), new actors (pedophile priests, corrupt bishops, complicit cultural Catholics, abuse victims, oppressed women), and new forms of moral action (disaffiliation, authenticity) and immoral action (institutional abuse, oppression, promotion of intolerant attitudes, convenient complicity). Thus she resolved to disaffiliate in the next census.

This situation, where muted objection yields over time to a new world in which respect and contempt are redistributed and where disaffiliation is an explicit and positive state, was perhaps best conveyed in yet another account related to me by a woman. Robyn, a 36-year-old atheistic ex-Catholic from South Dublin, was a single mother—in other words, somebody who would once have been seen as the worst possible Catholic. She believed it was impossible for people not from Ireland to understand the difference the scandals had made. She grew up during the transitional "respect without obedience" period, when the authority of the Church had declined but before its moral status had, for many, been inverted.[3] Some gesture of eternal deference—though distant and maybe even vaguely absurd when fully considered—was still the Church's due from a naturally Catholic population. Robyn remembered how, as a young teenager growing up in the early 1990s, she did not really *care* about religion (few of her generation did, in her view), but it was a force in her life all the same. People just "were" Catholics, and Catholicism was an environmental constant that was unquestionably endured publicly but could be subverted only in private when the opportunity arose. She took such opportunities, despite her protestations of apathy. For instance, she described how she once sneaked her boyfriend into the school chapel for sex as a way of profoundly trampling on the outwardly inviolable. Yet despite such obvious mental reservations about the Church, if Robyn saw a priest on the street, her lower status in the Catholic moral world would intuitively kick in. She described how a feeling of obscure deference would well up within her, and she would feel compelled to indicate submission to the priest's superior status: "I'd feel I had to look down or something." She believed this situation had been turned on its head in only a few short years. If out shopping in the Dublin suburb where she lived and a rare, fleeting clerical encounter occurred, she reported being conscious of the fact that it was *they* who manifested a sense of deferential awkwardness around *her*. In this new era, in Robyn's view, it was right and proper that the priest should bow his head before the atheist single mother. This is what it meant to live in an ethically reconfigured world. Other configurations might also exist, however, and might be experienced as impediments and a source of frustration.

The Frustration of Being Caught in Cultural Catholic Limbo

Ex-Catholic stances are supercharged by the new collective "secular revisionist" narrative described in Chapter 5: the dream of a new Irish freedom and the euphoric sense of escape from the nightmare of the Holy Catholic past. This narrative can associate Catholic affiliation with complicity, casting it as a shameful abrogation of moral responsibility. This was particularly clear in the personage of Emma, another woman in her 30s. Unlike Diane, Emma was an active, missionary secularist and a vocal member of a number of online groups. She very much adopted a mass complicity stance: "Everybody knew there was a darkness around Catholicism, but they didn't oppose it. It was like Saudi Arabia." She herself had been a believer until the age of 14 because of her grandparents' influence, though her parents were not particularly religious. She likened her grandparents' transmission of doctrines to her as "pretty disgusting, to the point of child abuse." Her evaluation of Catholicism blended the past into the present, described all nuns as "monsters," and used the present tense to describe past atrocities and culprits (this elision was defended with reference to the ongoing failure of religious orders to pay abuse redresses).[4] For Emma, the abuses of the past were alive in the present, because the Catholic Church still commanded loyalty. The attitudes of her grandparents were not merely anachronistic; they were living fossils of something terrible that should have gone extinct. When I interviewed her, Emma, ahistorical and at times vituperative, took the Church's claims to eternal moral truth at face value, demanding it justify every atrocity perpetrated in its name from the Crusades onward. She was hopeful, however, that the geography-defying powers of the internet might mark the beginning of an interminably deferred secular dawn.

> All your priests running around killing women and children. Like, separating women and children, selling babies, then burying them in mass graves and then, ugh, God! I just, I mean, is there, is there any end to it ever? Is it ever going to be something that's behind us? I mean I guess there is. Because when you look at it back when they did know about it but nobody was talking about it, where now everybody's talking about it and there's social media. I don't know maybe somebody's sitting in, I don't know, a little town somewhere in the middle of Ireland and actually they're the only person in their family who thinks, "Don't really believe in God but can't really talk about it," but they can go online and then they can be sort of emboldened to speak out and say, "Well actually maybe that's not correct," but I don't know.

Many ex-Catholics show sharp contempt for those who remain affiliated to "keep granny and grandpa happy," as one described it. Some maintain their own virtual networks of alternative social support to help them push back against the passive hegemony of cultural Catholicism that they cannot help but encounter in the "real" world—a point Emma alluded to in our interview. Perhaps, thanks to the cultivation of a robust online support group of like-minded individuals, Emma evinced a particular willingness to challenge existing social relationships with her family and peers. Her disgust overrode such concerns as the maintenance of social or intergenerational ties. For instance, her sister had recently had her child baptized. This prompted Emma to send an email to a radio station, in which she remonstrated with them about the fact that she could not officially "de-baptize" and sternly condemned her sister's actions. Her email described her feelings about the matter in vivid detail.

> Yesterday my sister baptized her second child. I am disgusted. I'm sure it was the first time she has been in a church since the baptism of her first child, before that, her wedding. I'm sure the real reason is to fit in, or to please my older family members, not that they would have asked her to do it. Maybe because she's not sure about what to believe. Maybe she wants to be able to get the kids into a school more easily. The reason is definitely not because she believes, although she would argue that it is, to defend her actions.

This email contains the first round of arguments against cultural Catholicism, encountered again and again among ex-Catholics, especially where they congregate in online groups. It places an emphasis on "authentic belief" and derogates action not motivated by this factor as a form of hypocrisy. From this perspective, concerns with intergenerational harmony or the maintenance of tradition cannot be considered legitimate motivations. The key idea here is the highly individualistic emphasis on values such as personal consistency, coherent standpoints based on explicit beliefs that have been arrived at through a process of individual reflection, and autonomy to behave in full accordance with these beliefs (so long as nobody else is harmed). Here, cultural Catholicism is portrayed as a form of "unwoken" or self-deceptive atheism (at least regarding Catholic religious beliefs). Above all, ex-Catholics portray themselves as *authentic*. For example, one online commentator noted that she "had always been 'the brave one' for not conforming" and that she had "lost respect" for her friends because of their willingness to go through with Catholic rites of passage because they were "just easier": "When you don't stand up for what you believe in, you lose integrity." In judgments of cultural Catholicism—and as per much public discourse (e.g., Donald Clarke or Atheist Ireland in Chapter 5)—inauthenticity is then compounded by a second factor: complicity. This was demonstrated in the continuation of Emma's email:

> I was complaining to a group of friends and one of them said, "Well, what's the harm?" Well, let's see, what is the harm? Ignoring the whole paedophilia, Magdalen[e] Laundries, homophobia, sexism, crusades, Inquisition, cover-ups and scandals question, there is a very large community who believe the Church should have no hand in education, healthcare or politics. Even people I know who are like my sister believe it should be separate. So, surely baptizing your child is a vote to keep the reins in the hands of the Church? Surely there is a lot of harm being done and perhaps people should think about what the hell they are doing before they throw another baby on the list of original sinners?

The phrase "what's the harm?" is a bête noire of moralized ex-Catholics. "What's the harm?" and other similar phrases ("Sure, it's grand," "You know yourself," and so forth) pepper Irish talk and are used to encourage turning a blind eye to any potential threats to interpersonal harmony. In certain cases of ex-Catholic discourse, it is used as shorthand for an ahistorical and irresponsible obliviousness. This is often described among online groups as stemming from conformity, cynical self-interest, and, at times, cognitive dissonance. This last item is a popular term of dismissal hinging on the disparagement of cultural Catholics for what is perceived as their personal inconsistency. Emma's email also deploys the argument that, besides the failure of individual religious orders to contribute seriously to restitution for historical abuse victims, Catholicism is an ongoing source of harm in that it denies secularists—"a very large community"—their rights. The secularist harm claim is thereby amplified with reference to past abuses. Connection to Catholicism is a form of complicity because it keeps an evil institution responsible for harm—past and present—in power. The inauthenticity charge feeds back into and exacerbates this; the cultural Catholic is seen to have no good reason for providing the support that they do (as one atheist man put it, "If there was a god, I'd imagine he'd be happier with the likes of me standing by my convictions, than those idiots paying a fortune for a meal and a bouncy castle and ignoring him for the rest of the year").[5]

Cultural Catholicism cannot be easily convened into a tight defensive formation to respond to this, but it often does not have to. As we saw in Chapters 3 and 4, much cultural Catholicism is implicit, operating according to an unspoken ethic of harmony and comprising rule-of-thumb-style values such as keeping family and community happy, privatizing potentially socially disruptive opinions, avoiding conflict, balancing respect for social traditions or local clergy with contempt for the Church as a whole, pretending to take absurd things seriously as and when necessary or advantageous, and swallowing resentment. These aspects of cultural Catholicism can never really be ideological because they are accommodationist. In this diffuse spectrum of strategies for compromise and equivocation, not having a fixed position *is* the position of much cultural Catholicism. "Ah sure, what's the harm?" may have bluff pragmatic logic, but it is hardly an inspiring manifesto. Cultural Catholicism, however, does not really need a manifesto, in part because religion is not a salient concern for moderates clustered around the middle of a spectrum that reaches from devout orthodoxy to ardent disaffiliation. Furthermore, it seems that cultural Catholicism's very amorphousness and detachment impart a kind of strength; its breezy flexibility helps it to continually adapt and endure. This casual persistence elicits powerful denunciations from ex-Catholics, featuring the use of strong moral terms that usually center on disgust and hypocrisy and are often expressed in language suggesting heightened emotional affect. Such denunciations may then expand out to encompass the entire "Catholic" country—for instance, "This is what we're living with in this country. This attitude. People who won't trouble themselves to think about what any of that [Catholic rites of passage] actually means. It's disgusting."

Parents for Secular Schooling: Coping with the Catholic Education System

The quote in the previous paragraph about Catholic rites of passage being disgusting is from the closed online group Parents for Secular Schooling (PSS), to which Emma gave me access. At the time, PSS comprised almost 3,000 parents who wished to see the Catholic Church's patronage of schools reduced to better represent changing religious demographics or, better yet, fully overturned in favor of a secular model of education where state-funded schools no longer have a religious ethos. For PSS members, religion should be a private matter. It is not something that should be taught in school, unless done so in a detached, anthropological type of way. The most significant bones of contention revealed in this forum were religious patronage of the vast majority of schools; the "baptism barrier" (schools having the right to discriminate on the basis of religion when awarding places, something that has changed in recent years but still not to the satisfaction of some secular parents who suspect that backdoor discrimination still operates through various loopholes);[6] the alleged presence of religious indoctrination both in religion classes and throughout the day; the difficulty of opting-out children from religious instruction; interference by religious authorities and devotees to thwart the secularization of the education system or to stymie efforts to opt out; and the inadequacy of politicians' proposals regarding what to do about all this. Discussions of these features of Irish Catholic education and how best to deal with them were carried out in meticulous detail, noteworthy for both the level of nuance involved and the high degree of moral indignation surrounding the topic. At this time, the group was strongly connected to Atheist Ireland, with high-profile Atheist Ireland leaders acting as vocal members. These members frequently posted stories concerning Atheist Ireland's contributions to the struggle to liberate Irish education from religious influence, updating members on their negotiations with the Irish authorities and, at times, using their expertise on the subject to guide the online discussion down more fruitful avenues or to overcome impasses.

Discourse in the group fell into six broad categories.

1. Practical advice regarding the secular education of children in the Irish school system and the avoidance of religious indoctrination.
2. Discussions of how the system might be changed at a systemic level, and the merits and deficiencies of various hypothetical and actual proposals, compromises, and ad hoc practices on the part of schools, politicians, and parents.
3. "Venting" threads revolving around the ridiculing or criticism of religion in general and Catholicism in particular, often involving memes or stories of hypocrisy, irrationality, abusive conduct, critical discussion of Catholic phenomena such as Marian apparitions or experiences of divine intervention among the devoted, or tastelessly materialistic First Communion or Confirmation celebrations among cultural Catholics. (The appropriateness and constructiveness of these venting threads were a constant source of friction in the group.)
4. Sharing news and opinion stories of interest pertaining to Irish secularization and Catholicism, and sharing opinions on these pieces. This sometimes involved sharing and endorsing ideologically compatible news and media articles, but it more often involved sharing and dissecting unpalatable Catholic utterances or promulgating information about Church scandals, which then served to galvanize opposition or bind the group in expressions of shared disgust, contempt, and outrage.
5. Communicating opportunities for practical action, such as petitions, protests, and the application of written pressure to local politicians, to further

the attainment of shared goals. Participation in these activities was often then reported back to the group, or excuses for nonparticipation expressed.
6. Sharing personal stories of injustices or impediments faced as part of living an openly nonreligious life.

At one end of the spectrum in this last category were what might be called low-level micro-aggressions faced by the nonreligious in daily life (such as nurses entering "Roman Catholic" on hospital forms without asking; the presence of Christian symbols or language in "secular spaces" such as building societies, parks, sporting associations, and so forth; the presumed potential for gory statues of Jesus or violent biblical stories to traumatize children; and unwanted Catholic literature such as the *Alive!* newspaper arriving through the letterbox with its condemnations of secularism). At the other end of this spectrum were larger disputes or experiences of victimhood (persistent family or local tensions revolving around Catholicism; discrimination suffered at school by children either at the hands of "indoctrinated" peers or the school system itself; and difficulties surrounding both exclusion or participation during sacramental preparation—discussions that would wax and wane, reflecting ongoing events in the academic year, such as the approach of Confirmation). Category 6 in particular precipitated expressions of sympathy and support, the sharing of similar stories, and comments vilifying or analyzing Catholic aggressors and complicit culturally Catholic parents who would not take a stand. A common theme described how children from nonreligious homes were othered in the education system. They would be sent to the back of religion class with a coloring book, forbidden to participate but left to passively absorb religious messages anyway. Many accounts described how children would come back rattling off prayers they had picked up by osmosis while their peers learned by rote. There were also many stories of children having been bullied by their peers for saying they did not believe in God—these frequently involved being told they were bound for hell. A countervailing "weapons of the weak" trope consisted of stories that revolved around children's precocious skepticism toward or often forthright ignorance of religious content. These incidents were often framed as examples of plucky independence on the part of the child or successful shielding on the part of the parent and tended to elicit expressions of mirth and pride.

PSS members were drawn from all over Ireland and demographically skewed female. Overwhelmingly, members were motivated by the fear of having their children indoctrinated by the Church (what Catholic educationalists refer to as faith formation or, more recently and ecumenically, belief nurturing). In other words, they appeared often to be motivated by the danger of having their children turned against them. This was an issue of constant concern, and coping strategies would be discussed in detail. For example, Emma emphasized that "it's important when surrounded by religious people to not have any unanswered or mysterious cracks for them to fill." She described how she would attempt to imbue her child with a rational, questioning attitude, describing a world in which adults do not know everything. She would tell her child that people should be free to form their own judgments but that there were people who wanted everyone to believe in the Christian story even though they had no proof. She would also draw attention to a range of positive non-Christian exemplars in the surrounding environment who did not accept this pressure (such as the child's father, herself, and others in their peer group). She would finally equip the child with a number of scripts, for example, by role-playing conversations where another child told her son he would go to Hell ("I would hope he might say something like 'I don't believe there is a Hell or a God, and I'm sorry for you if you think there is. That must be scary for you'"). Finally, she would interrogate any interest in religious activities the child might display as a result of going to a Catholic school.

Catholic Scandal and the Ethic of Authenticity in PSS

Aside from practicalities related to the education system, the immorality of Catholicism was an omnipresent—indeed sometimes *the* omnipresent—topic of discussion in PSS. Sometimes it waxed even larger than the education issue, fully eclipsing it. In particular, the Tuam affair catalyzed a wave of highly moralized discourse. In its immediate wake a few prominent members transformed their profile pictures into confrontational images, such as a graffiti image of a nun sweeping bones "under the carpet," though many were unwilling to follow through on this example for fear of alienating cultural Catholic acquaintances on the broader online platform.

More common were resolutions to share hidden sentiments more openly with culturally Catholic spouses, workmates, neighbors, fellow parents, and others, rather than simply venting about them online. Raw disbelief was frequently expressed about those who would condemn the Church and Tuam and then promise to "pray for the little babies" or about neighbors who in one breath execrated the Church and in the next started to talk about their daughter's First Communion preparation. Petitions advocating the separation of church and state in various forms were created and circulated. Atheist Ireland released an official statement referencing the scandals as evidence that it was beyond time to separate church and state. Posts appeared where members encouraged one another to "strike while the iron is hot," that now was the time to capitalize on public outrage and channel it toward an actual outcome. Discussion arose about how this could be done. Someone even posted images of a performative protest ritual they had created in which a number of ex-Catholics donned black clothing and applied tear-stained black eye makeup and, led by a woman in a nun's habit holding a chalice of blood, carried a large black cross over a bridge in Cork City. They were verbally abused by motorists, one of whom demanded that they "have some respect." This was relayed back to the group, to further outrage. Outrage simmered relentlessly for a period of two months following Tuam. The atmosphere was strangely feverish; alongside percussive explosions of people reporting to feel distraught, sick, disgusted, nauseated, and so on, there was a palpable sense of online collective effervescence that change was possible, that the media wave could be ridden to some secular victories. *Father Ted*–type positing evaporated—it would have been tasteless and distracting—and talk instead became achingly earnest, outraged, and purposive.

This atmosphere precipitated some extremely emotional contributions. For instance, a nonreligious mother in her 30s described how she was married into a religious Catholic family and consequently was forced to regularly bite her tongue. At home, mild aspersions were cast on those who did not believe or on the spiritual impoverishment of post-Catholic

Ireland, or on the materialism of "young people today." People had been better and more moral in the past, so it was said. She put up with this, for the sake of peace. But eventually the mother found that suppressing her views was becoming more and more difficult in light of the Tuam revelations, which seemed to register not at all on the complacent Catholic rectitude of her extended family. Anger welled up in her toward her affines and their unshakable complacency. This was causing her considerable emotional distress. Comments she would once have shrugged off or rolled her eyes at now elicited "tears of frustration" and "blood-boiling anger." This was particularly difficult for someone who considered herself to be "open-minded," "tolerant," and in possession of a "live and let live" attitude. As her attitude toward Catholicism hardened, this aspect of her self-image came to be shaken. Who was she? The limits of her own liberal tolerance rose before her. Her quandary became more acute again after the death of one of her husband's aunts, an elderly woman who had been one of a number of nuns in that family and not someone she had previously had any bad feelings toward. When she thought of the deceased woman, though, she did not see Sister Mary. Instead, Tuam news stories would rise up in her mind, or celluloid representations of abusive nuns such as those in *The Magdalene Sisters*. She wondered what Sister Mary might have seen or what she might have turned a blind eye to. Given the circumstances—a death in the family—the path along which her mind drew her made her feel like a "terrible person." As she summed up her predicament, "I know I feel less sympathy about this woman's death because she is a nun and I am horrified by this generalized intolerance on my part."

Such self-reflexive disclosures depict how Tuam pushed the group in a more extreme direction. Focus shifted to confronting the perceived evil of Catholicism in its entirety and to holding struggle sessions to extirpate the residues of Catholicism within the self, rather than accepting the status quo and confining oneself to discussing pragmatics concerning the education system. As a result, the affordance of Tuam had implications for the strength of different factions in PSS. Crucially, PSS is not homogeneous, and it is not composed exclusively of those with a strongly New Atheistic worldview. This source of friction was scrupulously avoided by Atheist Ireland leaders but was regularly triggered by rank-and-file New Atheist excesses. Just before Tuam, a schism occurred whereby a large number of PSS members who had joined primarily to obtain practical guidance were alienated by some extremely long and emotionally charged discussions about whether or not it was right to ridicule the deeply held beliefs of others. This resulted in some members leaving the group. Differences primarily revolved around a pragmatic/relativistic ideology that held that religion should not be attacked, as everyone has a right to believe whatever they want, and a rationalist/New Atheistic ideology that held that religion and other beliefs must not be quarantined from rational criticism, particularly when they cause harm. Truculent New Atheist voices could be destructively intransigent on this topic and on their own right to challenge non-evidence-based beliefs of other group members (homeopathy, for instance, was a particular sore point). These debates were a real and constant threat to the cohesion of the group, risking that it would split into smaller coalitions.

Once Tuam occurred, proponents of the more combative rationalistic/atheistic outlook gained a distinct advantage in ongoing arguments. Discourse was taken over by strident proclamations that "live and let live" had gone too far. In one man's words, "live and let live" was not a "humanist approach." Instead, beliefs found wanting had to be challenged, even if those beliefs were encountered in the intimate sphere of the family. As another man said, "I openly judge my religious family members, past and present: if they support a barbaric institution, they are all part of the problem." He made the following central point: "Nothing will ever change if we keep responding the way we've always done. It's time to shake up everything to do with this vile cult. All it takes for evil to flourish is for good men to do nothing. Time for respect of people's beliefs is well and truly over." Beyond religion, Ireland's deep-rooted equivocal culture of "don't ask, don't tell," its willingness to stagnate in ambiguity for the sake of peace, began to enter the PSS crosshairs. There was frustration with a quintessentially Irish mode of "wink and nudge," of face-saving doublethink,[7] of talk but never action, and how this seemingly affable and tolerant cultural mode in reality prevented anything from ever getting better.

Catholic scandal thereby seemed to create cohesion in secular ranks by empowering the most strident voices and discouraging compromising stances. By way of further example from outside the group, an atheist newspaper commentator in *The Irish Times* courted controversy by revealing that he occasionally went to Mass because he enjoyed the sense of community, the ritual, the silence, the homespun moral wisdom of the parish priest, and other features that he reported made him feel good.[8] This elicited praise from Catholic theists and social-harmony-valuing cultural Catholics in the comments section beneath his article, drawing notice to his "unusual" tolerance for an atheist. Such comments in turn tarnished the writer's own "worldview group" by implicitly denying the legitimacy of secular grievances and suggesting "normal" atheists were all dogmatists and fanatics. This implicated the author in an act of betrayal and elicited boundary-policing expressions of atheist anger that drew attention to Catholic moral violations in an effort to shame the author and demand that he fall back in line. The last line of the following comment in particular is striking for its injunction against nuance.

> All you have written is a blatant propaganda piece for the most destructive, corrupt, hypocritical, powerful, richest institution ever known in this country. And by the way if I thought that FIFA [the Irish football organization] had been systematically protecting generations of serial child rapists, had enslaved thousands of women in laundry factories for "moral transgressions," I certainly don't think I would be taking "morality" lessons from them each Sunday, whatever about attending their under-9 football matches. You are either entirely dishonest or the most blinkered atheist I have ever read. For you to separate the good from the bad of that institution is a disgrace to journalism.

Abuse also acted as a bonding agent in PSS by allowing disparate factions to unite around a common enemy, the cultural Catholic. The PSS schism mentioned earlier was based on notions of whether or not it was right to criticize other people's beliefs. Despite the debate, both factions shared the assumption that people ought to have clear and consistent beliefs and that these ought to determine what they do. In this worldview, people are driven by the beliefs they hold; in a sense, they *are* these sets of beliefs. Beneath this was a normative prescription that authentic actions are those that are in keeping with one's interior and individual beliefs. For the relativists, individuals could not be criticized for any particular authentically held belief, but they could be criticized for *not* acting in keeping with their beliefs or indeed for not having any consistent body of authentic beliefs at all. The underlying moral emphasis of all members, no matter their ideological point of origin, was the rejection of relational values based on traditional bonds or obedience to authorities or hierarchies. For PSS, these were not moral motivations; they were forms of cowardice or irresponsibility that choked liberty and authenticity in the name of conformity, irrationality, and unjust power. The ideal antagonist against which to cohere, then, was one who could be characterized as not acting according to a principled set of beliefs. Outrage at abuse combined with consensus on the negative evaluation of cultural Catholicism to produce a kind of cohesive indignation at perceived enablers of discrimination against the nonreligious, *even though religion is something they do not really believe in.* Tuam drove up anti–cultural Catholic rhetoric to excoriating levels. Cultural Catholics were either constructed as rank hypocrites or even more often as too soft-headed to perceive and address their own dissonant internal contradictions.

Moral Disgust in Nonreligious Rhetoric

The Tuam revelations also brought the emotion of disgust even more front and center. Disgust is a complex moral emotion. Anger and contempt are more straightforward. We are angry when a norm violation happens, and it motivates us to punish the transgressor. Contempt (basically the absence of respect), unlike the passing fiery emotion of anger, is a habitual sentiment that determines how we subsequently act and feel toward certain others.[9] People develop contempt in a more general way toward another person or category of people, holding them beneath themselves, often because they believe them to be habitual violators of moral norms. Disgust is more ambiguous. We approach what makes us angry, but we shun what disgusts us. In evolutionary terms, disgust relates to the avoidance of pathogens and is not self-evidently linked to morality. Some observers say moral disgust is purely verbal and metaphorical and acts as a way of adding an extra layer of denigration to condemnation.[10] Others say that the emotion has actually been co-opted by our moral cognition, where it encourages us to withdraw from transgressors as though they were actually physically contaminated.[11]

Whatever the case, disgust is frequently deployed in rhetoric about the scandals and was amplified in PSS. In all these cases, though I have no reason to doubt the sincerity of people's claims to actually feel moral disgust, we are also dealing with something else besides the emotion itself: the public expression of disgust through language or other symbolic means. Disgust is being *communicated*. Emotions communicate themselves through bodily signals, but disgust takes this further. It is a highly legible emotion: the brow pushes down, the bridge of the nose crinkles, and the nostrils arch. It has also been noted that disgust has "the important positive affordance that its display and attendant behaviors communicate to third parties that the emoter recognizes and disapproves of a norm violation (or an actor having a history of such violations)."[12] During interviews, I noticed that Catholics frequently expressed disgust when asked about the scandals—indeed, they were notably swift to do so—and may unconsciously have been particularly assiduous in expressing disgust (both verbally and physically) to perhaps head off accusations of complicity by signaling extreme disapproval. Brows were furrowed and nostrils arched, and there was a tendency to recoil, holding the body back and away from the interview table, as though that was where the scandals themselves lay. Most were also eager to move on from the topic, deflecting as soon as possible to something else.

Not so those who opposed the Church. By contrast, they seemed particularly given to expressions of extreme disgust that could linger for quite some time once scandal was present. Although it was obviously not possible for PSS members to project facial disgust to one another, they instead had recourse to graphic verbal expressions that were recruited to perform the task of signaling this reaction. These expressions of disgust would soon escalate, starting with the (frequently "vile") institution itself and then expanding to encompass its (perceived as "sick") supporters, both active and passive. Part of this may constitute a shoring up of the boundaries between ex-Catholics and other groups in preparation for expected conflict with religious antagonists, as is often unleashed by outbursts of scandal in Ireland's secularization struggle. However, PSS was a group specifically concerned with the fair treatment of young children, and it is quite reasonable to surmise that the Tuam revelations might generate an especially heightened and sustained reaction among its members. But there is another possible reason that disgust signaling is so prominent and sustained among those in opposition to the Church, and this relates to a particular stigma that has developed around the idea of the angry atheist.

Recent psychological work suggests that disgust signaling lessens perceptions of self-interested motivation, thereby rendering personal moral causes more legitimate in the eyes of third parties.[13] Experiments have similarly suggested that people are more likely to choose to express disgust when they wish to signal moral concern and express anger when protesting a threat to their self-interest. Anger acts to intimidate; it can arise in response to the perception of harmed personal interests, where it dissuades future transgressions against the angered individual. However, anger also carries potential social and reputational costs, particularly if it is engaged in too readily. The angry person is often seen as unreasonable and, in the ongoing dispute around secularization, the prevalence of justifiable anger among some Irish secularists, atheists, and nonreligious individuals has duly produced a countervailing anger stigmatization among their opponents. On the Irish moral battleground, secularist anger can be harnessed and redeployed against them in counter-weaponized fashion. When this move is performed, those seeking to effect secularizing changes are portrayed as an unreasonable group intent on eroding the undemanding, kindness-and-love, religion-lite social glue that binds together contemporary, "post-abuse" Catholic Ireland. One of the most recurrent Catholic tropes is thus that atheists in particular are angry, "anti for the sake of being anti," "against everything and for nothing," and so on: They just want to burn down the Church. This framing nullifies the threat of atheists as rival moral agents whose interests deserve to be taken seriously. Instead, they become petulant nihilists motivated by selfish and destructive rage. This trope is widely present in Augustine-influenced Catholic discourse, in which atheist behavior considered to

FIGURE 6.1. This image from a Junior Certificate religion textbook perpetuates the angry atheist stereotype. Source: *A Question of Faith*, 3rd ed., by L. Wheland and N. McDermott (Edco Press, 2016), p. 273

be moral is attributed to latent Christian conditioning and "immoral" behavior is depicted as the natural consequence of the atheist's unchecked self-interest.[14] These stereotypes of atheist motivation have infiltrated the Catholic education system. Consider Figure 6.1. The image is taken from a religion textbook page depicting the global variety of beliefs. All religious belief types are illustrated with a benign, smiling face bearing some hallmark of the tradition in question (a beaming face with a bhindi, for example, or a turban and beard, or a yarmulke). The agnostic, by contrast, looks a bit confused. But it is the atheist who really stands out, depicted as an irate individual shouting the word no.

This image, extracted from a Junior Certificate religion textbook and circulated on PSS to considerable outrage, clearly deploys and promotes the anti-atheist angry trope. In a discursive environment saturated with prejudicial representations of atheists as selfish and angry and where legitimate moral motivation is more likely to be inferred from expressions of disgust rather than from expressions of anger, disgust signaling may play an important role. Although anger is probably the most accurate emotion attributable to many ex-Catholics with regard to lingering Church influence and the cultural Catholic passivity that supports it, ex-Catholics are acutely aware that the expression of this anger can be perilously counterproductive. The scandals here present themselves as a resource allowing secular aims to be displayed more effectively as comprehensive moral concern, and anger to be supplemented with, sublimated into, and expressed as disgust. It is possible that this contributed in part to the marked prevalence and vehemence of Tuam-centered disgust in PSS rhetoric.

The Difficulty of Maintaining Critical Velocity

And indeed, back in the outside world, outrage and disgust at the Tuam revelations did seem to catalyze some responses from the government to address secularist concerns, notably the hospital transfer mentioned in Chapter 5 and some small, gestural movements toward educational secularization. Yet, despite the marginal nature of these partial victories, within a matter of months conversation in PSS had returned to its prior equilibrium. There were no more petitions. The abortion referendum had been won. Anger and expressions of disgust had wound down somewhat. Arguments about the justifiability of criticizing others' beliefs started to resurface. Atheist Ireland's influence seemed to have diminished, in part as a result of the in-fighting about social justice issues (trans rights, in this case, arising from an internal schism between Atheist Ireland founders and younger, more "woke" individuals).[15] Some members even claimed to have dropped the moniker "atheist" because of its militant connotations and its failures relating to social justice issues (the Richard Dawkins "elevatorgate" incident being a notable example).[16] Discussions had a renewed focus on the micromanagement of daily pragmatic concerns rather than the overturning of church-state influence in toto. A spate of giddy conversations arose about deliberately equipping children's school lunchboxes with ham sandwiches on Good Friday. Without Tuam and without the abortion referendum to fire people up, things seemed to return to a small scale. Eye rolling at cultural Catholicism supplanted outright condemnation. It was back to the weapons of the weak, back almost to the brink of tongue-in-cheek *Father Ted*–style humor.

This illustrates a profound problem for secular ambitions to dismantle Church influence on state systems such as education, in the case of PSS: Reliance on the online world risks that medium's propensity to absorb and redirect outrage, channeling it toward in-group-directed signaling predominantly active in a virtual sphere that is invisible to the world it proposes to remodel. Anger is stoked to fever pitch, but it is also quarantined. As and when moral affordances such as the scandals begin to wane, ex-Catholic outrage may be suppressed as the business of conflict avoidance and social coexistence with the religious and nominally religious reasserts itself. Just as the virtual world offers a galvanizing community of the like-minded, it also comes with its own inertial forces, providing insulation alongside radicalization and innumerable opportunities for the fruitless expending of rage. When a unifying surge of outrage subsides, people return to low-level strategies of everyday resistance, leaving a smaller core of dedicated secularists to await the next tectonic lurch in Irish Catholic disgrace to push things forward a little. Although it is difficult to imagine now, a day may come when there are no more such lurches.

Rationalist Wrath

Some ex-Catholics claim that morality is peripheral to their disaffiliation. The survey I conducted suggested that a subset of the nonreligious (especially male self-identified atheists) were particularly prone to adopt this stance. In the narratives of these informants, the main thing was that the representational content of Catholic doctrine was simply downright implausible. This dismissal of a religious affiliation on the basis of unconvincing ontological content can be termed rational rejection. Most nonreligious informants presumably dismissed Catholic beliefs as irrational as a matter of course. However, the complication lies in whether such beliefs were first found irrational and then dismissed or whether rational rejection was undergirded by prior factors.

Because Ireland was so recently theocratic, religion in the country is an emotive topic, and this likely inhibits people from entering into the consideration of a religious proposition in a purely detached manner as a kind of legacy curio. Through adult influence, even children are aware that there are things they *should* or *should not* accept as true, and people do not tend to report the rational rejection of theistic propositions on the first hearing in early childhood. They tend to reject them at least somewhat later than this and, by this stage, they have likely already become bound up with a multitude of other experiences and associations. Some rational rejection narratives I encountered clearly exemplified this, leading from moral withdrawal to a process of searching that then produced outright rational rejection as a form of validation, as in the following example:

> Initially it was boredom with church services and how irrelevant they were to me personally as a young teenager. When the divorce referendum happened it crystallised for me how much I disagreed morally with them. I questioned their moral stance more and more after that and found myself disagreeing with their doctrine on pretty much everything moral. Later in life—probably late twenties and into my thirties—I read a lot of literature about how inconsistent the Bible is, about how large tracts were left out, the big congress in the early centuries that just sort of decided on various issues, and how these changed hugely over the years. The hypocrisy was clear to me then, and I questioned the real motives of the church and came to some unsurprising conclusions. It is all about power and wealth, simple as. I really gave up all belief in God then in my early forties, purely because it makes absolutely no sense whatsoever.

In other cases, rational rejection is given causal priority, and these accounts should not be dismissed. It could well be that some people are simply more analytical than others, and this lends itself to primarily rational rejection.[17] It is telling, though, that rational rejection as ultimate cause tends to be claimed most in circles where the primacy of reason is an important ideological commitment; this is particularly the case with committed New Atheists, who tend to hold reason sacrosanct.[18] The responses of Atheist Ireland members to open-ended survey questions also illustrated this, where 37 of 98 respondents described their rejection of Catholicism as purely rationally motivated, and a further 27 reported their rejection as simultaneously rational and moral. This is unsurprising in a community like Atheist Ireland, where rationality itself is highly normative as the foundation that must guide all belief and action; the primary evil of religion from this perspective is its subordination of rationality to faith (which then subsequently enables manipulative, authoritarian, and harmful behavior). Reason reigns supreme, and acting on it *is* moral.

As with religious conversion narratives,[19] this lends a somewhat script-like quality to some Atheist Ireland deconversion narratives. Many involve a moment of doxastic awakening, generally situated in the teenage years or early 20s, when the individual shook off the "brainwashing" or "indoctrination" suffered at the hands of the Catholic education system and, in some cases, "brainwashed" parents.[20] Sometimes, this moment of realization was described as taking place almost automatically when the individual's critical faculties suddenly came online at a point described by some as the "age of reason": "When I say I used to, that was as a child—as I reached the age of rationality I also left superstitious beliefs behind." Sometimes this awakening was portrayed as an emergence from mindless conformity rather than belief, which is retrospectively posited to have never actually existed at all: "Up to my teen years I was part of the usual Catholic family upbringing, Mass on Sunday, Christian Brothers school, etc., but never thought about it. I do not think I ever really believed any of it. When I started to use my brain the brainwashing to which I had been subjected for the first sixteen years of my life began to be undone."

Although a number of respondents left it at this, the doxastic awakening was in many cases accompanied by a description of the particular pathway to rational rejection. At this point, rationalist deconversion narratives became more individualized by opening up and allowing the rejecter to express a particular favored argument, such as theodicy, evolution, or learning about other religions. This initial precociousness was sometimes presented as isolating the individuals from the religious society around them. They became outsiders; they were there, but the social world grew absurd and was viewed from an internal distance. Later, their initial rational "seeing-through" may be validated by subsequent encounters with atheist or secularist literature and arguments. These gave the individuals a sense of recognition, revealed that they were not alone, and in some cases led to a sense of purpose around the need to combat harmful religious dogma. At this point, some firmly took hold of atheism not just as a philosophical position but as a new identity ("In my final year of college, I would have been about 22, I began to watch debates online by some of the great atheist debaters such as Hitchens and Dawkins. It was around then that I finally came around to calling myself atheist").

A number of other factors seemed to play into rational rejection. Catholic school was one of them. As we have seen, exposure to religious doctrine is tightly associated with school years in Ireland. This in itself may make it appear infantile, as the comments about growing out of brainwashing could be taken to imply. In some cases rational rejection was reported not just as being the result of the implausibility of the ideas themselves but also of the inability or unwillingness of religious proselytizers to provide any kind of coherent explanation or defense of the content in question. This picture of unpersuasive models hawking paper-thin fables as truths was also emphasized by religious Catholic informants in relation to the education system. Their critiques tended to be twofold: that "faith formation" course content was intellectually underdeveloped, which encouraged rejection (this mapped onto existing critiques of Irish Catholicism as a paternalistic "peasant religion" that was never successfully adapted to the demands of an increasingly educated populace);[21] and that it was frequently taught in a rotelike manner by co-opted teachers with no real interest in religion, their indifference being palpable to students. It is possible that the decline in lived religion at home formed a particularly toxic combination for Catholicism when combined with this intellectually underwhelming, by-the-numbers experience at school. One conservative clerical informant found "this Catholic ethos thing amusing" because "the religion program is so dumbed down as to be ridiculous. There's no transmission of the doctrines of the faith and people aren't actually worshiping and they're not going to Mass. They're learning some sort of fairy tale stuff in class. There's no effect." The testimony of some other informants suggested that such perceptions of religious authorities as rationally inadequate were compounded by domestic circumstances that, in contrast to the Catholic school environment, encouraged free thought and debate. For instance, some rational rejecters were second-generation nonbelievers or else grew up in a house where they were "encouraged to think for themselves." These kinds of situations led to a variance between the home environment and religious environments such as school, from which the religious milieu seldom emerged victorious.

However, the longer and more detailed rationalist narratives became, the more difficult it often was to sustain the impression that rejection was purely a matter of rationally dispensing with implausible content. Longer narratives frequently revealed a process whereby rational rejection was triggered or accompanied by other factors. Although there were many examples of this among the Atheist Ireland respondents, the strongest example was provided during an interview with Michael, a retired civil servant and committed atheist in his late 60s. The interview began with a fairly standard expression of rational rejection based on a teenage moment of awakening: "Well, I suppose, as soon as I started thinking I gave it all up." However, although Michael seemed happy to be interviewed, his primary imperative was to shut things down quickly by emphasizing how Catholicism meant nothing to him and that he could not even remember anything about the subject anyway. He became quite brusque, but at the same time, his cheeks also grew red: "You see I've got to explain. I mean it's a total irrelevance to me. So, I haven't given much thought to it in recent years. I'm not involved." But this picture of the Church as an irrelevance was belied by the obvious anger he was experiencing just talking about it: "I think it's repressive. It has too much power. The sooner we're rid of it the better, you know." On the subject of the scandals and whether he thought they had had much influence on the decline of the Church's status, Michael revealed that he had personal knowledge of clerical abuse: "Well, I mean I went to the Christian Brothers and that sort of thing was well known in the sense that I heard plenty of stories. Never happened to me personally . . . [but] I know people who were physically attacked by Brothers, sexually."

Although he prioritized rational dismissal, it seemed clear that Michael felt personally affronted by Catholicism. Not only did he perceive the Church to be venally motivated and an ongoing repressive influence, but he also remembered abuse suffered by his peers and his own helplessness in the face of what he described as a deferential society and family who "would not have listened to him and may even have blamed him." He confessed that he "got a certain amount of pleasure out of seeing the whole thing come out, you know, in recent years. . . . It's nice to see them getting their comeuppance to some extent." It is difficult to say why exactly these experiences may have led Michael to frame his antipathy as unemotional dismissal when, as his face grew more flushed, it was so clear that it was a charged topic for him. It could have been a form of empowerment; as with Elie Wiesel's famous dictum that the opposite of love is not hate but indifference, sometimes the most powerful riposte to a despised force may be to feign dismissiveness. Framing Catholicism as patently absurd also allowed Michael to force priests into the unfavorable dilemma of being either stupid or self-interested hypocrites. It could also be that his dismissal was simply a means of avoiding talking about something that upsets him. However, a final, intriguing possibility is that the dismissive stance is actually a means of maintaining smooth social relations while retaining face. Michael's wife, once also alienated from the Church, recently returned to a more personalized, "spiritual" form of Catholicism; it may be that Michael's front of apathy serves to ease this point of tension by ignoring it.

Overall, Michael's rational dismissal seemed grounded in an extreme version of what one scholar has termed inauthentic ambivalence, essentially a façade of religious apathy that conceals stronger underlying disapproval.[22] This was particularly clear on the topic of celibacy, which made Michael shift from his customary protestations of apathy into the final admission that he *did* have strong negative feelings about Catholicism.

> I mean so I'm not too surprised that it should result in deviant behavior. What the hell do they expect? But as I say, remember I'm not involved so you know I don't have really strong feelings on it beyond having a certain amount of . . . negative feelings. I live in Ireland, don't forget. So, I don't have much choice. It's sort of in the culture.

The Core Stance of Ex-Catholicism: Anti-Nostalgic Moralized Authenticity

"It's sort of in the culture." Herein lies much of the fire beneath Ireland's version of nonreligion. Overall, I found that ex-Catholics are a loose category of generally individualistic and frequently but not always atheistic progressives who feel that their visions of an ideal society are stymied by the factor Michael pinpointed: the deep cultural and institutional embeddedness of Catholicism in what they perceive as being once almost a Vatican colony and the lingering power that this continues to give the Church over aspects of non-Catholic lives. They have a particularly keen sense of the repellent nature of clerical abuse and hypocrisy, but though this has likely contributed to some departures, outrage is often also partly instrumental, a means of heightening and justifying the rectitude of their stance in the inevitable moral conflict that follows. Whatever their internal divisions about the rectitude or otherwise of criticizing religion, they are, as a whole, driven by an ethic of authenticity: People should have clear beliefs; they should make these beliefs public and act in accordance with them, and they should stand up for them. This ethos is rendered imperative by the evils brought into being by the submissive, hierarchical, accommodationist past. By highlighting Catholicism as a source of moral harm, and the Church as self-interested and morally disgusting, ex-Catholics render cultural Catholics a complicit and enabling group, conjuring up an image of an infernal alliance of convenience between an intellectually lazy mob and a calculating, power-hungry institution.

Ex-Catholicism is propelled by what we might call anti-nostalgic moralized authenticity. Oblivion (often apathy) about the past gives way to acute consciousness of harm, unfairness, and often disgust. A sense of an impinged self mingles with a sense of violated societal purity: "Just because water was poured on my head, who are they—with all the contaminating filth of the past that encrusts them—to claim me as their own?" At times, ex-Catholics can feel almost as though they have been tainted by the Church's intrusion into their identities. Redemption can be found through struggle, and an unwanted essence can be purged by confrontation. Like the snakes banished by Saint Patrick, the last few integralists and neo-conservatives must be chased from their final church-state holdouts; no more will they sink their fangs into the innocent and inject them with a Catholicism they never asked for. This can get quite trivial when emotions run high, because cultural Catholicism can wend its way in at a psychological level when ex-Catholics are not on their guard. Occasionally overwrought threads would spring up in the PSS comments about how people could purge habitual "God language" from their lexicons ("thanks be to God," "please God," "God bless," "Jesus, Mary, and Joseph," "Ah Jaysus," "For Christ's sake," and all the rest of the legacy Christian phatic language that unconsciously peppers Irish speech). Despite such troubles, ex-Catholicism is in possession of a powerful and cohesive normative stance. It has been empowered by scandal. The opposite is true for devout Catholicism, where scandal has had a corrosive and fragmenting effect.

CHAPTER 7

"BLESSED ARE THOSE WHO ARE PERSECUTED BECAUSE OF RIGHTEOUSNESS"
COPING WITH A SPOILED RELIGIOUS IDENTITY

Contempt Switches Sides

Religious Catholicism manifests in many different ways. Some devout Catholics wish to see Christianity regain its everyday influence as a source of moral guidance in people's lives and view its increasingly peripheral importance with deep disappointment. A substantial number perceive a world without God to be rudderless, immoral, hollow, hopeless, or meaningless. Some hope that the Church can recover its relevance by engaging with the world and, in the process, guiding it along a more Christian path once people have been encouraged to embrace what is often described as the beauty of Christ's message. Others believe the opposite and place greater emphasis on preserving Catholicism rather than disseminating it; they believe that the Church should stand apart from the world, keeping its culture pure and acting as an unwavering voice of Christian conscience. Others simply wish to see Irish people recognize the rich spiritual resources derived from faith in times of personal need. All these hopes are currently growing more brittle, and much of this is attributable to the Church's moral taint.

Once, a person's respectability could be gauged by their depth of involvement with the Church. But now, the taint has spun that metric of status on its head. This means that the devout can find themselves objects not of respect but of contempt.[1] To be an object of contempt means the opposite of being respected; it is to be held in low esteem, to be looked down on. Whereas emotions (such as anger or disgust) relate to a particular situation and dissipate quickly, contempt lingers. It is a cold, long-lasting disposition, sometimes referred to as a sentiment, and it determines a range of downstream actions toward those deemed unworthy of respect. Contempt can manifest in a wide variety of ways: in hostility, in barely contained intolerance, in dismissiveness, in mockery or derision, in disrespect, sometimes even in dehumanization. When the tides of history turn, people and things held contemptible may change. In Ireland, thanks to its rapid transition from a dominant ideology of fortress Catholicism to one of progressive cosmopolitanism with romantic nationalist trimmings, those who were once objects of national contempt can suddenly find themselves eulogized (even if adequate redress for their sufferings seems less forthcoming). An example of this is found in Derek Scally's *The Best Catholics in the World* in his description of the Dublin Honours Magdalenes event, held in 2018. This event was a two-day festival organized to recognize the plight of those who had survived incarceration in the Magdalene laundries and to express sorrow and shame for the way they had been treated. President Michael D. Higgins gave a speech in honor of the Magdalenes at the event, and attendees crowded around them and reached their hands through railings to gain a fleeting touch of the women as they passed. In the new post-Catholic Ireland, the once-contemptible found themselves adulated as celebrities or venerated as living martyrs.

We have seen that the scandals have long since infiltrated the attitudes of those retaining a Catholic affiliation, allowing the emergence of disengaged relationships between clergy and laity and the reversal of the traditional current of power. The scandals have also greatly enhanced the power of secular rhetoric and the viability of secular objectives. But what of the devout? The moral status of religious Catholicism has been deeply affected as a result of the scandals. Even though religiosity was waning before the scandals came to light, some kind of connection to Catholicism, even an attenuated one, was always more normative than no connection at all. Today, however, one of the most normative stances is to reject the Church. Not only can Catholic doctrine be openly challenged, but so can committed contact with the institutions of Catholicism, particularly if they suggest the deference of the past. A new dynamic has emerged whereby religious Catholics can be asked to justify why they remain Catholic at all. Why would they allow themselves to be so close to the center of something so corrupt? This new onus has created a defensive self-consciousness about religious Catholicism. According to sociologist Erving Goffman's description of stigma, Catholics have learned to perceive themselves from outside and to consider how they might look to non-Catholic eyes. Goffman argues that the challenge facing the stigmatized is how best to manage their "spoiled identity."[2] In this chapter I examine the various strategies by which devout Catholics manage a religious identity that has been spoiled by scandal. One important factor in this management is that it has not been a uniform process. The Church is riven with its own internal schisms. In the arena of social interaction—and in their own minds—devout Catholics must legitimize their status as adherents of an institution perceived to be tainted. There are no set rules governing how to go about this. The resulting reactions have built on existing fault lines to further fragment the devout Catholic field.

The Experiences of Innocent Priests

The moral taint is at its most acute with priests. Through the actions of a few, they have become linked to what is viewed today as one of the most inexcusable of crimes: the sexual abuse of children. Clerical abuse has forged an associative bond between one category of person, formerly the most respected, and a category that may be the most morally unforgivable. To the public eye, especially since the 1980s, pedophiles are the vilest monsters, the ultimate pariahs.[3] They elicit moral disgust. One clerical informant framed public moral attitudes toward child abuse thus: "There's no contrition. . . . And you know when you flogged him, do it again please, and then, you know, quarter him, and then burn him, and then take out the ashes and flog them again. Like it's insatiable, absolutely insatiable, the need for revenge." This unprecedented blurring of what were once total opposites has profoundly altered the experience of being a priest. It also illustrates another aspect of the clerical abuse saga: the understanding, common among some clergy, that innocent priests are overlooked victims, the final casualties of Holy Catholic Ireland whose stories have yet to be told.

One consequence of clerical sexual abuse is that priests themselves, once considered a celibate moral elite, have become a dubiously sexualized category of person. This is notable in the taunting that some priests report. In Goode and colleagues' 2003 study on the effects of clerical abuse scandals, one informant reported an encounter with "a group of lads, about sixteen, sitting on the grass at the front of the Church. 'Here's the fucking priest, come over here Father and play with us. We won't tell the newspapers' . . . that kind of taunting."[4] Nonoffending priests themselves have reported widespread experiences of stigma, demoralization, guilt, awkwardness around parishioners and children in particular, and loss of confidence in Church leadership.[5] Although many nonoffending priests report sympathetic responses from parishioners, most also have stories of public hostility, and many report concealing their clerical status in public. For example, one of Goode and colleagues' interviewees said, "I rarely go into town because I'm so conscious of it now. It's almost like I'm wearing a paedophile uniform at this stage. . . . It's almost as though I've become ashamed of what I signify."[6] After exposure to media content detailing clerical sexual abuse, people were "more suspicious that joining the priesthood was an indication of sexual problems," "less willing to look to priests for moral guidance," and "less willing to encourage their children's participation in the Church."[7] Fifteen years after Goode's study, the strength of the stigma may or may not have abated; whatever the case, some priestly informants suggest that it has transformed clerical culture.

I interviewed six clergy individually, in addition to a number of attendees at a pastoral council meeting and some clergy after religious services. All these men reported to some degree a stigma attached to the priesthood. This was corroborated by other experiences that rendered striking the degree to which the collar—the archetypal symbol of the priest—has become associatively intertwined with pedophilia (I have heard it sometimes referred to as a pedo-collar). Perhaps the most emphatic illustration of this was at an intergenerational social gathering (mostly consisting of people who considered themselves Catholic in one way or another) where, during an increasingly bawdy game of charades, a number of sexual terms were put into the hat, including the word *pedophile*. When the word was pulled out, the performer first arched his eyebrows in an evil gesture and made lascivious facial expressions. He then attempted to demonstrate something of small stature with his left hand. Everyone was baffled. That was when a brainwave hit him. He brought his hands to his neck and traced out the clerical collar. The clue was instantly effective.

Such is the strength of this association that parish priests now exist most comfortably within the quarantined bubble of their parishes, where they are seen as individuals rather than tainted archetypes and where they are sheltered from negative sentiment by local recognition and devoted, mostly older, parishioners.[8] Outside these bubbles, the association between priests and pedophiles might manifest in displays of hostility and aggression. As with Goode and colleagues' study, being called a pedophile or being spat at was a common theme. For example, one elderly priest reported how, when he was "going up to visit someone in the hospital, [I met] this fairly young fella and he said 'Fucking priest' and spit at me, you know." It must be emphasized at the outset that, in raw numerical terms, a tiny minority of people would ever actually do something like this, but it is (or was, depending on the informant) common enough for it to have motivated priests to alter their behavior. Most notably, it has led them to conceal themselves. Most no longer wear the collar in public. As one priest, Father Toland, said, "I think most priests have gone underground when they go into public places. Yeah, wearing clerical dress has gone way, way, way down. I mean a tiny number of priests now wear clerical dress, other than maybe in the church—and even then, they don't. That's very much an Irish thing." The inner city of Dublin in particular was portrayed as a gauntlet to be run for priests. Father Dunphy, a parish priest from a working-class suburb in North Dublin, described the tension around the Mass of the Chrism on Holy Thursday, an annual ritual held in Dublin's Pro Cathedral, which necessitated wearing clerical garb outside the safe confines of his parish.

> If I get the bus, which I always do, I'm now a cleric, dressed as a cleric on a bus and going through the city center, Marlborough Street, and there are a lot of homeless and a lot of people who are displaced and on the streets and it's difficult because they do react. They'd be shouting, oh, you know

"you're only abusers," this sort of thing. It hasn't died down, not really, you know. There'd be an animosity. There's just something there.

There was some disagreement between priests as to the current extent of public hostility. Father Toland, a conservative diocesan priest working in a middle-class area, echoes certain elements of Father Dunphy's account but dismisses others. Primarily, he treats the ongoing hostility of the underclass as irrelevant and emphasizes that the form of overt antipathy he considers to carry weight—that is, soundly argued, middle-class denunciations in public—has died down.[9] Another priest, Father O'Connor, generally agrees with Father Toland. They are opposites in many regards, with Father O'Connor being liberal in orientation and critical of the Church's conservativism in many respects, such as being anti-celibacy (although he abides by the rule). Like Father Toland, however, he temporalizes overt hostility, maintaining that it crested in the past. Because of personal experiences in a challenging parish, his point of reference is far more extreme.

> It was from the mid-'90s until the mid-zeros, I would say, mid-noughties. Then guys would be afraid to wear collars and go around in public. I mean mainly it would just be kids. The last church I was in in Kilcluane, they tried to burn it down. I mean literally. €75,000 worth of damage done with barrels of petrol in the middle of the night. And they went down to burn four churches. I mean I know it's only young fellows who thought they were killing pedophiles. The whole Church was pedophile—nuts stuff, you know. It's like going for the Jews or something, you know. Nothing ever happened down there. There was no pedophilia: there was no nothing, nothing ever.[10]

Even if this kind of overt hostility is in decline, an undercurrent of raw anger remains. Some described how they feel hostility directed at them, even if it does not erupt. Father O'Connor said, "You can see just by the body language [of] some people, that they're saying in their head, '*you, you know,*' and just hate priests and basically that's it."

Priests regularly feel themselves disapproved of and distrusted. More specifically, they shared vivid accounts depicting a kind of heightened self-consciousness about being a priest that clearly persisted to this day. As Goffman tells us, this is the essence of stigma—to be "induced" to see oneself as a "type" and to become keenly aware of how others view that type.[11] This external eye of judgment is replicated within in a sense of shame. Even the conservative Father Toland, deeply proud of the Church and its heritage, recalled how "I would have felt it myself, very embarrassed to appear as a priest—so terribly embarrassed about what had happened. You know, ashamed, not just embarrassed, but ashamed of the priesthood because of that." This sense of heightened self-consciousness about categorical status was exacerbated by a sense of being publicly tainted, avoided even by those who bear no particular hostility. Father Dunphy describes how he believes parishioners now avoid him in public: "Silence. Well, if I'm in Ballycairn, people will say 'Good morning, father' or 'Nice morning' or just silently walk by. They wouldn't engage. That's a huge thing, they don't engage. They're afraid to be seen to talk to the priest publicly, that would be a difficulty. Like, if I talked to somebody on the street in the last parish, they would be very uneasy. They would feel uncomfortable around me."

The stigma thus remains present in a quieter, more entrenched way; it has become part of Irish Catholic culture. The sense of self-conscious shame and stigma are at their most extreme around children.[12] Father Bourke, a priest in a religious order, must fill in for a number of parish priests who refuse to have anything to do with schools, such is their fear of dealing with young people, which he attributes to "paralysis around abuse." He vividly describes one typical incident, which he views as an ongoing legacy for nonoffending clergy.

> I go to a Christmas concert in a good Catholic school. I was chaplain. It's part-time work. They give you a few jobs. I was doing the work. The nuns give you a front seat. The kids were there, lovely kids, lovely people. And there was a child behind me sitting beside the mother and the dad. They didn't know me from Adam, nor I them. And full hall. And I thought the child couldn't see behind me. And I said: "Can the child see," pleasantly to him, you know. And the mother says something about putting her on her knee. Your man interpreted that as putting her on my knee, or something. He just said . . . he just let out a big expletive, you know. He

> just lost it. He obviously hated me, just being a priest. The place went silent. I just sat. I could have answered him 10,000 times: "What do I know about child abuse, or whatever." And I said nothing. It was just horrible, you know. That kind of thing of somebody who would look at you in the street and want to spit at you. I mean guys had a . . . went from being kind of . . . people presumed you were benign . . . and you went from that to this. So, it was horrific, and I think it still is traumatizing really, you know. It's like the North of Ireland. You have to wait until a whole generation has gone, a new one comes through that it can be looked at any way objectively and calmly, I think. My generation were ruined by it, I would think. I don't think you can actually overestimate what it did.

This account brings two things vividly to life. One is the sheer salience of clerical pedophilia in the popular imagination, given the nature of the man's assumption triggered by his comprehension error. The second is the total loss of clerical moral authority. Father Bourke is a caring minister to his parishioners, an active, strong-willed man with a keen sense of right and wrong, but he remained silent when humiliated.

In some cases, despite deep hurt, there was evidence of forgiveness, and the priests made much of this. These stories were almost painful to hear, such was the suffering involved. They provide insight into the fraught emotional terrain with which the contemporary priest must contend, the sheer damage that clerical abuse has wrought, but also the robustness of some devout Catholicism. Father Coleman provided a particularly poignant account.

> There was a case over here, Lord have mercy on her, Betty Flynn. Betty just died about three months ago, and she was a wonderful, wonderful, woman. Her son, David, was abused by Kearney. He went down to live in Balbriggan and he had a terrible life. He married, or was living with a girl, and a family, but he was a very troubled, troubled, man and he finally ended up committing suicide. Now Betty Flynn, I often sat in front of that woman. I saw her lips shaking. I saw her tears coming down her eyes. But she was an extraordinarily strong woman. She never lost her faith, and when I was accused, she went berserk and went into the Archbishop. And ah, you know, but it did awful damage to that family.

Father Coleman's was not the only account that included a moment of acceptance or reconciliation between someone affected by abuse and the (innocent, unconnected) priest. It seemed that these encounters were a source of hope for priests; they presented moments where they transcended their tainted status and were embraced once more as good individuals.

Apart from among their devoted parishioners, there is another somewhat surprising place where priests can be liberated from their stigma. Although speaking enthusiastically of their encounters with young people in schools, some priests hold that Catholicism has generally become irrelevant for them but that this also means that clerical abuse is less relevant. Father Dunphy would visit a number of schools during sacramental preparation to talk with the students during their religion classes. He mentioned broaching the subject of clerical abuse with a class of preteens.

> They were looking at me, and I said, "You're going to go from here and I know you won't be back," and I said, "That is a great sadness to me, not only to me but to other people because you are the light of the world. You have so much to contribute, all your talents and all that you do," and I said, "I know it's been shameful," and hands went up and they said, "That's not our story at all." We've been told about that.

Father Bourke reported similar experiences and even used the same phrase, "That's not our story," perhaps suggesting that this anecdote had been shared around the diocese as a morale booster. In a strange way, this seemed to have been received with a certain mixture of sadness and relief, at least by Father Dunphy and Father Bourke. The apathy of the young was a respite from judgment; the silver lining of parental withdrawal, and of the evaporation of Catholicism as a lived religion and a source of daily routine and meaning, was that children's consequent obliviousness came with an amnesty.

The Contamination and Privatization of Devotion

Clergy are most directly affected by the moral tainting of the Church, but the scandals have also changed the experience of being a devout member of the laity. It is impossible to characterize in a representative manner all possible responses to clerical abuse among those who are part of the immensely broad category of believing lay Catholics. All that can be done is to describe some responses and observations derived from conversations with clergy, believers, and their relatives. The overall impression is that abuse exacerbated underlying frictions, causing greater fragmentation of the Catholic field. It did this by encouraging privatization and personalization; by causing committed believers to lose confidence in their moral status, especially in moments of conflict; by allowing the tenuously connected to pull free; by morally reinforcing cultural Catholic rejection of priestly authority; by triggering polarizing victimhood claims as a reaction to antipathy and criticism; and by driving the liberal and conservative wings of the Church further apart.

A first glance at the laity can invite optimism for the theistically inclined. Committed believers usually reported that their theistic belief did not waver in the face of clerical abuse. This was often attributed to the fact that only a minority of the clergy were abusers or that the Church is a flawed, human institution. This was particularly prevalent in open-ended survey responses. For example, one woman in her 40s said, "I was brought up a Catholic and I do not think the Church itself is to blame, it is the people that are 'employed' by the Church." Another woman in her 60s said, "I stayed with the Church because I believe that it is essentially good and pure. The majority of priests are good men and I'd hate to tarnish them all." Some reported a period of alienation, followed by return: "I lost interest for a while but I then decided that it is not the fault of the whole Church or all priests, just a few bad eggs, the message of Jesus is still there." In most of these cases, the organized involvement of the Catholic Church in prioritizing its reputation over children's welfare and the institutionalized policies of protecting and relocating abusers, dismissing or suppressing victims, and failing to report abuse to the Gardaí barely figured. The focus resided squarely on the direct perpetrators of abuse, the few bad apples who did not rot the barrel.

A resolute statement of abiding faith and a disavowal of doubt in the face of the Church's failings often also seemed not just normative but a symbol of the strength of one's relationship to God, a relationship that was, in many cases, described using the term *personal*. This was frequently accompanied by appeals to the benefits of religion commonly found among far more disengaged and nominal Catholics, such that religion was a source of comfort or community or that it imparted necessary moral structure which helped people to lead a better life. Many believers also had a set of personal religious paragons whom they could gesture toward as "counter-hypocrites"; sometimes a saint filled this role, or sometimes it was Pope Francis. Occasionally more local figures, such as Sister Stanislaus Kennedy or the retired Redemptorist Tony Flannery, would fit the role. These paragons helped to offset broad accusations seeking to tarnish any religious leader connected, presently or formerly, to the Church.

Some testimony suggested that the scandals had prompted a decline in what one informant, a Catholic journalist called James, referred to as "spontaneous trust in the clergy, that they will always do the right thing." For instance, a woman in her 20s said that a "small minority of people affected Catholicism. This did not change my beliefs or my bond with God. I am angry that I will never fully trust the main figures within Catholicism, but I still believe." Sustained fidelity under these circumstances came with something new: the realization that the laity were better Christians than some of the priests. In some cases, this reevaluation of moral status extended to encompass the institution itself. One informant, Roger, took a dim view of the mainstream institutional Church despite his orthodox beliefs. He portrayed them as a business, holding a monopoly on the Eucharist, something he valued highly: "I go there for one reason and one reason only and that is to receive Jesus in the holy Eucharist and if I could stay home, if I could say Mass myself, I would. And I wouldn't bother going to Mass." In many other cases, this disillusionment with the hierarchy or its elements prompted a reevaluation of belief and a move away from clericalist dogmatism toward something more personalized and self-reflexive. For instance, a man in his 60s typically described how "I want to retain faith in my life, whatever form that takes," as it "will ultimately keep me alive and [give me] some direction and drive in my life. I have questioned the Church, though, which has led to a more spiritual faith in myself."[13]

However, even if believers tended to confidently report within the limited, noninteractive confines of a survey that "a few bad apples don't rot the barrel," interviews suggested something more—a shift in moral power. This change is such that religious Catholics feel on the back foot and in the position of having to justify themselves, especially against the imprecations of their more liberalized offspring, but sometimes also to themselves. Clerical abuse is not something they are permitted to ignore in everyday discourse; it saturates the world around them and seeps into their identity as faithfully Catholic, including their self-perception as such. Some Catholics reported that abuse revelations created a feeling of complicity not just in the eyes of others but also within themselves. Bertrand, a devout liberal Catholic, described feeling "tainted." Máire, a woman in her 60s, said, "I felt I shouldn't be going to Mass because all those victims are out there. And this is a terrible sign to them that I haven't heard what they've gone through if I go along to the place where these priests [are] and how do I know that that one wasn't abusing them." James, a Catholic journalist, recalled how one old man "just said to me out of the blue, he said, 'Isn't it terrible because the way all the bishops covered up abuse, people think our religion is about abuse.'"

Devout laity exhibited clear personal negative affect when the subject of clerical abuse was raised, using heightened and often repetitive language that emphasized distance and strong moral objection. As with ex-Catholics, the emphasis tended to be on disgust, harm, and hypocrisy. James reported feeling "absolutely revolted and disgusted and completely and utterly turned off and angry, really, really, really angry." Whether the readiness of such responses was a straightforward report of sentiment or in some measure a social necessity predicated on the risk of contamination by association is not determinable, but degrees of both may apply.

All the priests maintained that some among the devout older demographic—"old, faithful people" in Father Coleman's words, perhaps with a "follower-style faith" (a euphemism for pre-1960s clericalism)—had reduced their attendance directly as a result of the scandals and that, unlike with other generations, this could not be attributed to "general secularization." It was a form of privatization driven by shame and, according to James, by accusations of complicity. Clerical testimony and other evidence indicate that some had lost the ability to argue for the Church, coming to view opponents as potentially justified—or at least in possession of unanswerable accusations—and losing the zeal to apply religious pressure to unenthusiastic younger relatives. In Father Dunphy's account, some seemed to mentally detach from their moral stance as observant Catholics, viewing their commitments from the outside perspective of a critic and wavering: "I would have known people here that would have been very faithful to the traditions of the Church, the stations of the cross, morning Mass, the legion of Mary—any events they'd be there in the church, but because of what happened they have distanced themselves and they would say to me, you know, 'My daughter doesn't attend church and maybe she's right.'"

Some unbelievers also reported observing the wavering of parental religiosity in response to the scandals. Sociologist Betty Hilliard's work also supports this, suggesting that the scandals have contributed to a loss of moral confidence in older Catholics and that they are connected to a breakdown in the transmission of religion. Although most of Hilliard's Cork housewife informants retained a "simple faith" or their "own faith in God," it seemed that the scandals combined with previous negative sentiments about the Church to bring about a more robust privatization of belief and rejection of specific doctrine, along with a decreased tendency to view religion as something that one was socially and morally obliged to transmit. When Hilliard re-interviewed her informants in 2000, she found that their feelings of "hurt, confusion, and anger" regarding their relationship to the Church were "further exacerbated by scandals exposing unacceptable sexual behavior on the part of certain religious [personnel]."[14] Hilliard describes the profound shock that one woman felt concerning the Bishop Casey scandal, especially after she was confronted by her daughter: "I sat there and I hadn't the answers for her but I said to be honest it is a bigger shock to me than it will ever be to you."[15]

Such experiences of domestic conflict because of the scandals might be quite commonplace for believers. Archbishop Diarmuid Martin, for instance, recounted that he had heard many cases of younger people "asking their parents how they could still be at home in an institution which was implicated in such filth." One ex-Catholic, Aisling, recalled just such confrontations with her father. At first, he would attempt to make theological justifications for the hierarchy's failures. Today, she attributes to him an outright refusal to engage, something that often aggravated her further, though they have since settled into a frustrating stalemate: "No, he's in a state of denial about that [clerical abuse]. He refuses to actually speak about it anytime I bring it up, but I would be quite self-righteous. Anytime I would broach the subject with him he just wouldn't engage. He would pretend not to listen."

Father Dunphy also believed that the scandals had produced another redistribution of moral power. By destroying the Church's moral authority, the scandals had reinforced the ability of cultural Catholics to use the Church in an occasional, utilitarian manner as a service provider for social rituals while resisting deeper commitment. Father Dunphy described how people would say, "D'you know what, we love each other and this is who we are. How dare you tell us how to live our lives after you've been entrusted with children and women and you've really messed it up." This would not impede the fact that they "want their child baptized," but it would come with a caveat: "Don't, please, say anything along the way, other than Jesus loves them and baby Jesus at Christmas and that's all ok. We'll turn the tap when we want it, turn it on and turn it off when we want to." He felt unable to push back against this; he likened the priest's current role to that of a social worker, and he seemed glad just for the opportunity to engage with parishioners. Under these conditions, explicitly Catholic beliefs had become remote and alien.

> I sense people really believe there is a higher power. They're naming God differently now, rather than God the Father. They're not quite sure but they would name God as the higher power, or entity, goodness, but to really and truly believe in the presence of God among us, the tabernacle, truly present among us in Jesus Christ, they're not quite sure. The tabernacle might be like a fridge for them. It's cold, it's distant, it's open when we want it. That's the image I have of it really.

Not all priests were as tolerant as Father Dunphy. Father Toland, the conservative, was of the opinion that the scandals had been a test of faith—one that left some believers wanting. He emphasized that the scandals were a winnowing process; true Catholics could see clearly that the failure of the Church's servants did not reflect on the truth of its message. He supported this argument with an observation on the stability of clerical dues.

> I don't think it's as big a factor as people might imagine. . . . I think people, it's fairly well documented here in the Dublin dioceses that there was a big fall off in Mass attendance after each wave of scandal. But a very interesting thing—and this is insider knowledge for you now—[was] that despite the noticeable decrease in Mass attendance, there was little or no decrease in the amount of contributions. . . . And what one concluded from that is that the people who stopped going to Mass were not among the more committed people because the more committed people will put their money where their mouth is. . . . So I think, if people were looking for an excuse to leave, they got it very nicely. But people who weren't looking for an excuse to leave were not so troubled by it. And people who were really committed weren't really troubled by it at all.

Sacred Victims: Taint Strategies for Salvaging Moral Status

As alluded to, a widespread perception among devout Catholics, both lay and clerical, is that the scandals provided people who were already disenchanted or only tenuously connected with an opportunity to sever or reduce ties. Archbishop Diarmuid Martin echoed this, saying the scandals "couldn't have fallen on a more fertile soil." Frequently, as with Father Toland, this was presented in a derogatory manner as using the scandals as an excuse. For instance, Father O'Connor said that "a lot of people would just walk away from it and say this is great, F them all, you're all pedophiles. And they know that isn't true but they're also secularizing so it's a way." Others, such as Father Bourke, delved deeper into the topic. He emphasized that this kind of absolute withdrawal was prominent in a certain age bracket, those in their 30s, 40s, and 50s, and that it was built on a prior anger. These people had long felt coerced, and they resented it: "There's certainly a cohort of people who stopped believing a long time ago but felt that for social, cultural reasons that they had to continue doing it." In Father Bourke's view, this was a response to being "controlled, dictated to, and judged . . . and the judging bit is probably the biggest thing." The scandals allowed people to free themselves from coercion and to return the judgment that they had experienced themselves: "It's almost like the whole sexual abuse phenomenon has given them permission to be overtly angry, and they couldn't be up to now." Or as James, a Catholic journalist, put it, "For the detractors that really was a kind of Eureka moment. Everything we've been saying about this organized religion just being mind control and just being obsessed about sex, obsessed about controlling people's bodies, look here's the proof."

This reinforcement of vocal moral opposition has led to a perception of victimhood among some contemporary religious Catholics. This was evident in the unusual personage of Roger, a 28-year-old man who is both a member of an old and famous sodality and gay. Roger goes to Mass daily and at all times wears a black 1950s-style suit and homburg hat, complete with badges identifying him as a member of the sodality. He cannot easily be pinned down; although he espouses strict pre–Vatican II orthodoxy in terms of theological belief and ritual practice, he advocates a liberalization of Church attitudes on divorce and homosexuality, condemning its intolerance in these areas. He has an immense knowledge of Catholic history and doctrine and is keen to become a priest but has so far been turned down twice. He believes that a "lot of Catholics" feel persecuted in Ireland today. Perhaps unsurprisingly, given the Church's stance on the issue of homosexuality, he describes how, in Dublin's gay bars, he experiences acute hostility for his beliefs.

> I suddenly get blamed for everything that's going wrong in the Church because I'm the only one there who's a practicing Catholic in that specific environment. And I have to tell people, you know, it's not my fault. That I go to Mass to receive the Eucharist. I'm not there to answer for the problems that the Church has been having. I don't know. It's not easy but that's what I do.

Roger added that "Jesus himself said blessed are those who are persecuted because of my name, you know, and that's the way I would look at it." He was not alone. Experiences of personal antipathy, especially insinuations of collusion by continued affiliation, were experienced as unfair by some devout Catholics, leading frequently to claims of victimhood. Focusing on these occurrences can act as a base for attempts to reclaim the moral high ground on two connected propositions. One is that secularists are motivated not by genuine moral outrage but by unreasoning hostility toward Catholicism. The other is that this hostility has led to the opportunistic instrumentalization of tragedy. If some secularists have weaponized the scandals, some Catholics have similarly weaponized secular weaponization.

Sometimes, this manifested in a tendency to redirect the conversation, after appropriate disclaimers, from clerical abuse itself to the detrimental effects of stigma, portraying the secular world as a place of unremitting aggression perpetrated on innocent Catholic believers, with priests being "spat upon" and "broken" by hate-filled accusers.[16] Those with true Catholic, Christian values are capable of forgiveness, unlike those from the "culture of despair" who have followed the path of hate and heaped further damage on top of the abuse scandals by unfairly victimizing innocent priests. The construction of ex-Catholics as blindly, unreflectively hostile and intolerant was a common trope. Áine, a 33-year-old Catholic schoolteacher, described how, in her view, it was the "cool thing just to hate the institution and hate the Church."

> Like they were incredible human failings and I cannot justify it. I can't be okay with it. I hate, absolutely hate, the fact that it happened . . . but I've had this conversation with other people who just shut down completely: anti-Church, anti-Catholicism, anti-priest. They're all pedophiles and whatever. And I wouldn't be able to speak as frankly as I can with you because I'll be judged then as if I'm defending them, as if actually all the abuse that's happened is okay because I still believe in the institution.

The motives of ex-Catholic antipathy are bypassed here, and such individuals are summarily deemed unreflective and rabid trend followers, "anti-everything for the sake of being anti."

The perception of victimhood is sometimes accompanied by deflecting strategies. One is that attitudes toward the Church are unbalanced and that all the good aspects of its legacy (charitable works, positive involvement in healthcare, social work, and education) are selectively ignored. Thus the mere raising of clerical abuse produces an associative saccade toward positive religious themes. For instance, Áine said that it is "too easy just to say the Catholic Church is, you know, a bastion of evil. Like, that is just too easy because the fact is it isn't. And the fact is it has done massive good to a lot of people's lives and it has brought a lot of education." Another connected argument is that the Church has been scapegoated for broader social ills. This means that the individual is not connected to a tainted institution so much as an institution that has been tainted unfairly. Father Bourke adopted an elaborated version of this argument. It essentially expands the taint of abuse to encompass all aspects of society, thereby making a victim of the Church, which has been forced to take on the entire burden of the taint.

> Well, it's, I mean, you know, on the one hand there was a stage where, you know, we were almost given to believe that this was part of the DNA of priests to abuse children. And that they were the only people abusing minors and vulnerable adults as well. I'd say we're still somewhere along that line in terms of we haven't got around to, like at the base of all sexual abuse is a desire for power and control and because that's what it's about. And that, you know, wherever you have human beings you are going to have one human being trying to dominate the other at some sort of level. It's very difficult to talk about clerical abuse without paralleling the reaction of those who are responsible ultimately: religious superiors, parish priests, bishops, anyone to whom a report of abuse was made and what they did. And that's what compounds this whole problem. But that in itself was not unusual either because that's what happened in swimming clubs, that's what happened in football clubs. That is what continues to happen in private homes. Sorry, a thought I often had throughout the whole, the height of the sexual abuse, and since, is that there are people out there who have been sexually abused within the sanctity of their own home, who wish that they were abused by a priest because, if they were abused by a priest, they had somebody to blame. And if it wasn't an individual, it was an institution who wouldn't take the responsibility once the complaint was made. It can't be expressed anywhere else and so instead of saying, you know, you fucking bastard Dad, it's you fucking bastard Father, you know.

Essentially, this argument works by accepting the evils of clerical abuse and institutional complicity but questioning why the Church and priests have been singled out when pedophilia is just as common in other institutions and among other categories of people. The scapegoat argument serves to distribute evenly across all social categories the crimes for which the Church and its representatives have been charged, meaning that in objective terms the Church no longer stands out as a uniquely tainted institution. Instead, it has unfairly absorbed all the blame for a sin present in the society around it.[17] In this conception, the destruction of its reputation is almost martyrlike: It has died for our sins, it becomes a victim. Catholic journalist James frames it as follows:

> Look, a lot of the anger that is there now, I mean a lot of it is justified. But a lot of it is, a lot of it isn't as wide as it ought to be as well. Sexual abuse was, and I think probably is, much more widespread in Irish society. But the Church in a sense because its sins were so public, so egregious, it was very easy to turn the Church into, like NAMA,[18] turn the Church into a bad bank, all the kind of abuse kind of went in there and everything that was, you know, that the Church did was kind of all this and were it not for this beastly Church, you know, the Irish wouldn't be fucked up around sex and you know we'd all be kind of fantastic and living very kind of liberal lives and all of this.

Factionalism, Localizing Blame, and Dancing with Schism

I came across a hard counter to the scapegoat argument, namely, the paragon argument: that a higher standard of behavior should be expected of "the Church of Jesus Christ," as Archbishop Diarmuid Martin phrased it. The paragon argument was deployed by secularists to deflect scapegoat claims but also by different groups within the Church who were vying for influence. These groups engaged it as a quarantining strategy, passing the taint to a particular sector of the Church, which was then constructed as no longer really "the Church of Jesus Christ," and localizing it there. This was used to claim that the Church should remodel itself according to the specifications of the claimant. In this way, abuse seemed to make liberals and conservatives in the Church surer of their positions, and very polarized. For example, for some conservatives, the Church was deemed to have strayed from its true path, and clerical abuse was regarded as a symptom of this.

Observers such as Gladys Ganiel and Derek Scally give detailed descriptions of devout deinstitutionalized Catholics who, often after a period of alienation from the Church, have found their way back to a more personal, more spiritual, and less dogmatic version of their Catholic faith. For these people, something often described by the term *spirituality* is usually an important component in their decision to stay. New initiatives, such as the Jesuit group attended by Máire, whom we met in Chapter 3, have sprung up to help encourage these kinds of healing relationships with Catholicism, winning back those disillusioned by the scandals by offering an alternative that addresses itself to the spiritual needs of the individual and lacks the rigid morality and authoritarianism of Catholicism under the command-and-control system of Holy Catholic Ireland. Many believers who find themselves in what Scally terms this "last chance saloon" of Irish Catholicism hold out hope that, although conformist participation and clericalist dogma may be in vertiginous decline, this may in fact have been a good thing all along. It clears the way for more low-key but spiritually rich versions of Catholicism to take its place—or at least take some of the market share—sometime in the future. But these benign visions of spiritual enrichment are not the only hopes for a postscandal Catholicism. In other visions, laissez-faire à la carte Catholics need to be cleared out of the away. The result may be a smaller but stronger and more militant Church willing to take on the hegemonic force of secularism. Often, congregations of this sort locate the blame for clerical abuse scandals not in the Church's organizational structure but in its loss of moral strictness.

The only outright optimist among the clergy I talked to was Father Toland, the conservative priest we encountered earlier. Alone among the clergy, his congregation was growing, albeit slowly. He described it as bifurcated between an older segment who had never really accepted the changes wrought by Vatican II and a younger, predominantly male segment who were attracted by the politicized sermons of some of the priests at his church. He linked it to the kinds of reactions visible in the United

Kingdom, the United States, and elsewhere against the perceived absolutism of globalism, multiculturalism, and politically correct attitudes (though he was swift to caution me against considering this group as simply "the alt-right at prayer").[19] When I attended Mass in his church, it was indeed notably full compared with some of the others I had been to. On one occasion, the priest, a powerful orator, expounded on the "disintegration of Europe," saying this was because it had forgotten its Christian identity. He told the parishioners that they must retain their Catholic identity because "this is who we are." Relentlessly, he condemned "the contemporary me culture" that was responsible for what he ambiguously termed the Church's "current crisis."

In Father Toland's congregation, people do not simply turn to religion for a sense of individual spirituality. Catholicism provides a sense of collective identity, and such identities become all the more salient under conditions of threat. The Ireland of the past, for all its cruelty, its suffocation of the individual, and its socially policed conformity, was also a place where people felt a reassuring homogeneity and a collective sense of rootedness in an ancient religious tradition. But this comforting image is now frequently derogated in a society that appears to value tolerant liberalism, multiculturalism, and consumerism above belonging and tradition. Some feel alienated by this new culture, and at times this alienation is joined by the sense that if they were to express their views to wider society, they would be met with derision and contempt. And, in feeling themselves to be objects of contempt, one of the only responses available is to return that contempt in kind. As Father Toland put it, "I would say that you could pick any younger person who comes to Mass here and you would find that [they] will have little or no time for political correctness."

Alongside the thrill of hearing political correctness trampled on and hearing their European Christian cultural identity affirmed, Father Toland identified another motivation behind his growing flock. The heightened Latin ritual provided them with a deep sense of historical rootedness, a feeling that one was not an individual adrift and alone in the atomized desert of late capitalist meaninglessness but rather a link in an unbroken ritual chain stretching back to the time of Christ himself.

It offered an eternal mission: perpetuate the chain, guard the purity of Christ's message. As the priest put it:

> You are seeing a ritual being done which has been done for hundreds of years and in a way immemorially. You really wouldn't know where to stop because you'd go presumably right back to the early Christian times, to the Last Supper, to the worship in the Jewish Temple, to maybe more primitive forms of sacrificial worship and, you know, you just wouldn't know. So and you can trace it back organically—this is the important thing—that at no point on that history could anyone say, oh, well now here on this day the whole thing was revised or restructured. It's not possible to do that.

With barely concealed contempt, he juxtaposed this against the early 1970s, when "you had priests encouraging the people to sing, to 'participate,' and I'm moving my fingers now to indicate inverted commas, and to shake hands with the person beside them and be folksy and relaxed." For Father Toland, this Vatican II version of Catholicism was a form of institutional suicide, and there was no wonder that it failed to command interest or respect among the young. Although there were no vocations to the priesthood in Dublin in 2016, by contrast three young men from Father Toland's congregation joined religious orders that year, and others intended to follow their lead.

From this perspective, secular society is not seen as something to aspire to; rather, it is perceived as vacuous and venal. A source of corruption and lax morals, it is the real culprit of the Church's moral contamination. Father Toland believed that both clerical abuse and widespread contempt for the Church were separable phenomena, but that both had their origins in Vatican II. He believed that the Church had sold out its traditions and was "widely held in contempt, not just for the bad things it's done, or its members have done, but due to its lack of self-esteem." Academics generally maintain that the explanation for clerical abuse can be found in some combination of the Church's secretiveness, hierarchical structure, clerical formation practices, sexual teachings, and demand for celibacy.[20] However, in the views of some conservative critics, such as Father Toland,[21] clerical abuse was made possible by a breakdown in clerical discipline, which occurred because of the laxity encouraged by the free-for-all of the *aggiornamento*. According to Father Toland, this encouraged people to see the Church's doctrines as "passé and therefore why would you bother living up to them even as a minister of religion because nobody really believes them, do they, you know? Whereas in the past we did believe them and we preached them and practiced them, or at least tried to."

In this view, the taint has seeped in from secular society. This argument thus displaces the taint, deflecting it back onto society more generally and also onto the mainstream Church. The Church is here seen as corrupt because secular society has corrupted it, and it allowed this to happen by abandoning its traditions and stooping to secular society's low moral standards in order to retain popularity. Father Toland and his flock are unsullied because they are prelapsarian Catholics and they know the value of obedience to the immutable law of the Church. The clock cannot be turned back, but they can act as the custodians of purity until such time as it can burgeon once more. This, essentially, allows for insulation from a fallen Church and the world that corrupted it.

When the Church Fails, Leave It to the Laity

Other voices in the Church see the problem quite differently and view the clerical abuse scandals as an opportunity not to push back against Vatican II but to take it further, diminishing the authority of the hierarchy in favor of a greater role for the laity, a promise that they feel never materialized. Father O'Connor, for example, believed that "somehow there's something providential [about the scandals] in that every time is a time of grace. Something good can still emerge—a new kind of church. Maybe the Church was meant to die." He was connected to two lay groups influenced by liberation theology that formed directly as a response to what was perceived as the mismanagement of clerical abuse scandals. These groups were small but active, holding monthly meetings. Each group consisted of about 50 people, generally 60 years of age and older.

Their rhetoric about clerical abuse was more reminiscent of the voices of ex-Catholics than those of other devout Catholics I had talked to. For example, Bertie, the leader of one of the groups, described the collective sentiment of the group as follows:

> Well, they felt betrayal. They felt the people, the figureheads, they had looked up to over the years in all their miters and their robes and all the rest had completely let them down. They felt a real sense of anger that innocent children had been the victims and that the people who had perpetrated the crimes had in some cases been protected and allowed to move around to repeat their crimes and so on. So, all that mismanagement and there was a real sense that what the Church had done was close ranks and tried to protect the institution and to hell with the victims.

His group consisted of "people who decided we are not going to get up and leave because of what has happened. We're going to stay in and fight, you know, and not leave it to the bishops, to try and challenge the whole clericalism of the Church and the hierarchy and all that sort of thing." One of the first things the group did was write to Archbishop Martin to express their outrage about how clerical abuse had been handled. Then they drafted a letter of apology and sent it out to organizations for abuse survivors across Ireland and the United Kingdom. Bertie recalls how "we had a very positive response back from them. Really because we were actually the first people to write to them from a Church background. We were the first people to write to them. And actually, *we are* sorry; the Church won't say sorry. *We* will say sorry."

Dónal, the leader of the other group, described a feeling of "guilt," adding that to stay almost felt like "collusion, in a sense." He wondered aloud, "Are we colluding in a system of injustice, perpetuating [it], you know, by our collusion? Is it not a more honest thing to leave, you know?" Separately, I asked both Dónal and Bertie why they stayed. Dónal, after all, had already described to me in detail how he rejected such shibboleths as transubstantiation. Part of their reason for staying was their feeling that it was incumbent on them to fight the influence of conservative Catholics and to push for justice from the inside. Bertie said "I'm just not bloody well going to leave it and leave it to them to make a complete ass of it. . . . If we pull out, Benedict spoke at one stage about [that] almost as his dream." Both men felt that they would have more impact fighting the Church from within than from without: "Those fellows should pay. Those bishops should be in jail, you know yourself. You wouldn't have the same [influence outside]. I can go to the press now. The laity are the real Catholic Church, the community of the faithful."

But the more fundamental answer seemed to be an inalienable sense of themselves as Catholic, leading to a need to redeem this identity because they could not separate from it. Dónal talked about how the group had discussed the possibility of walking away but could not bring themselves to "go down the road to the Anglican Church," concluding that "I suppose it's just ingrained in you that you don't feel like abandoning your own community." Bertie echoed these sentiments, describing "a combination of factors: our age, which also meant that we had a lot of years of commitment and service, you know; I suppose a faith that was obviously quite strong, and again related to the longevity of our time in the Church."

The irony was that the children of most of the members of the group rejected the Church outright, despite the example of their parents. This was a source of sadness for many members of Bertie's group; they did not understand why they were failing to "pass on the faith." One way they had of reconciling themselves to it was to describe their children as having absorbed a kind of latent Christianity, which they believed manifested itself in the altruism and moral concern for others that they displayed; this was glossed at times using the ever-flexible term *spirituality*. Unlike the other Catholics described earlier, Bertie and Dónal saw secular antipathy among younger generations in a positive light. The group members roundly believed that the refusal of younger people to go to Mass was primarily morally motivated. It was a righteous fury the Church had brought on itself; it was almost divine wrath. Perhaps, then, they *had* successfully transmitted their sentiments about Catholicism to their children, who had merely taken it further—they did not think the Church was worth trying to redeem. Bertie, for instance, who worked at a university, believed that "recent events would have had a huge effect" on young people "because they saw the hypocrisy."

> I find [with] young people here there's a high degree of sincerity in what they do. They don't go for phony stuff. They want something that's real,

and if you're putting up a kind of a false agenda, they'll see through it very quickly and they move away, and I think they looked at the Church and saw these guys are standing up on a Sunday and talking about mercy and compassion and forgiveness and all the rest and then look what they've done. You know. They're not living by example.

This failure of the Church to lead by example has contributed to an ongoing process of fragmentation. The scandals and others' reactions to them have destabilized the unquestionable rectitude of Catholic devotion. The devout have had to adjust to the fact that their motives and affiliations can be openly challenged. Priests are deeply associated with pedophilia and report acute stigma and shame, in some cases reporting that they are publicly avoided. Many observant laity report experiences of betrayal, anger, and disgust, in some cases leading to a personal reinterpretation of Church doctrine, privatization, and withdrawal from official practice. Some clergy report that Catholics of a less committed, more cultural sort have gained even greater autonomy from clerical stricture as a result of the Church's moral contamination, transforming the Church into an irregularly visited service provider for cultural rites of passage. At the core of this fragmenting process is the fact that Catholics now pursue a variety of idiosyncratic methods to salvage moral status. Among devout laity, methods for coping with the taint include localizing it in a rival Catholic faction, quarantining it to direct perpetrators, and counter-weaponizing it by deflecting to experiences of personal victimhood that portray secularists as opportunistic aggressors unmotivated by genuine moral concern. But perhaps most common is a kind of Catholic decoherence whereby Catholicism becomes amorphous, seeming to refrain from any definite meaning so that no stain can cling to its fluid and evanescent form.

Catholic Decoherence

Áine, a Catholic schoolteacher in her 30s, describes her worldview thus: "I think I'm justified in just the fact that I exist as a human. I have as much right to believe whatever it is I want to believe as anybody else. So, I believe in God." Áine's statement is here leavened with preemptive defenses that draw from a postmodern logic seemingly at odds with the Church's traditional claims of unique access to truth.

Religious commenters have observed that, since the 1990s, Irish Catholicism has become more polarized and fragmented, with greater disagreement about what it means to be Catholic. There is some talk of greater cognitive dissonance among Irish Catholics, with people holding "conflicting views at the same time,"[22] quarantining religion and separating it from other areas of their lives, in particular morality.[23] The same is not true for secularists. The scandals enhance and corroborate the progressive moral position of most secular people, confirming that the Church is indeed a source of harm to be opposed: They galvanize a sense of moral mission, the pursuit of that second, secularized Irish freedom. By way of contrast, for believing Catholics the scandals seemed to set moral intuitions against one another: Authority and loyalty went to war against purity and harm, and obedience and belonging wrestled with anger, disgust, and shame. This raises the interesting question of what happens when people's moral intuitions pull in different directions. The scandals seemed to unleash a new form of fragmenting psychological dissonance on Irish Catholics: not so much *cognitive* dissonance as *moral* dissonance. What happens when you must be loyal and subservient to something unmasked as potentially impure? There is no single set way to accommodate these warring intuitions, and each individual devout Catholic who wishes to retain their religious affiliation must embark on the lonely quest to do so in a bespoke manner. This moral dissonance could be described as adding a further cross-pressure to Irish Catholicism; one must reconcile the Faith with the Taint.[24]

Although the scandals themselves have been terribly damaging, the broad ambit and causal complexity they entail is their sole asset in the production of Catholic retention narratives. It means that, as has been said of moral conflict in general, there is always a lot of "choice about which thread in the tapestry of causation to isolate as culpable."[25] Blame attribution is not an unbiased process of causal unpacking; in most psychological accounts, it is deeply influenced by automatic judgments regarding the status or character of the blamed, where particular causal arguments are intuitively brought forth and others are pushed back to maximize the culpability of favored opponents or to deflect it from valued allies.[26] Such strategies were evident in the field and included efforts to quarantine, amputate, or deflect the taint. As we have seen, this led to a refractory process. Some Catholics invoked conspiratorial or "bad apple" theories focused on pedophilic infiltrators, quarantining the moral taint away from the institutional Church. Others refocused attention on good priests or Pope Francis; in such cases, abuse produced a direct, almost reflex motion toward positive exemplars. Others rejected the mainstream Church altogether and instead aligned themselves with splinter factions with an ambition to "cleanse" the taint, either by wresting power from the corrupt hierarchy and delivering it into the hands of the laity (if influenced by liberation theology or other left-leaning agencies within the Church, as Bertie and Dónal were) or by restoring and preserving austere "authentic Catholicism" in the face of a liberalized Church culture seen to have enabled the scandals by permitting internal decadence to bloom unchecked (as with conservatives such as Father Toland). Still others described a kind of paralytic tenacity; an incommunicable faith or distinctly Catholic experiences of divine intervention bound them to the Church despite its earthly flaws. Some co-opted the weapon for themselves, with traditional or conservative Catholics in particular alleging that people whose commitment to the Church had always been weak had exploited the scandals as an excuse to abandon religious participation; the scandals were a test, a winnowing event that had separated "true Catholics" from false ones, exposing rampant disloyalty. Many Catholic informants at times used anti-Church sentiment prevalent in the environment to deflect attention away from the scandals themselves and toward consequent Catholic-directed aggression: the counter-weaponization of weaponization. These many options and conflicts contribute to an endless process of idiosyncratic fissioning within Catholicism, just as ex-Catholicism appears to be taking form and consolidating under its own moral mission.

Let us now return to Áine to look at how dissonant moral intuitions and negative social feedback about shifting moral statuses has necessitated complex juggling for Catholics. Loyalty to family religious tradition is critical for Áine, but she has modified how this manifests to make it compatible with the attitudes of peers and a profoundly altered moral climate where these ties can be reconstructed as a form of contamination. She was once orthodox in her belief and more assiduous in her practice, but then the scandals emerged and she felt disgust, "a sickly feeling in [my] stomach." She felt "completely and utterly let down" at "the level of dishonesty and the total and utter hypocrisy and the power and the abuse of people. It was so anti the message—so completely contrary to what they should be doing." These intuitions became more urgent with input from the social realm; she experienced "anti-Church, anti-Catholic" ridicule at university, while also suffering philosophical doubts. In the wake of the pedophilia revelations, antagonists suggested that her faith made her complicit with a tarnished institution. These experiences combined to precipitate a period of shame and self-questioning, leading her to go to Mass and "sit there questioning, looking around going, 'God, am I a fool?'"

This period of doubt and conflict was overcome through the construction of a personal, relativistic, and doctrine-free redefinition of Catholicism as simply being a local manifestation of a universal spirituality. This seemed to be one of the most common ways of staying religiously Catholic under conditions of moral pressure. Here, Catholicism becomes something that exists in a state almost equivalent to quantum decoherence, shifting form as the Catholic moves between different contexts, cohering into traditional personal deism during prayer or while in church and cohering into flexible Unitarianism or psychological metaphor when placed under interpersonal duress in the secular realm. In Áine's case, Catholicism manifested as an inchoate meta-representational core[27] bonded to a traditional identity bequeathed by a more devout older generation, with this linkage then delimited by self-aware defenses to withstand incoming moral criticism. When she thinks of God, Áine says "that just means for me goodness and love and stuff." Áine also views the Eucharist as purely symbolic and quips that she is "basically a Protestant" who occasionally considers that she would "like to be Buddhist" but broadly regards all religions as the same ("It's all about love. It's all about God, or Mohammed, or Buddha. It's all the same thing."). She is adamant, however, that Catholicism is the "tradition that I like to still be a part of." It is evident that this version of Catholicism has evolved under conditions of moral conflict and in an environment where the secular narrative is increasingly normative. It has developed a kind of identity crisis both in how it presents and in how it self-regards, becoming at once unassailably shapeless and a vessel for an irreproachable universal good. Áine sought to reclaim Catholicism from the peers who had portrayed it as a complicit crutch; instead, it was for her a rich if ineffable experience that such detractors had closed off for themselves: "I do feel a little tiny element of, God, I feel really sorry for you that you're so negative about it and have such a bad impression of it and that you haven't access to what I had access to." The motivation to retain and recompose Catholicism in the face of moral repugnance, doubt, and considerable external social pressure seems largely to have been an inalienable sense of herself as Catholic, a firmly held group identity to which she must remain loyal. This could be primarily attributable to her upbringing by beloved and unusually intellectually Catholic parents, described by her as "role models": "I was brought up in a very nice tradition of love, family, and community and that on a weekly basis has meant a lot to me and that now maybe part of my link still to that Church is a fond memory of what it was for me."

Catholic believers, then, will find a way to stay Catholic, despite whatever feelings of moral repugnance they may have for the institution and even if this requires considerable acts of psychological contortionism. However, the sheer range of justificatory strategies indicates a problem for post-scandal institutional Catholicism. The moral narrative offered by the Catholic Church—that is, the story that draws on human emotion to craft a compelling, transmissible account of why one should be a member—has become fragmented and convoluted. Current narratives are frequently ill-suited to transmission and lack missionary zeal—there was much talk of "hanging on," with people often focusing on why it was acceptable for them personally, in their own unusual and idiosyncratic way, to be a Catholic rather than on why being a Catholic should be normative in general. With the exception of the marginal neo-conservative moral narrative about moral decay and incipient relativism (itself easily undermined by Church hypocrisy), there is no longer a clear, public defense of why Ireland, as a nation, ought to remain Catholic. Instead, there is a plethora of personal, reactive micronarratives produced by individuals about why their own version of Catholicism is good for the individual in question. The classic Catholic obligation to make other people more Catholic is seemingly being replaced by an emphasis on the nobility of one's own quiet perseverance. Whereas devout Catholicism is becoming further personalized, withdrawn, and idiosyncratic, disaffiliation has contrastingly become more moralistic in tone, more publicly acceptable, and more akin to a self-proclaimed inheritor of the venerable Irish schema of freedom from oppression. Given this climate, much of the scandals' power may lie not so much in inciting direct apostasy from devout Catholicism but rather in redistributing the balance of power in public claims to rectitude and moral status, thereby altering the appeal of (dis)affiliation for the undecided, the conflicted, the unwilling, the timid, the relatively apathetic, and the loosely connected—in other words, the majority.

EPILOGUE

"ANYONE ELSE NOT BOTHERED?"

Anyone else not bothered? My husband and I are born Catholic but don't practice any religion. My son thought churches were castles until he went to school and learned about religion. With him we bowed to pressure and he was christened though as MIL [mother-in-law] is very holy. With this one we aren't pushed and even more so now with the articles on the mother and baby homes I just think why christen a child into a religion that is so corrupt and nasty? But I am worried what it would mean if she had no religion growing up? I have no intention of baptising her into a different one or anything. But on those forms where you need to tick your religion what happens when you don't have one? Obviously we have morals and are strong advocates of being kind good people and teach our children the same but I don't think religion is needed to do that. Anyone else not baptising their children?

These concerns were posted to an Irish group on an international smartphone app for new parents. Across the different regional discussion groups on the app, talk tends to revolve around feeding, sleeping, and other practical issues relating to the care of infants that worry all new parents and tax their endurance. The Irish group is no different, with one notable exception. The topic of baptism arises regularly, and, when it does, it tends to elicit even more discussion than matters relating to the infant's basic survival.

This post crystallizes many of the considerations relevant to understanding Irish Catholic disaffiliation (and refusal to disaffiliate) and captures a good number of the tensions I have sought to describe in this book. One is the issue of ethnoreligious determinism. Catholicism is not just a religion in Ireland. Although the mother does not practice and it is doubtful that she believes, she has nevertheless been "born Catholic" and heavily implies that she continues to define herself as such "on those forms where you need to tick your religion." A second matter beyond this kind of intuitive essentialism is the business of pragmatic Catholicism. It is necessary to "have a religion" for forms, and in the discussion following the post, there was much talk of needing to be baptized to get into schools. Added to this is the issue of intergenerational harmony: Baptism is necessary to appease the mother-in-law, who is "very holy." To this can be added vague normative pressures sensed from surrounding society to maintain some kind of vestigial link, likely tied to fears of ostracism or social disapproval—"What would it mean if she had no religion growing up?"—and the evident concern that other people will believe that those without religion are immoral. These three factors could be described as the core triad sustaining cultural Catholicism: ethno-Catholic essentialism, pragmatic self-interest in an environment of institutionalized Catholicism, and relational concerns about maintaining intergenerational and local harmony and avoiding social disapproval. But despite these strong underpinnings, Catholicism is no longer a fully unconscious designation but an object of conscious scrutiny and dilemma. Although this particular individual still thinks of her own Catholicism as a fait accompli, she is considering breaking the link with her child. These kinds of considerations are critical to understanding the future demographic fortunes of Irish Catholicism and nonreligion.

These doubts occur because of factors that intrude on this baseline of cultural Catholicism and draw it into question—factors we have looked at in some detail. First is the breakdown of domestic religious transmission and the sheer peripherality of Catholicism as a religion or worldview. As distinct from a typical upbringing in Holy Catholic Ireland, religion is not a topic of interest at home, and all religious instruction is outsourced to the school system; until he learned otherwise in school, the son believed churches were castles. Second, it is primarily scandal-based moral concerns—in this case, the publication of the Mother and Baby Homes Report in 2021—that draw this thinned-out version of Catholicism into a state of conscious and acute scrutiny. Affiliation becomes morally questionable and somewhat contaminated by association, causing people to wish to pull back from Catholicism. The only aspect absent in the post is overt moral objection to the Church's current stances and influence, though the poster does call it "corrupt and nasty."

The overall intention of the post is to feel out which way social support leans for the decision not to baptize. It provides a good example of how ex-Catholics and the more distal sorts of cultural Catholics (such as this mother) are in fact close to one another. Both disapprove of the Catholic past and the Church. Both, typically, are already religiously disengaged. They are separated from one another by a hair's breadth. The difference between the two primarily revolves around whether the individual ends up prioritizing immediate concerns (e.g., holy mothers-in-law, institutional pragmatism, the risk of social disapproval) or more ideological projects (e.g., the goal of national secularization or the normative injunction to craft a public identity felt to be in "authentic" harmony with one's personal beliefs). If the ex-Catholic ethic of anti-nostalgic moralized authenticity described in this book establishes itself as the default national outlook (something that is well on its way to happening), then the cultural Catholic triad will become far less influential in deciding whether to stay Catholic or to baptize one's children. Cultural Catholicism will lose further ground to nonreligion. As the Church's power wanes further, more apathetic versions of nonreligion will then start to emerge, if they have not begun to do so already. Devout Catholicism will continue to develop into subcultural forms with little to no impact on the cultural mainstream for the foreseeable future.

This path seems plausible, but it is far from certain. Potent antireligious worldviews thrive in contexts where religion is seen to constitute a threat to secular freedoms and moral stances. The Church is rapidly losing influence and has already lost key battles on same-sex marriage and abortion. Educational reform is happening, and, though it currently seems unlikely that the system will ever be fully secular, Catholicism may become easier to avoid in the classroom and has already become less relevant to securing a school place. Perhaps paradoxically, the growing irrelevance of Catholicism in contemporary Ireland could quench the fire of anti-nostalgic moralized authenticity in the future and prevent the loose cultural link from evaporating. The second source of moral outrage—the scandals—may not be enough to drive widespread disaffiliation in the absence of a present religious "threat."

In this scenario Irish Catholicism could become something like Danish Lutheranism: an inoffensive, unobtrusive institution that acts as a carrier for collective identity without dictating moral values or worldview. This would be a difficult fate for the Catholic Church to accept, and no Catholic society has clearly developed in this direction. Ireland has parallels elsewhere, but no other country provides a perfect comparison that can shed an unambiguous light on the country's future trajectory. Scandal has happened everywhere, from Boston to Brisbane, but Catholicism elsewhere in the Anglosphere is a minority religion that usually exists in a context of secularized institutions and a thriving religious marketplace. The factors of cultural Catholicism and institutional influence, both critical in the Irish case, do not play as much a role in these contexts. That said, rapid institutional secularization has occurred in other hegemonically Catholic societies. Two good examples are the Quiet Revolution in 1960s Quebec and the institutional and legal reforms that took place in Spain after the fall of the Franco regime. Spain offers a particularly interesting comparison: Franco's oppressive dictatorship was staunchly pro-Church. Although post-independence Ireland was never a dictatorship, tight Catholic social control was a fact, and the period is increasingly cast in a kind of totalitarian light. Contemporary Spain may offer some insights into Ireland's future. Today, the nonreligious outnumber practicing Catholics in Spain, but the nonreligious themselves are outnumbered by nonpracticing Catholics. The divide between these two larger groups seems to hinge on attitudes toward a range of social issues, most notably immigration, on which nonpracticing Catholics are more conservative (than even practicing Catholics) and the nonreligious are more liberal. One Irish future could involve cultural Catholic nominalism as a kind of marker for a nationalistic, in-group-focused outlook juxtaposed against a kind of progressive globalism signaled by nonaffiliation. Actual beliefs about God or other cosmological matters would be fairly marginal to both sides.

Then there is the case of Europe's other great Catholic secularization outlier: Poland. Like Ireland, Poland also experienced an economic boom, and its nonreligious growth has recently overtaken Ireland's. The comparison stops there, though. Although the Church's hold is waning in Ireland, in Poland it is arguably growing under the influence of Poland's rightward Law and Justice Party. The Church in Poland is also able to benefit both from its recent historical role as a force of resistance against communism and its present role in potent cultural narratives about resisting Western cultural hegemony and preserving Polish values. There, a rapidly growing, youthful, and primarily urban ex-Catholic stance is in tension with a state-supported right-wing Catholicism that is prevalent among older people, the less educated, and the more rural and that draws on powerful emotions relating to demographic decline, fear of outside moral influences, fear of immigration, the looming threat of Putin's assertive Russia, and grievances about neoliberalism and economic globalization.[1] This potent force is almost the opposite of the scandal-afflicted, divided, and withdrawn version of committed Catholicism outlined in Chapter 7. An implication of Poland's greater polarization may be the smaller extent of any ambiguous, culturally Catholic buffer zone between its two extremes. Right-wing Catholicism is a far more marginal presence in Ireland, and the country feels like far less of a bifurcated religious battleground than Poland. Again, this difference contributes to the greater viability of disengaged cultural Catholicism as a social stance in any future Irish context.

Apart from the lack of exact comparisons, another difficulty in determining path dependencies in the development of Irish religious demographics is the country's uncertain future. At the time of this writing, the island of Ireland had been partitioned for 100 years. In part, the hegemony of Catholicism in the southern state eventually led to what we see today: the growing irrelevance of religious affiliation to personal self-conception. The same is not true of Northern Ireland, a society with a different history of sectarian strife between its proportionally equivalent Protestant and Catholic communities. Since the Good Friday Agreement of 1998, Northern Ireland has largely been at peace and, for some, religious identity has subsided somewhat. But current developments as a result of Brexit may pose a threat to the integrity of the United Kingdom, of which Northern Ireland remains a part. The prospect of a united Ireland directly endangers the sacred value of the Union for many Northern Irish Protestants. If it were to come to pass, sectarian conflict could reemerge and spill southward. People cleave to identities and in-groups when they feel threatened. Under such circumstances, disaffiliation may begin to look a lot more like in-group betrayal and a lot less like distancing oneself from a contaminated past. It would be a marked irony if the numerical decline of Catholicism south of the border was ultimately stalled by Ulster Unionism.

Irish secularization has been noteworthy for its active and institutionally unresolved status, for the extremity of the social and religious transformations wrought in such a short space of time, and for the complex roles played in this process by a heightened local version of the moral scandals that have globally blighted the Church. These circumstances have engendered a particularly potent and moralized sense of what it means to be nonreligious, a stance that is often predicated on ideas of personal authenticity and juxtaposed against "inauthentic" cultural Catholic complicity. Despite this, Catholic affiliation remains closely linked to ideas of the nation and the group. Given the fact that Ireland's geopolitical format may change and that this may have unforeseen implications for decisions about disaffiliation, nothing can be known for certain about future trends in Irish irreligion.

METHODOLOGICAL APPENDIX

This book has relied extensively on information gathered through mixed methods. The rationale and use of these methods are detailed in this appendix.

Surveys

Based on a series of preliminary interviews and secondary sources, I designed and ran two exploratory surveys, both of which probed attitudes toward the Irish Catholic Church, Catholic scandals, Catholic belief and identity, and Catholicism in general. The overall focus of both surveys was to understand the causes of affiliation to and disaffiliation from a morally contaminated religious tradition.

The first survey, conducted online in 2017 using the Qualtrics Panels participant recruitment service, consisted of 248 baptized-Catholic members of the Irish public, representative for age, gender, socioeconomic status, and urban or rural habitation. The response rate was 45%. Although small by the standards of representative surveys, the content was thorough (and quite time-consuming to complete—some respondents spent an hour on it). Stage 1 contained questions on the degree to which people identified with Catholicism. This was followed by questions on current Mass attendance, current religious self-description, dichotomous theism/atheism, levels of certainty in God's existence/nonexistence, acceptance of orthodox Catholic religious beliefs, perceived agreement with Catholic Church moral stances, whether or not they considered themselves to have overall rejected the Catholic Church as a source of moral and spiritual guidance and at what age, and the importance of various putative causes in this outcome. Finally, respondents filled out a

Catholic CRED scale measuring exposure to domestic religious behavioral modeling.

Subjects were then funneled into Stage 2, which asked more specific questions pertaining to the evaluation of the Catholic Church: whether it was a good, bad, or neutral influence on Irish society; a ranking task examining the degree to which the individual trusted clerical specialists as opposed to other categories of everyday people; and a section soliciting information about the participant's attitudes toward clerical abuse as a phenomenon, starting with self-reported emotional responses and followed by perceived percentage of priestly pedophiles, perceived causes, and whether the scandals had affected various forms of behavior that could potentially serve as behavioral modeling of religious belief (CREDs). Finally, participants completed Jonathan Haidt's Moral Foundations Questionnaire, as a greater emphasis on individualizing rather than binding moral concerns (i.e., "moral progressivism") was hypothesized to predict the rejection of Catholic belief and identity.

Of final note here, at the very beginning, participants were also asked to compile a list of swift associations intended to elicit gut reactions to the term "Irish Catholic Church" in a structured manner (cognitive anthropologists call this a free list). This was a particularly informative exercise. First, the results of the free list indicated stark differences in how different groups perceive the Church. Second, by beginning the survey with the free list, the signifier "Catholicism" denoted affiliation with a religious institution (rather than, say, ethnicity). I believe this played a large role in expanding the ex-Catholic category, probably at the expense of those who, through natal nominalism, would have put down "Catholic" on other measures (such as the census and the European Social Survey). Further studies should examine this possibility. Last, I employed two coders blind to the purposes of the study to standardize synonyms in the free lists.

I also circulated a similar survey around Atheist Ireland, asking members of this organization to provide descriptions of why they had rejected Catholicism. Ninety-three responded. The survey was similar in structure to the first survey but included additional questions relating to anti-atheist prejudice and feelings of implicit Catholic guilt. This second survey revealed some interesting trends: Atheist Ireland members are overwhelmingly male and, though often vitriolic on the subject of religion, strongly prioritize rationality in the rejection of Catholicism.

Fieldwork

I had originally intended to undertake my research in Ferns, but after lengthy negotiations, the Church there refused to cooperate. This was a problem, because I wanted to talk to clerical as well as lay informants. Instead, my initial fieldwork primarily consisted of a yearlong period spent in two Dublin parishes, one middle class and one working class, which I refer to as Sandhill and Kilbreagh, respectively, to mask their real locations. In both parishes I attended weekly Mass on a rotating basis to acquire an initial circle of believing Catholic informants. I also made initial contact with nonbelievers or cultural Catholics in bars and other locations where people gathered to socialize. Further informants were found by means of snowball sampling from these initial contacts (another reason for the survey, to offset any issues of representativeness). Aside from such nonspecialists, I also attended meetings organized by secularist and Catholic devoted actors, such as the secularist lobby group Atheist Ireland, the Iona Institute (a conservative Catholic think tank), and two reformist Catholic groups set up in the wake of the Murphy Report. I attended religious services, secularist gatherings, protests, general social occasions, and large-scale events, such as the papal Mass, anti–papal Mass protests, and pro-choice and pro-life rallies, all to observe behavior and ideology and to record the opinions of people predicted to have different stances and stories of interest with respect to Irish Catholicism. I variously used a notebook and a Dictaphone to record interactions, thematically coding these later.

Everyday life, too, was a permanent field site, both visually and in terms of everyday conversation. In general, I talked to as many people as I could—well beyond a hundred in fact—to gain as wide a perspective as possible on people's range of views on Irish Catholicism. Naturally I have not been able to reflect every attitude toward Catholicism that I came across in this book; instead I have focused on the most prevalent ideal-type responses. Over the three years subsequent to my initial fieldwork,

I returned to Sandhill and Kilbreagh regularly to catch up on local opinions relating to the fast-paced changes and events that were occurring at that time (2018 in particular).

Although the surveys provided some measure of representativeness, the fieldwork was intended to add nuance. The objective of my period of fieldwork was twofold. First, I wanted to get a sense of discourse about the subject of Catholicism from a range of different positions to gain deeper and more qualitative insight into how and why some people stay and others do not. The field allowed me to learn some of the different ways people understand and defend these decisions, especially in light of such phenomena as clerical abuse scandals. Second, I also wanted to examine not just these positions in isolation but also the tensions that exist between them, something that is lacking in existing descriptions, most of which follow Inglis's Geertzian lead and attempt to codify emerging forms of consensus around life meanings rather than moral conflict between rival coalitions vying for influence through rhetoric and narrative construction. Given the fractious image conjured up by the first survey, the field data proved instructive in depicting how different ideological positions and moral stances within a more polarized field interact with and construct one another. This shed light on the role that Catholic scandals play in such fields of interaction: They do not simply exist as neutral facts; instead, they are actively deployed and deflected in the pursuit of various agendas, driving up the salience of religious hypocrisy even more against a backdrop of contested secularization.

Interviews

Overall, I conducted and recorded semistructured in-depth interviews with 41 people: 10 believing Mass-goers, 10 clear ex-Catholic unbelievers, 10 people holding ambiguous stances perhaps best glossed as cultural Catholics, the Archbishop of Dublin, 6 priests (5 parish priests and 1 from a religious order), 2 high-ranking members of Atheist Ireland, and the leaders of two reformist groups who had split from the Church while retaining a Catholic affiliation. These interviews lasted between 30 minutes and 3 hours and were recorded by Dictaphone. They were then transcribed and thematically coded. I also had three initial in-depth guidance interviews with existing Irish academic specialists on Catholicism, but they declined to be named as informants. In this book pseudonyms are used for all people, places, and organizations to maintain informant privacy, with the exception of high-profile public organizations that are too distinctive to conceal in this manner. I also had informal conversations with scores of people over the course of the year while in the field, keeping notes in shorthand on these encounters in a series of notebooks. It was often these everyday encounters that proved the most informative, where I would be privy to the more natural attitudes of uncommitted people and those unprepared to deliver themselves of set stances. Taxi drivers were often particularly forthcoming, and I would like to express my thanks to them here. I always made my purposes explicit, both before formal interviews and when encountering informants in the field. What was clear was that, in general, contemporary Irish people are more than happy to talk (and complain) about matters of religion.

Virtual Fieldwork and Secondary Sources

The physical fieldwork was accompanied by extensive participant observation in online forums and groups, especially among committedly secular people, who are more geographically dispersed and more reliant on the internet as a means of organization and communication. I spent about 400 hours in such groups, focusing in particular on a thriving community of secularist parents who self-organize over Facebook to advise one another about how best to cope with Catholic educational influence but who also frequently discuss other topics pertaining to religion and Catholicism more generally. Observing discourse unfold in such venues was extremely informative; in many ways, it constituted enormous, ongoing focus groups. I used the software Evernote to capture particularly interesting dialogues for subsequent content analysis.

Finally, the Irish media is replete with religious news, and I consumed secularist, Catholic, and more neutral media while in the field, following such sources as Atheist Ireland's newsletter, mainstream newspapers such as *The Irish Times*, the *Irish Independent*, the *Irish Sun* and the *Herald*, and Catholic newspapers such as the *Irish Catholic* and *Alive!* Content from online groups and publications were (separately) thematically coded.

NOTES

Introduction
1. Molloy, 2009.
2. Parkins, 2020.
3. Ferriter (2009) is a particularly thorough treatment of the sexual culture of Catholic Ireland. In the work of James Joyce, Edna O'Brien, John McGahern, William Trevor, Tom Murphy, and numerous others, twentieth-century Irish literature also derived much of its transgressive energy from exposing the warping, hypocritical tug-of-war between the hollowness and judgmentalism of Irish public piety and the ineluctable fact of human sexual desire.
4. Any number of contrasts can be drawn, for example, between what was acceptable for the laity to read and what behavior seemed to be acceptable, or at least ignorable, for a member of the religious elite. Until quite a long time after its publication in 1922, booksellers were afraid to openly sell James Joyce's *Ulysses* in Dublin. Because of its sexual content, the book was sold under the counter in a brown paper cover; but, if you were an Irish Christian Brother, you could strip a boy in front of his peers and cane him until his buttocks bled and, by some accounts, experience a dark, enraged sexual gratification while doing so. When it comes to a cogent, deeply nuanced analysis of the various cultural, institutional, and personal factors that predisposed some priests to abuse, Marie Keenan's peerless *Child Sexual Abuse and the Catholic Church* is invaluable (Keenan 2012).
5. Topics of sex preoccupied many Irish clergy. From the nineteenth to the mid-twentieth century, Redemptorist priests in particular would tour from parish to parish, their mission to reinforce people's faith through rants about fire, brimstone, and fornication. In his essays the writer John McGahern describes how such priests were brought in to "purify through terror," but, in his experience, they were often instead "evaluated as performers and appreciated like horror novels," with satisfying Redemptorist performances being those that would "raise the hair on your head" (McGahern, 2009: 138).
6. Historians, rather than an anthropologist such as myself, are far better placed to offer more detailed accounts of how such high levels of clerical control, social compliance, and coercion were actually obtained in the past, as well as their limitations. Although I do provide simple overviews of what such scholars

have written to set the tone, I would advise readers who are looking for greater historical context to consult some of the scholars referenced in the early sections of Chapter 1. As an anthropologist, though I cannot ignore history, my focus must reside on the vision of the past in the present and the work that it does in contemporary social interaction.

7. To a far more limited extent, this faux pas still occasionally manifests. On a national level rather than a classroom one, there are moments when certain ecumenical and uncontroversial iterations of public Catholicism are treated with a kind of pious poker face. For example, despite their prominent role in exposing the failings and hypocrisies of the Church, the Irish press and the national television network RTÉ continue to prominently carry pious stories of religious significance, projecting an image of robust national religiosity. This arguably happens at the expense of other, perhaps more widespread, cultural trends. On Good Friday in 2017, for instance, RTÉ's 9 o'clock news featured solemn coverage of devotees following the Catholic and Anglican archbishops around Dublin's Phoenix Park in an ecumenical procession. However, the news neglected to report a quite different national story: The previous day, Ireland's off-license alcohol sales had achieved a historic spike. It had been widely leaked that 2017 would be the final year of the religiously motivated Good Friday ban on alcohol sales and pub openings, which had been in place since 1927. Over the years the ban had counterproductively created a transgressive annual festival of alcohol hoarding and home drinking, and the Irish public was determined to give the vanishing tradition an exuberant last hurrah.

8. A constitutional amendment to permit same-sex civil marriage was approved by a 62% majority in the referendum of May 2015. Amendments abolishing the offense of blasphemy and allowing the government to legislate for abortion were approved in the October 2018 referendum by 65% and 66% majorities, respectively.

9. The Commission of Investigation into Mother and Baby Homes could not find documented evidence of illegal adoptions at the homes, and this finding was met with considerable controversy and public consternation, including at least one High Court challenge, which was still ongoing at the time of writing. See O'Faolain, 2021.

10. Dalby, 2014.

11. Connolly also drew attention to the fact that the report had not been shared with mother and baby homes survivors in advance of being released publicly, despite government assertions to the contrary. The exchange can be seen at https://www.youtube.com/watch?v=KYGs7N1F7-E&ab_channel=CatherineConnollyTDCatherineConnollyTD (accessed April 29, 2021). The historian who brought the Tuam babies' fate to light, Catherine Corless, was also dissatisfied with the taoiseach's apology until it was joined by another issued directly from the Bon Secours nuns the following day.

12. Meskill, 2021.

13. John Charles McQuaid was the Catholic Primate of Ireland and Archbishop of Dublin from December 1940 to January 1972. McQuaid is famous for the repressive control he exerted over Irish society and the level of influence he held over Irish governmental policy.

14. During the Celtic Tiger economic boom, somewhat garish and generic paintings by the artist Graham Knuttel and his nephew Jonathan Knuttel proliferated throughout hip Dublin cafés and restaurants. These were invariably imbued with themes of status and suspicion. The figures in the paintings had haughty, masklike faces that were captured in the act of making sidelong glances loaded with judgmental anxiety and resentment. Although Celtic Tiger–era Dublin was splashed out on a number of flashy monuments, including a Calatrava bridge and a Libeskind theater, Knuttel's images of nouveau riche social unease and status competition are the truest cultural symbols of boomtown mid-2000s Dublin.

Chapter 1

1. The Penal Laws were a series of draconian persecutory measures implemented by the Protestant Ascendancy with the aim of forcing Catholics to switch to the King's Church. Catholics were banned from practicing their religion, getting an education, joining the professions, and owning any property of value (McGarry, 2006: 43). Although the laws demoralized and humiliated Catholics (Inglis, 1998), they also produced back-alley churches and illegal "hedge schools" (Connolly, 2001). Priests suffered such penalties as castration, branding, and execution, and their martyrlike perseverance further reinforced the Irish bond with the Church (Inglis, 1998). In place since the 1690s, the laws were gradually repealed beginning in the late eighteenth century. Many historians today argue that the Penal Laws were not applied as widely or as harshly as is popularly imagined (Scally, 2021), but in the nineteenth century their legacy contributed to the development of a more rigorously Catholic national consciousness.

2. According to some analysts, this increase in centralized Church power took place because of an uneasy détente between London and the Vatican over the Irish question. Subsidized by London, an Irish seminary was opened in Maynooth in 1795, and the Irish religious hierarchy, supported by an emergent native Catholic bourgeoisie, was given tacit free rein to mold Irish morality and notions of civilized behavior (Inglis, 1998). A critical component was the incorporation of Victorian morality and concern with respectability into Irish Catholicism, where they cross-pollinated with native interests among prosperous farmers in controlling fertility to prevent the fragmentation of landholdings among inheriting offspring (Inglis, 1998; Fuller, 2002; Scally, 2021). The resulting combination of inheritance interests, Victorian prudery, clericalism, and contempt for the flesh produced a uniquely potent culture of sexual abstention, shame, and control.

3. Scholars suggest that this century-long devotional revolution was fueled by such varied factors as the trauma of the Famine (D. W. Miller, 1975); the expansion of Church infrastructure alongside the disciplinary offensive of Ireland's

first cardinal, Paul Cullen (Connolly, 2001); the desire to be as "civilized" as the British, but not on their terms (Larkin, 1976; Inglis, 1998; Fuller, 2002); and the newly emergent and bankrupt nation's early reliance on religious institutions and personnel to provide mass social services such as education (Barr and O'Corrain, 2017).

4. Barr and O'Corrain, 2017.

5. From a cognitive anthropological perspective, the Irish religious system, as established during the period of Cullen's devotional revolution in the mid-nineteenth century and lasting to the 1960s, reads almost as a perfect mechanism for generating a particular form of collective identity oriented around widespread behavioral and dogmatic standardization. Irish Catholics would have regularly surrendered control of their bodies and voices to prescribed collective actions confined by ritual constraints. This shared relinquishment of control through physical and vocal entrainment may have both produced a cohesive effect (Wiltermuth and Heath, 2009) and primed congregations for the passive reception of dogma during sermons (Whitehouse, 2004; Schjoedt et al., 2013). This is paradigmatically akin to what cognitive anthropologist Harvey Whitehouse has theorized as the "doctrinal mode" of ritual, which serves to overcome critical resistance and encode shared religious dogma in semantic memory through regularized repetition. This then acts as a gelling agent in geographically dispersed collectives, extending beyond immediate face-to-face acquaintance to establish a shared sense of identity that is undergirded by common symbols and behaviors that indicate the acceptance of collective norms (Whitehouse, 2004; Whitehouse and Lanman, 2014). The form of centralized, hierarchical, standardized, embodied, and dogmatic Catholicism that came to define Irish notions of being a good group member—a good *Irish Catholic*—for most of the nineteenth and twentieth centuries is a striking example of the doctrinal mode in action.

6. Whitehouse and Lanman, 2014.

7. Foster, 2007: 50.

8. Scally (2021) was similarly drawn to this visual comparison between footage of the 1979 papal visit and Riefenstahl's *Triumph of the Will*, in which Hitler descends from the clouds to the adulation of the adoring masses gathered for a huge Nazi rally in Nuremberg.

9. According to Durkheim (1964), industrialization caused a shift in the nature of social bonds, precipitating the emergence of the individual as the new "sacred" entity. Recently, anthropologist Joseph Henrich has pushed the origins of individualism further back in time, proposing that Western individualism emerged in part as a somewhat ironic result of the Catholic Church's interest in dictating sexual norms through what he terms its "Marriage and Family Programme" (Henrich, 2020: 165–66). By banning such practices as divorce, polygamy, and cousin marriage, the Church inadvertently weakened the tightly interwoven kin networks found in most human societies. The Reformation and urbanization then further accelerated the process of individualization. By

mapping the expansion of the Church across Europe from roughly AD 500 to 1500, Henrich statistically demonstrates that the longer a society has been under the influence of the Church, the more its population's psychological attributes reflect an individualized pattern. These individualized societies are now generally the most secular, as people feel free to down-regulate or reject formerly socially ascribed affiliations. Ireland here provides a fascinating exception that may prove the rule. Early Irish Christianity was largely monastic and quite distinct from the hierarchical and dictatorial Roman model that imposed its "Marriage and Family Programme" across the rest of Europe. Once it did shift to a more diocesan structure, Catholicism was suppressed under British rule and remained too underdeveloped and understaffed to exert such control over the population, and this remained the case until around the turn of the nineteenth century, when the Irish Catholic hierarchy began to emerge with British support. To this it must be added that Ireland remained poor and largely agricultural until the twentieth century, by which time its deeply deferent and anti-individualistic post-independence version of religious nationalism had taken hold. Thus the peculiar trajectory of Catholic Christianity in Ireland may in fact have inhibited the birth of the individualized self until very recently.

10. Secularization theory took off in the nineteenth century when August de Comte proposed that as science advanced, superstition and religion would naturally wither under reason's glare (Comte, 2009). Durkheim diverged from Comte: Religion would decline principally because its social roles would be usurped by rational, secular replacements as society became more complex and specialization increased, though a privatized vestige might linger for some (Durkheim, 1964). Max Weber later situated the origins of secularization further back within the rationalizing impulses of certain religious ideologies, most notably Calvinism (Weber, 1930). Peter Berger, a highly influential secularization theorist, fused Durkheimian and Weberian themes in his depiction of the disintegration of the religious "sacred canopy," followed by the relativization and compartmentalization of belief (Berger, 1967). Secularization theory remains strong, particularly as a description of European religious change, though the exact causes and timing differ from theorist to theorist (e.g., C. G. Brown, 2001, 2012; Bruce, 2002). Academic disagreement about the inevitability of secularization began to grow in the late twentieth century because of such factors as the robust religiosity of the United States, the rise of Islamic fundamentalism, and the emergence of the New Age, causing new forms of anti-secularizationism to become dominant. See Cannell (2010) and Asad (2003) for influential versions of the idea that secularization is a Western cultural myth based on a culturally particular division between sacred and secular realms, and see Davie (1994) for the idea that secularization has been overstated even in Europe. Today, few would say that secularization is an inevitability or that it is the direct result of something as simple as the spread of scientific knowledge. At the same time, more sophisticated quantitative work (e.g., Norris and Inglehart, 2011; Voas, 2009) and qualitative work (e.g.,

Casanova, 1994; C. Taylor, 2007) have renewed the case for some more sophisticated and less deterministic version of the secularization hypothesis.

11. Bruce, 2006: 38.

12. Mass attendance had begun to decline markedly among young people and those with third-level educations by the 1980s, "both groups that were increasing in Ireland" (Weafer, 2014: 41), but "modernisation processes" in Ireland were not judged to have been "accompanied unambiguously by secularization" (Hornsby-Smith, 1992: 289). The signs of reduction in Catholic piety were small but present, manifesting in particular around moral disagreement with Church attitudes but rarely in the rejection of theism or affiliation (Inglis, 1998; Weafer, 2014).

13. Tom Garvin's (2004) book *Preventing the Future: Why Was Ireland So Poor for So Long?* is good on these topics.

14. Inglis (1998) elaborates on this in particular detail. Callum G. Brown (2012) also puts it into international perspective, showing how the "demographic revolution" of the 1960s precipitated declines in religiosity as women were emancipated through contraceptive technologies and the opening up of the workforce, among other factors. In Brown's scheme, Ireland belatedly but inevitably follows patterns visible elsewhere in the post-1960s West.

15. Fuller (2002), Inglis (1998), O'Doherty (2008), and some more religious observers such as Twomey (2003) are illuminating here. Vatican II was carried out with a certain level of iconoclastic philistinism in Ireland. Sacred traditions were zealously dismantled, altars ripped out and turned around. The elderly were confused and alienated, but the straying youth were not lured back by a God who now lacked the frightening powers of moral surveillance and punishment that he had once had.

16. Mulholland (2019) gives a thorough treatment of a long-simmering discourse of dissatisfaction with religious oppression stretching back well before the 1960s.

17. As one prominent feminist of the time recalled, there was a palpable sense of "female anger, subtle, veiled but there . . . the awful fifties are gone; things are going right for a change. Going right for the boys. But what about us?" (June Levine, quoted in Ferriter, 2009: 404).

18. See, for example, Foster, 2007; Ferriter, 2009; Ganiel, 2016; and C. G. Brown, 2012.

19. Sixty-three percent of the Irish population still opposed the sale of contraceptives in 1971 (C. G. Brown, 2012).

20. Changes should not be purely understood as the result of liberalizing ideologies, however. Tensions around the perceived harshness of the Church existed even in highly traditional enclaves where such ideologies as feminism would have been utterly alien. When Betty Hilliard revisited a number of her 1970s working-class Cork housewife informants in 2000, for instance, some recalled how clerical intransigence on the topic of birth control and the refusal of absolution had

prompted them to withdraw from participation in Mass and confession, and they spoke of the Church's influence on their lives with great anger and a sense of injustice. Liberalizing ideologies fell on fertile soil. See Hilliard, 2003.

21. C. G. Brown, 2012: 123–24.
22. Fuller, 2002: 227.
23. O'Doherty, 2008: 76.
24. Ferriter, 2012: 642.
25. McWilliams, 2005.
26. Although the 1970s saw greater liberalization and economic security (Ferriter, 2009), the decade also saw increasing wealth inequality (Weafer, 2014). What progress there had been was reversed in the 1980s, when more than a quarter of Irish people were living in poverty (Weafer, 2014).
27. See O'Toole (2021), though, for a discussion on the inflated and illusory nature of Ireland's high GDP statistics.
28. Coulter, 2003: 29.
29. Fuller, 2002: 232.
30. Norris and Inglehart, 2011.
31. Inglehart, 2020.
32. Zuckerman et al., 2017: 63.
33. McWilliams, 2005: 3.
34. C. Taylor, 2007.
35. Inglehart and Welzel, 2005.
36. By comparison, Latin America, long considered Catholicism's most unassailable bastion, was 69% Catholic in 2014 (Pew Research Center, 2014) and is 59% Catholic today. See also Latinobarométro, 2017.
37. Daly, 2017.
38. Scally, 2021.
39. Attendance figures in survey data frequently appear inflated compared with actual counts of attendance. For instance, in 1991, 2 million American Episcopalians claimed to attend weekly services in Gallup surveys, but actual counts of attendance put the figure closer to 900,000 (Hadaway et al., 1993). Hadaway et al.'s data suggest that across Catholics and Protestant denominations, attendance is in actual fact about half of what is commonly reported in surveys. This is particularly likely to be the case in a country where religion is normative, such as the United States or the Republic of Ireland (see, e.g., Ribberink et al., 2013).
40. Éamon de Valera (1882–1975) was the dominant Irish statesman in the early to mid-twentieth century, becoming president of the Executive Council, later termed taoiseach (prime minister), from 1932, and subsequently being elected as president (head of state) in 1959.
41. McGahern, 2009: 146.
42. The 2017 weekly Mass attendance figure also conceals internal complexities, being an awkward aggregate of particularly high (50%) attendance in the conservative border counties and far lower (<15%) attendance in Dublin

(Amarách Research, 2012), to which a further expected decline of 47% has been applied in relative terms between 2016 and 2030 (**O'Donovan**, 2015). This is to say nothing of the collapse in vocations to the religious life; for example, Dublin's priests, already under strain, are expected to reduce in number by a further 61% by 2030 (O'Donovan, 2015). Ireland now imports priests rather than exporting them and is considered a country of mission by the Church (Weafer, 2014).

43. Stack, 2017.
44. Ó Féich and O'Connell, 2015: 234.
45. Ó Féich and O'Connell, 2015: 240.
46. Inglis, 1998.
47. Ganiel, 2019b: 480.
48. Inglis, 2014.
49. Inglis, 2014: 123.
50. Central Statistics Office, 2016b.
51. Bullivant, 2017: 12. According to sociologist Stephen Bullivant's analysis, this "none" category breaks down into 11% ex-Catholics and 15% "cradle nones," but, given Ireland's demographics, a large number of these cradle nones are presumably the unbaptized offspring of a previous generation of ex-Catholics.
52. Central Statistics Office, 2016a; UCD Geary Institute for Public Policy, 2019: 27–28. It is also of note that even among those who continue to designate themselves as Catholics, not only Catholic moral stances but also Catholic religious representations appear to be diminishing in fidelity. In the 2017 Barna data, among the 70% of 14–25-year-old respondents identifying as "Christian" only 47% believed in the Resurrection, 31% in the Second Coming, and 15% in the proposition that "when you die, you will go to heaven because you have confessed your sins and have accepted Jesus Christ as your savior," all basic tenets of Catholicism. ESS data from 2008 on those specifically identifying as Catholic suggested that 10% did not believe in God and that 25.7% preferred the idea of a "spirit or life force" to traditional Christian notions. See Amarách Research, 2012.
53. WIN/Gallup, 2012.
54. In the 2008 European Values Study data, Ireland had the largest "pro-religious" majority and the most antireligious nonreligious minority. Bear in mind that the latter group has grown rapidly since 2008. See Ribberink et al., 2013.
55. For example, Cimino and Smith's (2014) *Atheist Awakening: Secular Activism and Community in America*; Lee's (2015) *Recognising the Non-Religious*; Zuckerman et al.'s (2017) *The Nonreligious: Understanding Secular People and Societies*; and G. Brown's (2017) *Becoming Atheist: Humanism and the Secular West*.
56. Zuckerman, 2008.
57. Bagg and Voas, 2009.
58. Hout and Fischer, 2014.
59. A topic of debate among sociologists studying Western European secularization is whether the decline of religion is stalling or is in fact accelerating.

Some, such as Grace Davie, believe that the combination of declining religious practice with comparably low levels of outright self-reported atheism heralds a new and potentially stable form of "believing without belonging," where theism remains both important and widespread in privatized form (Davie, 1994). Others, such as Abby Day, suggest widespread "believing in belonging," where religiously disengaged people nevertheless retain strong bonds to natal denominations as a means of maintaining social ties and differentiating themselves from other groups in society (Day, 2009). Those whom we might term neo-secularizationists, including C. G. Brown (2012), Steve Bruce (2006), and David Voas (2009), disagree with these positions. Some of these theorists focus more on those who are neither committedly secular nor religious—people for whom questions of belief or affiliation are matters of indifference, often sustained mainly through inertia. N. J. Demerath describes this as "cultural religion" and suggests that it may in some cases constitute a gully in which the momentum of purist secularism stalls (Demerath, 2000). David Voas, who has coined the term *fuzzy fidelity* to describe this state of attenuated religious affiliation, has compiled evidence from European Values Study data sets to show that this pattern is declining in most Western European societies. Some of this evidence further suggests that "fuzzy" cultural religion tends to evaporate if a tipping point is reached whereby the committedly nonreligious come to numerically outweigh the committedly religious (Voas, 2009). A further possibility is that future tensions in Catholic Europe will revolve around liberal secularists and disengaged "ethno-Catholics," who have been shown in Spain and elsewhere to have less tolerant attitudes toward immigration than either the nonreligious or the practicing religious (Pew Research Center, 2018).

60. The child's mother, Annie Murphy, published a book about the affair, *Forbidden Fruit*, in 1993 and made a now infamous appearance on *The Late Late Show* in April of that year. There, on the country's most-watched television show, her personal character and fitness to be a mother were publicly disparaged and she was repeatedly accused of fabricating a series of self-serving mistruths by a hostile audience and host. Despite the fact that Casey had admitted to being the boy's father when the scandal broke the previous year, the host, Gay Byrne, gave voice to the deep denial of a conservative Catholic Middle Ireland in crisis when he asked Murphy directly, "Is he Eamonn's child?" following up with "If your son is half as good a man as his father, he won't be doing too bad"—seemingly wishing to apprise her that, even if Bishop Casey were the father, he was still a good man and she the villain of the story. See https://www.youtube.com/watch?v=hvjZbxesEyU&ab_channel=KillianM2TVArchive (accessed May 7, 2021).

61. Ann Lovett was a Longford schoolgirl who, in January 1984, died at age 15 after giving birth alone at a grotto dedicated to the Virgin Mary. She had concealed the pregnancy, and her baby son died alongside her. In April of the same year, Kerry woman Joanne Hayes was arrested and charged with the murder of a newborn baby who had been found with multiple stab wounds on a local

beach. She had been in a relationship with a married man and was known to have been pregnant. Hayes was intimidated into making a confession but subsequently maintained that she had given birth to a different baby who had also died and whose remains were found buried on the family farm. The Gardaí were forced to drop the charges following a tribunal, but not before Hayes had been subjected to much public vilification. (In 2018 she was exonerated by DNA evidence and received apologies from the commissioner of the Gardaí, the minister for justice, and the taoiseach.) These tragic incidents drew national and international media attention, initiating fervent debate about Catholic-dominated attitudes toward unmarried mothers at the time.

62. The more recent case of Father Maurice Dillane provides a notable counterpoint. In 2006 Dillane resigned as a curate in Galway after he was confirmed to be expecting a child with a local schoolteacher. Commenting on the revelation, the chairman of the pastoral council said, "At the end of the day, they're two consenting adults. A child has been born, and that's something to be celebrated, not scorned." He further affirmed, "We have all moved on a lot since 1992," tacitly referencing the Bishop Casey scandal. Markedly, the public debate that followed centered on questioning the obligation of priestly celibacy. See Lavery, 2006.

63. Child sexual abuse by priests was being reported extensively in the United States beginning in the mid-1980s, raising questions about the possibility of its occurrence elsewhere (e.g., Rossetti, 1996). According to the Ferns Report (2005), "It is generally accepted that awareness of the nature of child sexual abuse in Ireland coincided with high profile cases such as the Kilkenny Incest Investigation in 1993 and the West of Ireland Farmer case in 1995. These cases demonstrated that child sexual abuse was a crime perpetrated by apparently upright and decent members of the community" (Ferns Report, 2005: 12).

64. "How a Government Sailed into a Storm over Clerical Abuse," *Irish Times*, August 23, 1997, https://www.irishtimes.com/news/how-a-government-sailed-into-a-storm-over-clerical-abuse-1.99378 (accessed March 8, 2021).

65. This was despite Archbishop Connell's statement that "I have compensated nobody. I have paid out nothing whatever in compensation" when questioned in May 1995 about compensating victims of clerical child sexual abuse in the archdiocese. He subsequently clarified, "I helped by giving the assistance of a loan. And consequently I have always believed the diocese did not compensate." See "Cardinal Connell: In His Own Words," *Irish Times*, April 27, 2004, https://www.irishtimes.com/news/cardinal-connell-in-his-own-words-1.1309742 (accessed March 12, 2021).

66. By way of a snapshot: in 1995 Daniel Curran was sentenced for child sexual abuse in the Northern Ireland; in 1997 Brendan Smyth was jailed in Dublin for abusing children south of the border; in 1998 Ivan Payne was jailed for the sexual abuse of boys, and fellow Dublin priests Gus Griffin and Thomas Naughton were convicted of the same crime; and in 1999 Tadhg O'Dalaigh and Eugene Greene received well-publicized convictions. A list of more than 90 Irish priests

and brothers who have been convicted of sexually abusing children or who were named in the Ferns, Murphy, and Cloyne reports has been published by the Boston-based group BishopAccountability.org (https://www.bishop-accountability.org/Ireland/).

67. It was not until 1996 that the Irish Catholic hierarchy formally prioritized the safeguarding of children in clerical sexual abuse cases by publishing its first ever child protection guidelines, *Child Sexual Abuse: Framework for a Church Response* (commonly referred to as the Green Book; https://www.catholicbishops.ie/1996/01/30/child_sexual_abuse_framework_church_response/). The Vatican's dismissive attitude toward this document was revealed in 2011's Cloyne Report.

68. Cullen, 2011.

69. Inglis, 1998: 2.

70. Amarách Research (2011). By contrast, academic research tends to give a statistic of between 3% and 6% (e.g., Keenan, 2012).

71. Monin and Merritt, 2012: 1.

72. Goode et al., 2003: 99.

73. "Mrs. O'Donovan," quoted in Hilliard (2003: 42). And as another of Hilliard's informants said of the secret child-fathering moralist Bishop Eamonn Casey, "He knocked all the religion out of people. It lowered the priests down to nothing" (42).

74. Keenan, 2012: 262.

75. Nic Ghiolla Phádraig, 2009.

76. Donnelly and Inglis, 2010.

77. Goode et al., 2003.

78. Bottan and Perez-Truglia, 2015.

79. Those who disaffiliated experimented with other denominations but three years later tended to report no religious affiliation (Bottan and Perez-Truglia, 2015). Irish sociological observers note that religious switching is a distinctly American phenomenon, with Irish Catholics tending instead to simply lose interest in religion while retaining Catholic affiliation (Egan, 2011).

80. Conversely, Britain and the rest of Europe were by this time moving toward the development of a welfare state to address social issues.

81. In addition to institutions run by religious orders, this also included state-run prisons, psychiatric institutions, and county homes (former workhouses). By 1951 more than 1% of all Irish citizens were resident within this system (J. M. Smith, 2007).

82. Garvin, 2004.

83. A small number of Protestant schools had also existed, with the last one closing in 1917.

84. "Industrial Schools (Ireland)," HC Deb 10 March 1884 vol. 285 cc1022-4.

85. Ryan Report, 2009.

86. The National Society for the Prevention of Cruelty to Children (now the Irish Society for the Prevention of Cruelty to Children) had highlighted that

higher social welfare payments would be cheaper than paying the capitation amounts to industrial schools, and numbers indeed declined after the introduction of "children's allowance" payments in the 1940s.

87. Ryan Report, vol. 4, ch. 1.23, http://www.childabusecommission.ie/rpt/04-01.php.

88. This included the 1936 Cussen Report, which criticized the large number of children in care and the inadequacy of education but led to minimal intervention by the Department of Education.

89. A number of industrial school survivors did publish openly autobiographical or fictionalized accounts of their experiences in the institutions as early as the 1980s. Notable examples include Gerard Mannix Flynn's *Nothing to Say* (1983), Paddy Doyle's *The God Squad* (1988), and Patrick Touher's *Fear of the Collar* (1991).

90. "'States of Fear' May Have Caused a Seismic Shift in Ireland, but More Needs to Be Done," *The Journal.ie*, March 2, 2020, https://www.thejournal.ie/readme/states-of-fear-5024180-Mar2020/ (accessed May 14, 2021).

91. "Irish Church Knew Abuse 'Endemic,'" BBC News, May 20, 2009, http://news.bbc.co.uk/2/hi/europe/8059826.stm (accessed April 26, 2018). For a detailed summary of the Ryan Report's conclusions, see Commission to Inquire into Child Abuse (2009).

92. In 2019, former president Mary McAleese revealed that Cardinal Angelo Sodano was deployed by the Vatican in 2003 to seek a backroom agreement that Ireland would not attempt to access Church documents as part of state investigations surrounding the handling of clerical sex abuse allegations. See McGarry, 2019a.

93. On the first day of the opening of the commission in June 2000, former justice Mary Laffoy, who had originally headed the inquiry, said, "There is no question of any person who admits wrongdoing to the Commission getting an amnesty, or any immunity from criminal or civil liability in respect of that wrongdoing." Ultimately, the inquiry held not one person accountable for crimes committed against children. See "Redress: Has the State Delivered for Abuse Survivors?" RTÉ, March 3, 2020, https://www.rte.ie/culture/2020/0302/1119661-redress-has-the-state-delivered-for-residential-abuse-survivors/ (accessed April 16, 2021).

94. Magdalene laundries were originally conceived in eighteenth-century England as workhouses for the "rehabilitation" and shelter of women in prostitution or those deemed at risk of prostitution. These early institutions were not confined to Ireland, nor were they exclusively Catholic established or operated. The first Magdalene laundry in Ireland was a Protestant asylum established in 1765 following earlier English examples that, in turn, were founded on a centuries-long tradition of refuges and asylums across Europe.

95. These categories of women were by no means found only in Magdalene laundries: Unmarried mothers and their children were in some cases retained in

county homes (formerly workhouses), and psychiatric institutions also housed significant numbers of women who had given birth to children out of wedlock.

96. No new Magdalene laundries were established after the foundation of the state; rather, they were part of what O'Sullivan and O'Donnell (2012) describe as "inherited networks of social control" (referring in that regard to industrial and reformatory schools, workhouses, Magdalene laundries, and psychiatric hospitals). See *Report of the Inter-Departmental Committee to Establish the Facts of State Involvement with the Magdalen Laundries*, http://www.justice.ie/en/JELR/2013Magdalen-P%20I%20Chapter%203%20History%20(PDF%20-%203824KB).pdf/Files/2013Magdalen-P%20I%20Chapter%203%20History%20(PDF%20-%203824KB).pdf (accessed April 24, 2021).

97. The *Irish Times* revealed that a ledger listed Áras an Uachtaráin, Guinness, Clerys, the Gaiety Theatre, Dr. Steevens' Hospital, the Bank of Ireland, the Department of Defence, the Departments of Agriculture and Fisheries, CIÉ, Portmarnock Golf Club, Clontarf Golf Club, and several leading hotels among those who used a Magdalene laundry. This wider social complicity in the practical functions of the Magdalene system has been suggested as one factor in explaining how the regime evaded mainstream public outcry until the 1990s. Frances Finnegan has speculated that "possibly the advent of the washing machine has been as instrumental in closing these laundries as have changing attitudes" (Finnegan, 2001: 2).

98. This is the estimated number of women admitted since Ireland's independence in 1922. Because of the policy of secrecy maintained by the religious congregations, their records remain closed and, though Ireland's last Magdalene asylum imprisoned women until 1996, there is no information for almost a full century of inmates admitted since 1900.

99. The religious order was selling the land to a property developer to alleviate significant losses it had incurred on stock investments (Gleeson, 2017, referencing Polman, 1993, and Raftery, 2003).

100. The discovery of the additional bodies and the lack of death certificates for so many of the women were investigated and reported by the journalist Mary Raftery in 2003.

101. Finnegan, 1998. It is notable that most such programs were produced in the United Kingdom, also including 1993's *Washing Away the Stain* on BBC2 and the 2002 film *The Magdalene Sisters*, directed by Peter Mullan.

102. The UN Committee Against Torture was responding to a shadow report submitted by advocates for Magdalene survivors frustrated with the government's long-held position of maintaining that the laundries "were privately owned and operated establishments and did not come within the responsibility of the State," as asserted by Ireland's then minister for education and science Batt O'Keeffe, when dismissing calls for an apology and redress scheme for Magdalene women at the culmination of the Ryan inquiry in 2009.

103. In March 2021, RTÉ screened *Redress: Breaking The Silence*, examining the state's response to survivors of institutional abuse and sharply criticizing the Redress Board's adversarial approach to victims. The program described the gag orders imposed on those who accepted offers of compensation as further abuses designed to prevent them from disclosing the full extent of what had happened to them.

104. The Department of Education stated in 2021 that, with regard to redress costs relating to industrial child abuse, the "offers made by congregations in 2002 and 2009 amount to €436.95 million, of which €239.93 million has been released to date," amounting to "approximately 16 per cent of the costs of redress to date, which are estimated to be approximately €1.5 billion" (McGarry, 2019b).

105. Beesley, 2021.

106. O'Sullivan and O'Donnell, 2012.

107. In her recent book *Republic of Shame* (2019), Caelainn Hogan coined the phrase "shame-industrial complex" to describe the networked complexes of coercive confinement of moral undesirables, and she attempts to decipher the public culture that permitted this to exist.

108. Haidt and Joseph, 2004: 55.

109. Graham et al., 2013: 61–67.

110. Haidt and Graham, 2007.

111. Lynch, 2012: 69.

112. Raftery and O'Sullivan, 1999. The abuse was described by people living close to the Christian Brothers School in Salthill, County Galway, and a similar school in Daingean, County Offaly.

113. Two groundbreaking series of articles by English-born journalist Michael Viney in *The Irish Times* are also noteworthy here, the first being his 1964 "No Birthright" series, which examined the stories of unmarried mothers and their children, including experiences of mother and baby homes. This was followed in 1966 by "The Young Offenders" series, which looked at Ireland's reformatories and industrial schools and included accounts of those who had been through the system. However, these articles did not incite widespread public reaction.

114. Indeed, it can be argued that the state took a similar position as the Church in its own management of child abuse issues in wider Irish society. As early as 1931, the Carrigan Report presented the government with conclusive evidence of widespread child sexual abuse in the country. The commissioner of the Gardaí at the time had testified that from 1924 to 1929 there had been more than 400 reported cases of the abuse of girls under 18, with an "alarming . . . number of cases of interference with girls under 16 and with children under 11 years of age." However, the response of successive governments to these shocking findings was to suppress the report and to make no further attempts at examination or intervention. Nationalist leaders had long depended on the argument that British rule was responsible for Ireland's failings, and the revelation of such a report almost a decade into independence would have gravely

threatened this narrative. Confronting the issue of widespread child sexual abuse would furthermore have destabilized Ireland's cherished reputation and identity as "a good Catholic country," which tragically took primacy over the welfare of its child citizens. See Dwyer, 2014.

115. Strikingly, two years earlier, in 1961, the Abbey Theatre had staged *The Evidence I Shall Give*, by Judge Richard Johnson, a play culminating in the revelation that a 13-year-old girl who had tried to abscond from an orphanage had her head shaved by the Mother Superior as a punishment. Johnson was a District Court judge and, according to his son, based the incident on true events that he had witnessed in the courtroom and wished to bring to critical public attention. See McGarry, 2010.

116. See Donnelly and Inglis, 2010.

117. Some evolutionary psychologists interested in the formation and maintenance of coalitions speak of a human proclivity for "offensive moral warfare," adding that the objective is often to cause a "moral cascade" that sways third-party bystanders by crafting and launching a "contagious representational bundle" that will leap from mind to mind. See Tooby and Cosmides, 2010.

118. See, for example, Asad (2003) and J. Z. Smith (1998) for two of the best known treatments of this hypothesis.

119. This approach is prevalent in the research area known as the cognitive science of religion, which often aims to understand cross-culturally recurrent aspects of religious social phenomena by breaking them down into more scientifically tractable components and explaining their prevalence in terms of universal evolved aspects of human psychology. See Taves (2009), Boyer (2010), and Whitehouse and Lanman (2014) for versions of this position.

120. For instance, see Tanya Luhrmann's *When God Talks Back* (2012) for a detailed ethnographic example of how social practices and psychological traits work together to make religion seem "real" (in the case of Luhrmann's study, to allow Vineyard Evangelical Christians to experience Jesus as a real presence in their lives).

121. See, for example, Berger, 1967.

122. In his recent work *Mass Exodus*, the sociologist Stephen Bullivant (2019) connects Berger's theory to Catholic disaffiliation in Britain and America since Vatican II.

123. Larkin, 1976: 77. To the list can also be added a proliferation of devotional paraphernalia (rosary beads, pictures, medals, and so on); an increase in Marian devotional cults encouraging intense religious experiences, which were interpreted as empirical reinforcement of religious dogma by investigating clergy (Hynes, 2009); and greater use of sensory props, such as music, candles, ornate vestments, and incense, which acted to increase affect during Mass and other religious occasions.

124. See, in particular, Mulholland (2019) for a detailed treatment of religiously inflected discourse in the Dáil.

125. Inglis, 1998: 249.

126. Inglis, 1998. Inglis makes much use of the concept of the Habitus, which is the term used by the French sociologist Pierre Bourdieu to describe the largely unconscious habits of thought, speech, and embodied dispositions that signal membership in a particular cultural group (Bourdieu, 1979).

127. For the original theory, see Henrich (2009). For an application of CRED theory to the topic of secularization, see Lanman (2012).

128. Although much earlier work on the psychology of religious transmission focused on cross-cultural regularities in the content of people's beliefs to argue that concepts such as unseen presences, teleological purpose in nature, or magical causation are in some way cognitively catchy or natural (e.g., Boyer, 2002), such explanations, though having some truth, have little purchase on why people believe the particular versions of these things that they do when so many options are available (e.g., W. M. Gervais and Henrich, 2010)—or why some people do not believe any of them at all (e.g., Lanman, 2012).

129. As Derek Scally notes, after Vatican II, the intellectual dimensions of Catholic theology were overlooked in favor of an "experiential" vision of religious indoctrination. The results were that cowed and unquestioning hellfire Catholicism was replaced, not by a more theologically satisfying alternative that could have proved compelling for a more educated and less insular populace, but by Hallmark Catholicism. Religious belief was far less commanding and demanding, but it was still something to be passively accepted rather than thought about. See Scally, 2021.

130. O'Doherty, 2008: 61.

131. See, again, Lanman, 2012.

132. This is not to say that secularized people inevitably become rationalists, as early secularization theorists such as Comte or Weber believed—far from it. As neo-secularization theorist Steve Bruce has noted, secularized societies remain awash with all manner of unsubstantiated and mystical beliefs. But these are no longer the output of socially mandated systems of belief standardization so much as tastes or bespoke choices, and they are largely unlinked to mass public identity. See Bruce, 2002.

133. Voas, 2009.

134. Orsi, 2017: 228–29.

135. Egan, 2011.

Chapter 2

1. For examples, see Greeley, 1994; Greeley and Ward, 2000; Cassidy, 2002; Andersen and Lavan, 2007; Donnelly and Inglis, 2010; and Ó Féich and O'Connell, 2015.

2. Financial constraints necessarily limited the sample size of this online survey. Within these constraints and in order to provide a more relevant and

representative sample, concomitant with the objectives of the survey, parameters were set in terms of age, gender, urban or rural habitation, socioeconomic status, and Catholic identification. In retrospect, measures such as education and income might have been more pertinent than socioeconomic status. This limitation, together with the small sample size, must be borne in mind throughout. More sophisticated surveys could be undertaken to enhance the analysis.

3. See, for example, Pew Research Center (2018) for data on religion in Western Europe.

4. Day, 2009.

5. This is certainly the conclusion of the organization Atheist Ireland, which has made considerable efforts in recent years to have the phrasing of the census question changed. See Chapter 5 for further details.

6. In the survey data, nine people rejected a Catholic identity but did not reject the teachings of the Church. This is an interesting position, but because of the small size of this group, they are not included in further analyses.

7. This difference in preference for dual identification between the two Catholic groups was a significant association, $\chi^2(1) = 17.553$, $p = .007$.

8. For example, Egan, 2011; Hilliard, 2003.

9. One piece of evidence that could be taken to suggest an ex-Catholic skew is Mass attendance statistics. In 2014 the ESS found that 34% of Irish Catholics reported attending Mass once a week or more. Only 24% of the current survey respondents reported attending Mass once a week or more. Although Mass attendance is in decline, a decrease of this magnitude in three years seems too steep. However, the differing setups also likely entailed differing demand characteristics.

10. This is something that could be fruitfully examined in the future with a quasi-experimental design treating free list exposure as an experimental condition.

11. Inglis, 1998.

12. The two magnets for hyphenation were "spiritual but not religious" and "Christian, no denomination." These are important. In a contemporary Irish context, being religious often connotes inflexible dogmatism or clericalism, such that many who appear quite traditional nevertheless hesitate to describe themselves using the term. *Spiritual* is often the preferred term, as it suggests a morally responsible, self-determined, "seeking" engagement with Catholic tradition, purged of derogatory connotations of slavish conformity. Supplementing *Catholic* with *Christian* is more ambiguous, intimating that the latter term is not entailed by the former. Perhaps this reflects perceptions that the Church has strayed from Christianity or has lost the right to determine what Christianity means for others, or perhaps by contrast it suggests an awareness of the prevalence of a "superficial" cultural Catholicism that flouts genuine commitment and persists in the absence of truly Christian belief and behavior. There are potentially several different motives that underlie Catholic hyphenation, and it warrants further study.

13. For example, Twomey, 2003; Goode et al., 2003; Donnelly and Inglis, 2010

14. W. M. Gervais et al., 2017.

15. Donnelly and Inglis, 2010.

16. $\chi^2(6, N = 239) = 77.16, p < .001$.

17. Romney and d'Andrade, 1964.

18. Manoharan and de Munck, 2015.

19. J. J. Smith, 1993. See also Quinlan (2019) for a good overview of free listing.

20. The prompt was as follows: "What are the first words you immediately think of when you read the term below? Please list as many as you can. List them in the order that they come to you, and please keep going until nothing more comes to mind. When you can't think of any more, click the button at the bottom of the page to move on. What comes to mind when you think of: the Irish Catholic Church?" This was the first component of the study, coming before any of the other items, so as not to contaminate the lists with artificial modifications of salience as a result of answering particular previous questions. Because traditional verbal probing was not possible in the online design, a question lock was included as a workaround, meaning that participants had to fill in at least 20 associations with the term before they could move on. Once the lists were collected, the terms garnered were categorized by two coders who were blind to the aims of the study. For example, "church," "cathedral," and "chapel" would have been categorized as "churches/buildings." This was done to standardize vocabulary, thereby facilitating comparisons of conceptual salience between groups.

21. The mean is the average of all values given; the median is the value that sits in the middle of the range; and the mode is the value that occurs most frequently. All three are provided here to demonstrate that, although the mean is affected to an extent by outliers, most people nevertheless significantly overestimate the extent of clerical pedophilia, generally gauged by scholars to be somewhere in the range of 3–6% (Goode et al., 2003; Keenan, 2012).

22. Interestingly, in a separate survey distributed to members of the secularist lobby group Atheist Ireland respondents provided much more accurate figures (mean, 13%; median, 9%; mode, 5%), presumably because their activist position meant that they were much more familiar with accurate reportage on clerical pedophilia.

23. Tangney et al., 2007.

24. W. I. Miller, 1997.

25. Hout and Fischer, 2014; Barna, 2017.

26. Data collected in the course of the survey using Jonathan Haidt's Moral Foundations Questionnaire indicated that ex-Catholics are concerned more exclusively with harm and fairness (the individualizing values emphasized by progressives) when considering whether an action is moral and far less motivated by

such factors as obedience, loyalty, or purity (the binding values emphasized by conservatives in addition to harm and fairness). See Haidt and Kesebir (2010) for a full treatment of moral foundations theory.

27. Zuckerman, 2008; Zuckerman et al., 2017.

28. W. M. Gervais et al., 2017: 1.

29. For example, one recent innovative measure that allowed people to out themselves as atheists in a subtler manner suggested that US atheists may have been underreported in religious polling by a factor of almost 3 (W. Gervais and Najle, 2018).

30. Ribberink et al., 2013.

31. Participants were asked to complete a scale designed to measure orthodox Catholic Christian beliefs (7-point Likert, α = .957, 6 items: transubstantiation, papal infallibility, the Resurrection, miracles, the virgin birth, confession). General theism was measured using a single-item Likert scale (0 = certain that some kind of God does not exist; 7 = certain that some kind of God exists).

32. A one-way ANOVA found that there were statistically significant differences between the groups ($F(2, 236)$ = 110.6, $p < .001$). A Bonferroni post hoc comparison found that both Catholics and deinstitutionalized Catholics scored significantly higher than ex-Catholics ($p < .001$). Catholics and deinstitutionalized Catholics did not differ significantly ($p = .371$).

33. To measure Irish Catholic CREDs, a Catholic version of Lanman and Buhrmester's (2017) CRED scale was developed (7-point Likert, α = .923, 8 items). This scale measures the degree to which people perceived their parents' behavior to have been motivated by religious belief. The Catholic belief scale was deployed for the purposes of establishing whether or not there is a link between Catholic CRED exposure and the acceptance of Catholic beliefs. CREDs were also assessed as a predictor variable for social identification with Catholicism, that is, the degree to which "being Catholic" is a valued part of one's identity, measured using a standard four-item social identification (FISI) scale (Postmes et al., 2013).

34. A significant multiple linear regression equation was found ($F(4, 243)$ = 12.028, $p < .001$), with an R^2 of .325.

35. CREDs: β = .465, $t(243)$ = 7.702, $p < .001$. Age: β = .149, $t(243)$ = 2.45, $p = .015$. Gender: β = .140, $t(243)$ = 2.61, $p = .01$.

36. In both cases the correlation between age and CREDs was strong, but collinearity statistics revealed that both variables were well within acceptable parameters for a valid regression equation (tolerance = .766; VIF = 1.305).

37. A significant regression equation was found ($F(3, 243)$ = 17.981, $p < .001$), with an R^2 of .214.

38. β = .449, $t(243)$ = 7.139, $p < .001$.

39. The main limitations of this inference lie with the scale itself. It could be prone to retrospective biases such that if people were more religious (or became so), they would be more likely to attribute religious motivations to parental behavior or selectively remember instances when parents behaved in a manner

suggesting underlying religious belief. These possibilities of reverse causation warrant further attention.

40. Go to Mass; go to confession; donate money to the Church or to Catholic charities; go to the church to light candles; receive ashes on Ash Wednesday; pray in front of other people; celebrate important events in my life or my children's with a traditional Catholic ceremony (marriages, funerals, christenings, etc.); bless myself while passing a church; give something up for Lent; confront family members or people in my community who were disrespectful to the Church; and hide the fact that I didn't really believe in Catholic teachings. (The last factor is the suppression of a CRUD rather than a CRED.)

41. Progressivism was measured in an established manner using Haidt's Moral Foundations Questionnaire. This questionnaire breaks morality into a number of different underlying concerns: harm/care, fairness/cheating, authority/subversion, loyalty/betrayal, purity/sanctity. According to Haidt and colleagues' research, progressives are concerned with the two individualizing foundations (harm/care and fairness/cheating), whereas conservatives are concerned equally with all five. By combining the two individualizing foundations (fairness/cheating and harm/care) and three binding foundations (authority/subversion, loyalty/betrayal, purity/sanctity) on Haidt's Moral Foundations Questionnaire and subtracting the binding foundations score from the individualizing foundations score, one generates a progressivism score. Because a large number of participants ($N = 49$) failed the stringent attention checks in Haidt's shortened Moral Foundations Questionnaire, these regression models use a smaller subgroup of the data ($N = 199$).

42. A highly significant regression equation was found for Catholic belief ($F(6, 193) = 37.792, p < .001$), with an R^2 of .540. Although there was significant correlation between independent variables, no collinearity statistic dipped below a tolerance of .675 (tolerance generally disqualifies the variable only if it dips below .2).

43. Among some theological observers, scandal is almost conspicuously sidelined as a lurid epiphenomenon more fit for lascivious tabloids than respectable academic literature. As historian Roy Foster observed, it "is striking, indeed semi-miraculous, that in a book by the editor of the Irish Theological Quarterly published in 2003 and called *The End of Irish Catholicism?* [Twomey, 2003], there is much about the dangers of the liberal agenda and not a single word about scandals" (Foster, 2007: 67). By contrast, sociologists and historians draw attention to the scandals but emphasize how they interact within a complex context and warn that Irish secularization should not simply be reduced to the scandals.

44. It is worth mentioning that the free lists were collected in 2017 before the Tuam affair began to occupy the news, suggesting the negative portrayal of the Church in the data is not the result of a transient surge in antipathy connected to this event.

45. For example, C. G. Brown, 2012.

46. Ganiel (2019a) analyzed 314 stories mentioning Francis in *The Irish Times* published between May and September 2018. Although the stories also covered such topics as the logistics of the visit and critical topics such as the Church's attitudes toward LGBTQ people, Ganiel found that it was abuse that dominated the coverage. The issue was already highly salient in the Irish media, but it was likely further amplified by the highly damaging Pennsylvania report on clerical abuse and cover-ups.

47. "Irish PM: Time to Move Catholic Church from Centre of Society," *The Guardian*, August 25, 2018, https://www.theguardian.com/world/2018/aug/25/arrival-of-pope-francis-in-ireland-brings-mixed-emotions (accessed August 25, 2018).

48. In reality, these were the end results of long grassroots-level campaigns to sway the center, and Fine Gael were quite cautious before allowing them to come to fruition during their leadership, acting only when they had determined which way the winds were blowing and that it would be in their political interest to collect some of the moral and political credit. See Drażkiewicz and Ní Mhórda (2020) for a detailed and nuanced treatment of the politics around the Repeal campaign.

49. Chang, 2018.

50. Mehta, 2018.

51. Ingber, 2018.

52. Ganiel (2019a) details the prominent and positive media coverage given to McAleese and Collins, juxtaposing this with the more critical coverage of the pope.

53. Martin, 2018.

54. Foxe, 2018.

55. By contrast, the Repeal movement's monochrome sweatshirts, Ireland's emblematic pro-choice apparel, were still in demand two years after the abortion referendum victory as a badge of moral elitism.

56. Ganiel, 2019a.

Chapter 3

1. McGahern, 2009: 143.

2. A significant area of atheist protest is the recruitment of teachers. Teachers in Catholic schools are expected to be able and willing to give religious instruction. Although this means that many unbelievers "of conscience" are thus unofficially disqualified from the education system, it also likely entails that a great many of those ultimately tasked with religious instruction have "fudged their faith credentials" in order to secure employment.

3. Weafer, 2014.

4. C. Smith et al., 2014: 190.

5. Bengston et al., 2013.

6. Sherkat, 2014.

7. For example, Atran, 2010.

8. For example, Durkheim, 1915; Sosis et al., 2007; Henrich, 2009; Lanman, 2012; Atran, 2010.

9. Máire's encounter with her Jesuits, who spoke the language of individualized therapeutic deism while gently corralling it back in a Catholic direction, is the kind of "post-Catholic" re-evangelism that Irish sociological commentators influenced by the religious economies model have proposed as a promising future avenue for the Church (Ganiel, 2016). It may be so, but its prospects may also be limited. If people treat religion as private therapeutic meaning making rather than as public ritual obligation, the potential result is lower CRED exposure. Combined with a religious marketplace in which the number of religious consumers with CRED-heavy traditionalist foundations such as Máire's are dwindling and in which negative moral evaluations of Catholicism abound, it is uncertain whether the future bodes well for the competitiveness of such Catholicism-inflected supernatural products, even if we were to grant the religious economies model its presupposition of invariant religious demand.

10. For example, Berger, 1967.

11. Mulholland, 2019.

12. Diarmuid Martin, "'Keeping the Show on the Road': Is This the Future of the Irish Catholic Church?" Speaking notes, Cambridge Group for Irish Studies, February 22, 2011, http://www.dublindiocese.ie/22022011-cambridge-group-for-irish-studies/ (accessed April 17, 2017).

13. For example, Twomey, 2003.

14. *Woo* is a term used in New Atheist circles to denote vaguely defined supernatural worldviews that do not form part of major institutionalized traditions and that are notable for their lack of rigor.

15. This outsourcing to the school system is not without detractors. Within the Church a number of clerics from left and right have advocated for faith formation to be taken back into the hands of parents, even if this were to drastically reduce Irish Catholics to a smaller demographic of purer believers. See, for example, O Kelly, 2019; and the proposed "Do This in Memory of Me" program (https://www.veritasbooksonline.com/brand/do-this-in-memory/).

16. This depends on whom one asks. Some maintain that issues of access for minority religions and the nonreligious have been resolved by recent policy changes, whereas others remain adamant that discrimination in the Catholic-dominated school system persists at a more covert level.

17. "First Communion Kids Apply for Covid Payment," *Waterford Whispers News*, May 6, 2020, https://waterfordwhispersnews.com/2020/05/06/first-communion-kids-apply-for-covid-payment/ (accessed May 9, 2020).

18. In *The Best Catholics in the World*, Derek Scally (2021) gives a particularly incisive description of the banal, patronizing, and intellectually underwhelming post-1980s religion classroom experience.

19. See McWilliams, 2019.

20. A Gaelscoil is a school where all subjects are taught in the Irish language. The schools are popular with a sector of upper-middle-class parents seeking to increase the cultural capital of their children.

21. Laura Whitmore, "Christmas Reminds Me Just How Ambiguous My Relationship With Religion Really Is," blog post, *Grazia*, August 7, 2019, https://graziadaily.co.uk/life/real-life/laura-whitmore-losing-my-religion/ (accessed August 11, 2019).

22. https://www.youtube.com/watch?v=RD8i4GICuyw (accessed October 12, 2020).

23. This came true (with added cocaine to boot). See Warrander, 2016.

24. Because of snowballing revelations about what actually goes on at night in the Vatican, this sketch looks far bolder today than it did in the mid-1990s. See, for example, *In the Closet of the Vatican: Power, Homosexuality and Hypocrisy* (Martel, 2019).

25. L. J. Taylor, 1995.

26. Today, further sources of irreverent cultural Catholicism can be found online that draw on the spirit of *Father Ted*, such as memes or anachronistic videos ridiculing aspects of the Holy Catholic past. One recent example is a video of an elderly couple driving frantically around Cork City with a statue of the Virgin bolted to the roof of their car and a megaphone blasting the Angelus in a desperate attempt to scour COVID-19 from the streets. These culturally Catholic in-jokes at the traditionalist Catholic's expense are often of the "Aren't we a daft bunch altogether" variety. In other words, they act, paradoxically, to bind the generations rather than divide them.

27. An interior locution is a form of private revelation defined by the online Catholic Dictionary as "a supernatural communication to the ear, imagination, or directly to the intellect." See https://www.catholicculture.org/culture/library/dictionary/index.cfm?id=34640 (accessed September 23, 2020).

28. Rooney, 2017: 113.

29. As of 2021, civil marriage ceremonies have overtaken Catholic ones. On the other hand, funerals remain overwhelmingly Catholic. For all the irreconcilable differences in cultural context, this emerging division of ritual duties is superficially reminiscent of the Japanese custom of being born Shinto, having a "Christian"-style wedding ceremony, and dying Buddhist.

Chapter 4

1. See, for example, UCD Geary Institute for Public Policy, 2019.

2. McGahern, 2009: 147.

3. Mulholland, 2019: 150.

4. Archbishop Diarmuid Martin and a number of priests regard these as particular areas of concern, with Mass attendance being as low as 1–2% of the Catholic population in some parishes. This has been ascribed to the dissolution

of traditional community bonds that occurred in the middle decades of the twentieth century, when urban working-class populations were moved from the city center out to new suburban council estates. There is general agreement that the best Mass attendances in Dublin are found in well-heeled middle-class parishes. However, I also heard the view expressed that suspected pedophile priests were more likely to be reassigned to working-class areas and that, in the wake of abuses, there were fewer pastoral initiatives to mollify affected working-class communities. If true, this may be a further factor in the lower attendance figures in these areas.

5. "Venerable Matt Talbot," *Franciscan Media*, January 18, 2020, https://www.franciscanmedia.org/venerable-matt-talbot/ (accessed March 25, 2020).

6. In many ways, this group of men constituted what Inglis (1998) and Stivers (1976) refer to as a "bachelor drinking group," a social structure proposed to have evolved as an outlet to compensate for the late marriage and permanent celibacy prevalent in Ireland since the nineteenth century and to provide a male refuge from the domestic sphere, which was increasingly ruled by religious morality through the "priest/mother" alliance. Scheper-Hughes's classic ethnography *Saints, Scholars and Schizophrenics* (2001 [1979]) also includes a number of bachelor drinking groups. Conversation and action are highly stereotyped in such groups, tending to revolve around safe topics and the mockery of those who exhibit unorthodox "showy" opinions or displays of arrogance. Social capital within the group accrues to those who can best "hold their drink," that is, maintain total control and appear as though they have not drunk at all. Although religion was not generally a spontaneous or popular topic of discussion in my group, within this traditional environment, conversation could be brought around to it without much trouble, everyone felt free to express an opinion on it, and the most acceptable position was that it was "a load of shite," indicating how uncontroversial it now is to openly criticize the previously sacred sphere of Catholic religion in Ireland.

7. This view had been cemented by an encounter with the undertaker, who had informed him that his father was gone—"It's a load of shite, this afterlife stuff"—but he did not generally relay that kind of information to his other customers.

8. Often these men would have children outside of wedlock, but they would almost always have them baptized. Some priests will not do this, but some—including the priest at St. Teresa's—are willing so long as the parents are deemed to show the intention to overcome the obstacles to full communion with the Church in the future and demonstrate sincere intent to raise their child in the Catholic faith. There were many children in Kilbreagh who were baptized but whose parents were not married.

9. According to John, this boy had been taken by the local priest in his car to another area of Dublin and "felt up." He was then left to find his own way home

from the other side of the city. This was also alleged to have happened to a second boy. John told me that when the boy's father found out about this, he hunted the priest down and punched him to the ground. The priest was subsequently moved to another parish. I was unable to verify this story.

10. C. Smith (2005) notes the emergence and spread of a relativistic, therapeutic conception of God among young Christians in the United States. He claims that this nebulous and personalized form of theism, which he calls "Moral Therapeutic Deism," parasitically occupies existing denominations and overwrites commitment to their specific doctrines.

11. It has often been claimed that, after Catholicism's post-Famine boom years, Ireland was distinctive in having no real tradition of widespread male anti-clericalism that was so prevalent on the continent (L. J. Taylor, 1995; Connolly, 2001) and that presented itself in ethnographic work on Latin Catholic cultures (Christian, 1989). The anti-clericalism of the Kilbreagh drinkers at times looks very much like that of Latin men opposing the effeminacy of the village priest and his collusion with women.

12. Perhaps excepting old people, who are generally constructed as both brainwashed and inordinately fragile regarding this matter, if put on the spot, one can—and indeed should—be perfectly candid about one's unbelief when the subject arises in ordinary conversation with another adult. Mutual tension can be defused with mollifying phrases that reposition ontological propositions as unverifiable opinions, such as "at the end of the day, sure, who knows."

13. This may also help to explain the high levels of ex-Catholicism found by my survey, where online respondents could reject a Catholic identity without concern for social consequences.

Chapter 5

1. D'Arcy and Pope, 2016.

2. The Citizens' Assembly was convened by the government in 2016 to debate a number of controversial political issues, one of which was abortion. It consisted of a chairman, 33 political representatives, and 66 "ordinary citizens" representatively selected by a polling company. Although previous polling suggested that the Irish population favored liberalization of abortion laws but not full unrestricted access, the assembly voted in favor of unrestricted access to abortion. As testament to the political dangers surrounding morally charged topics, the assembly was widely perceived to have been arranged by then-taoiseach Enda Kenny to deflect responsibility for a potentially divisive referendum that could have cost Fine Gael conservative votes.

3. "Time to Act! 6th Annual March for Choice," Abortion Rights Campaign, July 18, 2017, https://www.abortionrightscampaign.ie/2017/07/18/time-to-act-6th-annual-march-for-choice/ (accessed July 28, 2017).

4. D'Arcy and Pope, 2016.

5. Power, 2017.

6. A coalition of anti-abortion groups organized large public demonstrations under the Rally for Life banner. An anonymously authored report of the 2017 Dublin Rally for Life, written by a member of the movement, can be found at https://rallyforlife.net/dublin-2017/ (accessed June 2, 2021).

7. "Don't Stop Wiggle Wiggle" by the Outhere Brothers.

8. The cassock, a traditional clerical garment, is not commonly worn in public anymore in Ireland. See Chapter 7 for further details.

9. Specifically, "culture of . . ." phraseology. The idea of a conflict between a "culture of death" and a "culture of life" was promulgated by Pope John Paul II and revolved around a number of reproductive issues, most notably abortion, and today both of these terms as well as a broader variant of the binary, namely "culture of hope" or "culture of joy" versus "culture of despair," often appear in conservative Catholic publications such as *Alive!* newspaper to connote secularism and Christianity, respectively.

10. In her survey into belief and affiliation in post-Catholic Ireland, Ganiel (2016) was unable to recruit any believing Catholics below the age of 25 from the general population; thus to understand the views of young Catholics, she turned instead to university students who had been re-evangelized by a Catholic youth group. The new recruits generally cited the group's active interest in egalitarian economics-related social justice issues as one of the main factors behind their re-evangelization. This is an area where the social values of the Church and the young coincide, making it an optimal gateway to re-evangelization. However, I also found that a small minority with opposing "alt-right" sympathies are attracted to conservative Catholicism. Both of these groups are currently minuscule.

11. Savita Halappanavar was refused a medically necessary abortion in 2012 because of the presence of a fetal heartbeat. Her case became part of a series of high-profile incidents that served to underline the negative consequences of Ireland's strict abortion legislation. Other high-profile cases include the 1992 "X Case" involving a teenager ("X") who had been raped but was prevented from traveling abroad for an abortion, and the 2014 "Y Case," in which an asylum seeker who had been raped was forced to carry the child to term against her wishes.

12. These appear to be large-scale, organized examples of what moral psychologists refer to as moral reframing, namely, the effort to adjust the presentation of causes in a way that will appeal to those who might be alienated by them (e.g., Feinberg and Willer, 2015).

13. It was clear that, although both of these polarized positions could draw on large numbers of adherents to make a show, the differing ways in which they might publicly manifest indicated which way the wind was blowing. Adherents of the conservative narrative only ever signal their allegiance to their particular moral causes when protesting as part of a like-minded group; those with more liberal outlooks regularly walk down the street wearing "REPEAL" jerseys or "TÁ"

(yes) badges (the catchphrases for pro-choice and pro–same sex marriage campaigns, respectively) as components of everyday apparel. This appeared to be not just a matter of greater public relations savvy but of greater confidence in public acceptance.

14. The archbishop's point is not new. As far back as 1998, Inglis noted a growing trend to accrue political capital by challenging the Church. This becomes particularly notable in the aftermath of scandal breakouts, such as former taoiseach Enda Kenny's comments following the publication of the Murphy Report into abuses in the Archdiocese of Dublin (2010) or after the discovery of infant remains at the Tuam mother and baby home (2017). Like all long-lived politicians, Kenny is a smooth, calculating operator; his Tuam speech was noteworthy for the way it implicated a judgmental but vague "culture of the past," thereby spreading the blame widely across society while also confining it to history, something that allowed him to appear pro-secular while avoiding the alienation of contemporary believers and institutions.

15. Diarmuid Martin, "The Challenge for the Church in the 21st Century," Saint Kilian's Lecture, Archdiocese of Dublin, July 8, 2017, http://www.dublindiocese.ie/the-challenge-for-the-church-in-the-21st-century/ (accessed July 12, 2017).

16. One paper, though dated, offers an interesting account of ideological forces and their influence on Irish Catholics (Ruane, 1998). Two of these forces are described as widespread but largely inactive: *traditional Catholicism* (aging; fond of pre–Vatican II practices, highly orthodox beliefs; to be Irish is to be Catholic; a debt is owed to the Church) and *liberal Catholicism* (sentimental and social bonds to the Church, but the nation has moved on; theistic but decide for themselves about theological or moral matters). Two are politically active: *neo-conservativism* (small but influential, anti-relativism, anti-secularizationism, pro-Church influence) and *secular revisionism* (have either lost or shed their faith; the Church is an oppressive and authoritarian force which warped the emergent nation). Ruane believed that neo-conservative and traditional Catholic power was such that secular revisionists would precipitate a reactionary backlash if secularization was pursued too stridently. He defines "liberal Catholics" as a majority who exhibit (1) "a continued concern with the sacred and with the religious and moral dimensions of existence; (2) voluntary conformity to the forms of worship recommended or prescribed by the church; [and] (3) the exercise of personal judgement in theological belief and moral matters" (Ruane, 1998: 16). Today, this sounds like a description of the average Mass goer, not the average baptized Irish Catholic. At the very least, item 2 has certainly declined: Weekly Mass attendance was still around 80% of the Catholic population in 1998, and this "voluntary conformity" has lost ground (according to European Social Survey data, weekly Mass attendance is now around 34% of the Catholic population; UCD Geary Institute for Policy, 2019). In other words, the majority is shifting into a religiously disengaged state where it may be more receptive to courting by revisionists and less receptive to courting by neo-conservatives.

17. Ruane, 1998.

18. Ruane maintained that these groups primarily argue their cause on the following grounds: (1) moral-theological ("the will of God as made known through His Church"), (2) social ("the good of society"), and (3) political ("the will of the majority in the society"). My own field observations lead me to think that the moral-theological grounds have become largely concealed in externally focused campaigning and exists primarily in in-group discourse; that social grounds receive the most weight, as they are a point of meta-moral consonance with secular "human flourishing" (the means may be different, but the aim is the same); and that the political grounds are still widely recruited, with an optimistic reading of cultural Catholicism and opaque census figures often cited as evidence of majoritarian support for neo-conservative Catholic projects. However, after the repeal of the Eighth Amendment by referendum, the political grounds are much less compelling.

19. Ruane, 1998: 15.

20. "Change Was a Disaster for Church and Society," *Alive!*, July/August 2017.

21. See, for example, "How Unintended Religious Discrimination in Irish Schools Has Evolved Since 1965," Atheist Ireland, February 14, 2021, https://atheist.ie/2021/02/religious-discrimination-in-schools-since-1965 (accessed February 14, 2021). I also heard some parents report that religious education classes were deliberately timetabled in the middle of the school day so that parents could not bring children home early to avoid religious indoctrination.

22. "The state acknowledges the right to life of the unborn and, with due regard to the equal right to life of the mother, guarantees in its laws to respect, and as far as practicable, by its laws to defend and vindicate that right." *Bunreacht na hÉireann*, 40.3.3.

23. In 2017 interest in the blasphemy laws flared up with the Stephen Fry case, widely considered among both secularist and religious commentators to be an instance of a hoax aimed at exposing the absurdity and unenforceability of the laws. See H. McDonald, 2017. The blasphemy laws have also been criticized because they have been used as a model to cite precedent by religiously repressive states such as Saudi Arabia and Pakistan. See Greenslade, 2016.

24. McGarry, 2009.

25. "Homily of Bishop Leo O'Reilly at the Welcome Mass for the Relics of Saint Oliver Plunkett," Irish Catholic Bishops' Conference, June 6, 2017, http://www.catholicbishops.ie/2017/06/06/homily-of-bishop-leo-oreilly-at-the-welcome-mass-for-the-relics-of-saint-oliver-plunkett/ (accessed June 7, 2017).

26. Quinn, 2017b.

27. Ferns is forever associated in the public imagination with the depredations of Father Seán Fortune and the failure of the bishop at the time to bring him to justice, as detailed in the Ferns Report (2005).

28. "Block Sisters of Charity as 'Sole Owners' of National Maternity Hospital," petition, Uplift, n.d., https://my.uplift.ie/petitions/block-sisters-of-chairty-as-sole-owners-of-national-maternity-hospital (accessed November 27, 2018).

29. In 2020 it was made public that this promise was not fulfilled and that the "core values" stated in the constitution of the new company were identical to those that were to be amended and replaced, obliging the new owners to uphold the same ethos as other hospitals currently governed by the order. These hospitals do not provide contraception, sterilization, in vitro fertilization, abortion, and other procedures legal in Ireland but prohibited by Catholic teaching. See Boylan, 2021. Attempts to find a resolution to these issues, effectively caused by the state's continued dependence on Church-owned health infrastructure, were still ongoing at the time of this writing.

30. Cullen, 2017.

31. For example, Lakoff, 1987; Slingerland, 2011.

32. O'Toole, 2017.

33. Pine, 2011: 47.

34. O'Toole, 2017.

35. O'Gorman, 2003.

36. Scally, 2017.

37. The play was performed at the Abbey Theatre, Dublin, from September 26 to October 5, 2019.

38. Pierre Paulo Pasolini's 1975 film *Salò, or 120 Days of Sodom*, is an allegory about the Salò republic, the German puppet state within Italy where Mussolini clung on from 1943 until his eventual downfall in 1945. *Salò* is notorious for being one of the most difficult films to watch ever made, such is the utter depravity and sadism meted out by various state "officials," as, over the course of a weekend, they first abuse and then butcher a group of local young people captured for their debauched delectation. Far from being an exploitative video nasty, however, *Salò* is a deeply and indignantly moral piece of art, an unflinching meditation on the dehumanizing potential of unchecked power and the compliance that allows it to happen.

39. C. L. Murphy, 2019.

40. Luke "Ming" Flanagan, MEP, Facebook Post, March 8, 2017.

41. "Enda Kenny Describes Tuam Burial Site as a 'Chamber of Horrors,'" *The Journal.ie,* March 7, 2017, http://www.thejournal.ie/leaders-questions-30-3275086-Mar2017/ (accessed March 14, 2017).

42. The Coalition to Repeal the Eighth, for instance, reported to be a "growing alliance of over ninety organisations." See http://www.repealeight.ie/.

43. During fieldwork, Atheist Ireland had a central committee, about 300 core members responsible for regional activism and organization, several thousand paying members, and several thousand more "sympathizers." Its primary modes of message dissemination are its website (www.atheist.ie), further cause-specific sites (education: teachdontpreach.ie; blasphemy laws: blasphemy.ie; a provision for symbolically registering defection from the Catholic Church: NotMe.ie; and a "secular charitable initiative": goodwithoutgods.ie, presumably intended to combat the notion that atheists lack moral feeling), a weekly

newsletter *Secular Sunday*, its information booth near the historic General Post Office on O'Connell Street, and the presence of Atheist Ireland leaders in media debates. Atheist Ireland invites high-profile speakers to address its members and also hosts Atheist General Meetings a few times a year, which are open to all, but these latter events tend in practice to be small strategy-planning gatherings of a highly pragmatic and political nature with no more than a couple dozen deeply involved individuals present. Broader in-group discussion takes place online, primarily on the group's Facebook page. Atheist Ireland has similar demographic features to other ideologically similar groups—for example, less than 17% of Atheist Ireland members are female—and, though overwhelmingly liberal in orientation, the group has experienced a number of schisms and tensions around attitudes toward social justice issues. See Kettell (2013) and Taira (2012) for descriptions of New Atheist politics and activism elsewhere.

44. According to a former committee member Atheist Ireland has its organizational roots in the secularist wing of the now-defunct Progressive Democrats political party, which was formed from those alienated from the perennially dominant Fianna Fáil and Fine Gael political parties. This may account for its tight and hierarchical organizational structure, discipline, efficacy in campaigning, and keen sense of public relations.

45. It must be said, however, that Atheist Ireland is not without contradictions. Its growth from atheist awareness group to central secularist lobby group has created a tension between the specificity of its ideological origins and the scope of its current role. Its rank-and-file membership cleaves to New Atheism's core beliefs and values, and this can transmit a centrifugal undercurrent of instability where different secularists converge, particularly online. Atheist Ireland must therefore constantly balance an absolutist conviction in the supremacy of beliefs based on reason with a relativistic mission to secure an egalitarian social structure where all beliefs are treated equally, but it cannot ensure that its members reflect this doxastic egalitarianism in the public arena, which can lead to tensions in the broader secularist milieu.

46. For instance, a 2017 newspaper article on reactions to shifting census demographics contained the following quote: "My peer group, we'd all be of no religion, but for schools for our kids we'd all tick the box for Catholic. We're not practising though." The interviewee, a female student, nevertheless goes on to say, "I'd hope the rising figures of other religions would influence planning for schools, definitely." See Clarke-Molloy, 2017.

47. See, for instance, the introduction in Norget et al. (2017).

48. "The three sacraments of Baptism, Confirmation, and Holy Orders confer, in addition to grace, a sacramental character or seal by which the Christian shares in Christ's priesthood and is made a member of the Church according to different states and functions. This configuration to Christ and to the Church, brought about by the Spirit, is indelible; it remains forever in the Christian as a positive disposition for grace, a promise and guarantee of divine protection, and

as a vocation to divine worship and to the service of the Church. Therefore, these sacraments can never be repeated." *Catechism of the Catholic Church*, par. 1121 (Catholic Church, 2000: 290–91).

49. *Where Is Your God? Responding to the Challenge of Unbelief and Religious Indifference Today*, Concluding Document of the 2006 Plenary Assembly, http://www.cultura.va/content/cultura/en/pub/documenti/whereisyourgod.html (accessed April 2, 2017).

50. Until 2010 it was possible to officially declare defection. A website called CountMeOut.ie disseminated PDF forms to Irish Catholics wishing to symbolically sever themselves from the Church, especially in the wake of the 2009 Ryan Report into institutional abuses. The removal from canon law of the ability to formally defect is a sore issue for Irish ex-Catholics.

51. This interest in altering patterns of identification is present in other societies (the United Kingdom, for instance; see Lee, 2015), but it is perhaps particularly intense in Ireland.

52. The Central Statistics Office stipulates on its website that the "question is asking about the person's current religion or beliefs and not about the religion the person may have been brought up with," but critics hold that a large number of Irish Catholics tend to answer "Roman Catholic" simply based on the fact that they were baptized as such, thereby inflating support for Church patronage of schools, hospitals, and other services.

53. https://radio.rte.ie/radio1highlights/8-irish-catholics-said-dont-believe-god-low-hurdle-catholic/ (accessed April 20, 2017).

54. Quinn, 2017a.

55. Clarke, 2014.

56. Anonymous post on the "Time to Tick No" Facebook page (accessed March 15, 2017).

57. Drażkiewicz et al., 2020: 12.

58. Waters, 2018.

59. "More than Two Thirds of Voters Want to Keep the Angelus, *The Journal.ie*, October 27, 2018, https://www.thejournal.ie/angelus-exit-poll-4309296-Oct2018/ (accessed October 30, 2018).

60. Keane, 2015: 138.

61. See, for example, Liam Kennedy's (2016) work on the Irish cultural schema of MOPE (Most Oppressed People Ever).

Chapter 6

1. Beckett, 1990 [1955]: 83).

2. Keane (2015) argues in his book *Ethical Life: Its Natural and Social Histories* that narratives are a key ingredient in allowing new moral stances to emerge. They place us within a story and draw previously barely articulable issues into conscious scrutiny. Keane draws on anthropologist Naomi Scheman's work on US feminist consciousness-raising groups of the 1970s to exemplify this (Scheman, 1980).

Women discovered they had been angry for years; the groups birthed a situation where taken-for-granted subordination and simmering but inarticulable feelings of unfairness that had long accrued as a result were given form and redescribed as clear political injustice; in being articulated, resentment became legitimized and actionable, leading to the emergence of a reconfigured ethical world with new aims (liberation from oppression), new actors (male chauvinists, liberated women), and new forms of moral and immoral action (e.g., sexual harassment).

3. In a 2012 newspaper interview, sociologist Tom Inglis attempted to encapsulate how the Irish relationship to the Catholic Church had changed since the 1950s: "There was a sense in which the church was an authority to be obeyed, and there was a fear of not being obedient. Then you moved into a phase where it wasn't obeyed and it was respected. And now it has moved into a phase where the institutional church is not respected." This is a pithy rendering of the transition. See Sheridan, 2012.

4. "They're the same group of people. Now that's a good question. Are they individually the same people? Is that what people, why they're getting away with it? Cause they're like 'Oh well that was Sister, Sister. Very bad but she died, passed away.' I mean are those people dead? Then again, they don't pay. They're not paying their fine. So they must be the same people and in the Church they're covering up. So they must be on the same page as the people who did it or be the same people who actually did it. Like I don't know about that. I don't know, you know."

5. Renting a bouncy castle (an inflatable platform with surrounding inflatable walls) for children to play on has become a stereotypical festivity associated with First Communion in Ireland. One mildly popular derogatory term that I encountered online for cultural Catholics was "bouncy castle Catholics." McWilliams uses the term in a less disparaging way in *Renaissance Nation* (2019).

6. For instance, schools can still inquire about whether or not a student is Catholic, which some believe opens the door to unconscious or undercover discrimination. See O'Halloran, 2019.

7. See O'Toole (2021) for extensive reflections on the Irish capacity for doublethink.

8. Humphreys, 2017.

9. See M. Gervais and Fessler (2017) for a thorough treatment of the nature of contempt.

10. See, for example, the work of Paul Bloom on the subject (Danovitch and Bloom, 2009).

11. Kelly (2011) makes this argument in his book *Yuck! The Nature and Moral Significance of Disgust.*

12. Clark and Fessler, 2014: 5.

13. Kupfer and Giner-Sorolla, 2016.

14. See Twomey (2003) for a typical example.

15. Cimino and colleagues note that identity politics is a divisive issue in secular groups. Most are left-leaning, but often the membership lean more to the left

of the leadership, who may have attitudes that clash with left-wing attitudes toward identity politics and relativistic tolerance for Islam. See Cimino et al. 2020.

16. This was an incident that disrupted the New Atheist movement in 2011, producing a legacy that has lingered ever since. Rebecca Watson, a speaker at the World Atheist Conference in Dublin that year, described suffering unwanted advances from a male conference delegate in an elevator. Richard Dawkins, the "Pope" of New Atheism, belittled her position, spurring a movement-wide split of allegiance. The New Atheist world saw a schism between those who supported Dawkins and opposed "feminazis" and a more "woke" contingent who followed biologist P. Z. Myers. Issues about the treatment of women in the broader New Atheist community have dogged the movement ever since. See https://en.wikipedia.org/wiki/Rebecca_Watson#:~:text=The%20controversy%20that%20came%20to,movement%20on%20account%20of%20her (accessed June 20, 2019).

17. For example, W. M. Gervais and Norenzayan, 2012.

18. Cimino and Smith, 2014.

19. See, for example, Susan Harding's (2000) work on American fundamentalist Christians, which describes conversion as involving the application of a stereotyped narrative frame and vocabulary to one's own life experiences.

20. For example, one woman in her 30s noted that "I only believed in god as a child as I was indoctrinated by school and parents," and a man in his 50s noted that he "probably believed until I was 9—as we were all brainwashed to do." Another man maintained that he "believed as a child because I was brainwashed into it by our education system." A man in his 30s described how "I was brainwashed as a child into believing in a god made up by primitive Iron Age Middle Eastern peasants. I realized the scale of the nonsense in my teenage years."

21. For example, Twomey, 2003; McGarry, 2006.

22. Lee, 2015.

Chapter 7

1. See M. Gervais and Fessler (2017) for probably the most compelling academic work on the topic of contempt. Of further interest is that contempt is a tabooed sentiment in egalitarian Western cultures, where it tends to be performed as hate or pity, as these nonhierarchical responses are more socially acceptable.

2. Goffman, 1968.

3. Angelides, 2005.

4. Goode et al., 2003: 114.

5. Goode et al., 2003.

6. Goode et al., 2003: 117.

7. Goode et al., 2003: 68.

8. Many priests also feel unsupported by the hierarchy, further reinforcing the contraction of their worlds (King, 2017). During the tensions that followed post–Murphy Report investigations of the Archdiocese of Dublin, Archbishop Martin described how (innocent) priests would respond differently to proposals

depending on whether they were in their parish among their supporters or outside this safety zone. Although priestly views of Archbishop Martin were generally positive, especially with regard to his handling of the public, some priests felt that they had been unfairly treated, as though they were guilty before being proven innocent. One priest described at length how he was falsely accused and how, in his view, the accusation was dealt with poorly by the diocese. As he described it, his ability to bring pressure to bear from his devout parishioners was a key element in obtaining fair treatment.

9. Father Toland said: "In recent years nothing really, you know, apart from things I would consider of no importance, like the drunk who asks you for money . . . he'll say: 'Ah you old pedophile.' Well that's of no importance. The abuse I'm talking about from earlier years was sort of well-dressed people coming up to you on the street and actually, you know, denouncing you for what you are. . . . But it happened to me at least on two occasions where, I very definitely remember, very worrying events really which were not, sort of, just casual offhand things but were very deliberate and well thought out and very aggressive. But, no, I think at this stage we probably have gone beyond that."

10. A theme that emerges is that anti-clericalism is at its most intense in working-class communities, especially among young men. This assertion cannot be verified, but I heard a number of theories for why this might be the case. One, from a Catholic journalist, suggested that pedophile priests were more commonly relocated to working-class areas, because working-class people were less likely to "make a fuss" and involve the law. He also maintained that the kinds of working-class communities described were recent constructs that lacked a deep sense of communal bonds to the local church (e.g., West Dublin, where council estates sprung up after the 1960s to which uprooted people from inner city communities were exiled). The other reason, from Father O'Connor, was based on the role of the red-top media (*The Sun, The Star*) in whipping up outrage.

11. Goffman, cited in Keane (2015: 141)

12. For example, Father Bourke said: "It's in terms of reluctance and like in terms of the interaction with children, it's really, really difficult. . . . I was out for a walk with my good friend Anthony, my best friend, we've been friends since we were 14, and we walked the piers yesterday and we had a coffee in Starbucks and I was sitting on a seat and Anthony was sitting on part of a long couch and there was a woman beside him and there was a child in between, who was maybe two, a little girl. And Anthony was all chat with her and, because he's a huge extrovert, he'd talk to the cat. And he has three kids of his own. And he was engaged with the girl and I thought if I was dressed as a priest I couldn't do that."

13. Another typical example: "I have stayed with the Church because I still believe in God, and when I go to Church it's to pray to God, not to a priest. But I think a lot of things have to be reviewed by everyone, especially the fact priests cannot get married. They are only human; of course they have urges like

everybody else. That does not give them the right to do what they did, but if they were able to get married and have a sexual partner, maybe then none of it would have happened."

14. Hilliard, 2003: 41.

15. Mrs. Bohan, quoted in Hilliard, 2003: 42.

16. For example, one 71-year-old respondent said, "I have to forgive all the atrocities in one sense, and this is where merciful love comes in, otherwise it leads to hate, and if I go to hate, I am the opposite to love. . . . I saw priests being spat upon. . . . I've seen priests who are broken and had nothing to do with it. I have seen priests who have been ostracized because of false accusations, because there was a lot . . . I'm not defending the church, don't get me wrong."

17. The most extraordinary version of the scapegoat argument that I encountered was from a Catholic woman in her early 70s. She used the clerical abuse scandals to de-invert the moral status of the Church right back to its former paragon setting based on the conspiratorial view that the prevalence of clerical abuse accusations provided evidence of its moral purity because these accusations, in her view, proved that the Church had been singled out for destruction by an evil cabal led by the Rockefellers.

18. National Assets Management Agency, an Irish government body set up to buy toxic bank debts after the 2008 economic downturn.

19. "Alt-right" is a political catchall term originating in the United States to describe an acephalous, irreverent, anarchic, and nontraditional version of the political right that was incubated in online chatrooms as a response to the extreme political correctness hothoused in left-wing digital spaces such as Tumblr. Its members are predominantly male, and the movement is driven by a complex mixture of social conservativism, taboo baiting, antifeminism, 1990s era nihilism, Japanese *otaku* culture and the immersion in fictional worlds as an alternative to a real-world found to be underwhelming, and the loneliness of young men (often self-described "losers") stuck at home with falling job prospects. See Angela Nagle's *Kill All Normies* (2017) for a particularly concise and compelling account.

20. For example, Keenan, 2012.

21. Also see, for example, Fox (2012).

22. There is nothing cognitively unusual about this, especially in the religious realms (e.g., Astuti, 2007; Stringer, 2008). As Kurzban (2012) and Sperber (1996) suggest, people may be motivated to reduce dissonance in order to cultivate convincing public arguments and personae, not because they need inner consistency. However, the salience of this Catholic dissonance to third-party observers is what is most relevant here.

23. Weafer, 2014: 46.

24. Cross-pressure is a concept developed by the secularization theorist Charles Taylor to refer to contradictory forces that pull people in different directions with respect to religious belief and affiliation, rendering belief and unbelief

more self-conscious and promoting a fragmenting process marked by the endless generation of idiosyncratic compromise positions. See C. Taylor, 2007.

25. Tooby and Cosmides, 2010: 226.

26. Alicke, 2000; Alicke et al., 2008.

27. In this, Áine's religious identity was not very different from the kind of loose deism attested to by, for example, a large number of highly secularized Danes or nonreligious Americans.

Epilogue

1. See Krastev and Holmes (2020) on demographic decline and resentment of Western neoliberalism, and see Mishtal (2015) on polarization around Catholic moral and political influence.

BIBLIOGRAPHY

Alicke, M. D. 2000. "Culpable Control and the Psychology of Blame." *Psychological Bulletin* 126(4): 556–74.

Alicke, M. D., E. Zell, and T. Davis. 2008. "Culpable Control and Counterfactual Reasoning in the Psychology of Blame." *Personality and Social Psychology Bulletin* 34: 1371–81.

Amarách Research. 2011. *Attitudes Towards the Catholic Church: An Amarách Report for the Iona Institute.* Dublin: Amarách Research. https://www.ionainstitute.ie/wp-content/uploads/2014/11/Attitudes-to-Church-poll.pdf (accessed March 8, 2016).

Amarách Research. 2012. "Contemporary Catholic Perspectives." Survey commissioned by the Association of Catholic Priests. https://www.associationofcatholicpriests.ie/wp-content/uploads/2012/04/Contemporary-Catholic-Perspectives.pdf (accessed July 25, 2015).

Andersen, K., and A. Lavan. 2007. "Believing in God but not Obeying the Church: Being a Catholic in Ireland and Poland in the 1990s." In Betty Hilliard and Máire Nic Ghiolla Phádraig (eds.), *Changing Ireland in International Comparison.* Dublin: Liffey Press, 191–210.

Angelides, S. 2005. "The Emergence of the Paedophile in the Late 20th Century." *Australian Historical Studies* 36: 272–95.

Asad, T. 2003. *Formations of the Secular: Christianity, Islam, Modernity.* Stanford, CA: Stanford University Press.

Astuti, R. 2007. "Ancestors and the Afterlife." In H. Whitehouse and J. Laidlaw (eds.), *Religion, Anthropology, and Cognitive Science.* Ritual Studies Monograph Series. Durham, NC: Carolina Academic Press, 161–78.

Atran, S. 2010. *Talking to the Enemy: Violent Extremism, Sacred Values, and What It Means to Be Human.* London: Allen Lane.

Bagg, S., and D. Voas. 2009. "The Triumph of Indifference: Irreligion in British Society." In P. Zuckerman (ed), *Atheism and Secularity*, Vol. 2, *Global Expressions.* New York: Praeger Press.

Barna. 2017. "The Faith Crisis of Today's Irish Youth." https://www.barna.com/research/faith-crisis-todays-irish-youth/ (accessed October 12, 2017).

Barr, C. C. P., and D. O'Corrain. 2017. "Catholic Ireland 1740–2016." In E. F. Biagini (ed.), *The Cambridge Social History of Modern Ireland.* Cambridge, UK: Cambridge University Press, 68–87.

Beckett, S. 1990 [1955]. *Waiting for Godot.* In S. Beckett, *Samuel Beckett: The Complete Dramatic Works.* London: Faber & Faber.

Beesley, A. 2021. "Mother and Baby Homes: Up to €1bn Needed for 'Modest Redress.'" *Irish Times,* April 17. https://www.irishtimes.com/news/ireland/irish-news/mother-and-baby-homes-up-to-1bn-needed-for-modest-redress-1.4539794 (accessed April 17, 2021).

Bengtson, Vern L., Norella M. Putney, and Susan Harris. 2013. *Families and Faith: How Religion Is Passed Down Across Generations.* Oxford, UK: Oxford University Press.

Berger, P. 1967. *The Sacred Canopy.* New York: Anchor Books.

Bottan, N. L., and R. Perez-Truglia. 2015. "Losing My Religion: The Effects of Religious Scandals on Religious Participation and Charitable Giving." *Journal of Public Economics* 129(C): 106–19.

Bourdieu, P. 1979. *Distinction: A Social Critique of the Judgment of Taste.* London: Routledge.

Boyer, P. 2002. *Religion Explained: The Evolutionary Origins of Religious Thought.* New York: Basic Books.

Boyer, P. 2010. *The Fracture of an Illusion: Science and the Dissolution of Religion.* Götingen: Vandenhoeck & Ruprecht.

Boylan, Peter. 2021. "The RTÉ Investigates Programme Reminds Us of the Issues Facing the State-Funded National Maternity Hospital." *The Journal.ie,* May 6. https://www.thejournal.ie/readme/adoption-and-mother-and-baby-homes-5372535-Mar2021/ (accessed August 4, 2021).

Brown, C. G. 2001. *The Death of Christian Britain: Understanding Secularisation, 1800–2000.* London: Routledge.

Brown, C. G. 2012. *Religion and the Demographic Revolution: Women and Secularisation in Canada, Ireland, UK, and USA Since the 1960s.* Woodbridge, UK: Boydell Press.

Brown, G. 2017. *Becoming Atheist: Humanism and the Secular West.* London: Bloomsbury.

Bruce, S. 2002. *God Is Dead: Secularization in the West.* Oxford, UK: Blackwell.

Bruce, S. 2006. "Secularization and the Importance of Individualized Religion." *Hedgehog Review* 8(1–2): 35–46.

Bullivant, S. 2017. "Religion in Ireland: Recent Trends and Possible Futures." Paper presented at the Iona Institute, Dublin, August 24, 2017.

Bullivant, S. 2019. *Mass Exodus: Catholic Disaffiliation in Britain and America Since Vatican II.* Oxford, UK: Oxford University Press.

Cannell, F. 2010. "Anthropology of Secularism." *Annual Review of Anthropology* 39: 85–100.

Casanova, J. 1994. *Public Religions in the Modern World.* Chicago: University of Chicago Press.

Cassidy, E. 2002. "Modernity and Religion in Ireland: 1980–2000." In E. Cassidy (ed.), *Measuring Ireland: Discerning Beliefs and Values.* Dublin: Veritas, 17–45.

Catholic Church. 2000. *Catechism of the Catholic Church,* 2nd ed. Vatican City: Libreria Editrice Vaticana.

Central Statistics Office. 2016a. "Census of Population 2016, Profile 8: Irish Travellers, Ethnicity and Religion." https://www.cso.ie/en/releasesandpublications/ep/p-cp8iter/p8iter/p8rrc/ (accessed August 14, 2020).

Central Statistics Office. 2016b. "Religion." Summary of Census 2016 religion data. http://www.cso.ie/en/media/csoie/releasespublications/documents/population/2017/Chapter_8_Religion.pdf (accessed September 26, 2017).

Chang, Ailsa. 2018. "A Lot Has Changed in Ireland Since the Last Time a Pope Visited." Interview with Paddy Agnew, NPR, August 24. https://www.npr.org/2018/08/24/641706010/a-lot-has-changed-in-ireland-since-the-last-time-a-pope-visited (accessed August 28, 2018).

Christian, W. 1989. *Person and God in a Spanish Valley,* rev. ed. Princeton, NJ: Princeton University Press.

Cimino, R., and C. Smith. 2014. *Atheist Awakening: Secular Activism and Community in America.* New York: Oxford University Press.

Cimino, R., C. Smith, and G. Cziehso. 2020. "The Political Divide Between Lay and Elite Atheism." *Secularism and Nonreligion* 9, art. 5. https://www.secularismandnonreligion.org/articles/10.5334/snr.117/.

Clark, J. A., and D. M. T. Fessler. 2014. "The Role of Disgust in Norms, and of Norms in Disgust Research: Why Liberals Shouldn't Be Morally Disgusted by Moral Disgust." *Topoi* 34(2): 483–98.

Clarke, D. 2014. "If You Don't Approve of the Church, Then Don't Take Part in Its Rituals." *Irish Times,* June 7. https://www.irishtimes.com/news/social-affairs/if-you-don-t-approve-of-the-church-then-don-t-take-part-in-its-rituals-1.1823699 (accessed June 7, 2017).

Clarke-Molloy, J. 2017. "'People in Cities Just Don't Have Time for Religion.'" *Irish Times,* October 12. https://www.irishtimes.com/news/social-affairs/religion-and-beliefs/people-in-cities-just-don-t-have-time-for-religion-1.3254130?mode=amp (accessed October 15, 2017).

Cloyne Report (Report by Commission of Investigation into Catholic Diocese of Cloyne). 2011. Dublin: Department of Justice. http://www.justice.ie/en/JELR/Cloyne_Rpt.pdf/Files/Cloyne_Rpt.pdf (accessed March 12, 2015).

Commission to Inquire into Child Abuse. 2009. "Executive Summary." http://www.childabusecommission.ie/rpt/pdfs/CICA-Executive%20Summary.pdf (accessed December 1, 2021).

Comte, A. 2009 [1865]. *A General View of Positivism.* Cambridge, UK: Cambridge University Press.

Connolly, S. J. 2001. *Priests and People in Pre-Famine Ireland, 1780–1845*. Four Courts History Classics.

Coulter, C. 2003. "Introduction." In C. Coulter and S. Coleman (eds.), *The End of Irish History? Reflections on the Celtic Tiger*. Manchester, UK: Manchester University Press, 1–33.

Cullen, P. 2011. "Relations Between State and Vatican at Historic Low." *Irish Times*, July 21. https://www.irishtimes.com/news/relations-between-state-and-vatican-at-historic-low-1.605241 (accessed December 1, 2021).

Cullen, P. 2017. "Depiction of Sisters of Charity Like 'Elder Abuse,' Says Sr. Stan." *Irish Times*, June 3. https://www.irishtimes.com/news/health/depiction-of-sisters-of-charity-like-elder-abuse-says-sr-stan-1.3105759 (accessed June 4, 2017).

Dalby, Douglas. 2014. "Inquiry Urged on Site Called Mass Grave of Irish Babies." *New York Times*, June 5. https://www.nytimes.com/2014/06/05/world/europe/feared-burial-of-irish-babies-leads-to-call-for-inquiry.html?_r=0 (accessed June 17, 2015).

Daly, Greg. 2017. "Boost for Church as Research Reveals Irish Are 'Astonishingly Religious.'" *The Irish Catholic*, November 9. https://www.irishcatholic.com/boost-church-research-reveals-irish-astonishingly-religious/ (accessed December 18, 017).

Danovitch, J., and P. Bloom. 2009. "Children's Extension of Disgust to Physical and Moral Events." *Emotion* 9(1): 107–12.

D'Arcy, Ciarán, and Conor Pope. 2016. "Thousands Taking Part in Pro-Choice Rally in Dublin." *Irish Times*, September 24. https://www.irishtimes.com/news/social-affairs/thousands-taking-part-in-pro-choice-rally-in-dublin-1.2804559 (accessed September 25, 2016).

Davie, G. 1994. *Religion in Britain Since 1945: Believing Without Belonging*. Oxford, UK: Blackwell.

Day, A. 2009. "Believing in Belonging: An Ethnography of Young People's Constructions of Belief." *Culture and Religion* 10(3): 263–78.

Demerath, N. J., III. 2000. "The Rise of 'Cultural Religion' in European Christianity: Learning from Poland, Northern Ireland, and Sweden." *Social Compass* 47(1): 127–39.

Donnelly, S., and T. Inglis. 2010. "The Media and the Catholic Church in Ireland: Reporting Clerical Child Sex Abuse." *Journal of Contemporary Religion* 25(1): 1–19.

Doyle, P. 1989 [1988]. *The God Squad*. London: Corgi.

Drażkiewicz, E., and M. Ní Mhórdha. 2020. "Of Trust and Mistrust: The Politics of Repeal." in K. Browne and S. Calkin (eds.), *After Repeal: Rethinking Abortion Politics*. London: Zed Books, 90–106.

Durkheim, E. 1915. *The Elementary Forms of the Religious Life: A Study in Religious Sociology*. London: Allen & Unwin.

Durkheim, É. 1964 [1933]. *The Division of Labour in Society.* New York: Free Press.
Dwyer, F. 2014. "We Must Stop Claiming That 'We Never Knew' About Child Abuse at Catholic Institutions." *Journal.ie,* June 9. https://www.thejournal.ie/readme/column-we-must-stop-claiming-that-we-never-knew-about-child-abuse-649607-Jun2014/ (accessed December 1, 2021).
Egan, K. 2011. *Remaining a Catholic After the Murphy Report.* Dublin: Columba.
Feinberg, M., and R. Willer. 2015. "From Gulf to Bridge: When Do Moral Arguments Facilitate Political Influence?" *Personality and Social Psychology Bulletin* 41(12): 1–17.
Ferns Report [Francis D. Murphy, Helen Buckley, and Laraine Joyce]. 2005. *The Ferns Report: Presented to the Minister for Health and Children.* Dublin: Stationery Office. http://www.lenus.ie/hse/bitstream/10147/560434/2/thefernsreportoctober2005.pdf (accessed August 6, 2015).
Ferriter, D. 2009. *Occasions of Sin: Sex and Society in Modern Ireland.* London: Profile Books.
Ferriter, D. 2012. *Ambiguous Republic: Ireland in the 1970s.* London: Profile Books.
Finnegan, F. 1998. "Article Submitted to *The Irish Times* in 1998 in Support of Channel 4's Documentary *Sex in a Cold Climate.*" Piltown, Ireland: Congrave Press. http://congravepress.com/article/ (accessed April 16, 2021).
Finnegan, F. 2001. *Do Penance or Perish: Magdalen Asylums in Ireland.* New York: Oxford University Press.
Foster, R. F. 2007. *Luck and the Irish: A Brief History of Change.* Oxford, UK: Oxford University Press.
Fox, T. C. 2012. "Cardinal Burke Links Sex Abuse to Disrespect for Canon Law." *National Catholic Reporter,* September 2. https://www.ncronline.org/blogs/ncr-today/cardinal-burke-links-sex-abuse-disrespect-canon-law?_ga=2.29168828.1658419081.1506508478-1956651645.1506508478 (accessed November 25, 2016).
Foxe, Ken. 2018. "OPW Reveals Final Headcount for Papal Mass in Phoenix Park." *Irish Times,* September 19. https://www.irishtimes.com/news/ireland/irish-news/opw-reveals-final-headcount-for-papal-mass-in-phoenix-park-1.3634424 (accessed September 23, 2018).
Fuller, L. 2002. *Irish Catholicism Since 1950: The Undoing of a Culture.* Dublin: Gill & MacMillan.
Ganiel, G. 2016. *Transforming Post-Catholic Ireland: Religious Practice in Late Modernity.* Oxford, UK: Oxford University Press.
Ganiel, G. 2019a. "Negating the Francis Effect? The Effect of the Abuse Crisis in Ireland." *Research in the Social Scientific Study of Religion* 30: 335–57.
Ganiel, G. 2019b. "Religious Practice in a Post-Catholic Ireland: Towards a Concept of 'Extra-Institutional Religion.'" *Social Compass* 66(4): 471–87.
Garvin, T. 2004. *Preventing the Future: Why Was Ireland So Poor for So Long?* Dublin: Gill & Macmillan.

Gervais, M., and D. Fessler. 2017. "On the Deep Structure of Social Affect: Attitudes, Emotions, Sentiments, and the Case of 'Contempt.'" *Behavioral and Brain Sciences* 39: 1–77.

Gervais, W. M., and J. Henrich. 2010. "The Zeus Problem: Why Representational Content Biases Cannot Explain Faith in Gods." *Journal of Cognition and Culture* 10: 383–89.

Gervais, W. M, and M. B. Najle. 2018. "How Many Atheists Are There?" *Social Psychological, and Personality Science* 9(1): 3–10.

Gervais, W. M, and A. Norenzayan. 2012. "Analytic Thinking Promotes Religious Disbelief." *Science* 336(6080): 493–96.

Gervais, W. M., A. Willard, A. Norenzayan, and J. Henrich. 2011. "The Cultural Transmission of Faith: Why Innate Intuitions Are Necessary, but Insufficient, to Explain Religious Belief." *Religion* 41: 389–410.

Gervais, W. M., D. Xgalatas, R. McKay, M. van Elk, E. E. Butchel, M. Aveyard, S. Schiavone, I. Dar-Nimrod, A. M. Svedholm-Hakkinen, T. Riekki, E. K. Klocova, J. E. Ramsay, and J. Bulbulia. 2017. "Global Evidence of Extreme Intuitive Moral Prejudice Against Atheists." *Nature Human Behavior* 1, art. 0151. https://doi.org/10.1038/s41562-017-0151.

Gleeson, K. 2017. "A Woman's Work Is . . . Unfinished Business: Justice for the Disappeared Magdalene Women of Modern Ireland." *Feminist Legal Studies* 25: 291–312.

Goffman, E. 1968. *Stigma: Notes on the Management of Spoiled Identity*. Harmondsworth, UK: Penguin.

Goode, H., H. McGee, and C. O'Boyle. 2003. *Time to Listen: Confronting Child Sexual Abuse by Catholic Clergy in Ireland*. Dublin: Liffey Press.

Graham, J., J. Haidt, S. Koleva, M. Motyl, R. Iyer, S. P. Wojcik, and P. H. Ditto. 2013. "Moral Foundations Theory: The Pragmatic Validity of Moral Pluralism." *Advances in Experimental Social Psychology* 47: 58–130.

Greeley, A. 1994. "Why Do Catholics Stay in the Church?" *The Furrow* 45(9): 495–502.

Greeley, A., and C. Ward. 2000. "How 'Secularised' Is the Ireland We Live In?" *Doctrine and Life* 50: 581–617.

Greenslade, Roy. 2016. "Why Ireland Must Get Rid of Its Disgraceful Blasphemy Law." *The Guardian*, April 11. https://www.theguardian.com/media/greenslade/2016/apr/11/why-ireland-must-get-rid-of-its-disgraceful-blasphemy-law (accessed May 12, 2016).

Hadaway, K. C., P. L. Marler, and M. Chaves. 1993. "What the Polls Don't Show: A Closer Look at U.S. Church Attendance." *American Sociological Review* 58(6): 741–52.

Haidt, J., and J. Graham. 2007. "When Morality Opposes Justice: Conservatives Have Moral Intuitions That Liberals May Not Recognize." *Social Justice Research* 20: 98–116.

Haidt, J., and C. Joseph. 2004. "Intuitive Ethics: How Innately Prepared Intuitions Generate Culturally Variable Virtues." *Daedalus* 133(4): 55–66.

Haidt, J., and S. Kesebir. 2010. "Morality." In Susan T. Fiske, Daniel T. Gilbert, and Gardner Lindzey (eds.), *Handbook of Social Psychology*, 5th ed. Hoboken, NJ: Wiley, 797–832.

Harding, S. 2000. *The Book of Jerry Falwell: Fundamentalist Language and Politics*. Princeton, NJ: Princeton University Press.

Henrich, J. 2009. "The Evolution of Costly Displays, Cooperation, and Religion: Credibility Enhancing Displays and Their Implications for Cultural Evolution." *Evolution and Human Behaviour* 30: 244–60.

Henrich, J. 2020. *The Weirdest People in the World: How the West Became Psychologically Peculiar and Particularly Prosperous*. London: Penguin.

Hilliard, B. 2003. "The Catholic Church and Married Women's Sexuality: Habitus Change in Late 20th Century Ireland." *Irish Journal of Sociology* 12(2): 28–49.

Hogan, C. 2019. *Republic of Shame: Stories from Ireland's Institutions for "Fallen" Women*. Dublin: Penguin.

Hornsby-Smith, M. P. 1992. "Social and Religious Transformations in Ireland: A Case of Secularisation?" In J. Goldthorpe and C. Whelan (eds.), *The Development of Industrial Society in Ireland*. Oxford, UK: Oxford University Press, 265–90.

Hout, M., and C. Fischer. 2014. "Explaining Why More Americans Have No Religious Preference: Political Backlash and Generational Succession, 1987–2012." *Sociological Science* 1(4): 423–47.

Humphreys, J. 2017. "Why Did the Atheist Go to Mass?" *Irish Times*, December 10. https://www.irishtimes.com/life-and-style/people/why-did-the-atheist-go-to-mass-1.3311075?_vfz=c_pages%3D11000002670848 (accessed December 12, 2017).

Hynes, E. 2009. *Knock: The Virgin's Apparition in 19th Century Ireland*. Cork, Ireland: Cork University Press.

Ingber, Sasha. 2018. "The Pope Lands in Ireland, Overshadowed by Church Scandals." KRVS Radio Acadie, August 25. https://www.krvs.org/post/pope-lands-ireland-overshadowed-church-scandals (accessed August 28, 2018).

Inglehart, R. 2020. "Giving Up on God: The Global Decline of Religion." *Foreign Affairs* 99(5). https://www.foreignaffairs.com/articles/world/2020-08-11/religion-giving-god?utm_medium=email_notifications&utm_source=reg_confirmation&utm_campaign=reg_guestpass (accessed January 9, 2021).

Inglehart, R., and C. Welzel. 2005. *Modernization, Cultural Change, and Democracy: The Human Development Sequence*. Cambridge, UK: Cambridge University Press.

Inglis, T. 1998. *Moral Monopoly: The Rise and Fall of the Catholic Church in Modern Ireland*. Dublin: University College Dublin.

Inglis, T. 2014. *Meanings of Life in Contemporary Ireland: Webs of Significance*. New York: Palgrave Macmillan.

Keane, W. 2015. *Ethical Life: Its Natural and Social Histories.* Princeton, NJ: Princeton University Press.
Keenan, M. 2012. *Child Sexual Abuse and the Catholic Church: Gender, Power and Organisational Culture.* Oxford, UK: Oxford University Press.
Kelly, Y. 2011. *Yuck! The Nature and Moral Significance of Disgust.* Cambridge, MA: MIT Press.
Kennedy. L. 2016. *Unhappy the Land: The Most Oppressed People Ever, the Irish?* Dublin: Merrion Press.
Kettell, S. 2013. "Faithless: The Politics of New Atheism." *Secularism and Nonreligion* 2: 61–72.
King, W. 2017. *A Lost Tribe.* Dublin: Lilliput Press.
Krastev, I., and S. Holmes. 2020. *The Light That Failed: A Reckoning.* London: Allen Lane.
Kupfer, T. R., and R. Giner-Sorolla. 2016. "Communicating Moral Motives: The Social Signaling Function of Disgust." *Social Psychological and Personality Science* 8(6): 632–40.
Kurzban, R. 2012. *Why Everyone (Else) Is a Hypocrite: Evolution and the Modular Mind.* Princeton, NJ: Princeton University Press.
Lakoff, G. 1987. *Women, Fire, and Dangerous Things.* Chicago: University of Chicago Press.
Lanman, J. 2012. "The Importance of Religious Displays for Belief Acquisition and Secularisation." *Journal of Contemporary Religion* 27(1): 49–65.
Lanman, J. A., and M. Buhrmester. 2017. "Religious Actions Speak Louder than Words: Exposure to CREDs Predicts Theism." *Religion, Brain, and Behavior* 7(1): 3–16.
Larkin, E. J. 1976. *The Historical Dimensions of Irish Catholicism.* Washington, DC: Catholic University of America Press.
Latinobarómetro: Opinión Pública Latinoamericana. 2017. *Latinobarómetro Report 2017.* https://www.latinobarometro.org/latContents.jsp?Idioma=0&CMSID=InformesAnuales&Idioma=0&CMSID=InformesAnuales (accessed April 13, 2018).
Lavery, Brian. 2006. "Scandal? For an Irish Parish, It's Just a Priest with a Child." *New York Times,* January 22. https://www.nytimes.com/2006/01/22/world/europe/scandal-for-an-irish-parish-its-just-a-priest-with-a-child.html (accessed May 7, 2021).
Lee, L. 2015. *Recognising the Non-Religious.* Oxford, UK: Oxford University Press.
Luhrmann, T. 2012. *When God Talks Back: Understanding the American Evangelical Relationship with God.* New York: Vintage.
Lynch, G. 2012. *The Sacred in the Modern World: A Cultural Sociological Approach.* Oxford, UK: Oxford University Press.
Manoharan, C., and V. de Munck. 2015. "The Conceptual Relationship Between Love, Romantic Love, and Sex: A Free List and Prototype Study of Semantic Association." *Journal of Mixed Methods Research* 11(2): 1–25.

Martel, F. 2019. *In the Closet of the Vatican: Power, Homosexuality, and Hypocrisy.* London: Bloomsbury.
Martin, Michel. 2018. "'He Needs to Be Accountable,' Says 'Nope to the Pope' Activist." Interview with Lisa Breslin, NPR, August 25. https://www.npr.org/2018/08/25/641927173/-he-needs-to-be-accountable-says-nope-to-the-pope-activist (accessed August 29, 2018).
McDonald, Henry. 2017. "Irish Police Halt Investigation of Stephen Fry for Blasphemy." *The Guardian*, May 9. https://www.theguardian.com/culture/2017/may/09/irish-police-halt-prosecution-of-stephen-fry-for-blasphemy (accessed May 17, 2017).
McGahern, J. 1974. *The Leavetaking.* London: Puffin Books.
McGahern, J. 2009. *Love of the World: Essays.* London: Faber & Faber.
McGarry, P. 2006. "The Rise and Fall of Roman Catholicism in Ireland." In L. Fuller, J. Littleton, and E. Maher (eds.), *Irish and Catholic? Towards an Understanding of Identity.* Dublin: Columba, 31–45.
McGarry, P. 2009. "Church Faces Credibility Deficit, Says Archbishop." *Irish Times*, January 10. https://www.irishtimes.com/news/church-faces-credibility-deficit-says-archbishop-1.1233259 (accessed August 24, 2016).
McGarry, P. 2010. "Judge's Play on Abuse to Be Staged." *Irish Times*, June 11. https://www.irishtimes.com/news/judge-s-play-on-abuse-to-be-staged-1.676531 (accessed August 12, 2016).
McGarry, P. 2019a. "Cardinal (92) Who 'Sought Deal' to Bury Sex Abuse Documents Resigns." *Irish Times*, December 21. https://www.irishtimes.com/news/social-affairs/religion-and-beliefs/cardinal-92-who-sought-deal-to-bury-sex-abuse-documents-resigns-1.4122879 (accessed January 23, 2020).
McGarry, P. 2019b. "Religious Congregations Indemnity Deal Was 'a Blank Cheque', Says Michael McDowell." *Irish Times*, April 5. https://www.irishtimes.com/news/social-affairs/religion-and-beliefs/religious-congregations-indemnity-deal-was-a-blank-cheque-says-michael-mcdowell-1.3850063 (accessed June 10, 2019).
McWilliams, D. 2005. *The Pope's Children: Ireland's New Elite.* Dublin: Gill & MacMillan.
McWilliams, D. 2019. *Renaissance Nation: How the Pope's Children Rewrote the Rules for Ireland.* Dublin: Gill & MacMillan.
Mehta, Hemant. 2018. "When Pope Francis Visits Ireland, Protesters Will Greet Him with Empty Seats." *Friendly Atheist*, July 9. https://friendlyatheist.patheos.com/2018/07/09/when-pope-francis-visits-ireland-protesters-will-greet-him-with-empty-seats/ (accessed September 11, 2018).
Meskill, Tommy. 2021. "Not the First Time a State Apology Has Been Issued." RTÉ, January 13. https://www.rte.ie/news/analysis-and-comment/2021/0112/1189350-state-apologies-ireland/ (accessed October 23, 2021).
Miller, D. W. 1975. "Irish Catholicism and the Great Famine." *Journal of Social History* 9(1): 81–98.

Miller, W. I. 1997. *The Anatomy of Disgust*. Cambridge, MA: Harvard University Press.

Mishtal, J. 2015. *The Politics of Morality: The Church, the State, and Reproductive Rights in Postsocialist Poland*. Athens: Ohio University Press.

Molloy, Cian. 2009. "Dublin Report Leads to Calls for Bishops Resignations." *National Catholic Reporter*, December 1. https://www.ncronline.org/news/accountability/dublin-report-leads-calls-bishops-resignations (accessed October 23, 2017).

Monin, B., and A. Merritt. 2012. "Moral Hypocrisy, Moral Inconsistency, and the Struggle for Moral Integrity." In M. Mikulincer and P. Shaver (eds.), *The Social Psychology of Morality: Exploring the Causes of Good and Evil*. Washington, DC: American Psychological Association, 167–84.

Mother and Baby Homes Report [Commission of Investigation into Mother and Baby Homes]. 2021. *Final Report of the Commission of Investigation into Mother and Baby Homes*. https://www.gov.ie/en/publication/d4b3d-final-report-of-the-commission-of-investigation-into-mother-and-baby-homes/?referrer=http://www.gov.ie/report/.

Mulholland, P. 2019. *Love's Betrayal: The Decline of Catholicism and Rise of New Religions in Ireland*. Oxford, UK: Peter Lang.

Murphy Report [Commission of Investigation]. 2009. *The Report into the Catholic Archdiocese of Dublin*. Dublin: Stationery Office. https://www.documentcloud.org/documents/243712-4-murphy-report-entire-ireland.html (accessed July 23, 2016).

Murphy, C. L. 2019. "*Pasolini's Salò Redubbed* Review: Aims for Greatness but Falls Significantly Short." *Irish Times*, September 30. https://www.irishtimes.com/culture/stage/pasolini-s-salò-redubbed-review-aims-for-greatness-but-falls-significantly-short-1.4034991 (accessed October 11, 2019).

Nagle, A. 2017. *Kill All Normies: The Online Culture Wars from Tumblr and 4chan to the Alt-Right and Trump*. Winchester: Zero Books.

Nic Ghiolla Phádraig, N. 2009. "Religion in Ireland: No Longer an Exception?" *ARK NI Research Update* 64: 156–68.

Norget, K., V. Napolitano, and M. Mayblin. 2017. *The Anthropology of Catholicism: A Reader*. Berkeley: University of California Press.

Norris, P., and R. Inglehart. 2011. *Sacred and Secular: Religion and Politics Worldwide*, 2nd ed. Cambridge, UK: Cambridge University Press.

O'Doherty, M. 2008. *Empty Pulpits: Ireland's Retreat from Religion*. Dublin: Gill & Macmillan.

O'Donovan, C. 2015. *Archdiocese of Dublin: Projection of Position in 2030*. Dublin: Towers Watson.

O'Faolain, Aodhan. 2021. "Woman Who Gave Birth at Mother and Baby Home Sues over Commission Finding." *Irish Times*, May 21. https://www.irishtimes.com/news/crime-and-law/courts/high-court/woman-who-gave-birth-at

-mother-and-baby-home-sues-over-commission-finding-1.4571468 (accessed May 21, 2021).

Ó Féich, P., and M. O'Connell. 2015. "Changes in Roman Catholic Beliefs and Practices in Ireland Between 1981 and 2008 and the Emergence of the Liberal-Catholic." *Journal of Contemporary Religion* 30: 38–54.

O'Gorman, Colm. 2003. "State Has Put the Interest of the Church Ahead of Victims' Needs." *Irish Times*, February 8. http://www.irishtimes.com/opinion/state-has-put-the-interest-of-the-churchahead-of-victims-needs-1.348254 (accessed October 11, 2018).

O'Halloran, M. 2019. "Catholic Schools Can Still Ask Questions on Religion Despite New Law." *Irish Times*, August 1. https://www.irishtimes.com/news/education/catholic-schools-can-still-ask-questions-on-religion-despite-new-law-1.3974648 (accessed August 2, 2019).

O Kelly, Emma. 2019. "Dublin Archdiocese Embraces 'New Approach' in Preparing Children for Communion." RTÉ, December 4. https://www.rte.ie/news/education/2019/1204/1096864-primary-schools-religion/ (accessed December 8, 2019).

Orsi, R. 2017. "What Is Catholic About the Clergy Sex Abuse Crisis?" In K. Norget, V. Napolitano, and M. Mayblin (eds.), *The Anthropology of Catholicism: A Reader*. Berkeley: University of California Press, 282–92.

O'Sullivan, E, and I. O'Donnell. 2012. *Coercive Confinement in Ireland: Patients, Prisoners and Penitents*. Manchester, UK: Manchester University Press.

O'Toole, Fintan. 2017. "Ireland Is Still Defined by the Church's Mindset." *Irish Times*, March 14. https://www.irishtimes.com/opinion/fintan-o-toole-ireland-is-still-defined-by-the-church-s-mindset-1.3008295 (accessed March 14, 2017).

O'Toole, F. 2021. *We Don't Know Ourselves: A Personal History of Ireland Since 1958*. Dublin: Head of Zeus.

Parkins, Brianna. 2020. "In Oz, Marianne Would Have Told Connell: 'Get Stuffed, You Gutless Wonder.'" *Irish Times*, August 5. https://www.irishtimes.com/life-and-style/people/in-oz-marianne-would-have-told-connell-get-stuffed-you-gutless-wonder-1.4321748 (accessed August 5, 2020).

Penet, J. 2008. "From Idealised Moral Community to Real Tiger Society: The Catholic Church in Secular Ireland." *Estudios Irlandeses* 3: 143–53.

Pew Research Center. 2014. *Religion in Latin America*. https://www.pewforum.org/2014/11/13/religion-in-latin-america/ (accessed October 5, 2016).

Pew Research Center. 2018. *Being Christian in Western Europe*. https://www.pewforum.org/2018/05/29/being-christian-in-western-europe/ (accessed July 23, 2019).

Pine, E. 2011. *The Politics of Irish Memory: Performing Remembrance in Contemporary Irish Culture*. Basingstoke, UK: Palgrave Macmillan.

Polman, D. 1993. "Ireland's Forgotten Women Sparking Public Outcry." *The Record*, November 25.

Postmes, T., S. A. Haslam, and L. Jans. 2013. "A Single-Item Measure of Social Identification: Reliability, Validity, and Utility." *British Journal of Social Psychology* 52: 597–617.

Power, J. 2017. "Thousands March in Dublin in Support of Eighth Amendment." *Irish Times*, July 1. https://www.irishtimes.com/news/ireland/irish-news/thousands-march-in-dublin-in-support-of-eighth-amendment-1.3140573 (accessed July 1, 2017).

Quinlan, M. B. 2019. "The Freelisting Method." In P. Liamputtong (ed.), *Handbook of Research Methods in Health Social Sciences*. Singapore: Springer Singapore, 1431–46.

Quinn, D. 2017a. "The 'à la Carte Nones' Are the Counterpart of the 'à la Carte Catholics.'" *The Irish Catholic*, April 13. http://www.irishcatholic.ie/article/"à-la-carte-nones"-are-counterpart-"à-la-carte-catholics" (accessed April 18, 2017).

Quinn, D. 2017b. "Church-Bashing Is the New Brit-Bashing." *The Irish Catholic*, April 20. http://irishcatholic.ie/article/church-bashing-new-brit-bashing (accessed April 23, 2017).

Raftery, M. 2003. "Restoring Dignity to Magdalens." *Irish Times*, August 21. https://www.irishtimes.com/opinion/restoring-dignity-to-magdalens-1.370373 (accessed January 13, 2017).

Raftery, M., and E. O'Sullivan. 1999. *Suffer the Little Children: The Inside Story of Ireland's Industrial Schools*. Dublin: New Island.

Ribberink, E., P. Achterberg, and D. Houtman. 2013. "Deprivatization of Disbelief? Non-Religiosity and Anti-Religiosity in 14 Western European Countries." *Politics and Religion* 6: 101–20.

Romney, A. K., and R. G. D'Andrade. 1964. "Cognitive Aspects of English Kin Terms." *American Anthropologist* 68(3): 146–70.

Rooney, S. 2017. *Conversations with Friends*. London: Faber & Faber.

Rossetti, S. 1996. *A Tragic Grace: The Catholic Church and Child Sexual Abuse*. Collegeville, MN: Liturgical Press.

Ruane, J. 1998. "Secularisation and Ideology in the Republic of Ireland." In P. Brennan (ed.), *La Secularisation en Irlande*. Caen, France: Presses de Universitaire de Caen, 239–53.

Ryan Report [Commission to Inquire into Child Abuse]. 2009. *Commission Report*, 5 vols. Dublin: Stationery Office. https://www.dcya.gov.ie/documents/publications/implementation_plan_from_ryan_commission_report.pdf (accessed November 7, 2015).

Scally, Derek 2017. "'His House Was Always Filled with Children but as a Teenager I Shrugged It Off.'" *Irish Times*, January 26. https://www.irishtimes.com/life-and-style/people/his-house-was-always-filled-with-children-but-as-a-teenager-i-shrugged-it-off-1.2926797 (accessed January 28, 2017).

Scally, D. 2021. *The Best Catholics in the World: The Irish, the Church and the End of a Special Relationship*. Sandycove: Penguin.

Scheman, N. 1980. "Anger and the Politics of Naming." In S. McConnell-Ginet, R. Borker, and N. Furman (eds.), *Women and Language in Literature and Society*. New York: Praeger, 174–88.

Scheper-Hughes, N. 2001 [1979]. *Saints, Scholars, and Schizophrenics: Mental Illness in Rural Ireland—Twentieth Anniversary Edition*. Berkeley: University of California Press.

Schjoedt, U., J. Sørensen, K. Nielbo, D. Xygalatas, P. Mitkidis, and J. Bulbulia. 2013. "Cognitive Resource Deletion in Religious Interactions." *Religion, Brain and Behavior* 3(1): 39–86.

Sheridan, K. 2012. "The Irish Catholic: How We Differ from the German, Italian and Polish Churches." *Irish Times*, June 2. https://www.irishtimes.com/life-and-style/people/the-irish-catholic-how-we-differ-from-the-german-italian-and-polish-churches-1.1063511 (accessed December 12, 2016).

Sherkat, D. 2014. *Changing Faith: The Dynamics and Consequences of American's Shifting Religious Identities*. New York: New York University Press.

Slingerland, T. 2011. *Creating Consilience: Integrating the Sciences and Humanities*. Oxford, UK: Oxford University Press.

Smith, C. 2005. *Soul Searching: The Religious and Spiritual Lives of American Teenagers*. Oxford, UK: Oxford University Press.

Smith, C., K. Longest, J. Hill, and C. Christoffersen. 2014. *Young Catholic America: Emerging Adults In, Out of, and Gone from the Church*. Oxford, UK: Oxford University Press.

Smith, J. J. 1993. "Using ANTHROPAC 3.5 and a Spreadsheet to Compute a Free List Salience Index." *Cultural Anthropology Methods Newsletter* 5(3): 1–3.

Smith, James M. 2007. *Ireland's Magdalen Laundries and the Nation's Architecture of Containment*. Notre Dame, IN: University of Notre Dame Press.

Smith, J. Z. 1998. "Religion, Religions, Religious." In M. Taylor (ed.), *Critical Terms for Religious Studies*. Chicago: University of Chicago Press, 269–84.

Sosis, R., H. C. Kress, and J. S. Boster. 2007. "Scars for War: Evaluating Alternative Signalling Explanations for Cross-Cultural Variance in Ritual Costs." *Evolution and Human Behaviour* 28: 234–47.

Sperber, D. 1996. *Explaining Culture: A Naturalistic Approach*. Oxford, UK: Blackwell.

Stack, Liam. 2017. "How Ireland Moved to the Left: 'The Demise of the Church.'" *New York Times*, December 2. https://www.nytimes.com/2017/12/02/world/europe/ireland-abortion-abuse-church.html (accessed December 8, 2017).

Stivers, R. 1976. *A Hair of the Dog: Irish Drinking and American Stereotype*. University Park: Pennsylvania State University Press.

Stringer, M. 2008. *Contemporary Western Ethnography and the Definition of Religion*. London: Bloomsbury.

Taira, T. 2012. "New Atheism as Identity Politics." In M. Guest and E. Arweck (eds.), *Religion and Knowledge: Sociological Perspectives*. Ashgate, UK: Farnham, 96–114.

Tangney, J. P., J. Steuwig, and D. Mashek. 2007. "Moral Emotions and Moral Behavior." *Annual Review of Psychology* 58: 345–72.
Taves, A. 2009. *Religious Experience Reconsidered: A Building Block Approach to the Study of Religion and Other Special Things*. Princeton, NJ: Princeton University Press.
Taylor, C. 2007. *A Secular Age*. Cambridge, MA: Belknap, Harvard University Press.
Taylor, L. J. 1995. *Occasions of Faith: An Anthropology of Irish Catholics*. Dublin: Lilliput Press.
Tooby, J., and L. Cosmides. 2010. "Groups in Mind: The Coalitional Roots of War and Morality." In Henrik Høgh-Olesen (ed.), *Human Morality and Sociality: Evolutionary and Comparative Perspectives*. New York: Palgrave Macmillan, 191–234.
Twomey, V. 2003. *The End of Irish Catholicism?* Dublin: Veritas.
UCD Geary Institute for Public Policy. 2019. *Irish Social Attitudes in 2018/2019*. https://www.ucd.ie/geary/static/ess/ESS_Geary_Round9.pdf (accessed November 30, 2021).
Voas, D. 2009. "The Rise and Fall of Fuzzy Fidelity in Europe." *European Sociological Review* 25(2): 155–68.
Warrander, Ruth. 2016. "Blowman Catholic: Nazi Hoard Priest Snorts Cocaine in Shocking Video." *The Sun*, February 28. https://www.thesun.co.uk/archives/news/267554/blowman-catholic-nazi-hoard-priest-snorts-cocaine-in-shocking-video/ (accessed December 30, 2016).
Waters, J. 2018. "The Phony War on 'Taliban Ireland.'" *First Things*, June 25. https://www.firstthings.com/web-exclusives/2018/06/the-phony-war-on-taliban-ireland (accessed July 6, 2018).
Weafer, J. A. 2014. *Thirty-Three Good Men: Celibacy, Obedience and Identity*. Dublin: Columba.
Weber, M. 12001 [1930]. *The Protestant Ethic and the Spirit of Capitalism*. London: Routledge.
Whitehouse, H. 2004. *Modes of Religiosity: A Cognitive Theory of Religious Transmission*. Walnut Creek, CA: AltaMira Press.
Whitehouse, H., and J. A. Lanman. 2014. "The Ties That Bind Us: Ritual, Fusion, and Identification." *Current Anthropology* 55(6): 674–95.
Wiltermuth, S. S., and C. Heath. 2009. "Synchrony and Cooperation." *Psychological Science* 20: 1–5.
WIN/Gallup. 2012. "International Index of Religion and Atheism." https://sidmennt.is/wp-content/uploads/Gallup-International-um-tr%C3%BA-og-tr%C3%BAleysi-2012.pdf (accessed October 4, 2015).
Zuckerman, P. 2008. *Society Without God: What the Least Religious Nations Can Tell Us About Contentment*. New York: New York University Press.
Zuckerman, P., L. Galen, and F. Pasquale. 2017. *The Nonreligious: Understanding Secular People and Societies*. Oxford, UK: Oxford University Press.

INDEX

Abbey Theater, 170, 279n115
abortion, 24, 89, 154–56, 157–61, 181–85, 290n11
abuse, 70–75, 77, 136. *See also* child sexual abuse scandals
advancement, Catholic habitus and, 51
age of scandal, 2
agnostics, 61
Ahern, Bertie, 9, 40
alcohol, 266n7, 288n6
alt-right, 299n19
Angelus, 185
anger, 72–73, 209, 211–13, 214
anti-clericalism, 298n10
anti-nostalgia, 168
anti-nostalgic moralized authenticity, 220–21
antipathy, 92
apathy, 9, 32
Archdiocese of Dublin, 1, 35
Arnold, Matthew, 23
arson, 227
ashes, rejection of, 84
Ash Wednesday, 21
Atheist Ireland: alliances of, 174; campaign of, 178–81; female survey responses of, 194–95; influence decline of, 213; legacy of, 177; motto of, 174; overview of, 174–75, 293–94nn43–45; Parents for Secular Schooling (PSS) and, 202; ratio-

nalism within, 216, 218–19; report from, 162; scandal response of, 178, 205, 206–7; survey responses of, 215–16, 282n22
atheists/atheism: anger within, 211–13; distrust of, 65–66; ex-Catholics as, 77–79, 106–7, 117, 190; growth of, 32; within Kilbreagh, 149; New Atheism, 146; statistics of, 61, 176–77; stereotypes of, 212–13; stigma regarding, 77; survey for, 260–61; teachers, 285n2; viewpoint of, 131
Australia, 32
Austria, 29, 32
authoritarianism, 74

bachelor drinking group, 288n6
baptism: barrier of, 201; into Catholicism, 59; of children out of wedlock, 288n8; obligation of, 118, 141, 146–47, 148–49, 198, 199–200, 253; symbolism of, 294–95n48; "Time to Tick No" campaign and, 179–80
Beckett, Samuel, 191
behavioral reinforcement, 51–52
belief scale, 78
Benedict XVI, 160
benevolence, 149
Berger, Peter, 49, 269n10
The Best Catholics in the World (Scally), 223

Bhriain, Níamh Uí, 156
binding foundations, 45
bishops, trustworthiness score of, 65–67
black humor, 9
blame, 167–73, 240–44, 248–49
blessing oneself, rejection of, 84
Bon Secours Sisters, 7–8, 164
Bourdieu, Pierre, 280n126
Bourke, Father, 228–29, 230, 236–37, 239–40, 298n12
Boylan, Peter, 165
Breslin, Lisa, 91–92
Brexit, 258
Britain, 33, 269n9
Brown, Callum, 23, 24, 25, 26
Brown, C. G., 273n59
Bruce, Steve, 24, 273n59, 280n132
Buckley, Christine, 40
Bundoran, County Donegal, 47
Bundoran haircut, 47
Byrne, Gay, 273n60

Campaign to Separate Church and State, 174
candles, rejection of, 84
capitulation, 146, 148–49
carceral institutions, 39
Carlsberg, Father, 143
Carr, Marina, 171
Casey, Eamonn, 34, 275n73
Catholic Education System, 97, 101, 118, 177, 201–4, 217–18. *See also* education
Catholic guilt, 20–21, 105–6, 193, 245–46
Catholicism/Catholics/Irish Catholicism: aging within, 96–97; belief scale of, 78; characteristics of, 94; Charismatic, 108–9; Church viewpoint of, 67–75; cliericalist bent of, 20; commitment within, 19; commonality of, 111, 122; community within, 118, 119, 136; as contextual, 59; creative, 31, 63; CRED exposure within, 80–83; daily rituals of, 21–22, 50–51, 95, 284n40; decline of, 110; decoherence within, 247–52; defined, 59–60; deinstitutionalized, 62; discarded beliefs within, 100; disdain of, 10; disenchantment subcultures within, 133–37; dogma within, 52; as ethnic designation, 16–17; fragmentation causes within, 247, 248; fusion within, 21; group identity within, 21; Hallmark, 280n129; historical rootedness within, 242–43; hyphenated, 63–64, 281n12; identity within, 58–64, 175–76, 242; influence of, 21; lapsed, 101–2, 104–5; liberal, 62, 291n16; liminal, 60, 62, 67; men within, 14; new covenant of, 88–89; obligation within, 118, 141, 146–47, 148–49, 198, 199–200, 253; oppression of, 193; papal infallibility of, 19–20; persecution within, 237–38; population discrepancies of, 175–77; protests against, 25; redefining of, 250–51; rejection of, 60, 102–3, 109, 142, 148, 178–79, 189–97, 215–19, 246–47; relevance fading of, 31–32; reluctant, 102; rites of passage within, 30; scrutiny of, 33; secularization *versus*, 243–44; sexuality within, 20; significance of, 18; spiritually rich versions of, 241; statistics of, 29, 58, 60–61; traditional, 291n16; viewpoints regarding, 129, 222, 249. *See also* cultural Catholicism; devout Catholics; ex-Catholics; Irish Catholic Church; liminal Catholics
Catholic Men and Women's Society, 138

Catholic shame, 20–21
Celtic Tiger economic boom, 26–27, 168–69, 267n14
Chapel of Remembrance (St. Theresa's church), 138
Charismatic Catholicism, 108–9
children: Catholicism and, 103; class-based poverty and, 135; discarding of, 7–8; immoral family settings of, 46; within Mass, 96–97; protection for, 275n67; vaccine trials on, 8. *See also* education
child sexual abuse scandals: costs regarding, 278n104; example of, 265n4; innocent priests within, 224–30; lack of punishment regarding, 169–70; ontological dissonance within, 55; overview of, 34–48; reporting of, 274n63; secular empowerment following, 208–9; statistics of, 278–79n114; structural causes of, 243–44; theater works regarding, 170–72
Christian Brothers, 21, 24, 41, 105, 136, 218
Christianity, 272n52, 281n12
Citizens' Assembly, 289n2
Clarke, Donald, 177
Clarke, Harry, 114
Cleary, Michael, 34
clerical trust, 64–67, 85–86
Cloyne Report, 36
cognitive science of religion, 279n119
Coleman, Father, 229–30
Collins, Marie, 92
Come on Home (McMahon), 171
Comiskey, Brendan, 35
Commission of Investigation into Mother and Baby Homes, 7–8
Communion, 112–13, 119, 184
community, 118, 119, 136, 255
complicity, mass, 170–73, 179, 180–81, 199–200

Comte, August de, 269n10
confession, 83, 84
Confirmation, 112, 294–95n48
Connell, Desmond, 35, 274n65
Connolly, Catherine, 9
Connolly, James, 138
conservativism, 74
consternation, 9
Constitution, Irish, 89
contempt, 73–74, 222–24
contraceptives, 23–25
Conversations with Friends (Rooney), 128
Corless, Catherine, 7–8, 266n11
counter-hypocrites, 232
Cowen, Brian, 9
creative Catholicism, 31, 63
credibility-enhancing display (CRED): contaminated affiliation retention and, 80–83; as CRUDs, 105–7; domestic decline of, 100–105; domestic production of, 98; example of, 128–29; within families, 109–10; measurement of, 283n33; overview of, 48–55; religion and, 286n9; scandal's influence on, 83–85; significance of, 86, 87; survey regarding, 259–60
credibility-undermining displays (CRUDs), 54, 82–83, 105–7
cross-pressure, 248, 299–300n24
Cullen, Paul, 19–20, 268n3
cultural Catholicism: characteristics of, 120–21, 131–32; community within, 255; complicity of, 179; core triad for sustaining, 254; defined, 31, 199; education system and, 111–15; ex-Catholicism and, 151, 220; *Father Ted* within, 123–27; fear of missing out within, 115–20; inconsistencies within, 200; irreverent, 287n26; within Kilbreagh, 137–53; limbo frustration within,

cultural Catholicism (*continued*) 197–201; obstacle of, 175–77; overview of, 110, 200–201; popularity of, 129–30; religious indifference of, 190; scrutiny of, 10
cultural religion, 273n59
culture war, 152–53, 159
Curran, Daniel, 274n66
Cussen Report, 276n88

Dáil Éireann, 162
Danish Lutheranism, 256
The Dark (McGahern), 134
Dark Ages, 114
"The Darkest Corner," 170
Dawkins, Richard, 107, 297n16
Day, Abby, 59, 273n59
DDR Museum, 170
Dear Daughter, 40
The Death of Christian Britain (Brown), 23
deception, 52
decoherence, Catholic, 247–52
deconversion, rationalist, 216–17
deflecting strategies, 238–39
deinstitutionalized Catholics, 62
Demerath, N. J., 273n59
Denmark, 33
Department of Education, 40
desacralization, 57–58
devotion, contamination and privatization of, 230–36
devotional revolution, 19–20, 49, 267–68n3, 279n123
devout Catholics: contempt regarding, 222–24; devotion contamination and privatization of, 230–36; faith transition of, 241; motivations of, 244–47, 250–51; personalization of, 252; scandal effects to, 16, 223–24; subculture of, 255; viewpoint of, 222

Dillane, Maurice, 274n62
Diocese of Cloyne, 36
disaffiliation, 57, 64–67
disaffiliation, incentives of, 177–81
disbelief, 145
discrimination, 162, 203, 225
disenchanted Catholicism, 32
disgust, 209–13, 211, 250
distrust, 64–67, 72–73, 85
divorce, 24
doctrinal mode of ritual, 268n5
donations, 84, 106
Dover Beach (Arnold), 23
Doyle, Paddy, 172
Drażkiewicz, Ella, 183–84
Dublin, Ireland, 22, 26–27, 154, 261–62, 271–72n42
Dunphy, Father, 228, 230, 234, 235

East Germany, 170
economy, 26–27, 28, 168–69, 267n14
education: atheist stereotypes within, 212–13; atheist teachers within, 285n2; baptism barrier within, 201; Catholic control of, 29, 97, 101, 118, 177, 201–4, 217–18; cultural Catholicism and, 111–15; enrollment discrimination within, 162; industrial schools, 39–41; molestation within, 105; national identity representation within, 114; non-Catholic students within, 161–62; oppressive culture within, 135–36; post-Vatican II and, 113–14; rational rejection and, 217–18; reform of, 255; second priesthood within, 97–98; secular, 201–4; sex, 122–23; tertiary, 24
Eighth Amendment, 154–57, 174, 181–85, 187–88
Éireann, Raidió Teilifís, 123

Elizabeth I (Queen), 19
emotion, 108, 206, 210, 222–23
enchantment, 49
England, 23, 183
essentialism, 254
Ethical Life (Keane), 186, 295n2
ethno-Catholic divergence, 29–34
ethnoreligious determinism, 253–54
European Values Study, 176–77
The Evidence I Shall Give (Johnson), 172, 279n115
ex-Catholics/ex-Catholicism: abuse emotional responses of, 73; anger of, 213; as atheistic, 78–79, 106–7, 117, 190; belief scale of, 78; as black sheep, 108; characteristics of, 12–13, 15–16, 86–87; Church rejection by, 75–77; Church viewpoint of, 67–75; community within, 255; core stance of, 220–21; cultural Catholicism and, 151; defined, 60, 189; disaffiliation causes of, 214; distrust within, 12–13, 65–67; free list responses of, 70; overview of, 189–97; personal reflection of, 191–94, 195–200; in Poland, 257; rejection by, 84, 85; statistics of, 60–61; as unbelievers, 77–79
exploitation, 144

factionalism, 240–44
families, 96, 98, 104–5, 109, 254
Famine, 19
Father Ted, 123–27
fear of missing out, 115–20
feminism, 25
Ferns Report, 35–36
Ferriter, Diarmaid, 26
Fianna Fáil, 89
fieldwork, methodology within, 261–62, 263

Fine Gael, 89, 285n48
First Holy Communion, 112–13, 184
Flanagan, Edward, 47
Flanagan, Luke "Ming," 172
Flannery, Tony, 232
Flynn, Betty, 229
Flynn, David, 229
Flynn, Gerard Mannix, 172
Forbidden Fruit, 273n60
Fortune, Seán, 35, 124
Foster, Roy, 284n43
Francis (Pope), 56–57, 88–94, 232
Franco, Francisco, 256
free list, 69–72, 116, 191, 260, 284n44
Fry, Stephen, 292n23
Fuller, Louise, 24, 25, 27, 50–51
fusion, 21
fuzzy fidelity, 54

Gaelic Athletic Association (GAA), 151–52
Gaelscoil, 287n20
Ganiel, Gladys, 24, 31, 93, 241, 285n46, 290n10
gender norms, 28
The Genealogy of Morality (Nietzsche), 44
Germany, 32
God, 21, 25, 38, 53, 101, 129, 142–43, 289n10
The God Squad (Doyle), 172
Goffman, Erving, 224, 228
Good Friday, 266n7
Good Friday Agreement of 1998, 257–58
Graham, J. J., 46
Greene, Eugene, 274n66
Griffin, Gus, 274n66
group identity, 21
guilt, Catholic, 20–21, 105–6, 193, 245–46

habitus, 51, 280n126
Haidt, Jonathan, 45, 46, 282–83n26, 284n41
Halappanavar, Savita, 157, 290n11
Hallmark Catholicism, 280n129
harmony, intergenerational, 254
harmony, social, 137–53
Hayes, Joanne, 273–74n61
healthcare system, 162, 165
Heaney, Seamus, 114
hedge schools, 267n1
Henrich, Joseph, 51, 268–69n9
Higgins, Michael D., 223
Hilliard, Betty, 37, 234, 270–71n20
Hitchens, Christopher, 107
Hogan, Caelainn, 278n107
Holy Orders, 294–95n48
Holy Thursday, 226–27
Home: Part One, 171
homosexuality, 30, 237
Houlihan, Kathleen Ní, 154
Humanae Vitae, 25
humanism, 117
Humanist Association of Ireland, 174
Hungary, 4
hyphenated Catholic, 63–64, 281n12
hypocrisy, 37, 48–55, 143–44, 147–48, 193–94

Iceland, 32
ideal self, Western influence of, 132–33
identity, 58–64, 114, 175–76, 242
immigration, 27
individualism, 268n9
individualizing foundations, 45
industrialization, 268n9
industrial schools, 39–41
infants, discarding of, 7–8, 164, 291n14
Inglehart, Ronald, 27
Inglis, Tom, 24, 31–32, 36–37, 47, 51, 262, 288n6, 296n3

integralism, 160
intergenerational harmony, 199, 254
interviews, methodology regarding, 262–63
Iona Institute, 160, 174
Ireland: age of scandal within, 2; black humor within, 9; class distinctions within, 135; Constitution of, 89; cultural changes within, 242; de facto theocracy characteristics within, 59; economic growth within, 26–27, 28; Famine within, 19; immigration to, 27; materialism within, 5; moral priorities within, 45, 46; political climate of, 20, 186; pride within, 44; priest to people ratio within, 20; Protestant settlers within, 19; religious affiliations within, 2–3, 11; religious hierarchy within, 20; secularization within, 14, 22, 23–29; uncertainty within, 257–58; Wholly Woke, 11; worldviews within, 186
Irish Catholic Church: benevolence of, 149; blame absorption of, 1–2; business exploitation within, 144; challenges to, 291n14; coverups by, 34, 36, 41, 43–44; credibility deficit within, 163, 167; desacralization of, 2; dissolution of relevance within, 13; within education, 6–7; as family, 99; foundations of, 19–23; freedom struggle from, 185–88; free list for, 69–72, 116, 191, 260; healthcare system of, 162, 165; image alteration of, 1; influence of, 5, 33, 161–62; morality stance of, 2, 104; obedience to, 161; redress from, 43–44; rejection of, 75–77; scandal overview of, 34–48; sexuality within, 4–5, 20; staying power of, 152; submission pride within, 4; survey viewpoints

of, 67–75; trust decline within, 38.
  See also Catholicism/Catholics/
  Irish Catholicism
Irish Constitution, 89
Irish Society for the Prevention of
  Cruelty to Children, 275–76n86
The Irish Times, 208, 285n46

Jack, Father, 124
Jesuits, 136, 241, 286n9
John Paul II (Pope), 22, 26, 160,
  290n9
Johnson, Richard, 172, 279n115
Joseph, Craig, 45
Joyce, James, 265n4
Junior Certificate religion textbook,
  212–13

Keane, John B., 26, 186, 295n2
Keane, Webb, 186
Kearney, Peader, 151, 229
Kennedy, Stanislaus, 232
Kennedy Report, 40
Kenny, Enda, 9, 36, 43, 173, 291n14
Kilbreagh, 137–53, 261–62
Knuttel, Graham, 11, 267n14
Knuttel, Jonathan, 267n14

Laffoy, Mary, 276n93
language, deception and, 52
Lanman, Jonathan, 53
lapsed Catholic, 101–2, 104–5
Latin Christendom, 28
Law and Justice Party (Poland), 257
The Leavetaking (McGahern), 134–35
Lent, 84
liberal Catholicism, 62, 291n16
liberal nationalism, 187
liberals, moral systems of, 46
Likert scales, 75, 283n31
liminal Catholics: belief scale of, 78;
  Church rejection by, 75–77; defined, 60; distrust within, 67; free
list responses of, 70; hypothesis
  regarding, 62; rejection by, 83; statistics of, 60–61; survey viewpoints
  of, 67–75
Love Both, 182
Love's Betrayal (Mulholland), 135–36
Lovett, Ann, 273–74n61
Lutheranism, Danish, 256
Lynch, Gordon, 46

MacNamara, Angela, 122–23
Madden, Andrew, 35
Magdalene laundries, 42–43, 44, 91,
  223, 276–77nn94–102
The Magdalene Sisters, 168
majority compliance, within rites of
  passage, 112, 136–37
March for Choice, 154–55, 156,
  157–58
Marriage and Family Programme,
  268–69n9
marriage equality referendum, 89, 95,
  152, 183, 266n8
Martin, Archbishop, 297–98n8
Martin, Diarmuid, 106, 158–59, 163,
  234, 236, 240, 287n4
Martin, Eamon, 95, 119
Martin, Micheál, 173
Mary, mother of Jesus, 21
Mass: attendance of, 25, 26, 29, 30,
  38, 138, 192, 270n12, 271–72n42,
  271n39, 281n9, 287–88n4,
  291n16; children within, 96–97; of
  Francis (Pope), 92–93; obligation
  of, 107–8, 134–35, 141; rejection
  of, 84; significance of, 5–6, 21, 51
mass complicity, 170–73, 179, 180–81,
  199–200
Mass of the Chrism, 226–27
materialism, 5
McAleese, Mary, 92, 276n92
McGahern, John, 30, 134, 265n5
McMahon, Philip, 171

McQuaid, John Charles, 10, 134, 267n13
McWilliams, David, 26, 183
media, 168, 266n7
Micheál Martin, Taoiseach, 8–9
middle class, 111–12, 136
molestation, 105
moral authority of priests, 229–30
moral disgust, 209–13
moral dissonance, 248
moral foundations, 45
Moral Foundations Questionnaire, 282–83n26, 284n41
morality: contamination of, 177–81; as disaffiliation cause, 214; influence of, 27–28; religion and, 113, 149; survey regarding, 284n41; Victorian, 267n2; worldview formations regarding, 28–29
Moral Monopoly (Inglis), 31, 36–37
moral progressivism, 86
moral systems, construction of, 45
Moral Therapeutic Deism, 289n10
Mother and Baby Homes Report, 7–8, 43, 173, 254–55, 266n9
mother and baby homes scandal, 7–8, 163, 165–67, 177–78, 206–7, 209–13, 291n14
Mulholland, Peter, 106, 135–36
Murphy, Annie, 273n60
Murphy Report, 1, 36

natal nominalism, 59
national identity, within education, 114
nationalism, liberal, symbols of, 187
National Maternity Hospital (NMH), 165
National Society for the Protection of Cruelty to Children, 275–76n86
Naughton, Thomas, 274n66
neo-conservativism, 159, 160–61, 163, 291n16

Netherlands, 32
New Atheism, 146, 207, 215, 286n4, 294n45, 297n16
new covenant, 88–89
Nietzsche, Friedrich, 44
1916 Rising, 154–55
"No Birthright" series (Viney), 278n113
No Escape (Raftery), 170–71
"nones," 32, 59, 61, 177, 190, 272n51
nonreligion/nonreligious: antipathy within, 92; conflicts of, 205–6; cultural Catholicism and, 255; emergence of, 29–34; growth of, 2–3, 12, 133, 176; moral disgust within, 209–13; in Spain, 256; statistics of, 32, 58–59, 61
Norris, Pippa, 27
Northern Ireland, 257–58
Nothing to Say (Flynn), 172
nuns, 7–8, 156

O'Connor, Sinéad, 91, 227, 236, 244
O'Dalaigh, Tadhg, 274n66
O'Doherty, Malachi, 25–26, 53
O'Donnell, Ian, 44–45
O'Gorman, Colm, 90, 169
On Raftery's Hill (Carr), 171
oppression, 135–36, 191, 193
O'Reilly, Leo, 163, 164
Orsi, Robert, 54–55
orthodox Catholicism, 31
O'Sullivan, Eoin, 44–45, 46
O'Toole, Fintan, 168, 169

papal infallibility, 19–20
paragon argument, 240
parents: religious role of, 98, 109–10, 234, 283–84n39; scandal effects on, 234–35; secular schooling and, 201–4
Parents for Secular Schooling (PSS), 201–14

Pasolini, Pierre Paulo, 293n38
Pasolini's Salò Redubbed (Tighe), 171
Patrick, St., 114
Paul VI (Pope), 22
Payne, Ivan, 35, 274n66
Pearse, Patrick, 138
pedophilia, 70–72, 225–26
Penal Laws, 19, 267n1
Phoenix Park, Dublin, 22, 90, 92–93
Pine, Emilie, 168, 170, 186–87
Pius IX (Pope), 20
plausibility structure, 49–51
Poland, 4, 29, 257
political capital, 291n14
Portugal, 29
post-Vatican II, 113–14, 122–23
poverty, 135
priests: abuse by, 265n4; abuse statistics of, 72; child sexual abuse by, 34–48, 288–89n9; comic regarding, 166–67; convictions of, 274–75n66; devoutness of, 233–34; expectations from, 137; false accusations to, 299n16; garb of, 226–27; hypocrisy of, 143–44, 147; innocent, 224–30; moral authority decline of, 229–30; pedophilia statistics of, 72; under Penal Laws, 267n1; public opinion of, 1, 30, 48, 53; within Rally for Life, 156; ratio of, 20; Redemptorist, 265n5; sexualized picture of, 143, 225; symbolism of, 37; trustworthiness score of, 65–67
Primetime: Cardinal Secrets, 35, 36
pro-choice, 154–55, 156, 157–58, 166–67, 182–83
progressivism, 86
pro-life, 155–57, 158, 182, 184–85, 290n6
Protestant settlers, 19
protests, 25, 90–91
public prayer, rejection of, 84

Qualtrics Panels participant recruitment service, 57–58, 259–61
Quebec, 256
Quiet Revolution, 256
Quinn, David, 163–64, 176–77

Raftery, Mary, 40, 46, 170–71
Rally for Life, 155–57, 158, 290n6
rationalism, 216
rational rejection, 214–19
Redemptorist priests, 265n5
Redress Board, 40
Reformation, 268n9
rejection, data regarding, 75–77
religion: ambiguity within, 103; CRED exposure and, 286n9; crutch of, 145; cultural, 273n59; debates regarding, 48–49; decline of, 97, 272–73n59; emotion within, 108; as emotive topic, 215; expulsion of, 28; within families, 96, 98, 104–5, 109, 254; as form of support, 138–39; hypocrisy within, 48–55; influences to, 132–33; morality and, 113, 149; obligation of, 107; as personal, 232; secularization and, 269n10; statistics of, 272n52; viewpoints regarding, 139–41
Religious Sisters of Charity, 165
religious systems, suspicion within, 52
reluctant Catholicism, 102
Renaissance Nation (McWilliams), 183
Repeal the Eighth campaign, 174, 182–83
Republic of Shame (Hogan), 278n107
residential institutions, scandal within, 41
"respect without obedience" period, 196
Riefenstahl, Leni, 22, 268n8
rites of passage: complicity of, 180–81; majority compliance and, 112, 136–37; obligation of, 146–47,

rites of passage (*continued*) 148–49, 198, 199–200, 253; rejection of, 84; scandal effects to, 83. *See also specific types*
Rooney, Sally, 128
RTÉ, 40, 126, 185, 266n7, 278n103
Ruane, Joseph, 159, 162
Russia, 257
Ryan Report, 40–41, 44

sacraments, 119–20, 294–95n48
sacred canopy, 48–55
Sacred Heart, 21
Sade, Marquis de, 171
salience, measurement of, 69–72
Salò (120 Days of Sodom), 171, 293n38
Sandhill, 261–62
The Savage Eye, 126–27
"Say Nope to the Pope" campaign, 89–90, 93
Scally, Derek, 52, 167, 169, 170, 223, 241, 280n129
scandals: blame within, 167–73; as Church rejection cause, 77; communication of, 47; CRED performance and, 83–85; disconnection regarding, 167; dismissal of, 199–200; effects of, 178–79; emotional responses to, 206; guilt regarding, 245–46; innocent priests within, 224–30; moral disgust following, 209–13; overview of, 34–48; Parents for Secular Schooling (PSS) and, 204–9; public rhetoric regarding, 167–73; as rejection excuse, 236–40; sacred victims of, 236–40; secular empowerment following, 208; as secularization affordance, 161–67; secularized by, 26; structural causes of, 243–44; as unbelief weapon, 147–48; viewpoints regarding, 142–43
schism, 240–44

schools, 6–7, 101, 105, 201–4. *See also* education
second priesthood, 97–98
secularism/secularization: anger within, 211; characteristics of, 24, 92; components of, 28; development of, 18; developments in organized, 173–75; effects of, 256, 258; of Europe, 3; goals of, 159–60; of Ireland, 23–29; moral battlefield of, 14, 152; moral contamination through, 243–44; religious hypocrisy and, 54; scandals as affordance within, 161–67; security within, 53; theory of, 269n10; wealth within, 27
secular revisionism, 159, 162, 197, 291n16
security, levels of, 27
sex education, 122–23
Sex Education for Girls, 122–23
Sex in a Cold Climate, 43
sexual abuse, child: costs regarding, 278n104; example of, 265n4; innocent priests within, 224–30; lack of punishment regarding, 169–70; ontological dissonance within, 55; overview of, 34–48; reporting of, 274n63; secular empowerment following, 208–9; statistics of, 278–79n114; structural causes of, 243–44; theater works regarding, 170–72
sexuality, 4–5, 20, 28, 30, 104, 265n5
shame, 20–21, 73
shame-industrial complex, 278n107
skepticism, stoic, 137–53
Smith, Christian, 98
Smyth, Brendan, 35, 124, 274n66
social capital, 51
social harmony, 137–53
social institutions, 50
sodalities, 49–50

Sodano, Angelo, 276n92
The Soldier's Song, 151–52
Spain, 29, 256
The Spectator, 184
Stasi Museum, 170
States of Fear, 40
Stivers, R., 288n6
"St. Patrick" (plane), 22
Strong, Tom, 183–84
St. Theresa's church, 138–39
Suffer the Little Children, 35
Suing the Pope, 35

"Tá" campaign, 183
Talbot, Matt, 138
Taylor, Charles, 28, 299–300n24
teachers, 97–98, 285n2
Ted-talk, 124–25
tertiary education, 24
theater, abuse depictions within, 170–72
theism, 32
Tighe, Dylan, 171
"Time to Tick No" campaign, 178–81
Toland, Father, 226, 227, 228, 235–36, 241–42, 243–44, 298n9
traditional Catholicism, 291n16
transubstantiation, 99
Triumph of the Will (Riefenstahl), 268n8
trustworthiness score, 64–67
Tuam mother and baby homes scandal, 7–8, 163, 165–67, 177–78, 206–7, 209–13, 291n14
Twomey, Vincent, 52

Ulysses (Joyce), 265n4
unbelief, 149–50
unbelievers, ex-Catholics as, 77–79
UN Committee Against Torture, 43, 169

Unitarianism, 250
United Kingdom, 32, 258
United States, 27, 32, 33, 46, 183, 190
urbanization, 268n9

vaccine trials, scandal involving, 8
Varadkar, Leo, 9, 88
Vatican II, 25, 243, 270n15, 280n129
verbal statements of outrage, 47–48
Victorian morality, 267n2
Vietnam, 32
Viney, Michael, 278n107
virtual fieldwork, methodology regarding, 263
virus, disbelief as, 145
Voas, David, 273n59
Voss, Daniel, 54

Waiting for Godot (Beckett), 191
Watson, Rebecca, 297n16
wealth, secularization and, 27
Weber, Max, 269n10
West Dublin, 138
Whitehouse, Harvey, 268n5
Whitmore, Laura, 121
Wholly Woke Ireland, 11
Wiesel, Elie, 219
women, 7, 24–25, 50–51, 191, 194–95
woo, 286n4
working class, 138

"X Case," 290n11

"Y Case," 290n11
"The Young Offenders" series (Viney), 278n113

Zuckerman, Phil, 33

SPIRITUAL PHENOMENA
TANYA LUHRMANN and ANN TAVES, Series Editors

Spiritual Phenomena features investigations of events, experiences, and objects, both unusual and everyday, that people characterize as spiritual, paranormal, magical, occult, and/or supernatural. Working from the presupposition that the status of such phenomena is contested, this series seeks to understand how such determinations are made in a variety of historical and cultural contexts. Books in this series explore how such phenomena are identified, experienced, and understood; the role that spontaneity and cultivation play in the process; and the similarities and differences in the way phenomena are appraised and categorized across time and cultures. The editors encourage work that is ethnographic, historical, or psychological and, in particular, work that uses more than one method to understand these complex phenomena, ranging from the qualitative to quantitative surveys and laboratory-based experiments.

Alicia Puglionesi, *Common Phantoms: An American History of Psychic Science*

Yoram Bilu, *With Us More Than Ever: Making the Absent Rebbe Present in Messianic Chabad*

David J. Halperin, *Intimate Alien: The Hidden Story of the UFO*

J. Bradley Wigger, *Invisible Companions: Encounters with Imaginary Friends, Gods, Ancestors, and Angels*

Kelly Bulkeley, *Lucrecia the Dreamer: Prophecy, Cognitive Science, and the Spanish Inquisition*

Lightning Source UK Ltd.
Milton Keynes UK
UKHW012138150922
408931UK00002B/242